FROM SAMMY TO JIMMY

FROM SAMMY TO JIMMY

The Official History of
SOMERSET
County Cricket Club

PETER ROEBUCK

PARTRIDGE PRESS

LONDON · NEW YORK · TORONTO · SYDNEY · AUCKLAND

TRANSWORLD PUBLISHERS LTD
61-63 Uxbridge Road, London W5 5SA

TRANSWORLD PUBLISHERS (AUSTRALIA) PTY LTD
15-23 Helles Avenue, Moorebank, NSW 2170

TRANSWORLD PUBLISHERS (NZ) LTD
Cnr Moselle and Waipareira Aves,
Henderson, Auckland

Published 1991 by Partridge Press
a division of Transworld Publishers Ltd

All photographs supplied by the author, who
wishes to thank Roger Mann (pp 18; 19; 20, top and
bottom; 22–3, top; 24), Tony Steddall of the
Somerset Museum and Lord Rippon for their help.

ISBN 185225 0852

Typeset in 11/13 Times by
Falcon Graphic Art Ltd
Wallington, Surrey
Printed in Great Britain by
Mackays of Chatham Plc, Chatham, Kent

Contents

	Introduction and Acknowledgements	vii
1	Origins	1
2	Raising a team	15
3	Finding a pitch	23
4	Interlude – Sammy	38
5	Rolling a pitch	43
6	Off the mark	55
7	Consolidation	60
8	On the back foot	69
9	Tyke-bashing	81
10	Hiccuping along	92
11	A Daniell come to judgement	100
12	Stormy waters	103
13	Lest we forget	114
14	Post-war	117
15	A mixed bag	145
16	Last gasp of a dying world	155
17	Jack White downunder	166
18	Professional times	170
19	Led by lawyers	182
20	Professionals	190
21	A bright day dawns	195
22	War years	221
23	Post-war blues	224
24	More professionals	237
25	Captains courageous	242
26	Rebellion and rebirth	260
27	Australian revival	271
28	Our Fred	295
29	Up for the cup	316
30	Low points	320

31   Close endeavours   338
32   Roses all the way   349
33   Sweet and sour   369
34   Through fire   384
35   Having a go   394

Appendix – records and statistics   407
Index   437

Introduction
and
Acknowledgements

History is a mixture of fact, conjecture and interpretation. No effort has been made to pretend otherwise. Readers may disagree with judgements found here, and especially with the treatment given to those two most contentious issues, the rebellions of 1952 and 1986; affairs which were entirely different because supporters in 1952 were condemning complacency and obtuseness while the petitioners of 1986 were protesting about a radical solution to an intractable problem.

It is, of course, far too early for safe conclusions to be reached about 1986. So much, in any case, depends upon your starting point. Emotion fought with reason, past with present, foreign with local, Sunday supporter with diehard member, glamour with pragmatism, fact with fiction. Nor were blackmail and death threats absent, for bitterness is a debilitating emotion. Somerset's decline after 1982 brought pain and recrimination; views on whys and wherefores varied.

Of 1952 one thing can be said. Moore, Roberts and Hill were not, as they were portrayed, callous, ambitious reporters; rather they were bright, energetic men with a passion for Somerset cricket. Roberts died at the age of thirty-seven, by which time he had forged a brilliant career as a writer and an organizer of international cricket tours. Moore is presently charged with raising funds for Oxford University, and Hill has been a cricket journalist and a faithful supporter of Somerset cricket for fifty years. He had already, of course, shown immense courage at war. Had anyone upon Somerset's aged and unimaginative committee been as vigorous, those troubles need never have occurred.

vii

In so far as sides must be taken – and only a coward avoids them – this historian supports the rebels in 1952 and the club in 1986, on both occasions because, on balance, these men seemed to have the interests of Somerset cricket closest to their hearts. Both the rebels of 1952 and the apologists in 1986 absorbed vitriolic abuse for a cause in which they believed.

These are episodes isolated only in their scale. Both were explosions which had been building for years, years of neglect and deterioration, years of weak rule. Happy periods, of which there have been many, also took years to arrive. Somerset was strong in 1890 because Murray-Anderdon took the club in hand and built a side. They were strong in the 1920s because John Daniell took charge, and in the 1970s because Tom Cartwright and Roy Kerslake patiently forged a team with a blend of experience and youth. Administration plays its part.

Bowlers matter too. Somerset has won regular victories only when fielding 3 men, at least, capable of taking 5 wickets. In 1890 there were Sammy Woods, Ted Tyler and George Nichols. In the 1920s it was Farmer White and, sometimes Greswell, Robertson-Glasgow, Braund and Robson too. Professionals, if not professionalism, arrived in the 1930s, and Somerset could field Wellard, Andrews, Hazell and Buse. In the 1960s Somerset's attack was balanced and powerful; few batting teams escaped easily from the clutches of Rumsey, Palmer, Langford, Alley and Robinson. Afterwards, under Brian Rose, Somerset won its first trophies at last, and their batting was justly celebrated. Yet no cup was ever won until Joel Garner arrived, and none was won after his contribution slipped. Somerset's only serious challenges for the Championship during Rose's stewardship occurred when Garner played with a higher degree of regularity than was his wont.

Already two factors are common to those rare, if not exactly fleeting, periods of success: a dedicated, selfless administration and a dangerous attack. A third element is present too. Somerset can only sustain a challenge when fielding a mixture of local talent, providing passion, and imported players, providing brilliance. From Sammy Woods to Jimmy Cook Somerset has chosen outstanding men from overseas, men who have cheered crowds and won matches, and hearts too. Woods, Richards and Chappell have been saluted, Alley and McCool less so, yet they were just as colourful and just as important as Somerset recovered from the depths of 1952 to finish in the top three, and eventually to reach a Lord's final in 1967, one of the greatest days.

These matters apart, what sort of club has it been? A club is a product of its county. From the start cricket was a game weakly played in Somerset, especially at club level. Accordingly only a thin supply of indigenous talent could for decades be found. Somerset has had to forage around for players in universities, private schools and foreign parts, living and dying upon its wits. It is, too, a club expressive of character in which member and player are often on intimate terms, often meeting in a skittles alley, and a fellow is taken as a whole. Some men adapt to this intimacy, and are adopted by the crowd. Others do not feel the warmth and so miss the point.

So many people have helped in constructing this book. David Foot and Ron Roberts have already written splendid histories and these have been fearfully pillaged. David, in particular, wrote a book notable for its originality, his training as a reporter with a nose for a story expressing itself in his colourful recollections of the Rippons and of Albert Trott's murder case, matters lightly touched upon here, as have been the more private affairs of 1986, for a man may know things as an individual which a proper historian might choose to ignore. May Foot and Roberts forgive my pinching of their material. When it comes to figures, I have made constant use of the ACS' publication *Somersetshire Cricketers 1875–1974*.

Somerset's superbly efficient scorer David Oldam has provided a thorough statistical section at the end of this book and many players past and present gave of their time, and found photographs too. To mention them is to forget someone, so I will not even thank Neil Harvey and Eric Hill who were especially helpful! Robin Bush, distinguished archivist, historian and raconteur, provided lots of information about Somerset's cricketing life in the nineteenth century, and to him a bow is made. Finally, and most importantly, Caroline has done all the typing. You see, I have a degree, have written lots of books and am generally regarded as a somewhat distant if eccentric egg-head. But I can neither type nor write legibly. England contains about 55 million people, only one of whom can read my words: Caroline. She is a Trojan.

And so, good luck with this. If it is as much fun to read as it has been to write we will both be satisfied.

'Without any base reflection upon the many fine writers on the past, it is perhaps as well to unburden on your victims the facts of youth while youth is still with you, while memory is still memory "within the meaning of the Act", before narrow, but faintly discreditable, defeats have grown with the years into noble struggles against overwhelming odds, before straight half-volleys have assumed the guise of invincible shooters, before, as the decades add themselves, the truths of forty years ago become by a sweet but culpable process of entanglement, the romances of to-day.'

R.C. Robertson–Glasgow

FROM SAMMY TO JIMMY

1

Origins

Cricket arrived late in Somerset and took root, eventually, strictly as a recreation, one enjoyed by thousands of men and some women. By the time of its arrival there it had for decades been strong in the eastern, midland and northern areas, which thereafter scoffed understandably at the cricket of landowners and labourers in this distant farming country. Some prejudices die hard.

Cricket is still not a professional game in Somerset, though twenty-five or so men are paid various amounts to represent the county club in matches arranged between 1 April and 30 September. This fortunate group apart, it is hard to find a village, town or city between Bath and Minehead, Yeovil and Winscombe which has more than one professional player (and they are usually Australians whose wages are paid in scrumpy, a beverage for which most visitors to Somerset rapidly develop a thirst). Most clubs are as staunchly amateur as they were a hundred years ago; more so, if anything – for skulduggery is less common than it used to be.

Since the game was, somewhat belatedly, first played in these parts, it has bumbled along upon an occasionally crumbling foundation of friendly contests between urban and rural clubs, contests in which is commonly heard the old Somerset cry of ''ave a go at 'em!' In these matches pride alone is at stake, for Somerset has little taste, and too little money or skill, for the fierce leagues of the North or the flowery arrangements of the East. Temperamentally Somerset has been closest to the old amateur clubs of Middlesex, Sussex and Hampshire. As a club

Somerset has yearned for respectability, wanted to be accepted in the inner arches at Lord's in a way common amongst those on the fringe of society who urgently seek to be within its exalted ranks. Accordingly they have resisted the tide of professionalism and flown an amateur flag, longer and at a greater cost than could by any means be justified. Only reluctantly did Somerset finally abandon this rejection of paid players and begin to search for men capable of standing firm for the county as the old amateurs used to do. And even then, in the 1950s, when at last professionalism was adopted, nothing changed off the field. Other clubs – even Sussex – have succumbed to a tide of efficiency but Somerset has changed scarcely at all.

But already our story jumps far ahead of itself. To understand the history of cricket in Somerset is to find clues to the various dramas, tragedies and triumphs which permeate our story.

Cricket was not, of course, indigenous to Somerset, rather it filtered across from its birthplace on the eastern fringes of England and the western edges of France. Cricket was known, if not commonplace, in England in the 1550s, for John Derrick played as a boy in Guildford at around this time, and in 1598 Florio's dictionary confirmed the existence of *cricket-a-wicket*. William Bedle (1679–1768) was the game's first known expert practitioner and by 1720 matches were being played with some regularity in the south-eastern corner of England. And it was played by the nobility, including Frederick Prince of Wales, the Duke of Richmond and Lord John Sackville. Throughout the eighteenth century cricket spread in fits and starts, and in 1772 over 15,000 people attended the first day of a match between All England and Hampshire. By now bats cost 4s 6d (22½p); pads were not to be in common use for another fifty years.

Thanks to the growth of newspapers, cricket quickly spread to New York, Amsterdam, and provincial parts of England. At first Somerset did not take to it, partly because its rural population was too busy with the labour of the land to indulge in a game so demanding of time, and partly because they had pastimes of their own. Edward Goldsworthy, in his *Recollections of Old Taunton*, gives a vivid account:

When I was a boy, all classes enjoyed themselves more than they do at the present time. The rich amused themselves by eating, drinking, smoking, and gambling. Dining out meant, with them, drinking until they fell out of their chairs; those able to walk adjourned to an inn, and finished off by smoking, drinking, shouting, yelling, and singing, and were generally taken home, to use a mild expression, 'the worse for liquor'. Whist parties, smoking clubs, boating parties, and glee clubs were very fashionable with professional men. The lower classes imitated the rich, but in a coarser manner. Skittles, 'the devil amongst the tailors', all-fours, 'put', bawdy songs, and guzzling were their principal enjoyments. A pack of cards was found in almost every house and many carried them in their pockets. The most immoral songs were sung in the streets, to which crowds stopped to listen without shewing the least disgust. The walls of barbers' shops were covered with laughable and funny prints of prize fights, bull-baiting, wrestling, and fencing, and of gin shops, shewing the vagaries of 'Tom and Jerry', besides indecent pictures, which would not bear mentioning.

Cudgel playing was a particular favourite in the alehouses, not least with the landlords. Two men stood on wooden crates and belaboured each other with clubs until blood ran to within an inch of the eyebrows, whereupon the contest was stopped and wagers settled. It does not sound much fun and no doubt you had to be present properly to appreciate its quality. Billiards was popular too, and so was badger-baiting and cock-fighting, in which county contests were organized as early as the 1820s. Besides these loud and rough games (even billiards in the nineteenth century was not quite the cordial entertainment it has since become) cricket must have seemed dull fare.

It took a combination of publicity in newspapers, of trains permitting swift travel, and of an industrial revolution tolerating free Saturday afternoons, to allow cricket to establish a firm base in these parts. The first recorded cricket game in Somerset was played in 1751 in sophisticated Bath. According to Boddely's *Bath Journal*, on 13 July of that year a 'great cricket match was played in Saltford meadow, four miles below Bath in memory of his late Royal Highness The Prince of Wales, for on that day twelvemonth he died in the same meadow, and as His Royal Highness was an admirer of that diversion we hear that it is intended annually to

3

play this game'. Frederick, the aforesaid Prince of Wales, had died following a blow from a cricket ball, a misfortune which, occurring in 1751, had temporarily dampened the esteem in which cricket was held by the English aristocracy.

No further mention is made of this fixture in later years so presumably it faded away. Nevertheless it is plain that readers of this journal were acquainted with the game, even if it was deemed to be merely a 'diversion'. Plainly, too, cricket had for some time been played in Bath; no doubt in a rough and tumble manner, for clubs were still to be formed and the idea of regular fixtures between teams of Somerset men lay far in the future.

In August 1772 another cricket match was reported, this time one played in Wincanton, on the race-ground near Dropping Lane, between the gentlemen of Bruton and Redlinch, for a purse of 20 guineas. Local newspapers said 'players on both sides were active and alert' and after a long contest Bruton won by 'two notches'. Gentlemen from Middlesex and Kent were invited to stand as umpires (for in these domestic matters it is best to summon an independent view) and they proclaimed themselves 'greatly satisfied with the players'. Upon the contest finishing an elegant supper was provided at the Bear Inn where 'both parties regaled themselves with great cordiality and friendship'. For a further hundred years at the very least cricket in Somerset was to be a jovial occasion full of lusty hitting and jolly suppers. Matches were rather like fairs; they were days of celebration and festivity, and this in a time when men knew how to enjoy themselves. Later of course, cricket was taken up by clergy and educators, notoriously a fatal alliance, despite which it has never entirely been convinced of its own solemnity, especially not in Somerset. Alas, tabloid newspapers with their shocking prurience are now doing their best to ruin it, as they have ruined nearly everything else.

For years cricket stuttered along without any structure in Somerset, though soon enough Eton were playing Harrow and the Gentlemen commencing their annual engagements with their paid brethren. Cricket reappeared in the county newspapers in 1795, a match being played on Claverton Down in Bath for 11 guineas by 11 men against 11 youths of the City, a contest which was won by the former in one innings. Apparently 'the novelty of this manly exercise, in a regular match, drew together a great number of spectators'. Claverton Down was situated in the outskirts of Bath and it was to be here that Somerset played what is regarded by some as its first game. Time enough for that.

Club cricket in Somerset gradually sprang to life as one century turned into another. In 1819 Clifton beat Bath, though 'one of the Bath gentlemen gained 84 runs from his own bat'. Spectators were gratified at the skill evinced and they were 'no less struck by the harmony and decorum that prevailed'.

Soon cricket clubs were formed. By now wides and no-balls were penalized (1816) and wicket-keeping gloves had been introduced (around 1820 by J. Bernard of Eton). Lansdown is acknowledged as Somerset's most influential club in these early years, a position later to be challenged to telling effect by Taunton Cricket Club, which, carrying the day, brought county cricket to its home town, apparently for ever. Lansdown is recognized as the first club formed in Somerset, but this is only partly true. David Foot, in his colourful history of Somerset CCC, relates that a Bath club preceded Lansdown by a few years, Captain Thornhill lending his meadow, Sydenham Field, to this team a few times between 1817 and 1824. Lansdown's history, however, is unbroken, though their formation only just preceded that of less important clubs such as Glastonbury, Pennard, Street and Hinton Charterhouse (all 1826), and Frome and Shepton Mallet (both 1834).

Accordingly cricket developed here in its own inimitable way. At a meeting of the Gentlemen of the district held on 19 June 1829 Taunton Cricket Club was founded and 23 June appointed as the first 'set-too' in a field called the poor grounds, a few hundred yards from East Reach turnpike, a field provided by Mr Jeffrey of the London Hotel. Reports indicate that the players were mostly young beginners and add that cricket was not yet much practised in Somerset and that a high degree of skill could not be expected.

The Reverend James Pycroft, who lays claim to having founded Lansdown, recalled:

> being a small boy at school in Grosvenor Place, Bath, in 1824. I joined in a fund for bats and balls, played every half-holiday on Chornbury Down above Swainswick and afterwards, being joined by gentlemen of the neighbourhood, we shifted our ground to Lansdown about half a mile beyond Beckford's tower, and took the name of the far famed Lansdown Club.

Starchy and vain, Pycroft regarded himself as having 'as much as anyone else the right to be called the founder of Lansdown'. A graduate of Trinity College, Cambridge, who was called to the Bar at Lincoln's Inn, he was later to describe travelling professionals as 'a very serious nuisance, as superseding those annual contests between rural counties, making their living in a silly way'. He held a view of professionals which was to riddle Somerset cricket for 125 years, perhaps longer.

Lansdown quickly employed Somerset's first cricket professional, John Sparks, whose job it was to prepare pitches and to bowl to members. He is described in *Scores and Biographies* as 'a hard, slashing hitter, a splendid bias bowler of no great pace'. Lansdown's chronicler Dr Bradfield relates that he may originally have been a gamekeeper but that little is known about him as his daughter refused to furnish any account of him, stating that he played cricket against the wishes of his friends.

Ashby, a carpenter, succeeded Sparks but Carstown and others followed, including Tom Young, who lived by the gasworks in Bath, and Frank and Jack Lee. The Lees were to qualify by residence to play for Somerset between the wars.

In any event in 1830 clubs were being formed, some by aristocrats, others by farmers and shopkeepers who were apt to regard the local gentry as presumptuous. These clubs were creatures of fortune patently uncertain of their future and by no means central to either national or county life.

A team calling itself 'Somerset' had played a match on the recreation ground in Devizes in 1798, eleven gentlemen of Somerset being soundly thrashed by eleven gentlemen of Wiltshire. By all accounts both terms, 'Gentlemen' and 'Somerset' were misnomers for the teams were in no sense representative of Somerset; conduct following their defeat was somewhat questionable. A return fixture organized for the following week was delayed because Somerset players were, supposedly, ill. Historians relate that these Somerset Gentlemen wasted no time in summoning strong players from the counties of Surrey, Middlesex and Hampshire, a villainy compounded when another guest played under the name of John Thomas, a basket-weaver who said he had never previously tried his hand at this particular pastime. After the return match had been handsomely won, this adventurer was revealed as Scott, 'nearly the best player in England'. How the bets were settled history does not

6

tell, nor in what mood refreshments were supped that evening.

In truth these Gentlemen were a great deal more Bath than Somerset. Not that such licence was unusual, for in these times it was common for city and county to stand together, as in Devon and Exeter, or Cheltenham and Gloucestershire. Somerset cricket might have taken root in sophisticated, educated and rich Bath. Had it done so a very different club with a very different following would have resulted. Most will be thankful that Somerset happened, for it was largely a matter of chance, to stay close to its popular support, to turn away from cosmopolitan temptation.

History does not tell of any Somerset games played between 1798 and 1845. Games may occasionally have taken place, and an oil painting exists entitled 'Gloucester v Somerset August 1831'. Apparently the setting is near to the Duke of Beaufort's country house, and research indicates that the match is really between the Cliftonians and Lansdown. People were not, then, so concerned with labels or figures. In this picture a few gentlemen dressed in top and tails watch from the boundary as a ball is delivered underarm and with evident gentility. Plainly this game does not demand elevation into the august ranks of acknowledged county fixtures.

Somerset's first cricket match of any standing was played in 1845 against the Gentlemen of Dorset. These teams met twice that year, Somerset winning at Lansdown by 2 wickets and at Kingscote Park by an innings and 29 runs. As was the custom Somerset fielded 'given men' – 'ringins' in contemporary parlance – James Dean of Sussex and Samuel Redgate of Middlesex and were also 'assisted' by local clerics such as Rev J. H. Kirwan (Eton and Cambridge) and Rev W. Marcon (Eton and Oxford). Mr Charles Sainsbury, from a distinguished Bath family which was to serve Somerset cricket for years, also played. John Sainsbury, a brother, was one of Lansdown's best players, while Edward, a son, was to be an outstanding underarm bowler, an energetic and painstaking county captain and a steady batsman in the club's formative years. Already Somerset's team included a respectable clutch of clergy, a few rounded-up guests and a member of an important family.

Dorset won by 14 runs in 1846 after which nothing much was heard of Somerset cricket for years, though the game was capturing fresh addicts summer by summer. West of England (with given men) played MCC in 1844 and 1845 at Lords and at

7

Lansdown, winning twice and losing twice. Mr J. A. B. Marshall of Lansdown, who had a fine reputation as a long-stop, assisted the West on all four occasions and Fuller Pilch scored his tenth recorded hundred in the final contest.

Only from 1860 onwards did the Gentlemen of Somerset start playing with any regularity, Devon being their most frequent opponents, while Gloucestershire were met in 1863 and Dorset in 1871 and 1876. For Somerset Mr E. J. P. Cassan of Kings Bruton and Oxford (a blue in 1859) took many wickets and helped to lay the foundation of Somerset cricket, aided by Mr C. G. Elers of Crewkerne, by Rev E. T. Daubeny, an Oxford blue, who hit a capital 78 against All England in 1866, and by Mr S. C. Voules of Marlborough and Oxford (a blue from 1863 to 1866).

In 1861 Somerset played Devon at Martock and won, their team having been collected 'by the efforts of one individual', presumably Cassan. A scorecard survey of the 1861 game is shown opposite.

In 1862 Somerset and Devon gentlemen met at Exeter but only seven Somerset men turned up. Devon were victorious once more in 1863, and were clearly far better organized than their neighbours who were a thing of shreds and patches, a state to which they were to return from time to time.

By now cricket in England had evolved from a recreation enjoyed by aristocrats and ruffians into a game in which industrial workers and landed gentry fought not so much for power as to find a way of mutual survival. For cricket was no longer a mere pastime, it was an important game, a game good for the character in some opinions, in others a game in which a man might make a living. Since mid-century a battle had raged between those prepared to play for money and those bred not to do so. It was a class struggle and an economic struggle too and to survive it relatively unscathed has been one of cricket's greatest triumphs. A soccer amateur association and professional league separated for a time, reuniting only when the amateurs, realizing their irrelevance, retreated. Nevertheless the separate traditions of association and league endure. Rugby split into two camps, apparently for ever, while athletics and tennis were rent asunder for decades until, at last, two separate arms of the river merged into one swelling, flowing mass the directio nof which was determined, for the most part, by money rather than principle.

In cricket, too, these different forces struggled for control

8

in the nineteenth century, though the ripples were barely felt in distant Somerset, where club cricket was so weak, and the industrial base so thin.

SOMERSET *v* DEVON

There was very little cricket in Wells in 1860 and 1861, owing to the great interest which was taken in the Rifle Volunteer Movement, but I am able to give the following score of one of the earliest contests between Devon and Somerset. The match was played on Thursday and Friday, the 1st and 2nd August, 1861, at Martock. Somerset won by nine wickets. –

DEVON

First Innings		Second Innings	
Kindersley, b. Cassan	0	b Cassan	1
Eaton, b. Cassan	0	b. Voules	4
Coplestone, b. Voules	0	c. Voules, b. Cassan	3
Magendie, run out	10	b. Voules	4
Curtis, b. Cassan	13	run out	1
Arundell, c. Muttlebury, b. Voules	4	c. Newman, b. Cassan	8
Milford, c. Voules, b. Cassan	0	c. Ainslie, b. Cassan	11
Bartlett, b. Voules	0	b. Voules	0
Archdall, b. Voules	1	run out	3
Almond, b. Voules	2	not out	1
Blackburne, b. Voules	0	b. Voules	9
Extras	4	Extras	20
	Total 34		Total 65

SOMERSET

First Innings		Second Innings	
E. Wilkins, c. Bartlett, b. Kindersley	8	c. Magendie, b. Curtis	5
G.B. Voules, c. Kindersley, b. Archdall	3		
S.C. Voules, b. Arundell	21	not out	8
C.M.H. Fryer, c. Arundell, b. Copplestone	7		
Ainslie, b. Coplestone	5	not out	16
E. Cassan, b. Arundell	4		
Pencarves, run out	4		
J.W. Richards, not out	5		
Muttlebury, b. Eaton	2		
Newman, run out	1		
Sparkes, b. Eaton	0		
Extras	11		
	Total 71		Total 29

Until the 1840s professional cricketers had peddled their wares in a random manner, playing for a club here, coaching at a school there. As cricket spread, thanks not least to *Bell's Life* (the principal sporting newspaper of the period), which took advantage of the cheap and rapid transmission of match reports permitted by a revived postal service. In 1846 William Clarke formed the first All England eleven, a travelling band of select cricketers who moved from town to town playing against the odds for a fee of £65; Clarke paid his men £5 each, most of these professionals emerged from mines and lace-making factories in Nottingham, unsurprisingly so because Nottingham was the home of Chartism which argued for universal male suffrage, a secret ballot and an annually elected parliament. Workers in this area were of independent mind and could see no reason why their cricketing skills should not be used to fill their stomachs. As late as 1847, Fergus O'Connor still stood as a Chartist member of Parliament for Nottingham.

Soon Clarke's team was immensely popular, and its arrival an occasion for festivity. Gentlemen paraded their ladies at these infrequent games. Fireworks were lit, and gambling and drinking were widespread.

By 1854 there were 110 professionals in England, most of them from Nottingham, Yorkshire, London, Kent and Cambridge. No Somerset cricketer was good enough to join the ranks of the professionals, save Voules, whose background prevented any such move. In fact Somerset was not to produce a distinguished professional cricketer until 1935 when a youngster appeared from Bicknoller who might, in an earlier age, have been an amateur, for he had been to a minor public school. Club cricket in Somerset has never been strong enough to produce a supply of professionals in the manner of, say, the Yorkshire, Birmingham and Lancashire leagues. Somerset cricketers usually emerge from public and private schools, or else their talent is permanently lost.

Since Clarke and his team were earning well and leading the life of Reilly (though days of reckoning were, sadly, to arrive) other professional troupes appeared. John Wisden broke away from Clarke to form his United England eleven, bringing his team to meet 22 or 18 of Lansdown as early as 1852. That game ended in a draw, while All England won in 1853. In 1858 Wisden and his men played against Bath, and in 1860 they met Lansdown again.

10

Wisden, a small fellow who bowled quickish off-cutters, brought with him Thomas Hayward, the finest professional batsman of the day, and Julius Caesar (no relation). A year later Lansdown won by 13 wickets, E. J. Morris finishing with analysis of 13/65.

Besides various professional touring teams, lots of amateur travelling clubs appeared too, including Eccentrics, Anomalies, Vagabonds, Anythingians and I Zingari, one of whose eminent and colourful founders was one day to be Somerset Cricket Club's first president. Few of these teams, paid or otherwise, ever visited so farflung a part of the cricketing empire as West Somerset, for no one considered the game to be well or seriously played on the rough fields of her towns and villages.

Cricket in Somerset developed in its own inimitable way. In 1857 Milverton bowled out Wiveliscombe for 8 and Martock fielded a 'pro' called Cater who took 7 wickets against Taunton (who nevertheless won). On 29 August that year Wellington played Milverton, winning by 44 and 41 to 23 and 14 after which both teams repaired to the Globe Inn and partook of a 'substantial repast'. When Bishops Lydeard played Milverton the players adjourned to the Cricketers Arms where they partook of a 'collation'. On 19 September the swift underarm bowling of W. Maynard was praised in the contest between Taunton and Wellington, a large crowd gathering to watch 'this old English game' which was being played as part of an archery fête. A band played too and a fireworks display followed. Cricket in Somerset was neither organized nor strong, but it was fun.

During the 1860s professional touring teams began to fade and county clubs to grow. It was not a question of quality, for the professionals were still far superior to the amateurs, regularly winning their biannual engagements in London. But the professionals had fractured into so many parts and, moreover, cities were growing. In 1837 only six cities could boast more than 100,000 people; by 1891 the number had risen to twenty-three. This strengthened club teams and led to rejection of contests between eighteen locals and an amorphous bunch of strolling players. Pride in city, town and county rose and with it a demand for genuine matches between teams representing different areas.

Somerset began to awaken. In 1865 enthusiasts in Yeovil formed a committee and decided to begin a Yeovil and County Cricket Club. It was a reaction to inactivity elsewhere as much as a

11

challenge to Lansdown. More working class than most Somerset towns, Yeovil never really had a chance, for Somerset, as a farming community, was certain to produce an amateur club either in aristocratic Bath or amongst the country set around Taunton.

Anyhow, Yeovil was having a go. A field near Pen Mill railway station was bought and a concert held to raise money to build a pavilion. Mr Wadham, the secretary, announced: 'We're busy levelling the ground and three county matches have been arranged – against Devon, Dorset and North Wiltshire.' Unfortunately Yeovil and the County played badly in an early match against Shaftesbury, which, as David Foot has related, prompted a pointed remark in the *Western Gazette*: 'A professional from Oxford has been engaged for the Yeovil Club and we trust that members will come out to practise as the professional is now on the ground and ready for bowling.' In June when the club went to Montacute they were three players short and it emerged that the missing men had joined these rivals a day earlier. Cricket was not quite a proper game in 1865.

These were club fixtures, and it was not until Devon arrived that a county match was played. Somerset made 73 and 142, Devon 46 and 28/1, whereupon it rained. Alas, 'few bothered to turn up to watch', much to the disappointment of officials. No doubt curiosity was dampened by the somewhat rudimentary facilities at Pen Mill and by grim weather too, for English cricket followers had not yet been trained to a life of sitting in neglected misery while flannelled fools do their stuff upon the greensward.

Was this Somerset's first game as a county club? Certainly the team contained several respected names and several obscure ones, thereby setting a trend determinedly followed ever since. The Somerset team was C. Newman, Rev C. Ainslie, E. F. Henley, H. Lang, S. C. Voules, J. P. Gundry, A. A. Kenley, H. P. Doddington, G. B. Voules, C. Pencarves and H. Monk.

Mr Ainslie had been an archdeacon in Taunton and served as vicar of Corfe from 1854 to 1871 and of Over Stowey from 1871. Besides being an eager cricketer he was a first-class scholar who had travelled to India, Egypt, Turkey and Greece. In later life he was embroiled in the hot debate over Church discipline in 1903. More importantly he was to preside at the meeting in 1875 at which the modern county club was formed. Plainly a fellow with whom to reckon.

Doddington (more correctly Marriott-Doddington) was to be a familiar name too. These Doddingtons were a military and politically Conservative family who used to raise a team to play against Somerset on their ground in Horsington. Somerset lost there in 1881. Things were going well until a refreshing tea was widely enjoyed after which 'a mighty change came over the game'. This Doddington was no fool. Somerset club colours are those of the Marriott-Doddington family.

S. C. Voules cannot be ignored either. Another vicar, Voules entered the Church after leaving Oxford where he had taken his blue four years in a row, winning each time, and taking 7/26 in 1863. He also played for the Gentlemen against the Players in 1863 and 1864, but it was at university that he earned his nickname 'Rat' and where his captain, R. A. H. Mitchell, stopped him as he walked out to bat on a bad pitch and said: 'Now, Rat, steady for the first hour.'

He was a good cricketer, Stirling Cookesley Voules, and in 1875 he was the only Somerset player deemed worthy of inclusion in *Lillywhite's* list of significant cricketers, where he is described as 'one of the very best all round cricketers. He is now Headmaster of Sidney College, Bath.' It fell to Voules, in that year of 1875, to captain a team of Somerset Gentlemen in Sidmouth in the game which led to the formation of a county club.

Cricket was changing. Overarm bowling had been authorized (1864) and nets and a heavy roller used at Lord's, where in 1872 the pitch was covered before the game by way of experiment. Registration rules determining qualification to play for a county were introduced in 1872 to prevent men playing for whomsoever they chose whenever they liked. No man could play for more than one county in a season and soon a two-year period in residence was necessary. With these rules in place a county championship was deemed to exist, by historians at any rate, and newspapers printed tables until, finally, Lord's bestowed its blessing upon a championship to be contested by the most distinguished county clubs, a sextet to which Lancashire, Gloucestershire and Derbyshire had been added by 1871.

Having so little indigenous cricket of any merit, Somerset could hardly expect to mingle in such company, and they did not. Until 1885 Somerset cricket was in a chaotic state with brief periods of promise being undermined by years of hope-lessness. What is astonishing is that such a transformation was wrought over Somerset cricket from 1886 to 1890 that they won almost unanimous support for their application to join 'the sacred angels' in the championship for 1891. It was a change for which much credit must be given to three men: Murray-Anderdon, an honorary secretary, and two professionals, Tyler and Nichols.

But we jump ahead of ourselves. It is time to go to Sidmouth and to form a club.

2

Raising a team

In August 1875 eleven cricketing gentlemen of Somerset ambled down to Sidmouth to play eleven gentlemen of Devon. Somerset's team consisted largely of men from the western part of the county, for Sidmouth was an awfully long way from Bath, too far to travel upon the hope of a day's cricket.

Somerset won the game, bowling Devon out for 33 and 117, and scoring 141 and 10/2 themselves. Rev Frank Reed took 7/18 and Edward Fortescue Wright, an eighteen-year-old, 3/12. Reed, born in Ottery St Mary and educated at Oxford, bowled firstly medium pace with a round arm and was a good enough batsman to carry his bat in 1884. He fielded at short slip from where he was apt to remark on the game in Latin, a custom no doubt continued later by another classical scholar, Victor Marks. Reed's elder brother William, also a vicar, played occasionally for Somerset and their father was headmaster at Fullands.

Besides these two, Somerset's team included W. W. Palmer, H. P. Doddington, E. Cassan, S. Poole, Tristram Welman from Norton Manor (who was to play cricket until his hair went white – another Somerset tradition), E. Western and W. H. P. Greswell, who had made his fortune by growing tea in a thousand acres of jungle he had cleared in Ceylon and who was to bestow upon Somerset cricket two sons, one of them an outstanding player. Three other vicars played a lot for Somerset. Rev Parry Woodcock, from Corfe, Rev G. Eden Peake, rector at Holford, and Rev W. W. Pulman at Wellington.

Welman, by the way, had been born in Taunton and attended Oxford before work took him to London and Middlesex's perfumed embrace. He played for the Gentlemen in 1884, his skills having been noted at university, and he eventually returned to his native county, playing occasionally until hanging up his gloves after playing against South Africa in 1901 at the age of fifty-two years and three months. Only three other men played for Somerset after their fifty-first birthday, two of them wicket-keepers, and all relics of the late Victorian period.

Following this game Voules called a meeting, asked Ainslie to take the chair and Edward Western, who had been Somerset's highest scorer in the match, to record such resolutions as might be passed, which he did in his best copperplate handwriting. Western taught at Fullands School in Taunton (where General Gordon of Khartoum was educated), which had been a private school since 1839, having abandoned its previous existence as a lunatic asylum following the abrupt disappearance of the owner who had absconded to America taking £900 belonging to a patient. Fullands School was already famous for its cricket; a splendid pitch had been laid out on Bowling Green Meadow to the north of the distinguished main house, which had previously belonged variously to a Roundhead major (1640) and to a First Lord of the Admiralty (early nineteenth century). For a time Fullands House had served as an overflow for prisoners awaiting trial at Taunton Assizes; then as an asylum; now as a school where cricket was keenly played. Criminals, madmen, teachers and cricketers. It is not so bad a lineage. A pavilion had been built and a scoreboard on a carefully mown field. (Most clubs bothered to mow only their cricket square, everything else resembled a cow paddock.)

'Teddie' Western was a noted sporting figure in Taunton and he enjoyed a game of cricket, usually keeping wicket though his talents in this and other games were slender. Nor, it emerged, was he a capable administrator, for Somerset cricket did not flourish when he was at the helm. Perhaps he was simply a willing fellow who could offer a pitch at his school.

The *ad hoc* committee decided that

> 1. It is desirable to organise Annual Matches against the neighbouring counties and against first-class Clubs, such as the Incogniti, &c.
> 2. The Secretaries of leading Cricket Clubs in Somerset be communicated with upon the subject, and their co-operation invited.

16

3. The Clubs which possess first-rate grounds, in convenient situations, be requested to allow the use of their grounds
for County Matches.

Western at once sent a letter to potential benefactors amongst
the landed gentry of Taunton:

NEVA HOUSE, ILFRACOMBE

SIR, – I beg to enclose a copy of the resolutions passed
at Sidmouth in August 1875, relative to the establishment
of a county cricket club in Somerset. The following is the
scheme:
　　1. That there shall be no county ground.
　　2. That the club shall depend upon its support by voluntary
subscriptions.
　　3. That county matches shall be played on any ground
in the county that may be selected by the Committee.
　　4. That a president, vice-president, treasurer, and secretary
be nominated, and a committee consisting of nine gentlemen,
three from each division of the county, shall be appointed.
　　This appeal is being made throughout the county, and
it is hoped that the result will be such as to prevent the
great expense of county matches falling too heavily on the
individual players; otherwise many good men are excluded,
and the county cannot do itself justice. – I am, Sir, yours
faithfully,

EDWARD WESTERN, *Hon Secy.*

Nominations for president, vice-president, treasurer and secretary were requested and a committee of nine was to run the
club affairs. Oh, happy days! In Somerset's entire history this
was the only time when such a reasonable constitution was in
place. With minor changes in structure and even personnel it
served Somerset splendidly until 1930, after which came a series
of altercations which transformed a family club into an institution
run by a vast and self-perpetuating committee. The first club rules
were not especially democratic but at least they provided authority and accountability rather than the curtain of red tape which
so frustrated later secretaries – some of them, admittedly, only
moderately shrewd men.

Taunton was a sporting town, having raced horses on and
off since 1829 and continually fielding all manner of hunts. A
strong response to Western's announcement was expected. In the

17

event Somerset's newly formed club attracted only 112 subscribers, including John Bonamy Challen, a Welsh boy of thirteen who was to play for Somerset from 1884 to 1899, and soccer for Wales too. Each subscriber paid half a guinea and when various bequests were added £70 17s 0d was deposited into the first bank account of Somerset CCC. No doubt the bank manager considered this a somewhat unimpressive sum upon which to commence trade but Somerset officials waxed lyrical, arguing that better times were just around the corner, an argument which has been used so often since that it is fortunate bank managers change from time to time.

Somerset's first opponents as a proper club were Incogniti, who were met at Fullands on 7 August 1876, a contest closely followed by two other matches at Fullands, against Devon (Somerset winning by 200 runs) and the Civil Service. So began what was to be a long tradition of cricketing fortnights in Taunton during August, when the students and schoolmasters were free to play. Only with the growth of fixtures forty years later, was this happy fortnight lost.

Reports of this first season of 1876 indicate that 'much interesting cricket was seen but owing to weak bowling successes were not as numerous as could have been desired'. *Plus ça change . . .*! But Somerset did record a profit, so 1876 was not entirely a typical year. Of the £70 raised only £40 13s 11d was spent, 5s 6d of it on a scoreboard and 6s 9d on telegrams. (Such parsimony set an unfortunate example because officials of later generations were expected, more or less, to keep telegraphic costs below 6s 9d.)

Not that Somerset cricket was the talk of Taunton, let alone the pubs. A mere £1 15s 8d was taken on the gate in 1876. Tauntonians were more interested in a game between sixteen men who had never played cricket before and eleven experts armed with broomsticks. A big crowd of sightseers gathered and seemed to enjoy the spectacle, the broomsticks winning by 5 wickets in their second innings. Certainly in Somerset cricket was by no means yet prepared to abandon its rollicking, gambolling ways.

Australian cricketers were different. Reports indicated that they were 'steady and abstemious men who never give up till the last run is made'. Some, one astonished critic observed, 'are total abstainers', whereas 'our men live too highly'. Australians took bowling seriously too, crowds clapping a triumphant bowler no less than a productive batsman, which was not the English custom, for here the game contained echoes of master and servant as well as professional and amateur.

If Somerset cricketers were abstemious in 1877 it was a singular occasion in an epicurean history. Sober or drunk, William Morton Massey, born in Scotland, buried in New York, hit an unbeaten 120 for Somerset against Sussex in 1877 and is accordingly the club's first centurian, though this was not a first-class game. Massey was a devoted cricketer who, having scored 1,998 runs in all matches one summer, arranged an extra game in October, raising both teams so that he might score his 2,000th run. Unfortunately he bagged a pair. In 1882 Massey played one first-class game for Somerset and in 1883 he played another match for someone else and that was it.

Mr M. Lloyd hit 110 against Dorset, in 1877, Somerset's team including Welman, Alfred Pontifex, William Roe (aged sixteen) and the promising fast bowler Alfred Evans, who was born in Madras and was to captain Oxford University at Lord's in 1881, bowling them to victory. In his four university matches Evans took 36 wickets for 471 runs, besides which he won a rugby blue as a clever half-back, and played for the Gentlemen. In time he went to Winchester College as an assistant master and eventually moved on to be a preparatory school headmaster. Blue, rugby player, schoolmaster and holiday cricketer, Evans was very much the sort of fellow to be found in Somerset's cricket team in the nineteenth century. Such another was John Winter of Bishops Lydeard, who sometimes helped Somerset. He brought attention to himself by bowling out every member of a village team for a total score of 2 leg-byes.

In 1877 Taunton held its first open athletics meeting at Vivary Park. Undeterred by heavy rain, 130 men competed, following which an Athletic Society was formed. Within a few years this society had combined with a cycling club (founded in 1878) and the town cricket club to share a field. Sports were, at last, being organized in Somerset.

Ted Sainsbury and Hamilton Ross (who was born and died in Grenada in the British West Indies, and who also kept wicket for Middlesex) scored runs in local club cricket and in 1878 Sainsbury hit a hundred for Somerset against Hampshire, adding 114 for the 8th wicket with the Rev Frank Reed. Somerset's team included Western, Massey, Newton, Winter and Bill Fowler, a ferocious hitter of whom more was to be heard.

By 1879 the presence of such talents as Evans, Sainsbury, Welman and Stephen Newton was deemed sufficient to give Somerset a start in better company and matches were arranged against Surrey and Gloucestershire. Unfortunately Somerset played badly and sceptical local newspapers advised them either to drop two important words from their title – Somerset County Cricket Club – or to find a better team. Somerset beat only Hertfordshire and stood accused of measuring a cricketer by the length of his pocket. Journalists pointed out that the county's best men could not afford to play. Somerset was a team founded upon breeding rather than skill.

Money was tight, of course, and plays were staged in local theatres to supplement club funds. Nevertheless it is plain that Somerset's new club had failed to win support, had failed to grow beyond its origins as a simple, and occasional amateur outfit with no genuine desire to represent the county's strength. Somerset lacked drive off the field and were competent on it only in the matter of fielding, for Welman shone and Stephen Newton was regarded as being as superb a cover point as the celebrated Vernon Royle, against whom he had played in the 1876 Varsity match. Newton was a useful batsman, wrote Roe, whose reminiscences have survived, 'but I never saw anyone, except Barker, who played so many balls with his pad'. Roe added that 'by far the best batsman in the side was E. Sainsbury, the old Sherbornian'.

Perhaps, as Somerset stumbled along, caught midway between being jolly amateurs and earnest competitors, it is time to say more about William Roe, earliest chronicler of the club's affairs.

Though born in Somerset, Roe went to school in Canterbury where, as he was apt to recall in his dotage, he played against Chatham lunatic asylum and was chased from the field by an inmate who took exception to losing his middle stump. Roe was a mathematician too, and could recollect every shot of his innings, rather as might a boring golfer, even recalling every detail of his 415 in a college game at Cambridge. A keen cricketer, he was described by *Lillywhite's* as a hard-hitting batsman and as a 'plucky and sterling ex-Cantab'. Upon leaving university he took to teaching, which prevented him playing regularly. His career took him to Elstree and then to Stanmore, where he helped Vernon Royle to found a preparatory school. A heavily built man who sported a brush moustache, he was given to wearing an I Zingari cap and blazer. Fred Poynton, a doctor who occasionally assisted

Somerset, wrote of him as being 'not easy to know as is so often the case with schoolmasters'.

Roe was still a schoolboy when he made his first-class début for Somerset at The Oval in 1882. His first ball beat H. Jupp and led to a boisterous appeal and a kindly 'Not so fast young man, can't you see you've bowled him?' from the umpire. Next he played against W.G. at Clifton and was at once bowled neck and crop. 'He fairly mesmerized you, youngster,' said umpire Thomas, whereupon Grace invited the boy to practise next morning, bowling to him for a quarter of an hour. Roe scored an unbeaten 23 in the second innings.

Never should the capacity of men such as Grace to mesmerize and to hoodwink lesser men be underestimated – for only by these powers can men such as Jack White and Ian Botham have taken so many easy wickets.

Roe liked to remember his numerous trips to Manchester – where, he said, out of twenty-one days it rained on seventeen and snowed on another: 'We used to spend most of our time at Manchester Zoo and amused ourselves by throwing hard biscuits down the neck of the Hippo who seemed to enjoy it thoroughly though the smack when Sammy Woods was throwing could be heard a long way off.'

A public school boy, a schoolmaster, a paragon of respectability, a man who ended his days writing upon school cricket, he was a familiar figure at Lord's before his death in a London nursing home after an operation. Roe was scarcely less a typical Somerset cricketer of this period than Evans. Clerics and teachers, they were both men inclined to earn their living apart from trade and eager to spend as much of their summers as possible in idle pursuits, and amongst men of like mind. These were companionable days, and Somerset's new club was a reserve of conservative gentlemen who liked their cricket and were determined to play it properly.

Roe left this tribute to his years at Somerset:

> I doubt if any county ever had a happier band of cricketers than those who played for Somerset in the late 'eighties and 'nineties. There was never the slightest jealousy or ill-feeling, and though we often got beaten we also brought off many surprising victories. They were happy days, indeed, those twenty-one years during which I played for Somerset. What would I not give to have them all over again!

In 66 first-class games (played between 1882 and 1899) for Somerset Roe scored 2,404 runs at an average of 22.47. Handicapped by infrequent appearances and little helpful practice, Roe, like so many Somerset contemporaries did not score enough runs to support his reputation. Indeed few Somerset cricketers – certainly fewer than fond memories and parochial analyses would indicate – can truly stand beside those from powerful northern, eastern and midland counties. Somerset has produced hardly any indigenous cricketers capable of challenging for an England place.

Meanwhile in Taunton a multiplicity of small clubs had appeared and local cricket mixed enthusiasm with chaos. Deputations from various sports clubs met with a view to finding a field for their joint use and word had it that John Winter was willing to offer part of his farm. Mr Western promised that county games would be played upon such a field if provided, and plainly a pavilion must be built. Things were beginning to take shape. Somerset was beginning to take cricket seriously.

3

Finding a pitch

In 1880 Gladstone won a general election, Ned Kelly was captured and, in Taunton, duck shooting was the main crime, though more lurid affairs from afar were colourfully reported in local newspapers.

Somerset cricketers had a much better year, winning five and losing three games. Hampshire were beaten in Bournemouth thanks to 78 from Stephen Newton. Furthermore, Somerset beat Sussex while in the return fixture Sainsbury hit a hundred to take his team to a 2-wicket victory, following which he was carried on the shoulders of his confrères to the pavilion. It was a dry summer and despite these high scorers, Somerset depended heavily upon their first professionals, Brooks and Fothergill, to bowl opponents out.

Little is known about A. J. Brooks save that his career was short and somewhat disappointing, so that he never played a first-class game for Somerset, who were not granted such status until 1882. Arnold Fothergill was to be Somerset's first Test cricketer though really his caps were rather bogus. A left-arm fast bowler, he was a Londoner who had learned his trade on the Lord's groundstaff. Between 1882 and 1884 he played sixteen games for Somerset and by 1888 he was a veteran work-horse who might be picked for a few friendly matches, notwithstanding which he was taken by Major Warton, who had just retired from the Army after five years of service in South Africa, to tour the veld in a mixed team of professionals and club cricketers.

It was, by all accounts, a jolly trip and early defeats led to observations that 'generous hospitality had a bad effect'. Fothergill's Test

23

career consisted of two games played against weak opposition in South Africa. England's team was in no way representative and really it is nonsense to elevate these contests to Test match status. In any event Fothergill took 4 cheap wickets as England won the first encounter by 8 wickets, whereupon they dismissed South Africa for 47 and 43 in Cape Town to take the series. Fothergill played only one more first-class game but Somerset rewarded him with a benefit match against Middlesex in 1891.

Fothergill took 11 MCC wickets at Taunton in 1880 and Somerset won, having lost at Lord's by 10 wickets. Fixtures against 16 of Frome and Will o'the Wisps were also arranged, and the Gentlemen of Devon were trounced at Fullands where Mr C. J. Wilson hit 3 sixes out of the field. 'Somerset', wrote the critics, 'now ranks high amongst the cricketing counties' – an unduly generous statement for they had not yet been measured against England's strongest teams; besides which, they had little structure off the field and a woeful lack of depth on it.

Cricket in Taunton was 'in a sorry plight' according to the *County Gazette*, for there was little interest and lots of discontent. Somerset played Clifton College, could field only eight men and deservedly lost. Athletics was all the rage and it was a combination of Taunton athletes, cyclists, football players and cricketers all searching for an appropriate arena which eventually concentrated Somerset CCC's mind upon building a cricket ground during the winter of 1880.

By a great stroke of luck a field was found almost at once and in an ideal location to boot. John Winter, a local gentleman farmer, was short of money. Lambrook Farm had been in the Winter family for at least 150 years and Watts House (now Cedar Falls) was the family home from where was run a property spreading from Bishops Lydeard round the River Tone to where the sewerage works are to be found. But John Winter was a spendthrift and a man of consummate imagination, especially in business matters, a man who involved himself in all manner of extravagant schemes of a military type (armour for horses and suchlike), none of which proved nearly as lucrative as had been hoped. Accordingly he needed ready cash and his offer to let his Rack Field of 7½ acres on the outskirts of Taunton did not spring merely from a kind heart. In the course of a few years he was to dispose of Priory House, with its garden, stables and 70 acres and

Lambrook Farm with its 72 acres and two cottages in St James Park.

In any event an amalgamation of sporting clubs in Taunton, all wanderers hitherto, agreed upon common use of Rack Field. A cricket pitch and a cycling-track and running-track had to be laid down; no easy task, for fields in this area were low-lying, undrained and produced little besides bulrushes and prickly plants. Moreover near by was to be found a wide open black and stinking ditch which couples tried to ignore as they enjoyed their afternoon walks. The lease cost £50 per year. Edward Western promised that County games could be played there but acknowledged that so far as cricket went Rack Field belonged to Taunton Cricket Club.

Rack Field was opened in some style on Whit Monday 1881. An athletics fixture was organized to mark the occasion, excellent times being recorded on the new running-track, which was perfectly laid. It was a 440-yard track built in a D shape with a straight of 150 yards. Taunton was bedecked with flags and it was a gala day. The Great Western Railway provided extra carriages and cheap fares to bring Somerset families to the celebrations. Four thousand people arrived to mark the occasion and they were treated to a firework display by Wilder & Co, the well-known Birmingham pyrotechnist.

Some cricket was played on the Rack Field even in 1881, Mr Morley having 'provided a tolerably good wicket'. Of course it was by no means yet ready for first-class cricket; nevertheless plans were afoot. Taunton Athletic Society promised to erect a grandstand on their ground and to this end Western raised £400 on a personal guarantee, £150 of it being used to pay debts and the rest put towards the costs of a pavilion and grandstand.

On 15 August the new ground stood witness to a bicycle race between the French Champion De Civry and John Keen, the Champion of All England. They were to race over 15 miles with De Civry being given a one-mile start. A grandstand for 1,000 people was erected and the contest eagerly awaited, for cycling was popular, and a handicap race even more so.

Sadly it was a flop. A big crowd arrived but Keen was injured and withdrew after 9 miles having made no headway. 'From malice or ignorance,' the *Gazette* reported, 'some mischievous busybodies have been concocting the extraordinary statement that the man who raced under the name of Keen was not Keen.' It was also rumoured that not only was De Civry not De Civry, but he was not even French. Luckily some Taunton gentlemen had been to France and upon interviewing the cyclist were satisfied that he passed muster.

Somerset had a moderate cricket season. They met Gloucester-shire at Lansdown where 1,000 people watched play. When Sussex arrived in Bath for their fixture confusion reigned in the Somerset ranks, Scott failing to appear and the telegraph service failing to track him down. Apparently no one had been certain if Lansdown or Fullands was to stage the game. Earlier Fothergill had been the cause of a dispute which led Somerset to apologize for the 'rough treatment of the Kent team due to the misconduct of one man'. Kent had arrived in Bath, unusually enough with ten professionals in their ranks and led by Rev C. I. Thornton. Finding that Somerset meant to play Fothergill, their new professional from Lord's, they objected strongly that he was not qualified and insisted that he be replaced. What ensued is lost in time. Fothergill did not play all summer and F. S. Coke, a nineteen-year-old, was summoned to take his place against Kent. As A. H. Evans did not play either Somerset was practically denuded of bowlers in this first meeting with a top county and they duly lost. Who meted out rough treatment to whom cannot at this distance be said, though Leeston-Smith was thought by some to have rather a heavy hand. In any event matches were resumed in 1884.

Somerset would have liked to play this fixture on the Taunton Athletic Ground but it had been a dry summer; besides, the running-track had demanded too much of the groundsman's time for a wicket to be properly prepared.

In that same season of 1881 Master W. W. F. Pullen played for Somerset at the age of 15 years and a few days – the youngest fellow ever to do so. He was never to play a first-class game for the Club, because W. G. Grace, a rascal who lived near by, hearing of Pullen's talent lured him to Gloucestershire where, surprisingly, his career faded into disappointment.

By 1882 the ground was in use though it was a rougher place than it is today, for a foundry and a tannery stood near by and when the wind blew from the east, which was a fortu-nately infrequent occurrence, a distinctive smell spread across the ground, reaching the cottages amongst the trees on the far side. Apparently in a strong breeze the stench could be overpowering. By now a handsome grandstand had been built by the Taunton Grandstand and Pavilion company at a cost of £800. Around 500 people could be seated in comfort to watch events unfold upon a surprisingly reliable pitch prepared by Underwood, Morley having departed. Inside the pavilion was a room in which up to 100 people could dine and adjoining it were a dressing-room, a committee-room, a cloakroom, a lavatory and a refreshment billet. Everyone agreed that this Pavilion bore testimony to the adventurous spirit of Taunton Athletic Society.

Somerset's gradual rise in stature was reflected in 1882 by a meeting arranged with the Australian tourists of that year. It was not, in truth, much of a contest for Somerset lost in two days, to the dismay of their treasurer, who had to present half of the £125 gate receipts to the visitors. Around 1,000 people attended each day's play, distinguished members sitting in some comfort beside the pavilion, and others on hard benches around the ground, or on the grass banks which rose in each corner of the field. Part of the ground was reserved for carriages and this area was fully occupied. Also a tent had been erected for the president while the scorers had a box to themselves. Mr A. Hammett kept a small printing-press on the ground and issued a card giving the state of play at the fall of each wicket. Considering all this it was sad not to see a larger crowd. Alas, Taunton was 'at the heart of a district where cricket is but slightly appreciated' (*Somerset County Gazette*).

Fred Spofforth – The Demon – took 9/51 in an innings and 13/113 in the game, bowling from first to last. Legend insists that Bill Fowler, a local hitter who could bowl fast and who was given to playing in a flannel shirt boasting MCC colours, lofted Spofforth's first delivery over the pavilion. It is a story, and a hit, which has gained something in the telling. In fact Spofforth's opening ball hit Bill Murdoch, his captain and wicket-keeper, in the eye and his opening over was a maiden. Fowler did thereafter twice hit Spofforth over the carriages which were stationed around the enclosure. But he who laughs last laughs longest: Fowler's was not a productive innings.

Australia made 245, Somerset 96 and 130, Evans and Fothergill taking wickets. William Roe recollected facing Spofforth, and striking 2 successive boundaries through cover:

I can remember thinking to myself that he wasn't such a terrible bowler at all, but my illusion didn't last long, for I had hardly begun to play at the next ball before my middle stump was halfway to the screen. I had never before come across such a change of pace with no change in the action.

Only Ted Sainsbury with 16 not out resisted Spofforth for long. Bill Fowler, a Londoner, was to be a figure of some importance in Somerset's story though not as much as his younger brother Gerald, who was to play 119 games for Somerset (Bill played 15) and stayed to serve for years as treasurer.

Both were men of bulk. Bill was tall and powerful, a man capable of clearing any pavilion, hitting shots measured at 157 yards at Lord's and 154 against W. G. Grace at Gloucester. He played golf for England against Scotland in 1903 and 1905 and later designed courses in England and America. He was, too, one of the trustees upon whom the freehold of Rack Field was vested upon its acquirement by Somerset in 1896. Bill played regularly for MCC later in his life.

Gerald was a big man too, and a hard striker especially through cover. An Oxford blue in 1888 (he took 5 wickets with his fast stuff), he played for Essex for a time, and upon moving to Somerset he began an interesting cricket career, once scoring four ducks in a row, and ending with 3,472 runs (17.62) and 76 wickets, taken at a reduced pace. He acted as treasurer to Somerset from 1896 to 1916, the year in which he died.

These Fowlers were formidable men, alarming at first but with a bark far worse than their bite. It was typical of Somerset in this period that two brothers should play for them and continue to help for decades afterwards, for Somerset cricket was, until the Great War at least, essentially a family affair, albeit a family which included some rather chilly uncles and several sons of a sort commonly dispatched to Australia – one of whom had in fact travelled in precisely the opposite direction.

Somerset played Lancashire at Old Trafford in that year of 1882, a game generally regarded as its premier first-class match. As a début it cannot entirely be deemed a triumph for Somerset was dismissed for 29 and the northern professionals won by an innings and 157 runs. George Nash, a clever slow left-arm merchant with an action some thought to be dubious, took 4 wickets in successive balls and 8/14 all told. Fothergill and Scott were Somerset's pros and this first team included W. Fowler, E. Sainsbury, H. Tate, F. Welman, Fothergill, H. F. Fox, F. J. Potbury, W. Trask, H. Hall and Scott. It is a list rather short of class.

H. F. Fox was a Cliftonian born in Somerset who was to play ten games. Henry Fox was educated at Sherborne, played three times for Somerset and died in Russia in 1888 at the age of 32. Trask had been to Sherborne too, and formed part of the distinguished Trask clan in Bath. John Trask played four games for Somerset between 1884 and 1895 before dying of cholera when serving as a surgeon captain in the Sudan. William Trask was a good golfer whose partners included William Roe. He was to play forty-seven games for Somerset during which he failed to leave an indelible mark upon Somerset cricket.

Somerset played Lancashire again, and Hornby was moved to complain about Bill Fowler's shirt with its harlequin colours, for Fowler was crouching near to the bat. Hornby was bowled and complained that he had not kept his eyes on the ball because 'the only thing I could see on the field was Fowler's shirt'. Decades later batsmen used to ask Arthur Wellard to put his teeth back in as they were finding his appearance somewhat off-putting. Once again events echo through the ages.

Plotting an unpredictable course, Somerset did not do much in 1883, losing twice to Gloucestershire despite wickets from Fothergill and a new slow left-arm spinner who, frustratingly, was to have time for a mere trickle of county games, Edward Bastard. Rather stiffly *Lillywhite's* reported that 'certain counties are trying to force their way to the front, notably Somersetshire, but professionals not being indigenous to the area it is feared that their advance is only temporary'.

And *Lillywhite's* was right. Somerset could not depend upon its own resources to survive, could compete only by living on its wits, by adding imported players to such local talent as might emerge. Club cricket could not be relied upon to produce players. None the less Somerset was thought to be on the threshold. As it turned out, 1884 and 1885 were grim years lightened only by the occasional arrival at the County Ground of the clown cricketers, a group of failed professionals who travelled around playing entertaining games. Shops were closed early but crowds were disappointing and money was lost.

Somerset lost five games in 1884 and fielded twenty-seven men.

29

Their plight would have been worse had not Bastard, Roe, Stephen Newton and J. B. Challen played with some skill.

Edward Bastard was a local man who, like Fox and Trask, had been educated at Sherborne. From the start, Somerset was fortunate to have the pick of so many distinguished schools in its area. He won an Oxford blue with his slow left-arm spinners, twice taking a hat-trick, played for the Gentlemen, and once took 8/59 for his county. Unfortunately he could not play regularly and trapped just 57 men in his three seasons of occasional cricket. He died in Taunton at the age of 39 while engaged in scholastic work.

Only S. C. Newton, the captain, Charles Winter, a Londoner who had little impact, Trask, Sainsbury, and Francis Terry, a capable batsman and wicket-keeper who had been born in Wells and attended Oxford University, played in every game in that dismal year of 1884.

Hampshire scored 645 at Southampton, the first but by no means the last big total struck against the Cidermen. A year later, shamefully, Somerset 'was able to send only 9 men' to Southampton and, despite the efforts of Bastard and Winter, lost by 8 wickets. Major E. H. Murdoch played in this match, one of only two in his career. A capable wicket-keeper, he died forty-one years later with his pads still on, victim of a heart-attack in the pavilion at Bristol where he was playing a club game.

So appalling was Somerset's effort in Hampshire that a contemporary report and scorecard must be printed.

HAMPSHIRE v SOMERSETSHIRE

Somersetshire was only able to send nine men to Southampton on Thursday last for its return match with Hampshire, and the home team had, in consequence, a great advantage, enabling them to secure an easy victory with 8 wickets to spare. The chief features of the match were the good batting of Messrs Radcliffe and Winter for Somersetshire, of Messrs Powell and Calder for Hampshire, and the effective bowling of Mr Bastard. The Oxford slow bowler indeed did a capital performance in the first innings of Hants, taking eight of the ten wickets at a cost of only 59 runs. Mr H. W. Forster, of the Eton eleven, made his first appearance for Hampshire in this match.

HAMPSHIRE

First Innings

Mr. D. Duncan, b Bastard 25
Mr. R.G. Hargreaves c Murdoch,
 b Bastard 8
Mr. E.O. Powell, c Sainsbury, b Bastard 33
Mr. H.W. Forster, c Spurway b Roe 20
Mr. H. Calder, b Bastard 10
Dible, b Bastard 8
Mr. H.J. Mordaunt, b Roe 0
Leat, c sub, b Bastard 4
Mr. C.E. Currie, b Bastard 26
Lieut. Col. Fellowes, b Bastard 23
Willoughby, not out.............................0
B 1, lb 2 3

Total 162

In the Second Innings Hargreaves scored (run out) 1, Calder, b Roe, 43, Powell (not out), 54, Duncan (not out), 10; b 12, lb 3 – Total 123.

SOMERSET

First Innings		Second Innings	
Mr. O.G. Radcliffe, run out 34		c and b Dible....................................29	
Mr. E. Sainsbury, c Fellowes, b Willoughby....................................9		c and b Forster 10	
Mr. E.P. Spurway, b Currie................10		b Forster...1	
Mr. W.N. Roe, c Calder, b Currie.........12		c Powell, b Dible................................1	
Mr. H.F. Reed, c Fellowes, b Currie 4		c Willougby, b Dible 10	
Mr. C.E. Winter, b Dible....................22		b Dible..62	
Mr. E.W. Bastard, c and b Currie 0		c Powell, b Forster 3	
Mr. E.H. Hall, not out 11		c and b Willoughby............................23	
Mr. E.H. Murdoch, c Dible.................4		not out 5	
B 5, lb 3 8		B 14, lb 3, w 5............................22	
Total....................117		Total....................166	

BOWLING ANALYSIS
SOMERSET

	O.	M.	R.	W.		O.	M.	R.	W.
Willoughby.......	12	6	21	1		20	8	36	1
Dible...............	35.3	21	32	2		32	18	43	4
Currie.............	27	12	49	4		15	9	14	0
Fellowes..........	5	1	7	0					
Calder............						12	4	19	0
Hargreaves......						3	0	10	0
Forster						17.2	9	22	3

Hargreaves bowled one and Forster four wides.

HAMPSHIRE

	O.	M.	R.	W.		O.	M.	R.	W.
Bastard............	35	15	59	8		27	12	38	0
Winter.............	7	2	35	0		2	1	4	0
Hall	7	1	20	0		2	0	8	0
Roe.................	19	10	37	2		26.3	13	42	1
Sainsbury	1	0	8	0		1	0	13	0
Reed............						2	0	13	0

Nor was this all. Somerset had played a man short at Lancashire a year earlier, W. H. Fowler being absent following 'an emergency' and clearly the club was in a parlous state. Unsurprisingly, heavy defeats were suffered through 1885: Surrey scoring 635 at The Oval; Gloucestershire (of all people) winning twice; and a solitary victory over Hampshire was won largely thanks to Bastard's 11/81.

Morale was dreadfully low. Support was dwindling. It was enough. A meeting was arranged after the Gloucestershire game in Taunton to review the business workings of the club. Rules were amended and influential vice-presidents sought. Western resigned as secretary, owing to pressure of work it was said, and Mr Murray-Anderdon was elected as honorary secretary, a position he was to occupy until 1910. He succeeded Sir Spencer Ponsonby-Fane as president in 1915.

So arrived at Somerset a man whose contribution to the club was to be enormous. Inheriting a factional and practically bankrupt club he managed to revive finances, buy a lovely ground and build a team strong enough to enter the County Championship in 1891. And all within ten summers, and this in a town where cricket of only modest pretension was played.

It was not done easily, these things never are. Henry Murray-Anderdon is an extraordinary and somewhat elusive figure. Eldest son of a vicar in Kent, he attended Oxford and inherited Henlade House, just outside Taunton, from an uncle. Significantly he added 'Anderdon' to his original name in 1873 for he was a man who combined style with liberal patronage. In Henlade he married the daughter of a vicar and served more or less as the village squire, supporting the church, sitting on committees, employing numerous servants, one of whom, Toothy Maltravers, used to scrub his front step at 7 a.m. every morning, after which she would be invited to breakfast downstairs. Anderdon dressed for dinner, served as a magistrate in Somerset, had connections with a local bank, was wont to drive to Taunton in his pony and trap or, later, in his Daimler – a custom continued by his no less impressive wife after his death.

He wore a dark, bushy, spade beard because his horse had shied up on seeing a steamroller and an arm had been trapped and injured, so that Henry could not tie his bow or cravat. And he was a dedicated cricketer who kept a picture of his beloved Somerset team in his bathroom at home. For nearly forty years he gave unstinting service to Somerset cricket, paying debts and building a fine club. Suave and hard working, under his guidance, said the *County Gazette* in 1890, 'the club has been gradually improving its position in finances and in play'. He is one of a handful of giants in the story of Somerset cricket.

Murray-Anderdon's reward for driving Somerset cricket onwards was to be respected by supporters and players alike. On the occasion of his Silver Wedding anniversary in 1902 he was presented with twelve miniature solid silver bats and the replica of an ancient bowl which had been unearthed in a nearby village five years previously. He also received a book made of silk inscribed with the names of every member of Somerset Cricket Club, a rare tribute.

Under this new and energetic steward Somerset set about claiming Rack Field for itself, for the old rule about having no home ground had been abandoned. A meeting was arranged for April at Clarkes Hotel near the Castle, a hostelry soon to be a regular drinking hole of Somerset cricketers and already notorious as a place where ladies of lively disposition might be met (it is not, of course, suggested that these facts are in any way related). Athletics, cycling and cricketing interests were present and Murray-Anderdon took the chair, as he was uniquely qualified to do, being a noted and respected supporter of all these clubs. Motions were passed allowing Somerset to assume the nineteen-year lease from Taunton Athletic Society at a cost of 100 guineas a year, plant and pavilion to stay in place.

Rack Field was in somewhat poor condition, being pocked with holes, and time was needed to prepare the turf, cover the running track and build extra stands. Local cricket clubs were invited to subscribe and those which did were represented on the committee. Murray-Anderdon was asked to find a competent groundsman and he engaged Hortop, while Nicholls, the Yatton bowler, was to be a ground professional. Subscriptions reached £204 3s 6d that year and no extra charge was made for athletes or cyclists beyond the original half guinea membership fee. Taunton and Somerset cricket clubs had separated, electing different officers and Taunton members had to pay 2s 6d for the privilege of joining their own club.

Only one reservation was made concerning the right to use the County cricket ground: 'Wheelers and runners will be required to provide all lavatorial necessities.' Money was tight. Amateurs were paid £1 a day in expenses, while the professionals cost £40 all told. People wondered if these burdens were too great. By and large the amateurs did not claim their expenses, which was just as well.

Edward Sainsbury was captain by now – appropriately so, for he was Somerset's senior player and a staunch servant too. Somerset had a quiet year on the field in 1886 and were said to be 'not flying so high as usual'. Off it, things were afoot, especially in the estranged eastern part of the county.

Mr Tankerville-Chamberlayne ran a team which played upon his estate, a team variously called Yatton and – defiantly – East Somersetshire. Upon Taunton electing itself home of Somerset cricket this gentleman wrote to the newspapers regretting that

> My efforts during the past 10 years in the interests of our national game have not been of more benefit to the County Club, but I myself am certainly not to blame for that! Thousands of pounds have been spent yet my ground has never been visited by those who preside over the destiny of our county cricket for the purposes of discovering any promising players.

It was plainly a sentiment keenly felt in the area, for Yatton's two strongest players, O. G. Radcliffe and Leeston-Smith hardly played for the county and Radcliffe went so far as to join Gloucestershire, following an exodus which had already taken away S. C. Newton, A. H. Evans and several less important contributors, mostly for business reasons.

Leeston-Smith had begun life as F. A. Smith, changing his name after attending school in Malvern, Christ College and Brecon. A right-handed hitter and slow off-spin bowler, he is chiefly remembered as a Somerset cricketer for featuring in one of the better E. M. Grace stories. F. L. Cole took a single off Grace's first ball whereupon Leeston-Smith hit sixes off every remaining delivery of the over. 'I am afraid it is over, doctor,' said the umpire. 'Shut up,' said Grace; 'I'm going to have another one.' And off it Leeston-Smith was stumped.

He probably was not really a county cricketer, anyhow; besides, Somerset already had smiters aplenty.

Octavius Goldney Radcliffe was a substantially better player and his loss was accordingly heavily felt. Having been educated privately, Radcliffe did not take up cricket till he was seventeen and it was through untiring practice and painstaking attention to the principles of the game that he turned himself into a capable batsman of dogged temperament. Somerset did not pick him until 1885 and one year later he was playing in Gloucestershire colours – thanks, said the papers, 'to a ridiculous prejudice against him'. When he scored 100 for his adopted county the *Gazette* grumbled, 'What a pity it was that Somerset did not recognise his talents when he was anxious to qualify for his own county.' This reporter condemned 'the quidnuncs who did not think him good enough'.

That word 'quidnuncs' is significant for it points towards the marginal university cricketers who ran Somerset as an amateur club, for whose taste Radcliffe may have been somewhat dour. Most Somerset amateurs had attended a private school and one of the two great universities, and perhaps Radcliffe was caught betwixt and between as, in their way, were J. C. White and Harold Gimblett later. But was Radcliffe's departure such a loss? He played five times for Somerset and another 129 first-class games elsewhere. He scored 5,426 runs at an average of 21.36. If Somerset's neglect was not vindicated neither does it stand conclusively condemned. Radcliffe could have been useful, nothing more.

Despite these grumblings from the east, Somerset was now established in Taunton, a town of independent men which had defied sundry royalist sieges to support Cromwell, had even supported Perkin Warbeck in 1497, and of course the Duke of Monmouth nearly 200 years later. In other words Taunton had no taste for authority in London and was apt to welcome whomsoever rose against it. And yet Taunton was also a town of conservative rural instinct. This combination of mistrust of 'those beggars in London', and of dandy trends too, percolates through Somerset cricket history. Somerset likes to think of its players as good men, whose colourful traits will be absorbed so long as they are game. They want London to mind its own business and accuses it of neglecting their choicest sons.

Somerset did beat Hampshire at Wellington towards the end of 1886, thanks to a leg before decision off Bastard 'which the batsman did not seem to appreciate'; and a grand victory over Warwickshire followed, so that the season ended with a bang. As one reporter, whose range of adjectives was somewhat limited, put it, 'the Secretary of the County Club has tried a good many men this year which is not a good plan permanently but is a good

35

way to start in office'. E. J. P. Cassan, now fifty, played a few games, as did Fothergill, so plainly Somerset were hard up, in every way.

Help was at hand, for the most important cricketing events of the season were the arrival of George Nichols and the first appearance of Samuel Moses James Woods. William Roe recalled Sammy's opening delivery:

> When Warwick went in to bat Sammy bowled the first ball to Rock. It was a terrifically fast yorker on the leg-side. Rock missed it and was stumped by A. E. Newton. It was one of the very finest bits of stumping I have ever seen. In the second innings Rock had got 12 and looked like staying. Sam, however, bowled him with one of his slow balls, which bounced twice and Rock was yorked by the second bounce. Sam afterwards swore that he had bowled a double bouncer on purpose, as Rock seemed able to play any other kind of ball, but of course no one believed him.

Woods never left Somerset, though from time to time he was said to be contemplating a return to his native Australia whence he had been sent for an English education. Player, jester, secretary of sorts, and beloved *éminence grise*, he was the epitome of what Somerset cricket wanted to be, jolly, informal, colourful, and occasionally heroic.

Nichols deserves a chapter to himself, as does his partner in business and bowling, Edwin Tyler. Nichols's contribution has been somewhat neglected, partly because he was a professional in a period of extraordinary amateurs, and partly because he was an undramatic cricketer. Yet his contribution was vital as Somerset fought for substance and recognition.

Fred Poynton said of Nichols that he was a 'cricketing character, nerves rather shaky but a really good bowler, quick off the pitch. A hardworking pro, I never heard what became of him though told he had died. There was a rumour he wrote plays. He was amusingly cynical.'

He did indeed write plays. Arriving at Somerset from Gloucestershire (a move hastened by a rash of dropped catches off W.G.'s bowling), Nichols played 134 games and then took to writing for the stage. An imaginative fellow, he had shared a flat with Fothergill upon arriving in Taunton, and in time joined his shrewd and entrepreneurial chum Tyler in a gentlemen's outfitters

36

shop in North Street which included a sports department on one side and a tobacconist across the stairs, and to which every sporting fellow in Taunton was apt to go – 'up the stairs', they called it – for a chat and a smoke.

But Nichols had no head for business, being one of those who wear the caps and bells. Accordingly he began composing after-dinner speeches for his chums at the Nag's Head. Presently the Moonlighters, a mixture of cricket team and music hall, was started with Nichols as its leader on and off the field. His recitations in song and prose found favour and drew crowds when staged in Taunton. Alas, they were too full of parochial winks to travel well and though one play, *A Boer War Tale*, did reach the Elephant and Castle theatre in London it was too little to sustain him.

Nor were his compositions, such as *Zaachi the Barbarian*, written for Mr Fred Conquest's music-hall act, remunerative enough and so Nichols was forced to take to the road as a clothing salesman. He died in Dublin in 1911, aged forty-eight.

As a cricketer, Nichols bowled a tight line and length and did not bother much with variation. Bowling ferociously long spells, he took 291 wickets for Somerset at an average of 23.43 and played his part in taking his club into the championship, with Tyler as his main support, for Woods missed lots of games at critical times. Nichols only scored 2,793 runs, and hit a second-class hundred against Leicestershire when suffering with a dislocated finger. Never a dasher in the field, later in his career he was constantly berated for his sluggishness in every department by those sections of the crowd which had forgotten his early days. Towards the end he served as a handyman cricketer, summoned from his shop at the last moment, when no one else could be found. Fellows of infinite jest so often end badly. A grand fellow, with Tyler he provided much of the hard work around which others could build their reputations. And, like Tyler, he bowled too many overs, lost his nip and slipped into decline, though not before Somerset had joined the mighty.

4

Interlude – Sammy

Let us begin with Dr Poynton and William Roe. Poynton wrote of Sammy's passing in 1931:

> With his death our cricket died for we had known him in his prime as a superb athlete and as a most lovable cheery man with a kind heart, a pleasant light tenor voice and a teller of good tales who'd never admit defeat and was the life and soul of all parties.
>
> A fast bowler with a good slow ball he worked hard for Somerset and, as so often happens, strained himself bowling and so eventually lost his pace. His fielding at mid-off to Tyler's slows was a marvel both for what he caught and what he stopped. At first his batting was erratic but he became most dangerous and rose to greater heights when others failed.
>
> The last time I saw him was in my consulting room in Harley Street just before he went to see the surgical specialist who was to let him know his illness was inoperable. He was a broken man. In 1891 he'd been the picture of a great athlete.
>
> What a handicap is the average man to these athletes! They cling around and live in the cheap notoriety of having had a drink with X or Y who probably came in hot and tired after some great feat. It is so easy to stand a drink.
>
> There was a wonderful meeting of old cricketers at his funeral and the dear fellow was buried in sight of the scene of many of his sixes. He was just a big man child.

More simply, Roe said that he was 'a magnificent athlete and a glorious fellow to have in the side'.

Woods was born in Ashfield, Sydney, and was one of the thirteen offspring of John Woods, an Irishman whose father had been called Moses. John Woods married in Ireland in 1853 and upon arriving in Sydney he set about building his fortune by transporting railway tracks. In time Woods bought a lovely house in the village of Manly, now a beach suburb of Sydney. Woods Senior was something of a martinet and it was partly this which kept Samuel in England. One brother, Harris, also a cricketer, kept a diary during the Boer War which can be found in the Australia Museum.

As a boy Sam Woods played cricket and boxed with the local Aboriginal Champion, who knelt for the fights. Sam was game for anything, be it playing cricket in the South Seas, pinching stone gods from natives and being chased in canoes, or running truant from school to watch Billy Murdoch and taking his punishment in good heart.

At thirteen young Sam was sent to England to be trained as a proper gentleman. He never really got the hang of it. Starting at a prep school in Kent he moved to Brighton College where he played soccer and hockey for Sussex. Already he had powerful thighs and a back of knotted muscle so that rugby and fast bowling were more his caper. During school holidays he stayed in Bridgwater with a friend of his father's.

Being a gentleman Woods duly applied to attend Oxford University. But being a gentleman was his sole qualification. Sam could roll a skittle, pot a billiard-ball, shoot, fish, drink, sing, bowl and turn a lady's eye with the best of them. A scholar he was not. He could not spell and had never heard of Julius Caesar, a distinct handicap for familiarity with classical works was demanded at entry. Riding high in university games, Oxford turned him away. Cambridge was more sanguine.

Passing exams was another matter. When Sam approached the examination room in the Corn Exchange half the student body went with him. A giant figure with a shock of thick hair and a tiny, tatty gown, Woods was morose on such occasions. Few fancied his chances. Inside he would bite his pen, scribble a little and then walk out early, crestfallen. It is said on one paper he wrote his name and college, misspelling one word, from which slender evidence his authorities detected sufficient learning to allow him to survive his four years, during which time Cambridge won three university cricket matches and were denied only by rain in the fourth.

Rather than return to Australia upon leaving Cambridge, Woods stayed in Bridgwater for already he was a name in Somerset cricket and English rugby. In 1888, by replacing the injured Jones, Woods became the only man to play Test cricket for Australia without ever playing a first-class game at home. He nearly played for England in Australia on a rare visit to Sydney in 1902 – when S. F. Barnes broke down; Woods was summoned and only a possibly diplomatic chill caught in a Turkish steambath the night before stopped him playing. He did play three Tests for England in South Africa.

Woods did not have a distinguished test career, and there were those who considered his selection foolhardy. Somerset were not pleased either, for in 1888 they were pressing for recognition and thought Woods might have shown greater commitment to them. Test cricket was not, then, the be-all and end-all of life.

But Somerset soon took Woods to its heart. He played rugby thirteen times for England, captaining them in 1892–3 and he fished and hunted as a country gentleman (and said he had shot hounds and keepers in his time, though he was probably joking). As a cricketer he had no time for draws – 'you can bathe in 'em but that's about it' – and he hated dishonesty, telling one dubious umpire, 'In twenty years' time it won't matter to anyone who won this game except you.' Before batting he was apt to sip a double whisky and smoke a cheroot, once bellowing 'This must stop' as Somerset collapsed on a bad pitch, striding out to smite his first three deliveries over mid-wicket and to score 70.

As captain he led Somerset downhill with glorious style. Gilbert Jessop relates that upon enquiring why Sam had picked one individual of quite breathtaking incompetence Sam replied, 'Oh, he is not much of a bat, he doesn't bowl, and he can't field – but, by George, what a great golfer he is!' He did not so much pick a team as raise one. Robertson-Glasgow recorded:

> The great and only Sam Woods used to tell how he was captaining a Somerset team to play in the North country. He found himself three short. 'So,' he remarked in tones like the roll of a drum, 'I picked up a couple of my godsons, who had nothing better to do; and that made ten. With which we started by train. On the way I got talking to a fellow who said

he'd made hundreds and hundreds in club cricket. So I made him our eleventh man. He made nought and nought, and it turned out he hadn't played since he was ten, but wanted to get a close view of the game for nothing. He was a very good whist-player.'

Nor did he ever take life entirely seriously. He did try once to learn a trade, paying a surveyor £50 to instruct him in the mysteries of roods and perches. After one lesson the fellow went home and shot himself. Woods used to say, 'It would not be expedient for anyone to pay me for measuring a plot of ground.' In the war he served with the 6th and 9th Somerset Regiments and became a captain in the 20th Devon Regiment. Apparently he visited the Nile, for which he did not care, and a camel bolted from under him, permanently damaging his back. 'I was in charge of a bunch of those sods,' he said, 'when they stampeded and made for a cactus forest, so off I rolled and fell a bit wrong.' Neville Cardus pictures him loading cannons in the Dardanelles while all around are dying – with what authority cannot be said, save that the image fits the man.

Afterwards Woods was, for a time, paid £200 a year to act as an assistant secretary at Somerset, a post for which he was wholly unsuited and which he left in some dudgeon, and with an abiding sense of betrayal. In later life he was a shadow, for his blood depended on the rush of sport. Nevertheless he was a familiar figure at the ground, roaring at people walking in front of the sightscreens, and applauding when he chose, seldom when anyone else did, and usually when an edged stroke sped to the boundary.

If Sammy sounds rather a caricature he has been done a disservice. Most of all he was a fine cricketer, scoring 12,637 runs (at 25.07) and taking 554 wickets for Somerset at an average of 23.78. Not that he worried about figures, which he dismissed as so much fiddle-de-dee. Despite all those stories he was regarded as an astute captain and as a clever bowler. C. B. Fry said he was perhaps the most scientific and artistic of fast bowlers, and a man with an unrivalled knowledge of the game. As with Ian Botham, a calculating brain ticked beneath the jovial manner.

Woods did not marry, but apparently had an accommodating lady in town, for groundstaff boys were under strict instructions not to disturb him on certain mornings. By and large he lived in local pubs, and walked to the ground, passing by the shopkeepers and farmers driving their cattle through the streets, and always enquiring after their children, their aunt's lumbago or whatever. Crippled by arthritis, he stopped playing in 1910. Should anyone be injured he would immediately offer to wrench their dislocated shoulder back into place, usually with disastrous results, or alternatively offer a large glass of brandy which, in his opinion, was a remedy for every ailment. He stayed in his adopted county to the bitter end and all Somerset attended his funeral. Remembered as a man who hit hard, was prone to scampering desperate singles (often without warning his partner) and would bowl his heart out. Two final points on Woods. He could play 'the draw', a Victorian shot executed by deflecting the ball between one's legs as it were. Modern thought condemned it as too risky. Woods liked a challenge and variety. And he brought a glass of water to a friend suffering a heart attack. They say it was the only time he carried this particular refreshment.

His end was, in its way, glorious. Family histories indicate that Woods's splendid constitution deteriorated sharply after he plunged into freezing water in the English Channel to save a boy from drowning. At heart he was, through and through, a Somerset man.

5

Rolling a pitch

At the beginning of 1887 Somerset was still rather low in the lists yet by the season's end they were said to be 'a ship heading out for an ocean of prosperity'. Eight games were played and four won. Middlesex were beaten as Hewett, a new man, slogged 60 in 45 minutes. With Sainsbury scoring 417 runs, Roe 272 and Albert Clapp of Yatton, who was sometimes an amateur and sometimes a pro, hitting 212, Somerset's batting was more solid than usual. Moreover Woods and Bastard took 70 wickets between them, while the 'great wag' Nichols began with 19 at 9.1.

Yet Somerset had started badly, losing disgracefully to Lancashire by 395 runs, a loss blamed on bad captaincy by reporters who concluded that the club had fallen on evil days and mourned the apathy of Taunton supporters who were just as indifferent to the arrival in town of a free library. Incidentally, Taunton already had electric lighting and officers arrived from Bath – 'those wise men from the East', they were called – to study it.

Then Sainsbury scored 164 to beat Hampshire, and Roe 89 and Hewett 98 in a sensational display of hitting to beat Warwickshire at Taunton. Hewett was unbeaten overnight on 94 and a big crowd thronged to the ground hoping to see his hundred, but alas he fell short. Warwickshire did not take defeat well. 'Their conduct was a disgrace,' boomed one correspondent; 'they disputed decisions without the slightest reason and made themselves generally unpleasant. We are quite sure the Somerset secretary will make no further engagements with this county until they know how to behave like cricketers and gentlemen.'

Roe also recalled an occasion when Whitehead, an MCC bowler, dropped a ball he was about to deliver to Hewett.

> Whitehead left the ball where it was, and Hewett came prancing down to hit it, pursued, for some unknown reason, by the wicket-keeper. When he got to the ball, instead of hitting it, he simply patted it back to Whitehead, who picked it up and threw it at the wicket, but missed and we ran three. I asked Hewett afterwards why he didn't hit it, he said. 'It felt like shooting a sitting rabbit.'

Somerset was still a small club and though cricket was now high on the agenda of local newspapers, especially the *Somerset County Gazette*, whose editor enjoyed the game, it had not yet captured public imagination, and was still the preserve of rich gentlemen and their ladies.

Further advances were made under Sainsbury in 1888, with the previously faulty fielding improving so much that 70 catches were taken. Starting poorly as usual, Somerset found form once the schools emptied and six matches were won as the county rose to be strongest of those not yet amongst the sacred angels. Tents were erected for ladies and for journalists, a performance of *Pygmalion* was staged to fill the coffers and amateur athletic meetings, cycling championships, an archery competition and a Somerset Lawn Tennis Championship were held at the county ground. A shower was built to wash the horse which pulled mowers and rollers for Godsmark, the new groundsman, who was engaged for a year and paid 25s a week. Somerset had not yet entered its period of dedicated and long-serving groundstaff. Godsmark was a drunkard.

Gate receipts in 1888 brought in £44 11s 6d, Essex at Taunton providing the biggest draw (£18 6s 6d). Subscriptions amounted to £593 2s 3d, while professional expenses were £244 10s including £90 for ground bowlers. A deficit of £79 18s was recorded, and settled by Murray-Anderdon. To save money amateur expenses were reduced to 10s a day, Murray-Anderdon being empowered to give more in special cases. Bats were given to Bastard and Fothergill in respect of their bowling, a reward commonly reserved for men who hit hundreds. Rack Field was thoroughly dressed and the holes were filled. Despite a poverty which never really threatened extinction, efforts were being made to improve matters at Somerset Cricket Club.

In 1889 the deficit fell to £16 and Somerset enjoyed another splendid year, winning six games and losing two. It was Sainsbury's last year as captain and player, his 'services being lost', though the minutes are silent as to why. In any event Sainsbury moved to Gloucestershire, joining Radcliffe, and never played for his home county again. Perhaps it was the old East–West divide, or perhaps playing for Gloucestershire was simply more convenient. But he had been a Somerset man for years and it is hard to imagine that his departure for a neighbouring county was entirely without rancour.

As for the County Ground, a wooden open-fronted shanty situated beneath the Coal Orchard Cottages served as a scoring-box and as a press box, though only one reporter ever attended in the seasons before Somerset rose to the heights. The ground was bordered by ordinary wire fencing so that there was an unob-structed view to Priory Lock and towards the Quantocks. At one time a skittle alley ran behind the pavilion, and in later years tennis courts were marked out on a piece of ground in front of the pavilion (though nets soon took their place), and later still (in 1910) the Taunton bowling club used this patch as their green. It was a lovely ground, hardly spoilt by enclosure, one used by complementary sports, and it improved.

In October 1889 the cinder cycling- and running-track was finally removed. Domestically the accounts relate that £2 10s was paid to 'Trollope keeping gate' while Godsmark was told that if he was found again intoxicated he would be given a week's wages and promptly dismissed. Godsmark took the pledge at once.

Attendance at the Warwickshire game (for relations had not been severed) was 'numerous and fashionable', while Essex were beaten in a second-class game, W. A. R. Young, the Old Harrovian, adding 69 for the last wicket with Tyler, whose appli-cation for a pay rise had been rejected on the grounds that his services were already sufficiently recognized. Hewlett was chosen to succeed Sainsbury as captain, a task he carried out with verve if not diplomacy. Hewett was already a significant sporting figure locally, having been elected as first president and honorary captain of the newly formed Taunton Association Football club.

Somerset cricket was rising. Murray-Anderdon had found two good professional bowlers in Tyler and Nichols, and in Sammy

Woods, not yet adopted as a folk hero, he had that rare beast, an amateur who did not consider bowling to be a labour best left to professionals. Woods, of course, being an Australian had little time for old English ways. Grounds are filled by batsmen, matches won by bowlers.

Time enough for Edwin James Tyler from Kidderminster. He had played for Worcestershire without success and had accepted Somerset's invitation to join them in 1885, working on the ground-staff and playing for Taunton while he qualified by residence. He was probably the slowest bowler of his generation, sending his left-arm slows high into the air with a curious action not unlike that of an athlete putting the shot. So slow was his pace that had his temperament not been stoical and his command of length unwavering first-class batsmen would have demolished him. Yet he played once for England, under Lord Hawke in South Africa in 1895–6 (Sammy Woods was playing too and the England party was scarcely representative, though C. B. Fry and George Lohmann were in it), and though he was no Rhodes or Blythe he did take 864 county wickets at an average of 22.34. And he did bowl all day, day after day, for as Fred Poynton said, 'A cheerful, big-hearted bowler, he does not care how much he is hit, he always applauds a good stroke.'

Tyler played 177 games for Somerset, the last being an ill-advised comeback in 1907, but in truth his career was over when he was called for throwing during the agitation of 1900. In his obituary a discreet commentator wrote that

> upon the question of his action there is no need to say
> very much. It is fortunate for him that he came out at a
> time when great laxity prevailed with regard to throwing.
> He was too slow to hurt anybody, and so his action, though
> often talked about, passed muster for years. Many offenders
> ten times worse were allowed to practise their evil ways quite
> unchecked till the hour of reform arrived.

Woods had little time for such arguments, dismissing talk of chuckers with a roar of laughter, adding that 'there's only 2 or 3 of 'em around. Not enough to worry a bloke.'

Tyler was not much of a bat, did not take batting seriously at all, his shots scurrying towards point no matter where they were aimed. Unsurprisingly he was the third victim when Charles Townsend took a hat trick against Somerset, each man being stumped. Roe recollected:

> Tyler, who came in last, was stumped by yards. I was in at the other end and, as we went out I asked him why on earth he had rushed out like that. His reply was 'the poor boy's tired to death and may never get the chance again'. Just like Tyler, but we won the match so it didn't matter.

On another occasion Tyler joined Roe, who was unbeaten on 93. As he passed he said, 'It's all right, I'll let you have the bowling.' Directly the ball was released Tyler rushed down the pitch calling 'Come on!' Alas . . . he forgot to play the ball and was clean bowled. Roe 'couldn't help laughing. He was a cheery fellow and a great trier.'

But he was much more than an amusing companion who bowled slow and did not care for batting, for Tyler was an entrepreneur. Within a few years of arriving in Taunton he owned a clothes shop, a tobacconist's, sold insurance, ran a travel agency selling tickets for steamships going to Japan, India or Turkey, and acted as mine host in the Fleur de Lis pub two miles from the ground – a hostelry previously called The Jackass Tavern, because as many as fifteen or twenty jackasses were commonly to be found tied up outside. These donkeys came into town from Broomfield loaded with brooms then much used in stables and gardens. In any event, Tyler served lunch for 1s 6d ($7^1/_2$p). Later he was appointed cricket coach at Taunton School, and he showed his tricks to J. C. White.

Plainly Tyler was a considerable and energetic man who supplemented his meagre cricketing wage, which Somerset were loath to increase because funds were low, with all manner of bright schemes. He was regarded as a lovely man, genial, sympathetic and stable. When he was buried, play was stopped on the County Ground and players wore black armbands. His colleague Lionel Palairet sent a wreath and a note saying 'in affectionate memory of a great trier'. Other wreaths were sent by the Conservative Club and various bowling clubs. Not bad for a professional, and evidence that in Somerset the divide between paid and amateur players was narrow.

With Hewett and Lionel Palairet to the fore, Somerset's batting was now more dependable too. Cricket was beginning to take itself

47

seriously. Apologists said it was better for the character and, what is more, more beautiful to the beholder than any other game. In any event style was all the rage in this Golden Age of amateur batting. It was a time of high back lifts, of flowing off-drives, of timing, a time when the ugly and crooked were rejected by such as Spooner, MacLaren and Jackson. And the epitome of style was Lionel Palairet of Somerset.

He was, perhaps, the *only* stylist ever to play for the club, though Peter Wight had similar traits. Not that Palairet was a local. He had been born in Lancashire, attended Repton with C. B. Fry, played soccer for the Corinthians, and was five times champion archer of England. Having been schooled for a time in Somerset, having married a Wiltshire girl he had West Country links and it was the cider county he joined upon leaving Oxford.

Playing for a strong team, including several like-minded and well-bred men, Palairet was happy in those early years at Somerset, for whom he scored 13,851 runs and struck 27 hundreds in his 222 matches. He was an offside player, whose arms 'seemed to follow the bat rather than lift it', according to Fry. But he was no mere stylist for he carried his bat three times for Somerset and scored five hundreds against Yorkshire and four against Surrey. He was also in the top twenty of the national batting averages in eight of the eleven seasons between 1891 and 1901, finishing 6th in 1892 and 5th in both 1895 and 1901. And, though he failed when he played for England on a damp pitch in the miserably wet if dramatic series of 1902, Palairet was a fine player on a spoiled wicket, too. He scored 49 runs in his innings for England. Fry and Ranji scored even fewer in those same Tests. Palairet could easily have played more often for his country – he probably deserved to do so more than Gimblett – but he was handicapped by a reluctance to tour during the winter.

Colleagues found Palairet somewhat aloof, a reserved fellow incapable of inspiring affection save amongst his closest friends. He moved in distinguished circles, being prominent in the golf and angling worlds and he served as a land agent for the Earl of Devon's estate. Palairet captained Somerset in 1907 and was elected president in 1930, leaving his pedestal occasionally to deliver to the world his regrets that 'the new generation did not come into cricket with the traditional principles' – a change for which he blamed the First World War.

Somerset's new captain in 1890, Herbert Tremenheere Hewett,

was a bird of a different feather, though his background (Harrow and Oxford) was not dissimilar. Poynton regarded his skipper as an outstanding player who suffered 'from a deep, difficult nature, which once upset, took long to recover'. Hewett had a short fuse and it was this which condemned him to a brief if brilliant career.

As a batsman Hewett was a fearless hitter who did not bother much with style, to the dismay of aesthetes at Lord's. A left-hander, he saw it as his task to conquer whilst others tended their gardens. A forceful leader, respected and feared, Hewett took Somerset into the championship, was regarded as England's best left-hander in 1892 and left Somerset in a flare of hotheaded controversy a year later, never to return, as a player at any rate. By profession he was a barrister, and he joined the Western Circuit. Upon war breaking out he was much too old to fight which did not prevent him serving as a provost marshal. He did return to Somerset in the end, for his passion was born of care and despair rather than loathing and he ended his days sipping whisky with Lionel Palairet and Sammy Woods as Somerset fought another rearguard action.

By 1890 Somerset had a fearless leader in place, three good bowlers and as effective a pair of opening batsmen as the county ever fielded. Down the list they had Roe and Challen (nickname Venus), a small, neat, alert and active sportsman who had been educated at Marlborough, was a fine cover fielder, an aggressive bat (1,656 runs in 52 games), a schoolmaster and, though he played soccer for Wales, a thorough English bulldog type.

These were the men who were to bring glory to Somerset cricket between 1890 and 1893, a period of success matched only by Brian Rose's team in 1978–81.

In 1890 the breakthrough was made. It is a year which merits close study.

Thirteen county games were played in 1890, of which twelve ended in victory and one in a tie. Tyler took 126 wickets, the first Somerset bowler to pass 100, Nichols snared 79 while Woods was dangerous when he played. Hewett headed the batting averages while Palairet and Nichols scored heavily and even Tyler concentrated enough to average 19. For once Somerset could field a regular team, albeit one which leant upon its only three serious bowlers.

It was a marvellous year during which interest in cricket in

Somerset gradually built towards fever pitch until cricket was no longer a private game for country gentlemen but was instead a matter of communal pride. Newspapers printed long reports of Somerset games and away matches were eagerly followed, telegraphed scores being posted in shop windows from Minehead to Wells. To such heights did Somerset cricket rise that by the year's end they were elected to the County Championship.

Somerset's season began at Lord's where, in Woods's absence, Tyler and Nichols gave their team a famous victory over prestigious opponents. Hampshire appeared next as Hewett's team, weakened by scholastic duties, won a tight contest by 2 runs, Vernon Hill rising to the occasion. Staffordshire were trounced, Tyler taking wickets and Lionel Palairet, still only 20, scoring runs; whereupon Somerset continued its winning ways in Birmingham, where Woods, who had promised to play, did not appear. 'Perhaps', wrote one critic, 'it would be as well not to risk this disappointment.' Tyler took 13/124 in 79 overs and Nichols 6/97 in 76 overs, also scoring 50 and 67. Upon hearing the result Murray-Anderdon sent a telegram saying 'Bravo! Nichols, well played'. Usually he travelled with the team, passing the evenings with billiards and dinner.

Warwickshire arrived in Taunton bent upon revenge, for relations between these teams were a trifle sticky. Reporters crammed into their dirty, draughty and uncomfortable box and hundreds of people paid their pennies to enter through a new patent turnstile which allowed takings to be carefully checked. Perhaps money had been slipping away. Progress was followed upon the Denings patent scoreboard purchased to help Somerset's scorer who had announced his intention of keeping a proper scorebook that year (for previously averages had been compiled from reports in the *Somerset County Gazette*).

Despite backing themselves with hefty wagers, Warwickshire were beaten by an innings, Tyler bowling at the river end, taking 5/9. Upon the last wicket falling, Somerset players were hugely cheered and hats were thrown in the air as these visitors left growling furiously that Tyler was not a proper bowler, merely an overgrown schoolboy. He had bowled his skyscrapers with consummate control, and they had proved irresistible.

Staffordshire arrived without two men, including their captain, Somerset providing their diffident and effective joint secretary,

Tom Spencer, and C. J. Robinson, an unorthodox tailender who once kicked a ball to the boundary and who was nicknamed 'the White Mouse' because of his complexion and hair, as substitutes. Alas, both dropped catches, saying that the sun had been in their eyes. Hewett, who scored 203 not out, hit a ball through a window and on to the tea table of a cottage in Coal Orchard (at 10 o'clock from the Old Pavilion) and all was set for the return of Middlesex.

Somerset's record was already a proud one, and it was celebrated in verse by one Taunton poet:

Eight matches played and eight matches won
That's what none of the first-class Counties have done
Tis clear that Young Zummerset knows how to do it
Bravo Palairet, Woods, Tyler, Roe and Hewett
Go on in this fashion and soon you'll be reckoned
Among the first instead of the second.
Wet wickets this season, boys, seldom a rummer set
But they anyhow seem to have suited Young Zummerset.

A weak ending, and perhaps not vintage stuff but plainly Somerset cricket had stirred strong interest and pride, for only mighty deeds were celebrated in rhyme and metre.

Fully £53 15s 3d were taken at the turnstiles during the Middlesex game. And it was a magnificent contest; Somerset scored 107 and 127, Middlesex 108. Things looked black for the hosts because their powerful visitors had an afternoon in which to score the runs. After lunch both teams were photographed, which delayed the resumption until 3 p.m. No true Somerset supporter could stoop so low as to regard this as anything more than a somewhat fortunate turn of events.

Middlesex advanced steadily toward their target and 14 runs were needed with 5 wickets left. It was now that Hewett made a tactical move which was to be celebrated. At Hampshire he had changed the bowling at a critical moment to bring victory. Here he removed Tyler and summoned Nichols. Yet it was Woods who struck first, captain A. J. Webbe, no less, being adjudged caught behind. Webbe was a superb player who had the game at his command. But was the decision correct? Webbe did not think so and forty years later, when he bumped into wicket-keeper Arthur Newton, the conversation opened with Newton confessing: 'It wasn't me who appealed, you know. It was Sammy.'

51

With 3 wickets left 6 runs were needed. Nichols took a wicket and amidst scenes of panic, in front of a crowd alternately shrieking and silent, 2 runs were needed with the last pair at the crease. According to Roe's account Dauglish cracked the ball to leg and tried to run a second. Richard Palairet, Lionel's brother, ran from slip, turned and threw in. It hit something on the way, struck Newton on his chest and fell on the wicket with Dauglish feet short. Players rushed for the pavilion and the home team was mobbed.

Two games remained, a meeting with Devon. After a wet morning Devon made 172 and in reply Somerset reached 159, Fowler swiping 26. Devon were dismissed cheaply leaving their opponents little time to score the runs. Roe, acting captain, ordered a forcing game to be played and sent out Challen and the elder Palairet who hit at everything and ran like hares. Excitement mounted, wickets fell and spectators hooted, complaining that Devon were not moving at the call of 'over'. To the contrary their venerable captain, a vicar, walked slowly from deep mid-off to deep mid-off without due celerity, so that Somerset supporters impatiently shouted, 'Play up!'

At 6.25 p.m. Somerset still needed 6 to win. Suddenly Rev Coplestone decided to bowl himself and walked to the crease, rearranged his field, studied the clock and pointed out that it was now 6.30 and they should all go home. Upon the umpire having none of it he proceeded to bowl underarm grubbers in a manner later revived by Trevor Chappell. Robinson hit a single and a 3 was scrambled too. Coplestone again pointed to the clock and again umpire Mycroft shook his head. Finally Robinson struck a single and Somerset had won. The *Somerset County Gazette* reports: 'Men threw up their hats, flourishing their walking sticks and shouted themselves hoarse. Ladies in the grandstand waved their handkerchiefs. It was a famous end to an epic season.'

Taunton laid on a banquet for their heroes, and a Rabelaisian affair it was. Flowers, fruit and trophies smothered the Castle Hotel and a vast congregation of distinguished guests dined upon oysters, mullet, venison and grouse and the tables were lit with handsome electric lamps of the newest design. Many jovial speeches were made, for the mayor was a keen cricketer. Toasting the army Mr J. E. W. Wakefield said that much was owed to those who had never worn flannels, and Sammy Woods praised Nichols, Tyler and his captain. Woods's speech, as reported by the local paper, was funny and ribald, and included typical digs at Gloucestershire and Lord's:

He attributed Somerset victories to the excellent bowling of Nichols and Tyler, and the admirable captaincy of Mr Hewett. Whenever he looked at a paper in the morning when he was away he knew what to expect. It was invariably Somerset 200 odd, and the rest caught somebody bowled Nichols, or caught somebody bowled Tyler – (laughter) – and when he came down here, and saw how, in the most critical part of the game, the captain said to one bowler, 'You can slope,' and puts on another and won the match by it, he could quite understand how Somerset had gone up. (Laughter and cheers.) He didn't believe in this tom-foolery about going on till '93 to grow into first-class counties – (hear, hear) – but then it could not be helped – they were 'Not in the know, you know.' (Laughter.) He thought winning ten fixtures and tying one was better than losing five and winning none. Somerset cricket was certainly much better than it had been before. They had a good team of bats, and could always trust Mr Newton to go in tenth and make 40. (Laughter.) They could also always trust him to catch a man out at the wicket when they wanted to win the match. (Laughter.) He would say no more about that – (laughter) – but they must remember that the umpire's decision was final. A great deal of this year's success was due to the untiring energy of Mr H. M. Anderdon [sic] – (cheers) – and too much praise could not possibly be given him for the interest he had shown in county cricket. (Cheers.)

For his party Murray-Anderdon hoped that people would come forward and help in the way of subscriptions and securing bigger gates, adding that every player save Mr Hedley, who was going away, and Mr Trask, would be available next year. He would 'like to see the lines swept away and counties allowed to play amongst themselves as they choose'. His assistant Tom Spencer also pleaded for Somerset and heaped praise upon the professional bowlers. Certainly, he thought, Woods deserved recognition but they 'must not forget that their earlier victories were due to the splendid bowling of the two professionals'.

Neither Tyler nor Nichols spoke of course, and this effort to acknowledge them has the air of an attempt to correct history before it sweeps facts away in a storm of romanticism.

One man was not present at this dinner: Somerset's president until 1915, Sir Spencer Ponsonby-Fane, whose family seat was Brympton House and whose family motto, appropriately enough, was 'Out of darkness, through fire, into light'. Ponsonby-Fane was an interesting and significant choice as president. A keen sportsman from a powerful family, he had played for MCC at fifteen and was described as 'a free and lively hitter, a fast runner, but ran himself and his partners out very frequently'. He was a member of the Old Stagers, who laid on convivial dramas during Canterbury week, helped to found I Zingari in 1845, occupied the office of Treasurer at the MCC from 1879–1915, worked at the Foreign Office after 1840, serving as secretary to Lord Palmerston, played a bit for Surrey and the Gentlemen (as a capable batsman from 1851–6), controlled the destiny of many London theatres, was a Privy Councillor and brought back from Paris the treaty which ended the Crimean War. Altogether the sort of man to be president of a cricket club.

Turning to lesser matters, Godsmark had lost his battle with the bottle and been replaced by Somerset's first great groundsman, Mettam, a grave, tall and dignified figure who would rise at 4 a.m. to mow the grass with an old-fashioned horse-drawn cutter. He provided pitches with turf as smooth as any bowling green. So docile were they that occasionally he had to be asked to roll them less conscientiously, to give the bowlers a chance. Nevertheless he was not a man with whom to meddle, and while he called the amateurs 'sir' he did so with a look reserving his position should they drop a cigarette butt upon his beloved field.

Since 1886 Somerset's young team – average age 24 in 1890 – had won twenty-seven games and lost six, this despite their customary slow start. In the opinion of authority it was not enough to permit entry into the ranks of the sacred angels. In 1887 a County Cricket Council had been formed and at a meeting in August 1890 it deemed that nothing should change. Another meeting was held in December and led to a hot debate during which A. J. Webbe rose to say that the Council should abolish itself – which it promptly did. A day later county secretaries met and arranged their fixtures. All of the sacred angels agreed to play Somerset who were, therefore, accepted into the hallowed championship by default. Murray-Anderdon had made it.

6

Off the mark

Somerset began 1891 with a series of practice games against club sides, none of which provided stern enough opposition. Nichols made 311 not out against Glastonbury and a local newspaper did not think it necessary to publish the analysis of the Glastonbury bowling.

Somerset's opening serious fixture at Lord's against Middlesex was spoilt by rain though Tyler and Nichols took wickets and Newton was in superb form behind the stumps. Over 4,000 people watched play on the Tuesday following a wet Monday and they were happy to see these supposed upstarts hold their own.

Surrey were second on the agenda and with Woods injured, the Palairets at university and Roe teaching, Somerset arrived severely weakened. They left much dismayed, walloped by an innings and 375 runs as, caught on a sticky dog, they replied to Surrey's 449 with 37 and 37. This dismal offering led critics to comment that Somerset's executive had been a little over-sanguine in seeking promotion into the major counties. Nichols and Tyler had bowled 151 overs between them.

A crowd of 1,500 watched Somerset's first home game, against Lancashire. Alas, Mold (later to be called for throwing, in the controversy that also claimed Tyler) took 15 for 131 and Somerset lost by 9 wickets. By now many hard and bitter things were being said about Somerset by less fortunate sister counties which had opposed promotion.

And then Somerset went to Maidstone and beat Kent. First Woods and Nichols used their pace to bowl Kent for 106, following which Lionel Palairet hit 79 and Challen 41 as Somerset took

55

a lead of 112, Challen's innings being a most creditable display of defensive cricket. Kent collapsed again and, though chasing only 49, Somerset stumbled for a time (much to the horror of Fred Poynton waiting to bat in the pavilion) before Richard Palairet and Challen took them to a 5-wicket victory saluted in the papers as 'no fluke' and as 'a clever triumph'. Archdale Wickham, vicar of Martock, had taken 4 stumpings and it had been a splendid team effort.

Somerset were trounced by Yorkshire and then beaten by Kent by 10 wickets. To increase local satisfaction, however, Gloucester-shire, W. G. Grace, Radcliffe, W. W. F. Pullen and all, were bowled out for 25 on a wet pitch at Cheltenham, as Somerset, for whom Palairet scored 100 and Challen 79, won by an innings. They beat Gloucestershire by 10 wickets at home.

So Somerset headed north after a mixed beginning. Unfor-tunately their fixture at Bradford coincided with the Yorkshire Agricultural Show and only a small crowd saw Somerset record a shock victory, Woods taking 11/126 and bowling at his fastest. Heavy rain across the Pennines led to defeat against Lancashire, who had dropped R. G. Barlow because of unattractive batting. Barlow vowed never to wear the Red Rose again.

Only a few games remained. Against MCC Tyler drove a six into the churchyard and was out next ball. He was not bowling so well, they said, a disappointment to his many friends who lament-ed he did not bowl a fraction faster. E. W. Ebdon played in the match, batting at 11 and failing to break his duck. Three Ebdon brothers from Wellington were to play a few games in Somerset colours.

And so to the climax of Somerset's first season in higher company, the return of mighty Surrey, who arrived at Taunton needing a victory to be certain of the championship. They had won their first meeting by a vast margin. Bar the shouting it was all over.

Matches in those days began on a Thursday. C. J. Robinson, the White Mouse, could not play because of a family match between the Robinsons and the Graces. Somerset won the toss, Hewett hit out for 55 and his team scored 194. Surrey slipped to 154 all out, whereupon Somerset batted consistently to reach 331, challenging Surrey to score 372 in under five hours. Sensibly Surrey played for a draw and, with half an hour left, 5 wickets

56

were still intact. Then Tyler suddenly struck twice in 2 balls, and Woods clean bowled Read so that the game was afoot. Roared on by a vociferous crowd, these sporting visitors showed no dilatoriness either in arriving at or in leaving the crease. With ten minutes left one wicket remained, and soon Sam Woods was bowling the last over. The first delivery to Sharpe rose over the batsman's head. His second was little better. Woods (according to legend at any rate) walked contemplatingly back to his mark and heard Wood, the non-striker, observe how well Sharpe batted for a man with only one eye – 'Which eye?' asked Sammy. 'His left,' said Wood; so Sammy bowled a round-arm delivery which crept through on the blind side and clean bowled Sharpe.

The scenes which followed beggar description, with caps being thrown in the air as if a tense coil had been released. Was Sammy's ball such a beauty? Reports vary. One writer called it 'a clinker'; others spoke of it variously as a long-hop and as a full-toss. No matter. The deed was done and quickly celebrated by Percy Graves, an ancestor of poet Robert Graves, in a narrative poem of some 133 lines, ending:

. . . Then Zammy rushes down the pitch in our wustest time o'
     need,
And swings a splendid yorker droo the stomps of Maurice Read.
And "Hurry up again," we cry, and "Come, look sharp!" ta Sharpe.
And quick and confident he comed, there was no need ta carp.
Then zeconds zimed like minutes, and minutes weary hours,
As Sharpe and Wood again wi'stood our bowlers' desperate
     powers.
Vive—vour—dree minutes—now were left; they vielders vlying pass
At every maiden over's end, like swallows o'er the grass.
Two minutes—one—vrom Zammy's arm a sudden yorker zails,
And passes Sharpe and like a shell explodes upon his bails.

Then we went wild! tha straain wur such—the pipple bust the
     barriers,
And went vor tha pavilion like a pack of huntin' harriers;
And one oald gent his hat a sent into tha river saailin',
Another like a coalt he jomps all vours across tha paailin',
And a fat old bloke went nigh to choake tell his buttons I undunned,
And then a blubbered like a babe vor joy that we'd a-wunned.

I moast vorgot to tell 'e dro' bein' in a vlurry,
Tha figgers o' our vectory o'er the Champion County Zurrey,
We gied 'em one vine wecket. I never likes to boast,
But I doant think 'twould a counted more'n a hunderd at the moast.
Still it warn't along o' weckets, 'twere by urns tha trick was done,
And our purty winnin' tottle read one hundred thirty-one.

Well, o' course we cheered vor Zummerzet as long as we could
    cheer,
And we hed out zplendid Zammy, our bowler wi'out peer,
And our clever Cap'm Hewett and our clinkin' pair of pro.'s,
Not forgettin' a good ringin' cheer vor our gallant Zurrey voes.

Percy Graves, by the way, attended many games at Taunton and
recalled the fine contingent of ladies, with pencils and scorebooks
complete, who used to sit in comfort in the old Hen Coop, where
the Ridley Stand was built years later. Included in this elegant
party were the Misses Palairet and Newton, and other friends and
relations of the amateurs. Apart from the pavilion it was the only
place where a lady might shelter on the ground.

In 1891 Somerset took £554 11s 9d on the gate, of which £233
was from the Surrey match, thanks in part to the Horticultural
Society which kindly arranged its flower show to coincide. In 1889
just £34 2s 9d had been taken, and in 1890 £138 9s 9d. These were
heady days.

Somerset included nineteen distinguished soldiers and sixteen
clerics amongst its 350 members, subscribers who paid 1 guinea
a year, as they were to do for decades. Murray-Anderdon under-
wrote the expense of fencing the northern and eastern sides of
the ground; an automatic bowling machine was purchased; and
an entrance costing £150 was to be erected at Priory Bridge. A
decision was made to build a ladies' pavilion. Rugby players
using the field were not allowed to use straw. Nichols signed a
three-year contract and was paid £2 10s a week, though Somerset stood firm against winter wages. And Mr W. W. Kettlewell
presided at the AGM. His son went to Eton, played one game
for Somerset in 1899, was wounded in the Boer War and twice
mentioned in despatches during the World War. Mr Kettlewell
Senior was a wise man. He told members he had not seen much
cricket and had arrived at one game in London (presumably the
Surrey match) to find it already over. He gave one opinion only:

'The best form of government for a cricket club is that which is as nearly absolute as possible.'

It is an observation Somerset has never taken to heart.

Hewett was presented with a handsome silver flask and everyone agreed that 1891 had been a most satisfactory season.

7

Consolidation

If anything 1892 was better still, eight of sixteen games being won and five lost. Captain Hedley returned to strengthen the bowling with his medium-pacers which spun sharply. Hedley, born in Taunton, first played for Kent, who had let him go because they considered his action to be suspect and their loudest voice, Lord Harris, was presently conducting a campaign against chuckers. Hedley twice played for the Gentlemen, once took 8/18 against Yorkshire and all told removed 254 batsmen at a cost of 20.77 in his 84 games for Somerset. Eventually he was drummed out of cricket, being condemned by eleven votes to one at the famous captains' meeting of 1900. He could bat too, scoring a county hundred. Hedley gave military service in the Boer and Great Wars, being mentioned twice in dispatches, receiving the Queen's medal with six clasps, winning the CMG and promotion to colonel. Poynton called him 'a great English gentleman'. He was not the only Somerset cricketer to be decorated during the Boer War, for F. A. Phillips and Captain Stanley were also honoured.

Plainly Hedley fitted Somerset's blend of university sportsmen, soldiers, professionals and vicars. Now they had four bowlers, talented batting and two splendid wicket-keepers. It is time to take note of Arthur Newton and Archdale Wickham.

Wickham was an outstanding fellow. Nicknamed The Bishop, he had arrived at the county ground by the usual route of public school and university. He was a curate in Norwich before arriving to be vicar in Martock, where he soon became a beloved character, a man ready for a gamble and for a game of billiards and yet one whose private collection of butterflies and moths was considered to be the best in the county.

As a wicket-keeper Wickham's skills were widely acknowledged. C. B. Fry commented upon his peculiar habit of standing with his legs very wide apart, his hands on his knees, and praised the alacrity with which he could pounce from this position. In fact standing thus was not unusual until 1902, when Hanson Carter began squatting to put less strain on his legs and the trend caught on.

Wearing a Harlequin cap and brown pads, Wickham missed little in his eighty-two games for Somerset spread over seventeen summers, during which he stumped 48 men and caught 81. He could not bat for toffee and his second nickname of 'Snickham' accurately conveys his talent. He ended his days as a romantic figure in the world of sport, regularly dipping into a rich fund of anecdotes and serving on county committees upon which, no doubt, he helped to keep men in their place and matters in perspective.

Wickham used to drive to a match in a horse and trap. Arthur Newton, a different sort of fellow entirely, was given to wearing clips and to riding a bicycle with a large basket upon it. 'A funny little man,' said one contemporary; while a relation observed that 'you could tell he'd been to Eton'. Born into an important local family aware of its position, Newton kept wicket for Oxford and toured Australia with Major Vernon's party, though for once he kept badly, winning spurs with his dashing and risky off-side play.

Rather like J. C. White, Newton was not the kind of man about whom warm tales are told: colleagues found him somewhat aloof and perhaps mistook correctness for coldness. Somerset likes its sons to be characters and is inclined hastily to reject those who cannot by dint of scowl, bumper or smite, readily win hearts. Nevertheless Newton's skills were of immense value to Somerset from his début at 17 to his reluctant retirement at the outbreak of hostilities in 1914 when he was 51. Even after the war he continued playing Somerset Stragglers cricket, to the dismay of sundry clucking relations, and opponents in the 1930s recall a dexterity and a precision extraordinary in a man half his 75 years. And, to top it off, Newton was a man so clumsy that he could scarcely tie his own shoe-laces.

Not that Newton could play every match for Somerset, for he had to earn a living and work as a land agent took him to Ireland and elsewhere. He tried to take his holidays during August week in

61

Taunton and so managed to play 197 county games, scoring 3,050 runs and claiming 415 victims. Wicket-keeping gloves were different in those days, being handmade in leather with a preparation of rubber rolled into the face. Finally linseed oil was used and the glove left to dry in the sun for an hour or two, a course repeated every few months. If a fellow's timing was right the gloves were perfect, if not the ball would return to the bowler with sticky substances upon it.

With these characters to take the edges Somerset rose to third position in 1892. They have never finished higher. Nottinghamshire, the champion county, were beaten by an innings and plenty, Vernon Hill striking 93 and Tyler taking 15/96, clean bowling Arthur Shrewesbury first ball. After a blank day Somerset lost at Old Trafford in one day, on a slow and treacherous pitch. Four thousand people saw 32 wickets fall. Recovering, Somerset beat Yorkshire at Sheffield by 87 runs. Surrey were too strong but Middlesex were vanquished in front of a large and noisy crowd, for Somerset were now attracting interest wherever they went, partly because they were new, partly because they were seldom dull.

And so Yorkshire returned to Taunton. Could the locals do the double? On 25th August Hewett and Lionel Palairet took guard against Jackson, Peel and Wainwright, a formidable trio perhaps rather tired at this time of year. Hewett cut his first ball to the boundary and, in their differing styles, this pair launched an unremitting attack. Palairet drove Peel into the churchyard for 6 but it was Hewett who reached his 100 first. Even Ulyett's lobs met with little success as Somerset plunged on, scoring at 100 runs an hour. They beat the existing record opening partnership, 283 by Grace and Cooper, and, though Palairet had been dropped on 28, Yorkshire rarely troubled them. Finally at 346, Hewett had an old-fashioned heave at Peel and the partnership was broken. Later the pair were pictured by the Dening patent scoreboard, which was now kept by the pavilion.

Hedley entered and hit a rapid 100 but rain saved Yorkshire.

Under Hewett Somerset seemed certain of a sustained challenge in the championship and now no one thought their victories a fluke. Nothing appeared more certain than that Somerset cricket was here to stay. And yet, of course, it was dreadfully thin really, for Somerset could produce few players and lived on its wits. If a couple of vital men departed there was no solid supply of talent to maintain strength. This, too, has never changed.

All was not solemn in 1892. Tyler took three bats on the northern tour and announced his intention of using them all . . . which he did, scoring 3 ducks and hitting the ball just once, an edge to slip, sufficient evidence, he thought, of supremacy in this weapon. The following year, 1893, saw an unusual match which is worth recording. Somerset played with 12 men at Oxford to give an extra fellow a chance. Hewett missed one game because a relation had died and G. R. Wood was summoned, hit 0 and 52 and played only twice more. Woods's second dismissal was interesting. Sammy recalled it in his memoirs: 'He was playing very well and had got over 50 when he hit a ball into the country where another reverend gentleman was fielding, a splendid bat but the worst fielder in Europe, and never known to make a catch. He picked it up on the long hop and chucked it up and the Umpire gave my Christian out. Worst decision I ever saw! "Christian awake!" said a man in the stand. As Palairet wasn't playing and this one was doing so well, I smiled some!!'

Fothergill's benefit match raised £74 including 5 guineas donated by the club. Hewett was the only man in England to score 1,000 runs in county cricket. And, with such as Fowler, Hill and C. J. Robinson lashing out, Somerset scored their runs much, much faster than any rival, striking at 54 per 100 balls.

Besides those already mentioned, Somerset had two significant players in this pioneering team.

Vernon Tickell Hill was from Wales but he had attended Winchester and won a blue at Oxford and he was to help Somerset cricket on and off the field for decades. His sons Evelyn and Mervyn played like their father, with as much vim as skill, Evelyn being a fast bowler and Mervyn a wicket-keeper.

By all accounts, Vernon, a great pal of the Palairets and Fowlers, was one of the cheery souls of cricket, a forthright fellow who gave the ball so fearful a clout that trained spectators were reluctant to stand in his line of fire at the nets. He played at a time when the individual counted for little in cricket, and his sole purpose at the crease was to hit every ball as far as he could. Sometimes it worked and in the 1892 Varsity match he smote 114 in 100 minutes, *Wisden* saying he hit with 'a power which was absolutely amazing'. Lean and hard-swinging, Hill hit skimming shots rather than steeplers and his triumphs were memorable, which advanced his reputation, though cold figures say he scored 3,785 runs in 120 matches for Somerset at an average below 20.

But Hill must not be dismissed as a simple thumper, for he was a man of substance. Son of a Conservative MP for Bristol he married the daughter of another MP, was himself a member of a ship-owning firm, a magistrate and churchwarden. He had been called to the Bar but preferred a rural life, and was a noted archaeologist who helped in digs at the ancient priory in Woodspring. A tough old bird, he volunteered for the Army much too aged, and served as a major in France. Sammy Woods was godfather to one of his sons.

Richard Palairet, a year younger than his brother, might have been as graceful and efficient a batsman had he not been handicapped by a fractured knee incurred while playing soccer at Oxford. Like Lionel he had been taught style by his father, who employed two professionals to bowl to his sons during the Easter holidays. Richard, they say, had been the better player at Repton, before that injury denied him ease of movement. Nevertheless he played with some regularity for Somerset from 1889 to 1902, scored 3,000 runs and occasionally forged brilliant partnerships with his brother.

Upon his retirement Richard served in India during the war, was appointed secretary at Surrey, went to Australia in 1932–3 as joint manager with Plum Warner, who found him 'very cross at times, and apt to be rude, especially to servants'. Returning to Somerset, he acted as president from 1937 to 1946.

Money was still tight and a row broke out at the AGM over a steep rise in amateur expenses. Murray-Anderdon explained that since Somerset was now an established club the amateurs felt able to collect an allowance which previously they had generously waived.

Charles Dunlop was one such amateur. A Scotsman educated at Merchiston, he was to play forty-two games spread over twelve years and be remembered chiefly as a dashing if seldom effective batsman and as a brilliant outfield. Being a Scot he was really a soccer player and he played both games despite heart trouble, two valves of which had been broken by a juvenile rheumatic fever. He used to visit Dr Poynton in London where he worked as a schoolmaster; but despite Poynton's tender ministrations he died of progressive vascular disease at the age of forty-one.

Naturally enough, Somerset's heroes of 1892 were celebrated in verse:

Alphabet on the Somerset XI, 1892

A for the "averages" hard to be beat,
B for the Batsmen so fleet on their feet.
C for the "centuries," Yorkshire's fate sealed,
  Also, for *Challen*, so deft in the field,
D for the "duck's-egg," that's never allowed,
E for the eagerness shewn by the crowd,
F stands for *Fowler*, a good useful hitter,
G is for Gloucester, whose feelings are bitter.
H is for *Hewett* and *Hedley* and *Hill*,
I for the "innings" prolonged by their skill.
K for the "knocks," that poor *Newton* bore,
L for the Leg that is sometimes "before!"
M for the "maidens," our *Sammy*'s just pride,
N is for *Nichols*, who ne'er bowls a "wide."
O for the "overs," that *Woods* makes renown'd,
P is for *Palairet*, a "clinker," all round!
Q for the quartet of bowlers so deadly,
  S.M.J., Tyler, Nichols, and *Hedley*.
R is for *Robinson*, ne'er caught at wicket,
S is for Somerset, *the* County for Cricket.
T is for *Tyler*, whose "slows," batsmen flurry,
  The terror of Notts. and the envy of Surrey.
U for the Umpire, whose ankle's quite sore,
  With stopping the drive that *Hill* meant for 4.
V for the "'Varsity Blues" in the team
  Of Cricketers verily they are the cream.
W the Wicket-keep, so smart with his catches,
X for the 'xtras, so rare in our matches.
Y for the Yorker, each bowler's ambition,
Z for the zeal which sent Notts. to perdition.

Somerset's hopes of continued success in 1893 soon faded, Yorkshire beating them easily thanks to a hundred by A. Sellers for which he won a canary from a colleague. Eight games were lost but there were some notable scalps too, with victory at The

65

Oval, a handsome win over Nottinghamshire at Taunton, Hewett scoring 120 and Tyler taking 9 wickets, and two over Gloucestershire, whose light was, for the time being, burning low. Sceptics were still to be found, Surrey's defeat being regarded as 'one of the wonders of cricket'.

But this was small fry beside the dramas associated with the visit to Taunton of the 1893 Australians, a visit which was to have sweeping consequences.

Australia had last visited Somerset in 1882, when the locals hardly had a ground or a team. Now Somerset were strong and boasted their own bluff and crafty antipodean, Sammy Woods. Seldom has a game been more eagerly awaited.

Torrential rain fell overnight and yet the morning dawned bright and warm. Thousands packed the streets of Taunton and thousands more arrived by rail to see the Australians who had not reached town until the early hours. At 11.00 a.m. the umpires inspected a sodden pitch and decided to abandon play, a premature decision for this county ground can dry in hours under a hot sun. Perhaps pressure was applied by the Australians and by Hewett, Somerset's captain, who was a decisive man.

Even the most docile members were angry at this feeble verdict, and those who had travelled for miles were outraged. They booed and heckled as the Australians packed their picnic baskets, hired a coach and wandered off to Cothelstone, a beautiful part of the Quantocks.

Meanwhile things were worsening at the County Ground so that Somerset officials, desperate to placate a seething crowd, asked the umpires to inspect conditions again, which they did at 2.00 p.m., promptly overturning their previous verdict and saying play could commence. Hewett was furious and a fierce argument began between the captain and his administrators. Hewett lost and an announcement was made that there would, after all, be some cricket that afternoon.

Of course it was not quite as simple as that. A messenger was sent on horseback to find the Australians and the telegraph between Taunton and sundry Quantock villages ran hot with urgent messages. Finally the tourists were located and brought back to Taunton, in what sort of mood cannot be said.

Play began at 4.00 p.m. between two teams neither of which were overly keen on this turn of events. Hewett, in particular, was in high dudgeon and upon Somerset being asked to bat he threw away his wicket for 12 runs, having been dropped once. Somerset made 119, no cricket was possible on the second day, and Woods took 6/26 as Australia collapsed to 107 in front of 5,000 people on the third. Then C. T. B. 'Terror' Turner took 7/26 to bowl Somerset out for 64. 'Terror', Spofforth's successor, could cut the ball venomously at medium-pace. In seventeen Tests he took 101 wickets yet he had never played till he was 16 when, watching a game, he told one captain his team would never 'bowl 'em out' whereupon for his cheek he was invited to have a go, which he did, saying, 'If I do any worse I'm going home'. He became a superb bowler.

Needing 77 to win, Australia lost early wickets to Woods but won easily enough.

For Hewett it was too much. He believed his authority had been unwarrantably defied and felt badly let down. To him the whole thing had been a farce. Friends thought he was making too much of it but he was extremely angry and unprepared to compromise. Accordingly he was lost to Somerset cricket at the end of the season, walking out never to return as a player. It was a dreadful blow, and an unnecessary one for plainly Hewett was being intemperate, for Somerset had feared a riot, and not without reason. Perhaps Hewett had too little self-control to survive as a county captain.

Typically he left in a blaze of glory, belting hundreds off Nottinghamshire and Gloucestershire, the second before lunch. His resignation was much regretted by Lionel Palairet and Wickham in particular.

Elsewhere Tyler and Nichols were to be paid £1 a week during the winter (a belated introduction of winter wages) and a Bath Festival was mooted but rejected because conditions were too poor at the various grounds. New practice nets were ordered.

Sammy Woods was chosen to replace Hewett as captain and he was to lead Somerset for thirteen years during which time his team finished in single figures on only three occasions, in 1894 (when it could scarcely be avoided, there being 9 teams), in 1895 (14 teams) and in 1902 (7th out of 15). Woods sits in history as an alert and imaginative captain but as a man incapable of building the strength of his team by finding outside talent. As it was, once Nichols, Tyler and Woods had lost their sting Somerset was condemned to many long hours in the field.

Woods's period as captain sadly suffered some abrupt defeats on the northern tour where matches supposed to last six days ended in two! Lancashire bowled Somerset out for 31, whereupon Sugg scored 86 before lunch. Percy Ebdon played in Manchester. No great shakes as a cricketer, he was a good enough rugby footballer to represent England. Soon Herbert Gamlin was playing too; Gamlin was 16 years old and was a professional earning 5s (25p) a week in winter and 10s in summer, 'such payment dependant on good behaviour'. Presumably they were a pair of promising local sportsmen who tickled Woods's fancy. Certainly neither was to distinguish himself in cricket.

Woods's captaincy had in fact begun encouragingly in June, when Somerset had recorded six county wins to set against seven defeats. They also beat the South Africans by 9 wickets. Highlight of the season was an incident at Bristol when by close of play on the second day Woods's men needed a mere 7 runs to win. Somerset pleaded with Dr Grace to allow the game to be finished that evening but he could not be budged. Next morning when play was resumed Lionel Palairet did not bother to change into flannels, appearing at the wicket in ordinary trousers.

More happily, at Hove, Somerset won by 1 wicket, Westcott, who had a handful of games as a pro, helping Wickham in the vital last wicket partnership. All told Tyler took 88 championship wickets, while Woods, Hedley and Nichols bowled well too. Palairet hit two hundreds, and R. P. Spurway hit Somerset's other ton. These Spurways were another of those circle of distinguished and sporting local families which helped Somerset at every opportunity and brought to their club an atmosphere of intimacy. Robert Popham Spurway had attended Haileybury and was to serve in Natal as a captain of his regiment. A splendid rackets player, his military career restricted his county appearances to sixteen before typhoid brought untimely death at the age of 32. His brother, Reverend Edward Popham, Rector of Heathfield, played twice too, once in 1885 and once in 1898, perhaps because he was such a close friend of Sammy Woods. Later the next generation of Spurways, Francis and Michael, assisted Somerset from time to time as wicket-keepers. Poynton wrote of R.P. that he was 'a delightful man and a good cricketer, helping the county when in difficulty' – which, perhaps, captures the Spurways in general.

But it is time to move on, towards another remarkable summer.

8

On the back foot

Somerset had its last remotely satisfactory season for years in 1895. As was typical in this period, only one victory was recorded until the end of July while in August five out of six games were won. Nevertheless these triumphs were the dying gasp of a weakening team, a team whose bowlers were on their last legs. Woods's men managed some valiant play this summer, yet in the following fifteen years Somerset's record was to be dismal, with 345 games played of which 33 were won and 202 lost. In contrast Yorkshire won 285 times and were beaten on 68 occasions – several of them, let it be said, by Somerset.

Having failed to recruit gifted cricketers, a knack which was not to return until after the Great War, Somerset could hope only to muddle through, never despairing, never losing temper, celebrating infrequent victory in style, and otherwise portraying character rather than quality.

Somerset's 1895 season included an eventful match against Kent at Blackheath. Middlesex were nearly beaten in the Whit Monday fixture at Lord's, Mycroft's benefit match. Both Palairets scored hundreds at Lord's, the scene of their spiritual home, while Stoddart scored 150 for Middlesex, though Vernon Hill dropped him twice in the deep whereupon rowdier elements (not in the pavilion) threw bottles of ginger beer at him.

Down in Brighton Sammy Woods struck 215 in $2^1/_2$ hours of belligerent strokeplay and provocative running. And then Somerset hit a bad patch.

At Bristol Gloucestershire exacted harsh revenge for rough treatment in recent years and W.G., displeased to hear that he was finished, took a fearful toll of Somerset's threadbare attack as he swept towards his 1,000 runs in May. Having already bowled 45 overs and taken 5/87 as Somerset were dismissed for 303, Grace put on his pads, marched out and struck 288 in five hours and twenty minutes. Archdale Wickham was keeping wicket and he wrote to a friend afterwards:

> I had the advantage of watching that innings from the closest quarters, and have no hesitation in describing it as the most marvellous performance with the bat that I have ever seen. I can never forget the way Tyler's good length slows, converted by W.G. into half-volleys pitching about a foot outside the off-stump, were driven – rather than pulled – over mid-on's head, and pitched over the ropes. He only allowed *four balls* to pass his bat; one was on the leg-side, and the other three were low ones on the off-side. But no matter how high the ball leaped – and Sammy Woods, who had 40 overs at him, could 'prance' a bit – W.G.'s bat dropped on to them. Some of them went for 4s, and others for a safe 1 or 2 to the man on the boundary; while those aimed at his head generally found the ropes on the leg-side!

W.G. had accepted an invitation to attend a dinner given in honour of A. E. Stoddart that night in London so he dashed from the field, changed on the train (which rather upset one old lady, whose objections were withdrawn when the reason for such conduct was explained), and arrived at 'Stoddy's' dinner to be given a prolonged standing ovation.

It was a crippling year for Somerset bowlers. During an astonishing week of cricket in Taunton in July Somerset lost two games by an innings and 317 runs and by an innings and 452 runs. First Essex scored 692 in little over seven hours and then Lancashire arrived, led by their patrician captain Archie MacLaren, who had not faced a bowler over fourteen years of age for weeks. Nevertheless his father was in the crowd and he was eager to do well. Only by a narrow squeak did he survive his first ball from Tyler and perhaps Wickham missed stumpings at 76 and 317, and certainly Stanley, a combative Etonian and a local landowner who staged county games at his estate, Quantock Lodge, dropped him at mid-on on 262; but these incidents apart, the young Harrovian cut and drove without mercy in an innings lasting 470 minutes which ended only when, with his score already 424, MacLaren lifted Gamlin to Fowler in the deep field. He had hit one six (a drive out of the ground), 64 fours, 10 threes, 26 twos and 80 singles. This innings was cheered with gusto by players and spectators alike and critics regarded it as one of the finest achievements ever witnessed on a cricketing field. Robert Bagehot Porch, a Malvernian who was to play 27 games for Somerset from 1895 to 1910, scoring 665 runs at an undistinguished average, later recalled the innings in a letter:

> I did not play a great deal of first-class cricket for a school-master is not free till August, and unless he is in the very first flight may, as I did, prefer something less strenuous and serious as a holiday, but I fielded out for Archie MacLaren 424 at Taunton. It was a fine innings, but poor Somerset went into the field with two of its bowlers already suffering from sprains and injuries, and we just had to take what was coming to us!

MacLaren was out at 792; Gamlin, the architect of his dismissal, was seventeen years old and had been a professional of sorts for a couple of years. In his brief cricket career he was to score 0, 0, 0, 0, 2, 5 and take 2 wickets for 207 runs. A Wellington schoolboy, he was, though, an outstanding rugby player and he was to represent his country as a full-back on fifteen occasions. Plainly he was one of Sammy's men.

Lancashire were all out for 801, the first time such a total had been scored in first-class cricket in England. MacLaren's 424 eclipsed W. G. Grace's 344 made for MCC against Kent in 1876, which stood hitherto as the highest individual total recorded in a first-class game. MacLaren's innings has never been surpassed in county cricket and until Graeme Hick marched to the crease at Taunton in 1988 it seemed certain to last for ever.

Somerset were bowled out by Mold and Briggs for 143 and 206.

To recover from such a lashing was remarkable and Somerset's five victories in a row speak of character. Those victories revived local interest, if not to the heady level of 1891, and much was owed to the indefatigable Tyler (a collection was taken and realized £35). Twice he conceded more than 200 runs in an innings and yet he fought on to take 10/49 against Surrey, 14 in a match against Yorkshire and 11 against Gloucestershire. Evidently a man of fortitude.

By no means were these exchanges upon the field the most

important event in Somerset cricket that summer of 1895, for on 6 February the executive committee received a letter from John Winter offering to sell to the club his freehold upon the Taunton Athletic ground at a price of £2,000.

Hard up for cash, intent upon looking a gift-horse in the mouth, Somerset began to haggle. A Mr Morris valued the ground at £1,360 and Gerald Fowler, in his role as treasurer, offered £1,700 for the freehold plus £100 for the plant. Could Mr Winter see his way to accepting this and could he remove the telegraph poles?

Mr Winter could not. Urgently in need of money to settle his debts, he stood by his price. Fearful that Winter might withdraw his offer, or ask for more, the Club quickly agreed to pay £2,000 and to raise an extra £150 to pay for a new entrance at Priory Bridge. At once twenty-two debentures of £100 were issued at 4 per cent interest and taken up by wealthy supporters in Taunton. Somerset now owned a cricket ground, an asset which has been of immense value in the decades since.

Somerset finished eighth in 1895 and played some good cricket too. Times ahead were to be much harder, for the bowlers were in decline. Woods was now really a batsman, Nichols had taken a benefit (against Yorkshire in 1895, takings at Priory Bridge being reserved for him) and though George Gill had arrived from Leicester, at a wage of 32s a week in summer and 10s in winter, he could not be expected to carry a county attack. Perhaps it is just as well that memory is selective. For the following ten years or so Somerset was to remember a few famous victories and to ignore frequent heavy defeats.

By beating Gloucestershire, Sammy's team started the 1896 season in deceptive style. Besides Gill, a new bowler, Ernest Robson, had arrived the previous year and was showing accuracy with his medium-pacers. He was to stay for twenty-seven years and to die more or less with his boots on. In 1897, a promising spinner would be found in Cranfield who worked wonders in the nets and failed dismally in matches, a characteristic not unique to Cranfield or even to Somerset cricketers. Nonetheless it was contributions from Captain Hedley which in 1896 brought bursts of glory to Somerset cricket.

Robson took 8/50 against Australia after Somerset had hit 219. Leading by 90, Somerset slipped to 49/6 and the game was nicely poised when rain came to spoil things. Then Surrey arrived, needing a draw to be certain of the championship. They had already won sixteen games but now collapsed to 172, Robson taking 5/47. Somerset slid to 56/8 when Tyler joined Hill; incredibly both men scored fifties and their team led by 10. Bowling his cutters with an idiosyncratic action, Hedley took 6/26 in 17.2 overs as Surrey were swept aside for 69, whereupon Lionel Palairet eased Somerset to a 9 wicket victory.

Apart from Palairet's magnificent form – he hit four hundreds, including 292 at Southampton and a century against Sussex at Taunton which was matched by one from his brother – Somerset had little else to boast of in 1896, finishing eleventh and with prospects gloomy. Douglas Smith, a young pro from Yorkshire, was tried, made a hopeful start and then faded. It is hard for a youngster to do well in a beaten team.

Not all was solemn. Nichols lost his wicket at Bristol after hitting the ball twice, which must have amused his numerous friends.

Bedevilled by poor fielding and with Woods and Lionel Palairet less prominent, Somerset did little in 1897 or in the following two summers.

Nine games were lost in 1897. Concentrating upon the three victories, Somerset beat Kent and recorded two scarcely believable triumphs over Surrey, one at The Oval by 224 runs, Tyler scoring a fifty and taking wickets, one at Taunton, where Surrey arrived once more needing a win to take the championship. Instead Tyler took 9/111 (to follow his 13/163 at The Oval) and Surrey lost by 66. For the second time Lancashire could thank Somerset for their championship success. Since 1891 Somerset had beaten Surrey on six occasions and lost eight times.

By 1898 crumbling walls on the eastern side of the county ground had been replaced with iron spikes but nothing could stop the crumbling in Sammy Woods's cricket team. Tyler was not catching so well. George Gill bowled as well as anyone. Tall and loose-limbed, he had an easy action but was inclined to bowl defensively outside off-stump and to rely upon change of pace to take wickets. Before returning home he scored 2,442 runs, and took 243 wickets for Somerset. In 1902, his most prized scalp was Victor Trumper, who wrote: 'I got a real thunderbolt from Gill in the first innings and was out for five.' Gill trapped his man in the second innings too, leg before for five. He was an honest journeyman in a struggling and poor club.

Charles Bernard was playing too. A correct public-school batsman, he was a good off-side player who, said C. B. Fry, 'is sure to be a great batsman if he has the necessary leisure to play regularly'. In fact he was to play just thirty-three first-class games and to score his runs at an average of 30, higher than most comrades and especially respectable considering how infrequently this locally born batsman could play. They say Sammy Woods found him and certainly Somerset's captain must have been sorry his discovery could play so much club cricket in Bristol and so little county cricket in Somerset. Bernard scored 94 and 56 against the Australians in 1899 but he was, alas, a poor fielder.

It was a time of comings and goings, as Somerset desperately tried to replace ageing warriors with men as impressive and as wholehearted, usually without luck. Frank Phillips, formerly of Oxford University and Essex, began playing in 1897 as a forthright batsman whose defence was brittle. A blue in 1892 he was to score 163 against Sussex in 1899 before abandoning his position as a schoolmaster to fight in South Africa and later in the First World War, from which engagements he emerged with a DSO. His cricket career embraced sixty-seven games for Somerset during which he scored four hundreds in the old manner and upon his retirement he served in Southern Nigeria as an Assistant District Commissioner.

Only one victory was recorded in 1898, to set against ten defeats. Thankfully *Wisden* felt 'little inducement to dwell at any length' upon this disastrous season. Somerset's supply of talented amateurs had run dry – or nearly so, for Bernard was certainly impressive – and more importantly the bowling was dreadfully weak. Robson and Gill simply could not carry it alone. Moreover Woods's team chopped and changed with unconscionable regularity and while Robson took a hat trick against Hampshire and H. T. Stanley tried hard it was usually to no avail.

Woods himself was appointed as a paid assistant secretary in 1898 at a wage of £200 a year. He did not do much administrative work and his appointment was simply a way of giving money to this amateur so that he could live in his customary manner and feel no call to go home.

Wisden did not feel inclined to dwell upon Somerset's season in 1899 either. 'The doings of the Somersetshire eleven in 1899 do not call for any lengthened criticism.' Major Poore (304), a massive man, a splendid swordsman and a noted polo player, added 411 in 260 minutes with his Hampshire team-mate Captain Wynyard as Tyler, who had not missed a game since 1888, bowled 63 overs and took 4/201. Cranfield, Nichols and Gill were harshly punished too. Major Poore was a somewhat eccentric and peppery cricketer. Upon being asked by undergraduates how Larwood might be played, he replied 'Sah, fix yer bayonets and charge him!' He was apt to field on hot days in a solar topee, which did not always help in his attempts to catch skiers.

Sadly Tyler's benefit game against his old foes Surrey was thinly attended. 'Poor recompense,' said *The Sportsman*, adding a hope that wealthy people in the area – 'and there are plenty of them' – would subscribe to a collection. It was a good game, Surrey scoring 499, Somerset 358, whereupon they followed on and were saved by Newton and a new youngster, John Daniell, who added 78 runs in 100 minutes.

Australia arrived and were held to a draw. Laver scored 143 as the visitors reached 532. In reply Bernard and Len Braund, a professional cricketer who had just joined Somerset having been rejected by Surrey, added 152 for the first wicket. With Lionel Palairet suffering from appendicitis and unable to play all summer, these runs were much needed. Woods, who batted well this season, was run out by Trumper as he tried to pinch yet another quick single, despite which the game petered out into a draw, though not before Australia's occasional bowlers turned over their arms. On snaring one wicket Iredale and his chums executed a sort of wild Indian war dance on the pitch which amused everyone.

Braund was to be one of Somerset's greatest cricketers and an outstanding all-rounder for England too. For the time being he had to twiddle his thumbs while he served a two-year stretch of residential qualification. He was a promising recruit, as was this Daniell fellow from Clifton College. Currently an undergraduate at Cambridge, he thrashed 107 off Lancashire, adding 174 in 115 minutes with his captain as Somerset recorded an astonishing victory by 10 wickets. Gloucestershire were beaten too, but a veil must be drawn over other fixtures for, in truth, Somerset was a soft touch. They lost by an innings at Lord's in a game which lasted just over three hours, Somerset scoring 35 and 44, Middlesex 86. Trask, Palairet, Roe and Tyler all recorded pairs, and only Woods reached 20. A newspaper accompanied its match report with the following timetable which graphically records the succession of events:

P.M.
12.05 Game started, Somerset batting
12.07 Robson, b Hearne, first over, 2-1-2
12.10 Palairet run out, second over, 2-2-0
12.11 Roe, b Trott, second over, 3-3-0
12.14 Phillips, b Hearne, third over, 5-4-1
12.16 Trask, b Hearne, third over, 5-5-0
12.20 Stanley, b Hearne, third over, 5-6-0
12.23 Nichols, b Trott, fourth over, 8-7-0
12.27 Tyler, c Hearne, b Trott, fourth over, 8-8-0
12.33 Newton, b Trott, sixth over, 17-9-7
12.35 Woods and Gill batting
12.50 Rain stopped play
 1.32 Play resumed
 1.35 Woods, lbw, b Hearne, fifteenth over, 35-10-20

 1.50 Middlesex started batting
 2.00 Lunch
 3.00 Play resumed
 3.02 Hayman, c Stanley, b Tyler, 24-1-13
 3.18 Warner, c and b Tyler, 33-2-14
 3.23 Ford, b Tyler, 35-3-2
 3.28 Cobb, b Robson, 35-4-2
 3.31 Trott, st Newton, b Tyler, 36-5-0
 3.52 Rawlin, c Stanley, b Tyler, 57-6-11
 3.58 Stogdon, c Newton, b Robson, 68-7-2
 4.03 Foley, c Phillips, b Tyler, 68-8-20
 4.08 MacGregor, c and b Tyler, 76-9-3
 4.24 Roche, c Woods, b Tyler, 86-10-0

 4.38 Somerset started second innings
 4.40 Phillips, b Trott, second over, 2-1-0
 4.42 Palairet, b Trott, second over, 2-2-0
 4.46 Roe, b Trott, second over, 2-3-0
 4.48 Robson, b Hearne, third over, 2-4-2
 4.53 Trask, lbw, b Trott, fourth over, 5-5-0
 4.58 Woods, c Rawlin, b Hearne, seventh over, 11-6-6
 5.03 Stanley, b Trott, eighth over, 18-7-5

76

5.06 Tyler, c Stogdon, b Trott, eighth over, 18-8-0
5.08 Nichols and Newton batting
5.23 Newton, lbw, b Trott, sixteenth over, 44-9-12
5.26 Nichols, c Roche, b Hearne, seventeenth over, 44-10-18
5.26¼ Tears and Triumph.

And this was the game Flowers had picked for his benefit! Six thousand people watched these dramas so Flowers was not entirely unrewarded.

Only one other memory lingered. Stanley hit 127 in the victory over Gloucestershire. Within fifteen months he was dead.

Apart from one sad affair which virtually ended a player's career, 1900 was not in any important way different from its recent predecessors. Somerset finished eleventh and critics found time only to praise Daniell's fielding, to rue the poor form of Palairet upon whom so much depended, to regret the decline of Bernard and to feel sorrow at the absence of some decent players (Phillips, Hedley and Stanley) in South Africa. Of course there were some highlights in this grim period of matches played on tranquillized pitches. Surrey were beaten twice despite nearly a score of palpable chances being missed off Woods who, for the first time in ages, found fire in his bowling. Sam Apted's Oval wicket had been turned by rain into a glue pot yet upon it Robson hit an outstanding hundred. At home Woods scored a century, and Vernon Hill hit 72 out of 75 in 35 minutes against Middlesex in J. T. Hearne's benefit match. Somerset's popularity is shown by the frequency with which they were chosen as opposition in benefit games.

Hampshire were beaten twice and had catches been held more matches would have been won, for Somerset lost two games in a row by a single wicket. One of these matches was played in Bath for Somerset was now arranging two of its contests a year to be played in the Recreation Ground, evidence that Bath had returned to the fold after the differences in 1885, and was now eager to play a full part in the county's cricket club.

The event of the year, in some respects anyhow, was the winning of an Olympic gold medal for cricket by Devon Wanderers representing England. They bowled France out cheaply in the final and their team included Montagu Toller and Alf Bowerman who had played occasionally if without distinction for Somerset.

But the sorrow of the year lay in the calling of Tyler for

77

throwing by umpire James Phillips, who had similarly called Ernest Jones in Australia in 1897–8 and C. B. Fry in 1898. For some years there had been rumblings about unfair bowling and in *Wisden* Sydney Pardon wrote: 'I cannot help thinking what a number of scandals and what an immense amount of grumbling would have been avoided if in the middle of the eighties the county captains had taken concerted action.'

Tyler was the first slow bowler to be condemned. Somerset were playing Surrey at Taunton and Tyler bowled 2.1 overs and took 1/6 in the first innings. He did not bowl in the second. Somerset won the game, the first victory at Taunton since 1897, but they lost Tyler. Mold of Lancashire was no-balled too, and no doubt both actions were suspect, to say the least. Perhaps Tyler and Mold were fortunate to have lasted so long. Having done so, both were sorry to leave.

Luckily Somerset had been grooming a successor to Tyler for some years. Beaumont Cranfield of Bath was a left-arm spinner who won praise from no less than Alfred Shaw, who said of him: 'He can make the ball turn either way just sufficiently to beat the bat. Practical experience will enable him to keep an accurate length.'

But experience taught Cranfield no such lesson, for he had a brittle temperament and his career was to be short. In part this was due to a decision not to change the leg-before rule. Shaw again:

> The Somerset left-hander's faster deliveries go sharply with the arm, and had the proposed alteration been adopted I should have had to give all the Worcestershire batsmen out in 3 overs. The bowler pitched the ball about four inches outside the off stump and would have hit the middle and leg stumps.

Nowadays, of course, this is *out*. Poor Cranfield! Appearing first in 1897, he had some marvellous games for Somerset, took 563 wickets and at an average of 24, and was good enough to play for MCC against Australia in 1902. Perhaps this was his undoing, for after 1902 he faded, taking only 88 championship wickets in 1903 and 71 in 1904 before illness took him away. Not every county cricketer, let alone every Somerset cricketer, welcomes attention.

Sammy Woods said: 'Cranfield could do more with the ball than any bowler I ever saw, but you cannot be a bowler if you ain't got a head.' Woods remembered him as a nervous little fellow and related that:

> Although he had £200 in the bank at Taunton he didn't like to apply for it. He didn't like the late Gerald Fowler, at whose bank his money was. He had an aged mother. It was a very cold winter, so Cranny, as we called him, got a barrow load of coal and went out selling it in Bedminster, where he lived. He shouted out 'Any coals! Any coals!' Some man poked his head out of an attic window. Cranny said, 'Do you want any coals?' 'No,' said the man, 'I don't and why do you want to wake me up at this time of day?' Cranny remarked, 'Then why the devil did you poke your head out of the window? Go to bed again, you blighter.' Curious fellow, Cranny.

Aged 35, his career long since over, Cranfield went to see a local football match, contracted double pneumonia and died. Like Nichols, and later Robson, he gave his best years to Somerset cricket. Included in Cranfield's rich repertoire was county cricket's slowest-ever delivery. So lofty was its flight that he was able to follow it down the pitch and to block any shot with his boot.

For the present Cranfield was an adequate replacement for Tyler. With Braund available to play in 1901, hopes could be held for a stronger showing, especially as Ted Lewis, another professional bowler, had arrived and was beginning to impress.

In the event Somerset finished a place lower. In his first full season Braund scored 1,064 runs and took 78 wickets, pressing his case for Test recognition, which was soon to come. South Africa were beaten easily, Palairet and Lewis scoring well, Lewis adding 119 for the 8th wicket with Gill (85) and 109 for the 9th with Cranfield (28). Yorkshire arrived in Taunton and despite Woods hitting a rollicking 90 and Robson reaching 58, Lord Hawke's men scrambled home in a desperate finish with their last pair at the crease.

These moments apart, it was mostly gloomy. Ranjitsinhji saved Sussex at Taunton by batting throughout the final day after being up all night fishing for trout, following a somewhat inaccurate tip from his opponents. Moreover Sussex amateurs had told Ranji that if he stayed in all day he might score 300, which must have added to his burden. As it happened, only a flurry of rain restricted him to 285 not out. Major Pridham, who was so keen a Somerset supporter that he gave his son the initials L C H P, recalled sitting in the front row of the seats, 'in the vicinity of square leg or danger zone . . . Time after time Ranji's famous leg glance came flashing, almost humming, from the flick imparted by those delicate wrists.'

So greatly did Ranji enjoy himself in Taunton that once on a visit, he volunteered to field as substitute for Plum Warner as Palairet and Lewis set about Middlesex joke bowlers in a dead game.

What else? Somerset amateurs cost £219 in expenses in 1901 and the pros £993 in wages. Beyond argument Jessop was right to say that 'the cost of an amateur compared with a professional is about one-third – in some counties even less. Impoverished counties use available amateur talent, which is where the rabbits creep in'. He added that 'an inclusion in first-class cricket does not constitute a first-class cricketer'.

Somerset's amateurs played for their expenses of £1 a day, from which dinner and accommodation had to be paid. Woods apart, there is no evidence that money was paid on the sly. They may have been rabbits but they were not crooks.

Subscriptions amounted to £1,091 and £1,050 was taken at the gate as Somerset continued to survive year by year, often balancing their books as precariously as in 1897 when a Mr J. S. Donne paid £25 towards clearing off the debt, provided the other £100 was found elsewhere. It was. To date it always has been.

Nothing remarkable about 1901? Yet one match played had cricket observers shaking their heads and poets reaching for their quills, for this was the year in which Somerset beat mighty Yorkshire. Typically these three improbable days were held to be quite enough to cheer up Somerset's long-suffering supporters. It is time to go tyke-bashing.

9

Tyke-bashing

Not since August 1899 had Yorkshire lost a county game. They had won the championship in 1900, and were to win it in 1901 and 1902. In those years they lost only two county games, both to Somerset. They were beaten again in May 1902, against which county hardly needs to be said. Another match was lost – to MCC at the Scarborough Festival. Nineteen of Yorkshire's wickets in that contest were taken by Cranfield and Braund.

Despite Yorkshire's narrow victory at Taunton in 1901, Somerset did not catch their train to Leeds with much enthusiasm, for their form was abysmal. They went because the fixture list insisted upon it. Sammy's team was much as usual, except that George Burrington, a thirty-seven-year-old from Tiverton was summoned to bat at 10 (he scored 11 and 15). Burrington caught Lord Hawke, played two more games and was heard of no more. Frank Phillips was back from the Boer War but had trodden on his hand during an earlier game at Lord's and rushed north only at the last moment, when Sam counted heads and noticed he was one short. Ted Lewis was included yet was not called upon to bowl, though he was in time to take 500 wickets for Somerset. Perhaps no one had told Woods he could turn his arm over. When Keith Jennings first played for Somerset he did not bowl, for Brian Close imagined him to be a batsman.

At least Somerset had a wicket-keeper. Playing Yorkshire at home, they had called upon Bill Price, a Tauntonian, to pull on the gloves as an emergency substitute. Price let through 23 byes and it was his one and only game. Not that he is unique in playing just one for Somerset, for emergencies are common. To date ninety-six men have enjoyed a solitary fixture, a list including A. J. Ricketts (a local spinner who played in 1936) and A. T. Sanders, a Harrovian who played in 1919 and died a year later aged 19, sadly having scored a duck in his only innings.

Arthur Newton was Somerset's keeper in Leeds and by now people were saying that only Halliwell, the South African, was his match. At first everything went as predicted. Gambling by batting first upon a wet pitch, Somerset were skittled for 87 by Wilfred Rhodes, with only Sammy Woods (46) contributing much. Hard though Cranfield and Gill tried, they could not prevent Yorkshire reaching 325, of which Haigh smote 96, adding 118 in fifty-five minutes with Rhodes, a partnership loudly cheered by a partisan crowd of 10,000.

Somerset's position was hopeless. A dinner party was held that night for home and visiting amateurs (though Newton did not attend) and as liqueurs were drunk, mostly by Woods, Mr Hepworth, the genial host, said he'd pay £100 to the county funds if Somerset won. Woods fancied a flutter and put £10 on Palairet to score a hundred at 10/1. Both bets were won but, alas, neither was paid.

Braund and Palairet had scored ducks in the first innings. Now, upon play resuming, they set off at a furious pace. Yorkshire missed a runout and an appeal for a catch at slip was denied, though Tunnicliffe went to his death-bed swearing it was fair. Yorkshire had missed their chance. Palairet batted with supreme elegance while Braund, England's finest all-rounder of the Golden Age save those from Yorkshire, hit a hundred which pulsated with life and colour. Soon Hirst was tired for it had been a long season and he told Woods 'My feet are so sore I can hardly run to the wicket'.

Somerset's openers added 222 in 140 minutes, opening the way for Phillips to strike 122, batting with Sammy Woods as his runner for he had strained a leg. Before play began Somerset had pessimistically arranged for an extra carriage to be tacked on to the afternoon train. In the event Somerset did not catch that 5.30 express.

In 155 overs of violent batting Somerset scored 630 as Yorkshire for once fielded badly. They were a beaten side. On a wearying pitch they could scrape only 113 runs on the third and final morning, losing their last 8 wickets for 16 runs to Somerset

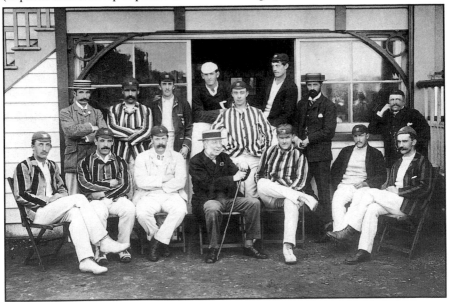

1890. T. Spencer, J.E. Trask, R.C.N. Palairet, S.M.J. Woods, J.B. Challen, E. J.
Tyler, H. Murray-Anderdon, T. Knight, L.C.H. Palairet, W.A.R. Young, W.N.
Roe, Hon. Sir S. Ponsonby-Fane, H.T. Hewett, G. B. Nichols, A. E. Newton

1891. E.J. Tyler, G. Fowler, A. Wickham, R.C.N. Palairet, S.M.J. Woods,
L.C.H. Palairet, V.T. Hill, C. Robinson, J.B. Challen, H. Murray-Anderdon,
W.N. Roe, H.T. Hewett, A.E. Newton, G.B. Nichols

1901. G. Gill, E. Robson, L. Braund, G. Burrington, F. A. Phillips, A. E. Newton,
S.M.J. Woods, L.C.H. Palairet, V.T. Hill, L. Cranfield, A. Lewis

1912. E. Robson, J. Bridges, A. Lewis, H. Chidgey, L. Braund,
M. Bajana, L. Sutton, E. Poyntz, J. Daniell, W. Greswell,
J. MacBryan

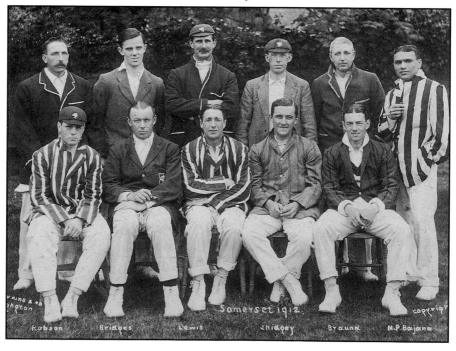

1922. A. Young, T.C. Lowry, M.D. Lyon, J. Bridges, S.G.U. Considine, E. Robson, W. Greswell, P.R. Johnson, J. Daniell, J.C. White, J. MacBryan

1927. W. Luckes, A. Young, G.E. Hunt, J.W. Lee, F.G. Lee, A.E.S. Rippon, C.C. Case, G. Earle, J.C. White, W. Greswell, R. Ingle

1936. F. Lee, H. Hazell, W. Andrews, A. Wellard, W. Bunce, H Gimblett, J. Watson, H.D. Burrough, R. Ingle, W.F. Baldock, W. Luckes

1949. H.W. Stephenson, E. Hill, G.R. Langdale, M. Tremlett, M. Coope, J. Lawrence, H. Gimblett, G. Woodhouse, H. Hazell, A. Wellard, H. Buse

1955. C. McCool, M. Walker, P. Wight, G. Tripp, T. Clements, C. Davey, K. Biddulph, B. Lobb, G. Lomax, L. Pickles, W. Andrews, J. Hilton, R. Smith, J.Lawrence, G. Tordoff, J. Baker, H. Stephenson, B. Steer, K. Palmer, G. Atkinson, G. Keith, B. Roe, G. Trump, R. Virgin

1960. R. Virgin, F. Herting, K. Biddulph, T. Tout (Scorer), A. Whitehead, K. Palmer, G. Atkinson, A.H. Baig, M. Tremlett, H. Stephenson, C. McCool, B. Langford, P. Wight

1963. D. Doughty, B. Lobb, M. Kitchen, R. Virgin, C. Greetham,
R. Kerslake, P. Eele, K. Palmer, B. Langford, H. Stephenson,
P. Wight, G. Atkinson

1967. G. Clayton, R. Virgin, M. Kitchen, F. Rumsey, R. Palmer,
T. Barwell, P. Robinson, K. Palmer, B. Langford, C. Atkinson,
W. Alley, G. Atkinson

1972. M. Hill, H. Moseley, S. Wilkinson, P. Denning, A.A. Jones, D. Taylor, A. Clarkson, J. Roberts, K.O'Keefe, G. Burgess, T. Cartwright, B. Close, B. Langford, R. Virgin, M. Kitchen, P. Robinson

1981. J. Lloyds, D. Breakwell, P. Roebuck, J. Garner, C. Dredge, N. Popplewell, V. Marks, P. Denning, D. Taylor, I. Botham, B. Rose, V. Richards, H. Moseley

1988. P. Robinson (Coach), D. Foster, J. Wyatt, G. Palmer, R. Harden, R. Bartlett, M. Douglas, G. Rose, N. Pringle, M. Cleal, R. Woolston, A. Phillips, N. Burns, N. Mallender, N. Felton, C. Dredge, M. Crowe, V. Marks, P. Roebuck, B. Rose, S. Waugh, J. Hardy, A. Jones, T. Gard

1990. A. Hayhurst, M. Cleal, P. Rendell, S. Priscott, R. Harden, I. Fletcher, D. Kutner, R. LeFebvre, N. Pringle, G. Townsend, R. Bartlett, I. Swallow, P. Robinson (Coach), N. Mallender, N. Burns, J. Cook, C. Tavare, R. Parsons (Chairman), J. Birkenshaw (Manager) T. Gard, A. Jones, J. Hardy, G. Rose, P. Roebuck

spinners to fall 279 runs short at that target. Yet Yorkshire were sporting in defeat, Woods and his chums being roundly cheered, a large crowd jostling around them so that they could scarcely reach their charabanc. Apparently Woods said nothing until he reached his hotel, whereupon he uttered one word: 'Magnum!'

It was one of county cricket's most extraordinary results, an unbeaten record lasting forty-eight games being ended after a large first innings lead had been taken. Naturally Woods and his men were heroes in Taunton, where the game had been closely followed, telegraphed scores being posted in shop windows.

SOMERSET

First Innings		Second Innings	
1 L.C.H. Palairet b Hirst	0	c and b Brown	173
2 Braund b Rhodes	0	b. Haigh	107
3 Lewis c Tunnicliffe b Rhodes	10	b Rhodes	12
4 F.A. Phillips b Hirst	12	b Wainwright	122
5 S.M.J. Woods c Hunter b Haigh	46	c Tunnicliffe b Hirst	66
6 V.T. Hill run out	0	c Hirst b Rhodes	53
7 Robson c Hunter b Rhodes	0	c Tunnicliffe b Rhodes	40
8 Gill c Hunter b Rhodes	4	st Hunter b Rhodes	14
9 A.E. Newton b Haigh	0	c Taylor b Rhodes	4
10 G. Burrington c Brown b Rhodes	11	st Hunter b Rhodes	15
11 Cranfield not out	1	not out	5
B 2, l-b 1	3	B 16, n-b 3	19
Total	87	Total	630

1-0   2-0   3-16   4-32   5-38   6-38   7-64   8-65   9-86   10-87
1-222   2-244   3-441   4-466   5-522   6-570   7-597   8-604   9-609   10-630

YORKSHIRE

First Innings		Second Innings	
1 Brown c Braund b Cranfield	24	c sub b Gill	5
2 Tunnicliffe c Newton b Gill	9	c Palairet b Braund	44
3 Denton c Woods b Gill	12	b Braund	16
4 T.L. Taylor b Cranfield	1	absent, hurt	0
5 F. Mitchell b Gill	4	b Braund	21
6 Hirst c Robson b Cranfield	61	l-b-w b Braund	6
7 Wainwright b Gill	9	c Lewis, b Cranfield	1
8 Lord Hawke b Robson	37	c Burrington b Cranfield	4
9 Haigh c Robson b Cranfield	96	not out	2
10 Rhodes c Lewis b Robson	44	st Newton b Cranfield	0
11 Hunter not out	10	c Woods, b Cranfield	0
B 13, w 5	18	B 12, n-b 2	14
Total	325	Total	113

1-13   2-33   3-44   4-51   5-55   6-86   7-142   8-167   9-285   10-325
1-14   2-57   3-97   4-99   5-104   6-109   7-109   8-109   9-113   10-113

BOWLING ANALYSIS
SOMERSET

	O.	M.	R.	W.		O.	M.	R.	W.
Hirst	12	5	36	2		37	1	189	1
Rhodes	16	8	39	5		46.5	12	145	6
Haigh	4	0	9	2		20	4	78	1
Wainwright						34	3	107	1
Brown						18	1	92	1

YORKSHIRE

	O.	M.	R.	W.		O.	M.	R.	W.
Cranfield	27	5	113	4		18	5	35	4
Gill	23	2	105	4		4	1	23	1
Braund	5	0	33	0		15	3	41	4
Robson	10	1	35	2					
Woods	5	1	21	0					
Palairet	1	1	0	0					

Umpires – Wright and Mycroft

Naturally, too, the poets were back to record this magnificent feat:

SUMMERZET GIN YARKZHEER*

I 'ad a vunny dream las' night,
That put me in a dreadful vright
I zeed as plaun as tho' t'were light,
   An' clear, an' vine,
Leb'm vellers dressed in cricket cloaze,
The tears a urnin' down each noaze,
An' loud a doleful cry aroze,
   "Two zemty-nine."

Thinks I "whatever be um at?"
For zum were leun, an' zom were vat,
An' down upon the grass they zat
   All in a line,
An' cussed, an' zwared, an' zobbed, an' zighed,
'Till 'pon me live I thought they'd died,
An' then they altogether zighed
   "Two zemty-nine."

They groaned as if in anguish zore
"Oh we ant bin about avore
An' think 'ow high our 'aids we bore,
   An' cut a zhine;
An' now they men vrom Zummerzet
Our equilibrium 'ave upzet,
Thie number we zhant zoon vorget
   "Two zemty-nine."

An' then I 'eeurd a veller zay,
"As you've bin 'urnin' 'bout all day,
I thought that p'raps as 'ow you may
   Think it were kine,
If zumbody 'ud stan' a quart
A zider for to cheer yer 'eart:"
That zeemed to ztab 'em like a dart:
   "Two zemty-nine."

Then I waked up, an' course I knowad
What 'twere that in my dream were showad,
'Twere Zammy 'Oods, the artvul toad,
   Wi look benign,
A askin' 'Awk if 'e ud taake
A mug a zider for's stummick's zaake,
An' if it wadd'nt the stuff to maake
   "Two zemty-nine?"

Then 'ere's a 'ealth to Pallerett,
Cranfield, an' Braund, an' all the zet,
As zmart a team as ever met
   To do or di(n)e.
In every match they've got to play
Let's wish 'em luck, and hope they may
Win in a zummat zimlar way,
   "Two zemty-nine."

ZEKIEL HOMESPUN.

Tanton, July 18th, 1901.

*Reprinted from the *Somerset County Gazette* Saturday 20 July 1901

Somerset won again a year later in Sheffield. On a bad pitch
Jackson, just home from the Boer War, took 6 cheap wickets

in Somerset's first innings and Haigh 6/19, five of them clean bowled in the second. And Yorkshire lost! Braund took 6/30 and 9/41 and hit hard with Palairet to give Somerset two good starts. Chasing 119, Yorkshire failed abysmally and for years afterwards when West Riding babies were unduly troublesome, 'Fratching and tearing in their mother's arms,' as A. A. Thompson wrote, their mothers would say, 'You 'oosh or Len Braund will come and get you.'

It is time for Braund. For Somerset he scored 12,222 runs (average 25) and took 674 wickets (28), and this in a bad side. He was also an outstanding slip fieldsman. C. B. Fry paid him handsome compliments.

> He was one of the greatest all-round cricketers and to think Surrey let him go. The thing about Len Braund was that he was a big match player. I have never seen a better slip fieldsman. He had such a delicate hand. MacLaren would never take the field without him . . . he was as cool as a cucumber.

Braund's temperament could not be faulted. In Somerset's heroic victories over Yorkshire he snared 55 victims (at 14.6) and hit 399 runs. He did well against Australia too, for Archie MacLaren's team of 1901–2, scoring a hundred in Adelaide and taking 21 wickets. Two later tours downunder were hardly less successful, Braund scoring 102 in Sydney in 1903–4 as R. E. Foster plundered his famous 287. He played twenty-three times for England between 1901 and 1908. Of Somerset cricketers only Ian Botham has been capped on more occasions.

As a man Braund had some style. Never ruffled, faintly quizzical in manner, he was regarded as cricket's most debonair and dashing player. What he made of Somerset cricket cannot at this distance be told but certainly it never wore him down. Perhaps he was simply a fellow who took life as he found it.

Braund did the double in each season from 1901 to 1903. Leg-spin bowling was in its infancy and Braund's combination of puzzling flight, sharp turn and phlegm was too much for most opponents, and persuaded Fry to salute him as one of the three or four best leg-spinners in history. Later, when his fingers thickened and his body began to creak, he lost his bowling and had to depend upon his batting skills, which led him to abandoning his old panache for a more cautious approach.

Curiously Braund is not much celebrated in Somerset mythology. It cannot be that he was unpopular, for when his legs were amputated in 1943 Herbert Sutcliffe launched an appeal which won immense support, £7,000 being raised. He coached at Cambridge too, and was held in high esteem, as he was when he took up umpiring. In so far as Braund is obscure it is because he was never really a Somerset man, simply a cricketer playing for Somerset. It is a matter of attitude rather than birth. Woods was a Somerset man, and so were Harold Stephenson and Bill Alley. Significantly all these fellows stayed to live in the county, adopting its mores. Braund was simply a shrewd observer, a detached commentator, and while he was respected he was never taken to heart in the manner bestowed upon numerous lesser sons.

Beating Yorkshire was not the only highlight of 1902 for Somerset rose to giddy heights in the championship, finishing seventh. Curling his deliveries, Braund took 97 county wickets, while Cranfield took 123, 27 of them in two games against Lancashire. Woods, in the evening of his career, had a wonderful game against Middlesex at Lord's as Somerset chased 313. Wickets tumbled until 3 were left, including those of Peter Johnson, and Cranfield. Sixteen were needed as making his championship debut Cranfield took guard and, disobeying orders, lunged hugely at his first delivery, sweeping it from outside off-stump to the boundary at square-leg. Greatly alarmed, Woods hit out and was unbeaten on 88 as Somerset won by one wicket.

Inexplicable things happened too. Out of the blue Mr C. A. H. Baily (from Glastonbury) and Mr Oswald Wright (educated at Malvern) appeared in the Surrey game, batted at 10 and 11 and promptly disappeared.

Somerset made a profit too, which cheered everyone up, for plainly they could afford to keep all five professionals, Braund, Lewis, Robson, Gill and Cranfield.

By 1903 it had come to be regarded as part of the natural order of things that Somerset should beat the County of Broad Acres. This time Somerset beat opponents weakened by injury at Taunton in front of thousands of supporters who greeted victory with a 'deafening roar' as at 5.35 p.m. Woods sliced a shot over the slips. Hirst had broken down, Brown had dislocated a shoulder and Tunnicliffe had spiked a hand, so Somerset's victory was less noble than its predecessors. Woods, incidentally, served as substitute for Hirst when Yorkshire took the field.

If Somerset's latest triumph owed something to luck it was nevertheless saluted across England, for the game was keenly followed. A contemporary cartoonist's comment is reproduced in the photograph section, while a poet wrote:

> In a zecond-class carriage a cricketer zat
> Zighin' "wickets, zix wickets, zix wickets"
> An' I zed "My poor veller, whatever be at
> Zighin' wickets, zix wickets, zix wickets."
>
> 'Ave e' 'ad too much zier, or Zommerset ale,
> That yer looks be so zad, an' your cheeks be so pale?
> Wi' a zorryful shake o' is 'ead e' did wail
> "Oh, wickets, zix wickets, zix wickets."
>
> 'E glared up in me vace wi' a tear in 'is eye
> Zighin' "wickets, zix wickets, zix wickets."
> Be 'e couldn't zay anything, tho' e' did try
> 'Cept, "wickets, zix wickets, zix wickets."
>
> An' once e' got up wi' a wild look o' pain
> As if e' could drow isself out o' the train
> But e' settle back into the coushan again
> Zighin' "wickets, zix wickets, zix wickets."
>
> Now I know what t'were zat this there chap groans so
> "Oh wickets, zix wickets, zix wickets"
> 'E'd bin playing agin Zammy, an Pal'ret an Co
> Wi' their "wickets, zix wickets, zix wickets."
>
> Zo I just gied 'im all the good cheer I could gie
> An 'e zimmed more resigned when I told 'im that 'e
> Mid beat all the tothers if he couldn't beat we
> Wiv our "wickets, zix wickets, zix wickets."

Somerset's team on this auspicious occasion included North, a young fast bowler from Bedminster who did not bowl a ball but was to play another 14 games in which he took 24 rather expensive wickets. And Sammy picked two wicket-keepers too! Actually this was not so unusual, for both Newton and the Devonian Henry Martyn were fine cricketers; besides which, Martyn could bat, and he scored 62 important runs.

Martyn may have been Somerset's best-ever wicket-keeper. Born in Devon he was an Oxford blue and he played for The Gentlemen in 1903, 1905 and 1906. Tall and blessed with long arms, Martyn wore two pairs of gloves, stood up to everyone including Walter Brearley and was a fearless and effective batsman. 'If', one contemporary observed, 'there was a greater cricketer with bat and gloves than he amongst the amateurs I never saw him.' Woods regarded Martyn as charming and recalled that he was nicknamed Admiral Beaune, after his favourite after-dinner drink. Apparently he was full of optimism from the start of a game until its conclusion, and full of advice as well. Martyn stood up to everyone, and once had his teeth knocked out by a bumper from Gill, whereupon Woods ordered his keeper to hold his head still and promptly 'shoved them back into their sockets, they are still there, although a bit discoloured'.

Alas, Martyn could play for only a few years before business commitments took him away, leaving a legacy of 74 games, 2,934 runs (average 24) and 113 victims. Keeping his word, he returned for Braund's benefit match in 1908, a notable tribute and yet an unavailing one for it rained and though Braund commandeered blankets from his hotel in a desperate effort to dry the Bath ground it was no good. Later Somerset offered him another benefit and he declined saying he could not afford it.

If Martyn was not Somerset's best keeper this accolade may belong to Leslie Gay, who played a few games in 1894 before moving to Hampshire. Gay played once for England, under Stoddart (who had never seen him at work) in 1894–5, helping to win a sensational Test in Australia. He also kept goal for England and so stands as one of Somerset's double internationals.

Rain reduced the 1903 Bath Festival to one day and unsurprisingly (for it was a dismal summer) Somerset suffered a loss of £412, which provoked Ponsonby-Fane into telling subscribers that to remain first class Somerset needed more money and better bowlers. Woods's men managed to win six games and to finish tenth in the table, though Woods himself was a virtual passenger, for he had incurred a bad knee after being walloped by a lady wielding a hockey stick (and few sights are more terrifying) during a winter game.

Not that Woods was downcast. At a dinner given by Somerset

men in London he apologized that his 'men are not talkers', whereupon, disproving the point, he spoke of Somerset's great following which was due to never playing dull cricket and always trying to 'rip things along'. They were, he said, 'a British Bulldog kind of a team'. Certainly there was a drama about them which gripped the popular imagination.

Woods, by the way, ended this dinner by singing the humorous song 'The Frenchman', following which Braund gave 'The Blind Boy' in an agreeable voice. Then everyone drank still more cider and sang 'Auld Lang Syne'.

By 1904 Braund and Cranfield were being terribly overbowled and soon both were burnt out. Woods's team carried more passengers than the Minehead railway line and though Lewis confirmed his promise and Palairet recaptured the magic of his youth, especially in his 203 against Worcestershire, Somerset could rarely field their strongest eleven and were, accordingly, doomed to days of thankless toil.

Ted Lewis scored 101 and 97 against Hampshire at Taunton. He was perhaps the first, though by no means the last, Somerset professional who refused to be drawn into the jovial, blundering, valiant world of Somerset cricket. A hardened sceptic, Lewis was an impassive, imposing character given to smoking big cigars and walking around Taunton with a gold watch chain and a rose in his lapel. A tall, striking figure with a waxed moustache, he had dark, fierce eyes and a proud, haughty air which men such as Daniell, his sometime captain, found intolerable. Lewis did not care for the old amateur spirit, thought loyalty merely a word employers used at their convenience and set about grafting hard to build his career. Accordingly Daniell in particular considered him to be 'a bolshie character – bloody awful bloke'.

Lewis, a bachelor with a roving eye and considerable charm, had kept goal for Everton, Sunderland and Bristol City and was once regarded as an England candidate. As a cricketer he played 208 games for Somerset from 1899 to 1914, when he broke down so badly that retirement was certain. In this time he struck 7,633 runs and took 513 wickets (average 22) with his medium-pacers which he would bowl all day beside his comrade Ernie Robson. He was a careful, persevering cricketer rather than a dasher, and he collected runs and wickets as assiduously as he constructed his hundred breaks at snooker, which he played extremely well and often, decades later, with young Eric Hill as his partner.

Lewis – who was referred to as 'Talbot' – opened a sports out-fitters shop with the scarcely less magnificent Mettam, still Somerset's groundsman. This store flourished for years, posting the county scores in its windows as soon as they arrived, so that people hurrying by would stop and see how their team was doing. He carried on playing snooker, in a dingy smoke-filled room above Burtons where men used to go after The George closed, and later still in St Andrews Men's Club, where he'd tell Hill: 'You go for the pots and I'll attend to winning the match.'

Somerset did beat Surrey in 1904, Lewis hitting 118, Daniell 50 and Palairet 49. Albert Bailey arrived from the Surrey groundstaff to take 11/78 against Middlesex with his left-arm spinners. He played forty games, took 129 wickets at a respectable average and then departed.

Naturally Somerset were scouring the metropolitan capital for bowlers. Braund had already made his mark, and while Bailey was of a lesser standard he was nonetheless a handy replacement for Cranfield. Nor were Somerset necessarily scrupulous in their poaching of players. After all, Surrey could pick their men from all London and its surrounds . . . Why, if a couple crept over to Somerset, they'd hardly be missed, would they?

Once bitten twice shy. Bill Montgomery had played fourteen games as a professional for Surrey when he suddenly packed his bags and moved to Somerset – who were, of course, astonished by this turn of events! Surrey protested strongly that Somerset had broken one of the rules governing county cricket and upon Montgomery appearing in the Cider colours they cut off sporting links and refused to play Somerset again, a break which lasted until 1908. Montgomery in fact, played just ten games for his adopted team, barely scoring a run or taking a wicket. No doubt Surrey still seethed over Braund. Somerset men wondered if they had appreciated being beaten in 1891, 1895 (when Surrey were champions), twice in both 1900 and 1904 and on other occasions besides.

Perhaps it was just as well Somerset did not play Surrey. They were in no fit state hereabouts to play anybody.

10

Hiccuping along

From 1905 to 1914 Somerset won 22 games and lost 115. At the heart of this decline lay a distaste for professional cricket and a determination to survive somehow without employing too many supposed mercenaries. Time and again, at area meetings and AGMs and on the executive, where Newton, Palairet, and others from the old school ruled the roost, praise was heaped upon the amateur game. Significantly it was these men who, at a meeting held in the tea room of the ladies' pavilion in 1900, formed The Somerset Stragglers Cricket Club, with the specific purpose of encouraging amateur cricket within Somerset.

Within a year this club had 105 members. The Rev E. P. Spurway was the prime mover and men such as Gerald Fowler and Lionel Palairet played as often as they could. Soon the Stragglers had their own enclosure and by 1924, when money was not so tight, they were asking for a plot of land upon which to build a pavilion, a request which was granted and which led to the erection of the Somerset Stragglers Pavilion which still stands in a lovely corner of the County Ground.

Plainly Somerset's governors meant to depend upon amateur talent, a dependence which brought a flush of interesting cricketers in the 1920s but which otherwise failed to bring strength to Somerset cricket. For the next thirty years or so Somerset played as few professionals as possible, winning recognition as the truest amateur club in the country, surpassing even Middlesex and Sussex. Somerset's attitude to professional cricketers was underlined by Ponsonby-Fane's statement at the 1905 AGM that his club had no intention of paying any winter wages because to do so was to 'pay a man to idle away 8 months out of 12'. Surrey had introduced winter money in 1894 and it had spread quickly, and for a time Tyler, Nichols and others were duly rewarded. But attitudes had hardened and the new professionals were not as much part of the family. Local club cricket being weak and their coffers usually empty, Somerset employed few professionals and by and large these men were treated as employees rather than intimates. This disrespect for professionals has echoed throughout the decades of Somerset cricket since Ponsonby-Fane, who was, after all, merely reflecting widespread contemporary opinion. Only when economic depression and a growing fixture list caused the supply of amateurs to run dry did Somerset search for men like Wellard and the Lee brothers to augment such amateur sporting talent as might appear. Somerset wanted to fulfil the amateur ideal more than it wanted to succeed – an attitude still prevalent, especially off the field; for Somerset folk are immensely patient with their own, and ask only that they ''ave a go'. They too set a high store by spirit and pay less attention to efficiency. Accordingly Somerset County Cricket Club has never, save by chance, taken on a lean and hungry look, and has been content to potter along twenty years or so behind rivals taking heed of their world. It is the characteristic which has made Somerset cricket lovable to its acquaintances and exasperating to its closest friends.

By 1905 Somerset's powerful eleven of 1891 had almost disappeared. Woods was near the end, and Palairet able to play only occasionally. *Wisden* felt 'no temptation to write at any length upon . . . a deplorable season' in which ten games were lost and no cheery surprises occurred. Poor form upon the field brought a decline in interest, matches at Taunton being very badly supported, nor was Somerset any longer so attractive a team away from home, for they were so often simply inadequate. No longer could Somerset find robust sportsmen such as Challen, Roe, Fowler and Hill, tough men willing to try their hand at any game, to support their leading players. Cricket was ever more a game for specialists, not for men with a keen eye for a ball. Bluster was not enough unless it was complemented by skill and concentration, two qualities rarely evident in Somerset cricket at the turn of the century. Somerset gave woeful support to its few good cricketers.

For the Australian visit to Bath Somerset was reduced to calling upon Tom Richardson, a great bowler now running a nearby pub. Richardson had drunk too many bottles of beer and was now a military medium-pacer, the very shell of a once great bowler. Warwick Armstrong scored 303 not out, Monty Noble 127 and Trumper 86. In reply Braund struck 117 and 62, while Henry Martyn hit a fierce and unbeaten 130 to save the game. After 4 wickets had fallen in Somerset's first innings, Kelly, who had already taken a catch, retired injured, whereupon his name was scrubbed and his place taken by Howell.

Richardson died of congestion of the brain in France in 1912, leaving £629, reward for a thousand wickets.

Major Trestrail, DSO, a Somerset man, made his solitary appearance in 1905. Oswald Samson, a local amateur educated at Cheltenham College and boasting an Oxford blue, was also playing some of his forty-five not especially productive games as a left-hand batsman. Samson was killed in action in France in 1918.

Other ordinary cricketers were appearing too, notably Fred Lee from Kent and Percey Hardy, a great trier from Dorset. Educated at Uppingham, Fred played seventy-seven county games, scored a few runs (average 20) and died in Devon in 1914. Percey struggled desperately for ninety-nine matches as a poorly paid professional, scoring 2,696 runs at a dismal average. Tragically he took his own life during the war.

Somerset lost £926 in 1906, a formidable deficit and one which could not be sustained. To raise funds a bazaar was held, and wealthy supporters rallied round. Ever since its creation Somerset had relied upon concerts, dramas, and dances to pay their bills. For county cricket has never been able to support itself. Later, whist drives, raffles and lotteries were introduced and when times were hard rich patrons were appropriately generous, for cricket was certainly beloved of the aristocracy and of the county set.

Nevertheless severe economies were made. Robson, Braund and Lewis were to be the only professionals – others such as Hardy might play as amateurs. It was Woods's last year as captain. In it he 'distinguished myself by not getting a wicket'. Palairet played in only one game, scoring well, and he was sorely missed. Woods wrote that

> At the end of the season I thought it about time I gave up the captaincy. I had been captain for 12 or 14 years, I don't know which. We were a very weak team except in August. Still, we were a happy party all the time and when we did win we did enjoy the victory.

Somerset won at Portsmouth and beat Middlesex by 10 wickets at home. More typically they lost to Yorkshire at Bath by 389 runs. Avenging his 1/189 in 1901, Hirst hit a hundred in each innings and took 11 for 115 in the match, a performance grandly cheered by locals for Hirst was popular wherever he went.

Rumour had it that Woods meant to return to Australia but he stayed in Taunton, living as a sportsman and doing no work at all. He was not without funds, for when he died in 1931 he had some Japanese bonds and £641, which he left to Amy Deane, though Massey Poyntz received his gold watch and chain, and his gold cuff-links.

Nothing changed under Somerset's new captain, Lionel Palairet, in 1907. Palairet had been released by the Earl of Devon to help Somerset but he was to be captain for only one season, and was not an ideal choice for he was too apt to dwell upon the giants of yesterday, grumbling at the AGM that Somerset cricket lacked 'the old spirit of playing together which was the secret of our success'. Finances allowed only nineteen matches to be arranged, which was perhaps just as well for interest was low and so was morale.

Nevertheless it was not a season bereft of incident. For a start, this was the year of Albert Trott's benefit match. Trott was a marvellous cricketer, who played for Middlesex, a powerful hitter and a crafty bowler. Although he was Australian, he was left out of Australia's touring team in 1896, a team led by his brother Harry. Perhaps he knew Albert too well, for besides being a brilliant cricketer this Trott also lived somewhat high. David Foot relates that on every visit to Taunton Albert renewed his acquaintance with a local girl for whose services he paid, or so prurient locals believed. Later she died brutally, and though Trott was innocent still the rumour-mongers gossiped.

Gradually Trott declined, undone by drink, and by 1907 he needed a substantial benefit instead of which he twice took a hat trick in the course of a single innings. Somerset needed 264 to win. They began well, reaching 56 before Palairet was caught at cover. Phillip Trevor's report takes up the tale:

Mr Johnson came in, made a few hits, and was then finely caught by Trott off Tarrant's bowling, the second wicket falling with the total at 74. Lewis succeeded him, and this was the beginning of the end. He was leg-before-wicket to Trott after making a single. Then Mr Poyntz came in, only to be deceived in the flight and bowled first ball by Trott. Mr Woods suffered a similar fate next ball, apparently trying to make a chop stroke. With the defeat of Mr Woods Trott accomplished the 'hat trick', but his success did not end there. Robson was the next man to face him, and his fate was the fate of his predecessors. He was, too, clean bowled, and he was, therefore, Trott's fourth successive victim. It was only by an accident that Mr F. M. Lee did not become his fifth. He hit at the ball bowled to him and missed it. For the moment it seemed from the pavilion that that ball had hit the wicket as well. Mr MacGregor, the wicket-keeper, evidently thought that that was so, for he did not take it, and four byes were the result. It was a wonderful over, and one is scarcely likely to see one like it bowled again in a first-class match. Mr Lee made seven runs before being caught at short slip by Trott off Tarrant's bowling. Then Mr Mordaunt, who had made four runs, faced Trott. He made a poor stroke to mid-off, and was easily caught by Mignon. Mr Wickham succeeded him, and was bowled first ball. Bailey, the last man in, had to take the one ball of the over which remained to be bowled. He hit it up into the air, and Mignon made another easy catch. Thus Trott did the hat trick for the second time in the course of half an hour. Neither the excellence of his bowling nor the failure of the Somerset batting is to be explained away, but it is only fair to state that the light was very bad at the time. But that defective light was even the primary cause of Trott's success was not the case. Two or three of his victims he deceived in the flight of the ball, and the uncomfortable necessity of batting under unpleasantly dramatic conditions no doubt was responsible for the rather poor efforts which some others of his victims made.

By bringing the game to so abrupt an end Trott had 'bowled himself into the bloody workhouse'. Seven years later he was found dead in his dingy digs at Willesden. He had shot himself.

His room was littered with empty beer bottles. He left his clothes and £4.00 to his landlady.

More happily Bert Bisgood of Glastonbury made a first appearance in 1907 which was scarcely less dramatic than Harold Gimblett's twenty-eight years later. A wicket-keeper and a batsman of modest pretensions, Bisgood made a 'sensational debut' at the age of twenty-six, hitting 82 and 116 not out at Worcester. Bisgood was to play another sixty-six games for Somerset without ever again doing anything remotely as dramatic. Those whom the gods wish to destroy they first give promising starts.

Upon Palairet's resignation as captain at the end of the 1907 season Somerset appointed in his place a rumbustious rugby player, John Daniell. And, as Woods comments, 'a nice time he had. We only won two matches. More than 30 people played, some, as you may imagine, very poor performers.'

Daniell had not played for a season, having taken himself off to India to ride elephants and shoot. In Somerset he found little material with which to work, and once again county spirits were kept up only by rare spurts of success which usually sprang from professionals excelling themselves. More typically Kent scored 601, while Lancashire bowled Daniell's men out for 33 at Liverpool. Somerset's batsmen averaged 18 runs per dismissal, their opponents 32.

Somerset were in dreadful trouble and their executive contemplated a return to Minor County status. They had no money, dwindling support and little sign of emerging talent, for their hopes had been dashed too often for any faith to be placed in two teenage debutants, Bill Greswell (1908) and Jack White (1909). Certainly the failures of Somerset's team had a disastrous effect upon crowds and finances.

Bearing in mind this depression, noting Somerset's dire weakness in batting and bowling, observing the absence of romantic victories over such as Yorkshire and Surrey – and even being thankful for such absences, since they would merely serve to cloak incompetence – it is nevertheless possible to recall a few happy times in 1908. Somerset managed to beat Hampshire after falling 163 behind in the first innings. Hoping to rest their bowlers, Hampshire did not enforce the follow-on, whereupon Greswell took 7/42. Needing 292 to win, Somerset lost early wickets only for Woods to join Braund. Woods recalled: 'We began to

97

run short runs, what I call bustled 'em up. Some shocking runs we ran. We had quite a lot of overthrows, chiefly from Llewellyn.' Sam also told one young Hampshire spinner to stop appealing for leg before. Then: 'Len [sic] and I went on and got the runs, he 120 and I 105. Braund was a splendid judge of a run but with me it was the worst running I have ever seen and my poor old legs did give me trouble that night.' Luckily he bumped into a farmer friend who had some whisky.

Apart from this day of glory, only one cricketer showed his true form, Peter Randall Johnson who hit 164, 131, 117 and 126 in consecutive games. Rather priggish in his magnificence, Johnson was a cut apart from the common run of Somerset amateurs but he could bat, on occasion, like a Greek emperor, so much so that supporters said he was an England player lost to the stock-market.

Educated at Eton, Johnson was sneaked into the Somerset team thanks to a certain economy with the truth. Upon his application, Lord's asked where he had been born. Somerset replied 'In Wellington' and did not add 'New Zealand'. Accordingly Johnson was adjudged a Somerset man and he played 229 games for the county.

A negligent fielder and erratic bowler, Johnson was given to batting in I Zingari colours and with a silk handkerchief knotted round his neck, for on and off the field he was a picture of sartorial elegance. At the crease he would belabour bowlers with panache, especially the faster men, whom he could drive through cover with a flick of the wrist. In form he was a champion, and he was invited to go to Australia under J. W. H. T. Douglas – an invitation he declined because of business commitments.

Yet was he really so fine a batsman? His career average of 25.83 denies it, though of course he was severely handicapped by the irregularity of his appearances. Nevertheless, tall and graceful as he was, he cannot be counted as a major batsman because he did not score enough runs. To assume that he could have been outstanding simply from a fist of outstanding innings is to assume too much.

Nor was he a universally popular cricketer. Dressed to the nines, he was apt to stride into the pavilion saying he had just been doing a spot of work. Colleagues found him mannered and distant, though they respected his batting. Johnson did not mix much, preferring a game of poker on a Saturday evening and a

Dickens novel on a Sunday afternoon. He was really a London businessman of hardened temperament rather than a cricketer devoted to his county's cause. In Taunton he lived in a large house near the police station. Two beautiful daughters shared this abode but his eldest son lived in the pub opposite and did not return home even for parties.

Recovering from a severe illness suffered while serving in Mesopotamia during the war, Johnson continued playing occasionally until 1927 and his final hundred against Surrey in 1926 was probably his best.

Had Johnson been able to play regularly Somerset's new captain might have had a chance in 1908. As it was, Daniell's first five years in charge were singularly unsuccessful, Somerset finished bottom three times, 14th once and 11th once. It is a curious fact that Somerset's two most celebrated captains, Sammy Woods and John Daniell, presided over teams that lost with great regularity, though Daniell's second period at the helm (1919–1926) was certainly more successful. Quite simply neither man had a match-winning bowler, until J. C. White settled in 1919. Perhaps only one captain – Maurice Tremlett – was able to defy weak bowling, and even he could not keep it up for long.

Nonetheless Daniell did his best and was to be as influential a figure in Somerset cricket as Murray-Anderdon, who was still acting as honorary secretary. Daniell was a man of powerful character and trenchant views who felt no inclination to bow to contemporary opinion. Brave and unapologetic, he set the mood of Somerset cricket between the wars. It is time to pay attention to him.

A Daniell come to judgement

Few top sportsmen courted popularity less than Daniell. Dogged and determined, he treated every man, amateur and professional, alike and had no time for a shirker. As a captain he possessed a forcefully picturesque vocabulary when things did not go as expected but he was scrupulously fair and accordingly much respected. Starting as a teenager in 1898, he was to dedicate much time and energy to driving Somerset cricket onwards. Tough as old boots, an amateur who never took a penny even in expenses for his contributions, Daniell was a rock upon which Somerset cricket was built during an especially parlous period.

Born in Bath, he was educated at Clifton and at Cambridge, where he won blues in cricket and rugby. Returning to his beloved Somerset he was lost for a time to school teaching and to tree-planting in India, reappearing as captain in 1908. Appointed to office he continued to curse like a trooper and to lead from the front, crouching at silly point rather in the manner of Brian Close, and playing his best innings in tight corners. His leadership qualities were so admired that panic-stricken England selectors contemplated asking him to captain their team in 1921, though Daniell himself was by now a selector. Having served as a fierce leader of the England rugby pack and winning praise as a man capable of turning a mediocre outfit into a good one, Daniell also assisted the rugby selection committee and was often to be seen wearing trilby hat, pipe in mouth, hands clasped behind his back, striding towards the dressing-room to announce that it had been 'the worst perishin' game I've ever seen'.

As a cricketer Daniell was never much above average, for by

temperament he was really a rugby man and cricket's technical and tactical requirements were not to his taste. For his county he scored 9,824 runs, including two hundreds in a game as a forty-six-year-old in 1925, but his figures suffered from Daniell's 'fits of thinking he was Jessop, whereupon he would be comfortably caught at long-leg. And when he holed out he was apt to ask why "that ruddy captain can't keep his fieldsmen where he put 'em"'. Robust and brave, he needed to copy Braund's care to score runs but was seldom inclined to do so.

Daniell was the embodiment of Somerset cricket. Not interested in money (it helped that he had private means) he was a fighter whose game rose to a challenge. In everything he did he entered the old Somerset idea of having a go, of playing with pride and character no matter what the odds. Fielding in a soft fedora, shepherd of a strange flock which he used to call 'our music-hall act', he was charismatic, impetuous and decisive. People tended to witter on less about man-management in those days.

Beyond doubt Daniell's experiences in rugby and his early years at Somerset helped to form attitudes which he never lost. Upon hearing criticism of his strictly amateur regime he was liable to explode and to condemn such words as the 'pettifogging criticism of pygmies'. When, years later, a sardonic supporter dared to observe that the Somerset committee, in which Daniell was very much the leading voice, was suffering from *rigor mortis* he bellowed back that such people had been notable by their absence in the grim days of struggle, adding that those benches around the ground had been good enough to sit upon in 1910 and they were good enough in 1936 too!

During the war he rose to be a captain in France and his son, Nigel, served as a major in the Second World War.

John Daniell was plainly a great man. Because his heart was large and his mind honest he was able to bring to Somerset, eventually, a colourful and capable band of amateurs who helped to restore the club's reputation in the 1920s. Nevertheless Daniell cannot entirely be excused from blame for its decline thereafter, for those difficult years from 1925 to 1931 when Somerset, though by no means poor, continued to depend upon amateurs and never once finished above thirteenth place in the table. It was only upon the outbreak of the Depression that Daniell, his supply of amateur talent nearly exhausted, reluctantly began to allow the employment of professional cricketers who, sensing this reluctance, did not have undue faith in his conversion. For his part Daniell probably found professionals too inclined to grumble about a penny here and a threepence there, and not sufficiently prepared to rough it.

It must, in part, be laid at Daniell's door that Somerset for so long endeavoured to defy the tides. Nevertheless his influence simply reflected an attitude prevalent amongst prominent Somerset supporters, those who had propped up the club since infancy. His attitudes have not been buried yet; understandably so, for they reflect a glorious world in which men overcame all manner of hardships and played not for themselves, not as a career, but for the sake of county and game. Daniell was a sportsman who liked other sportsmen, and loathed the damage done to his beloved game by narrow-minded and self-serving people. Accordingly, and perhaps unfairly, he resisted professionalism with every power at his disposal, for he believed such characteristics were to be found mainly in the professional game which is, perhaps, to forget that Gimblett, Wellard, Hazell, and Andrews were pros, and that MacBryan, White, and Johnson were amateurs.

Daniell's contribution lay in his unbending determination to keep Somerset cricket on its feet, rather than in his choice of direction once the club was mobile. A fair cricketer, a combative captain, an outstanding leader, and a man with the courage of two lions, he was, perhaps, as impressive a man as has ever taken an active part in the directing of Somerset cricket affairs. Picture him, if you will, fielding in his Homburg, cursing a negligent cover-point, glaring at a timid batsman, and waiting upon the arrival between overs (and carried by a telegraph boy) of news of a horse upon whose fortunes he had placed his shirt. Picture him, afterwards, chatting with Len Braund, a fellow enthusiast, and promising a scotch or two upon stumps being drawn.

12

Stormy waters

Having lost thirteen games in 1908 and won only two, Somerset's form improved somewhat a year later as only seven games were lost while four ended in victory, including a double over Gloucestershire. Braund and Daniell were to the fore as batsmen, and Lewis (74), Robson (76) and Greswell (76) were the leading wicket takers.

By now the County Ground was an intimate and lovely place at which people from all walks of life might congregate. Taunton's most important families had their own seats in the Hen Coop, where the Ridley Stand was to be built, and no one else ever dared to occupy these seats should those august personages be absent. Distinguished visitors from outside Taunton would leave their pony and traps at a stable in the back of the Castle at a charge of sixpence a day, a feast of oats included. From the Castle they'd walk to the ground, through the old marketplace and past the shops with their awnings. Trams and cars were to be found in Taunton in 1910 but still travel by horse and trap was much more common. On market day in Taunton there would be an 'incessant entry and exit of carts, waggons, traps, gigs, four wheelers and a large number of private carriages'. So it could be on cricket match days too, if the opposition were sufficiently enticing.

Nor was the County Ground merely the preserve of a class of idle rich. To the contrary, locals sat on the hard benches around the ground, or gathered near the chestnut trees by the Orchard Cottages where soon a public bar was to be found and from which, after the war, raucous shouts were to be heard. People simply congregated in their rightful places. Just as the professionals had their

103

separate and rather dingy changing room, a separate enclosure from which they watched play, a separate gate from which they took to the field, and separate train compartments and hotels too, so people were divided between rulers and ruled, rich men and tradesmen at the County Cricket Ground. A cricket club cannot be expected to be ahead of its times politically, philosophically or socially, and bygone eras cannot be judged according to modern thought.

In any case do not Somerset supporters still gather at precisely the same locations as in 1910? Do not old county families meet in the Old Pavilion, the toffs in the Stragglers' Pavilion and a rougher element in the bars?

Bill Greswell was Somerset's top cricketer in 1909, for besides taking 76 wickets he also struck a hundred out of 198 in seventy-two minutes against Middlesex at Lord's, an innings, E. A. Halliwell described as 'the best I've ever seen, fearless, free and correct'. Since his début as an eighteen-year-old in 1908 Greswell had made an enormous difference to Somerset cricket and it was particularly galling, not least to himself, that he was so seldom able to play in the summers ahead; notwithstanding which, he managed to accumulate 454 wickets (at 21) and nearly 2,500 runs for Somerset in 115 appearances spread over twenty-two seasons, and this despite war and work depriving him of his greatest days.

Greswell was a considerable cricketer and a considerable man, certainly one of the most challenging to play for Somerset. Writing nearly twenty years after his death, John, his son, recalled a man born in Madras whose father had worked as an engineer for the Ceylon and Indian Railways, retiring to Somerset in 1891. Bill grew up beside a boy called John Cornish White with whom he used to practise endlessly. Meanwhile an investment in a Ceylonese jungle which his father had cleared and turned into a tea plantation was paying dividends.

Bill, and his gifted brother Ernest (who played a few games for Somerset), attended Repton and played for Somerset in the holidays. Bill bowled at around Tom Cartwright's pace, and swung the ball back late – and to widespread consternation, for the inswinger had not yet really been discovered. Later Greswell was to dismiss Fred Root, its most noted practitioner, as a bowler who angled the ball in from wide of the crease. Besides swing and variety of pace Greswell had at his command an outswinger and even a googly. He had, according to Robertson-Glasgow, 'an exaggeratedly side-on action, throwing his head back almost at forty-five degrees from his body and continuing the swerve of the ball entirely by the way he held it'.

Unfortunately in 1909 his father sent him to Ceylon to earn a living, to the frustration of Somerset, and of England selectors who had taken an interest in him. Returning on leave in 1912 he played for the Gentlemen, bowling Hobbs for a duck, and missed selection for England only on the vote of one selector, who considered him too young, and whom Greswell never forgave.

During the war he had to drive around on a motorcycle sniffing for gas and in peace he returned to Ceylon, where he was an outstanding bowler, athlete, hockey and soccer player. Whenever the MCC stopped in Ceylon they found in Greswell a formidable opponent. He settled in England in 1928, too late to use his cricket talents to their fullest. According to his son:

> He was a man of great charm but with a poor opinion of his own ability. This self-depreciation led him to introspection and periods of acute depression later in life. Efforts to earn a living with a tea and rubber importer in London in the thirties caused him much unhappiness.

Greswell returned to Somerset, regretting that he had not been permitted to enjoy a time in the limelight. Others recall a competitive sportsman who liked to win and a saddened man who rued his lack of opportunity. Alan Gibson has captured Greswell in old age when, from 1962–5 he acted as Somerset president:

> a spare, venerable but approachable figure in a corner of the pavilion. I always called him, respectfully, Mr Greswell, for there was something of Victorian austerity about him despite his readiness for a chat.

Somerset needed Greswell and his absences were a bitter disappointment to both parties. Never has the club missed a man more.

Thanks in part to Greswell, and to fellow medium-pacer Robson, Somerset gave Australia a fearful scare at Bath during that summer of 1909. In a see-sawing game Robson took 8/35 but when Australia chased a meagre 66 for victory it was Greswell who struck, taking 4/11 so that the visitors needed 5 to win when their eighth wicket fell. Moreover W. J. Whitty was in bed with 'flu and it was only a couple of lucky snicks that won the day for the embarrassed guests. Upon the winning run being scored Somerset's wicket-keeper Harry Chidgey, burst into tears.

Economy measures had been taken, with fixtures again being reduced to the minimum of sixteen, and as a result Somerset recorded a profit of £300 this season. Money was a desperate problem and perhaps it persuaded Somerset not so much to pick a team as to raise one, and to neglect strength in favour of a tight budget. Players were not regarded as investments but as costs, and accordingly they were judged by their cheapness rather than their quality. And so things slipped from bad to worse as the executive committee awaited upon the arrival of some redeeming angel. Later they were to realize that waiting was not enough, and went searching universities and schools for good amateurs. For the time being Daniell was too young and callow to undertake such missionary work.

Wisden had nothing favourable to say about Somerset's performance in 1910. Fifteen games were lost and three were drawn. Only eighteen first-class games were played. Greswell was in Ceylon; Braund had a poor season; and Daniell suffered a knee injury which prevented regular appearances. With Woods and Palairet more or less finished Somerset constantly took the field with no hope of success. In Manchester they were dismissed for 157 and in the 145 minutes which remained Lancashire feasted upon an appalling succession of long hop and full-tosses, reaching 300 in 130 minutes. Tyldesley was out on the stroke of 6.30 for 158, one more run than Somerset had managed.

Inevitably all sorts of curious creatures appeared in Somerset colours that year. H. Forman of Minehead played against Worcestershire in front of a surprisingly big Taunton crowd, for the annual flower show was being held in town. He batted at 10, took 1/88, fielded well and was heard of no more. H. E. Hippisley played in seven games, batting down the list and scraping together 114 runs. Born in Wells, educated at King's Bruton, he was to die in France in a conflagration shortly to commence.

More exotically Prince Narayan, youngest son of the Maharajah of Cooch Behar, played too. He had been coached by Daniell in India in 1907 and had attended Eton, later representing the Somerset Stragglers, for whom he hit two hundreds against Devon Dumplings. Narayan was allowed to play against Australia while still qualifying in 1909, but he played little in 1910 and then went home. His career embraced seven innings and included 45 runs, slim evidence upon which to conclude, as newspapers did, that he had 'a taking style' and was 'probably a good bat.' Somerset's only genuine prince (others have considered themselves *de facto* royalty) died of influenza in Darjeeling at the age of thirty.

Who else can be included in this litany of incompetents? To mention Harry Chidgey in such company is to be unkind. Harry was from a Flax Bourton farming family and he was a safe wicket-keeper who claimed 188 victims in his ninety-eight games spread over a twenty-one year career. Chidgey could not bat but he once defied Yorkshire for 85 minutes with his pal Len Braund by his side. This pair used to stay with Ernie Robson and much time was spent debating the merits of various horses who were to meet that afternoon.

Bert Morgan was playing too. Son of a stonemason, he had qualified as a Somerset professional. Plum Warner said he'd be a good 'un. Alas, he was a difficult man with a fondness for brown ale and free speech. A fiery left-arm pace bowler, he was not quite good enough to carry these burdens and quickly faded.

Scratching around for a team, Somerset were not destined to finish higher than fourteenth before war began. In 1910 Murray-Anderdon retired as secretary, Gerald Fowler assuming the mantle for a couple of years, followed by Brooks-King until 1919. Upon his retirement Murray-Anderdon was given an illuminated address book and a gold watch, due recognition for years of selfless endeavour. He must have been saddened by the current plight of his beloved county. Not that he was lost to the club, for upon the death of Ponsonby-Fane he accepted office of president, serving until 1922.

Somerset managed to beat Hampshire at Bath in 1911 but this solitary win was not enough to raise them from the Championship floor. Daniell was fit, Lewis was injured and Greswell was overseas, Braund was out of sorts while Johnson and Bisgood were seldom available. And there was not anybody else, save a newcomer called Jim Bridges who was to shine and another called Humphrey Ramsay Seymour Critchley-Salmonson from Winchester College who had a long run, a windmill action and who was to play fourteen games for Somerset in eighteen years, work taking him to South America between times. Phillip Foy played in South America too, and took wickets for Somerset in occasional games from 1919 to 1930. Bridges was a gain, Foy a loss and the book must remain open on the standing of Mr Critchley-Salmonson, with his 24 wickets at an average of 29.

Understandably Somerset could detect little hope in its present state, though Daniell was never one to admit defeat. If only Greswell could play regularly! Somerset's rare periods of success have depended upon a combination of a handful of talented young locals and a phalanx of imported cricketers of high calibre, a combination which has in truth arisen in 1891, 1963 and 1978. Each team lasted four years or so and then darkness returned. Naturally none of these powerful teams could have achieved much without at least one match-winning bowler. Sometimes Somerset has fielded a useful team, and they were to do so from 1919 to 1924 during which time they never once fell below tenth in the table. Had the executive known in 1911 that White, Bridges and two other youngsters now beginning to appear, MacBryan and Young, would between them score 35,000 runs and take over 3,200 wickets for Somerset, they would have felt less inclined to shiver when *Wisden* pronounced that 'the outlook for Somerset is cheerless'.

A rise to the dizzy heights of fourteenth in 1912 was not sufficient to persuade John Daniell to stay in England and at the end of the season he sailed to India in search of riches. Two games were won but Somerset's improvement was due almost entirely to the return of Greswell, who took 96 wickets. Alas, Lewis broke down badly finally, unbalancing Somerset's attack and allowing only two wins to be recorded. Naturally all sorts of remedies were tried. Taylor, a fast bowler, was discarded because he was 'too slow and doesn't use his height'. Bajana did play. He had toured England with India in 1911 as a small, solid opening batsman. His name tickled local fancy, as did the red-spotted handerkchief he wore around his neck, and whenever he moved nimbly toward a ball in the fields shouts of 'Come on, Banana' rent the air. In a handful of summers Bajana found time for fifty-one games in which he scored 1,802 runs at an average of 20, a typical contribution by a contemporary Somerset batsman.

And a Bruce de la Coeur Hylton-Stuart played too. Harry Chidgey was hit on the head while keeping wicket against South Africa (a drawn match) and Hylton-Stuart happened to be on the ground. A Cambridge graduate from Bath, where his father was a vicar, he was to play thirty-three games before the war, to hit a hundred against Essex in his forthright way and to take 51 wickets at a respectable price, including an astonishing burst of 5/3 at Stourbridge. Unfortunately Bruce de la Coeur was hit on the head by a fast one in 1914 and was never quite the same again. Afterwards he served as music master at Marlborough and as organist at St James's in Piccadilly.

A loss of £327 was incurred in 1912. Daniell went off to India and in his place was appointed Edward Stephen Massey Poyntz, who had been playing for Somerset as a forceful batsman since 1905. Poyntz was from a military family which was very much part of cricketing life in Somerset. His father, Col. Poyntz, was a good cricketer and a distinguished warrior and Sammy Woods, no less, was Massey's godfather. David Foot has captured Massey Poyntz:

> He was a tall man who glossed his hair back with a distinctive parting in the middle. His brother Hugh also played, but less frequently because he was an officer in the regular army. No one had excessive regard for Massey as a cricketer. He would strike bellicose blows from the middle order.

John Daniell's son Nigel recalled:

> When father brought the family up to Bristol for the pantomime we all called on Massey, who lived in some style. It's funny when you remember. The housekeeper brought out the marrow and ginger jam. I was so nearly sick!

Jack MacBryan once stayed with Poyntz in his Bristol flat. 'I was confronted by this massive coat of arms. Massey told me he could trace his family back to William the Conqueror.'

Poyntz was associated with a wine business in Bristol which must have been some consolation for his difficult years as Somerset captain. He was not, in fact, the executives' first choice as captain, but after a period of deliberation Arthur Newton, now fifty years of age, had declared himself unavailable. It is a point worth repeating. Somerset had asked a fifty-year-old to serve as its county captain. Times were hard.

Wisden felt 'no temptation to deal at any great length with the doings of Somerset in 1913', a year during which two matches were won. Poyntz worked zealously but it availed not. In only 5 of 32 innings did Somerset creep past 200, including twice each against their weakest rivals, Sussex and Gloucestershire.

And yet one fellow scored 257 not out on his own! Ron Roberts tells the tale of an innings which rekindled for the admirers of Len Braund memories of former great days and it also enabled him to score 1,000 runs in the season for an average of 38 . . . Braund's knock so dominated the match at Worcester that in the same innings his colleagues mustered only 126 between them.

Bath week was a great success. Bill Hyman, a batsman from Radstock who had been playing occasional county games since 1900, had now turned professional and at thirty-eight years of age he hit his solitary century, doubling his previous best by scoring 110 in 155 minutes against Sussex. Once he settled his cricket was attractive and he was 'especially smart in turning the ball to leg'. Johnson hit a polished hundred and Hylton-Stuart made an unbeaten 72, as the tailenders Newton (aged fifty) and Jack White (twenty-two) tried to offer support.

Hubert Garrett, born in Melbourne, batted at 9 in this contest, one of his eight appearances for Somerset. Garrett was living in Bath and had been brought to the game by Hylton-Stuart, his friend. Upon hearing that Somerset were one short he fetched his creams and played for a month. Two years later a Turkish bullet took his life in the Gallipoli campaign.

Only this new spinner White offered hope, taking 93 wickets at a respectable price, relying upon deceptive flight rather than break. His dismissal of R. Relf at Bath was typical. 'Relf once hit White clear of the ropes for 6, and attempted to serve the next delivery the same but shied the ball and was caught.'

Neither Newton nor Hyman played after the war. White was a farmer and stayed on his land from 1914 to '18, a choice of which some colleagues took a dim view, driving White yet further into his shell.

Jim Bridges had good days too, using his neat run, smooth, sideways action and high arm to swing the ball back towards his clutch of short legs. Sadly it was Bridges's fate to be over-bowled and, very much like Cranfield, he was not suited by temperament to carry such a burden, for failure bit deep. He was no subtle thinker, simply an honest Somerset type who bowled long spells, some of which were inspired. Given a more phlegmatic personality he might have risen to the heights, but he did not care for the way Duleepsinhji swept his inswinger and his fuse was short. He nonetheless gave Somerset good service, first as a professional, then later as an amateur, enduring until 1929, once

110

reaching 99 not out and all told taking 685 wickets. And then he opened a pub.

Gerald Fowler (honorary treasurer) was gloomy at the AGM. A loss of £162 18s 8d was recorded and he could not see how this could be reduced in the forseeable future, for income was steady at around £1,600 and expenditure was rising towards £2,000. His notion of bequests in members' Wills brought the interjection 'You'll have to kill 'em first!' Finishing a day's cricket half an hour later, at 6.30 p.m., was contemplated, to bring more businessmen through the turnstiles. Mr R. Brooks-King, secretary, offered to work without wages and this generous offer was hastily accepted.

Fund-raising was important. A shilling fund raised £503 to which was added £191 donated by guarantors, enough to settle debts of £530.

Significantly supporters outside Taunton were demanding to join in the running of the club. Major Badcock proposed a scheme whereby the county was divided into sub-centres with local committees being formed to watch promising players. This was adopted. Bath complained long and hard about being neglected, a recurring theme in these early AGMs, and said they were hoping to raise money by copying the approach of festival organizers in Cheltenham and Canterbury. Major Simpson (in the chair) said he had held many 'At Homes' in Bath and been supported by society but had never succeeded in getting townspeople properly interested.

Now it was Weston-super-Mare's turn to demand attention. With support dwindling and money running out, officials felt obliged to take cricket to their public. This was a time when transport was less easy, for few had cars and though trains were regular they were used for excursions rather than everyday movement.

Nevertheless a festival week was arranged for Weston, and an area committee formed and given a free hand to act as it saw fit. From these festivals and talent-spotting groups sprang the area committees which were to bring devolution to Somerset cricket, spreading power and complicating the method by which decisions were made. Ever since an argument has raged between those in favour of a small committee duly elected by a postal ballot and a bigger committee upon which every voice in Somerset cricket can be heard. By and large the second opinion has prevailed, to the

111

detriment of Somerset cricket, in the opinion of this historian at any rate.

Upon the proposal of Bruce Hylton-Stuart and the seconding of Arthur Newton, Poyntz was reappointed captain for 1914. Newton thought that

> they might easily have been a little more successful in some of their matches. It was not the fault of their captain that they did not have a little bit more luck. Several matches were started very well, but they did not end as well as they began. With a couple of good batsmen they would be a really good team.

Fond hope! Poyntz's reply was a gem. It was 'owing to a lot of bad luck that they did not finish half way up the table instead of at the bottom'.

Heavy losses continued in 1914 and a special meeting was called, following which a finance committee was set up. But interest was low and only by fielding a stronger team could Somerset hope to move its accounts from red to black.

Happily £78 was taken on Whit Monday, as Somerset played Gloucester. Naturally rival entertainments were seeking to capture popular support on this bank holiday, railway excursions and sporting distractions being offered in various parts of west Somerset. For once cricket held its own, largely because their dreaded nearest neighbour was providing the opposition. Local derbies were, in those years, great occasions – a circumstance which was to endure until the world began to shrink after the Second World War.

These relaxed supporters saw two brothers, the Rippon twins, Dudley and Sydney, of King's College, Taunton, open the batting together for the first time in county cricket. Unfortunately Sydney was hit on the head by a bumper but it was an accident and the crowd did not demonstrate. So alike were this pair that Sydney wore a dark sash to help with identification. Not that they actually batted together: rather they went about their business of scoring runs at the same time. As a pair they were no great shakes between the wickets. If Dudley considered that Sydney had wrongfully denied him a run he would in turn refuse to answer his partner's call until family honour had been satisfied. They were curious men who were to intrigue a Somerset crowd, which liked its players to be interesting and was less inclined to worry if they

112

were good or bad, sane or mad as hatters. We shall hear more of the Rippons.

Bert Bisgood, who was playing for Richmond now, cheered up those Whitsun festivities with a display quite of holiday character. Ever belligerent, if usually ineffective, he smote 116 rapid runs, each one recorded on the new River Telegraph board donated by the Rippons' old headmaster, Rev G. O. L. Thompson. Veteran supporters cried out: 'This is how we used to win matches years ago'. Bisgood struck an unbeaten 78 as Somerset surged to victory in their second innings. Not that his efforts pleased everyone. He had on occasion played as wicket-keeper and performed indifferently in this role; besides which, while batting he was somewhat studied in attitude. In short, he was a poser.

Yorkshire arrived to give Weston its baptism. By now recruitment posters were everywhere, for war had been declared though as yet battle had not been joined. Alonzo Drake and Major William Booth bowled unchanged through each innings, Drake, the frail Sheffield United footballer, taking 10/35. Booth was an all-rounder who had already played twice for England. Two years later he was dead.

Bill Hyman of Bath Association played the last of the twenty county games in 1914. A modest batsman, Hyman is chiefly remembered for scoring 359 not out in a club game against Thornbury in 1902. Hyman hit E. M. Grace for 32 sixes and when some of his side asked the 'Little Doctor' why he did not take himself off he replied: 'I know d–m well if I can't get the blighter out no one else can.'

And that, for the time being was just about that. Somerset's game with Northamptonshire was abandoned. Somerset beat Derbyshire at Taunton, only the second visit by the Peakmen. White took 83 wickets, MacBryan and the Rippons were showing promise and some predicted an improvement if these resources were judiciously managed. Lancashire were less hospitable, proposing the relegation of some clubs, a question deferred until 1917. Plainly Somerset was fighting for survival. It had seemed a serious matter.

13

Lest we forget

A number of Somerset cricketers died in the war to end wars. **Cecil Banes-Walker** from North Petherton and Tonbridge School was killed at Ypres on 9 May 1915. He was twenty-six years old, played cricket for Long Ashton and had a handful of games for his county in 1914. **Charles Gerard Deane** from Oakhill died at the age of twenty-nine in Multan, India. Educated at Taunton School, he played thirty-six times for Somerset from 1907 to 1913, lending regular service in a difficult period. **Hubert Garrett** and **Oswald Samson** died, as has been mentioned, and so did **Hervey Tudway** (aged twenty-six) in 1914, four years after his solitary county appearance. **Harold Edwin Hippisley** was taken too, in the war's first year. He had been born in Wells, educated at King's Bruton and played seven games for Somerset in his twenty-four years of life. **Percy d'Aguiler Banks** of Bath and Cheltenham College also played seven games for his county in those far-off days of constant struggle. He scored only a few runs. A bullet took his life at Ypres in 1915. **Ralph Escot Hancock**, born in Wales and given a public school education, appeared in Somerset colours a few times just before the war before dying in France in October 1914. **Edwin John Leat** (two games in 1908 and 1910) was a local boy killed in action in 1918 at the age of thirty-three. **Leonard Cecil Sutton**, born at Half Way Tree, Jamaica in 1890, educated at King's Bruton, and a friend of Hippisley, played for Somerset seventeen times from 1909 to 1912 with precious little success, also died in action in 1916. He had emigrated to Canada in 1912 and had returned to fight. Everyone, and especially his school coach Percy Vasey, who played once for Somerset, against Yorkshire in 1913, mourned his death.

Hopefully no victim of this carnage has been omitted, though this is not easily verified for some men died at an early age in those war years who were not deemed to be military losses. Nevertheless plainly Somerset cricketers flocked to battle as willingly as everyone else, and their lives were sacrificed in this most terrible of wars. What can scarcely be believed is that it happened again twenty years later.

One more Somerset cricketer died a painful and dreadful death during the First World War. **Frederick Percey Hardy** from Blandford in Dorset had joined Somerset from the Surrey groundstaff in 1902 and had been struggling desperately to survive in the game ever since. After years of mediocre play down the order, Hardy, who also played soccer for Somerset, at last managed to score 46 and 76 against Lancashire in Bath. In 1910 he scraped up 700 runs (19.44) and 27 wickets to hold his place in a lamentable team. That summer he recorded his highest score, surviving two and a half hours against D. W. Carr, Kent's googly bowler, Fielder, and Woolley, a fine spinner, and scoring 91 runs. A contemporary team photograph captures Hardy in the back row, 'straw boater tilted towards the back of his head, blazer open wide, cigarette perched on his lower lip, hands thrust nonchalantly into pockets', as David Frith has written. He appeared to have not a care in the world. By 1914 Hardy had scored 2,696 runs in ninety-nine games at an average of 16. Despite failures he played as often as possible until war began and hoped to carry on afterwards too, though these hopes forced him to leave Somerset who no longer had any use for him, and to join the MCC groundstaff at Lord's.

During the war he served as a private in the County of London Yeomanry. Returning to London on leave in 1916, he decided he could not go back to the trenches. He told his wife that he was drinking heavily to relieve his anguish. On the morning of 9 March 1916 he was found on the floor of the public lavatory at King's Cross station with his throat cut and a bloodstained knife by his side. A verdict of suicide was returned.

Somerset had its war heroes as well as its victims for most Cider cricketers, regular and occasional, had joined the fight. In fact, the entire club was geared for battle. No fixtures were organized and the County Ground and buildings were lent to the military authorities for training purposes. Only by a narrow squeak had Somerset stopped its ground being ploughed up and

115

used as a vegetable patch. Everyone was relieved when the fire brigade and army agreed to use it as a parade ground instead. Inevitably damage was done for the Australian heavy artillery practised from there and slept in tents upon the turf. After the war it took Robson and Woods quite some time to flatten their beloved ground, and Sammy Woods had to launch an appeal for £500 to pay for repairs.

Rabbits bred with their customary enthusiasm and it was left to Ernie Robson, now assisting a declining Mettam on the ground, to control them. Ernie's spaniel hunted them out and the old pro shot them.

Ironically Somerset cricket was stronger financially at the end of the war than at its beginning. With few expenses to be met the finance committee was able to call upon the patriotism of members to help to settle its debts. In 1915 £325 was raised, and by 1916 the deficit had been reduced to £112.

At last it was over. Of course the world was never the same again.

14

Post-war

From 1919 to 1939 Somerset played 526 county games, winning 123, drawing 180 and losing 218. It was in keeping with tradition that Somerset should lose more games than anyone else for, as C. B. Fry used to say, Somerset cricketers were all right for an hour and then they started thinking about apples. A few games might end in handsome victory, but lots ended in calamitous defeat. Somerset seldom had the resources for a long struggle; they relied upon a cavalry charge towards heavy fire.

Times had changed, especially for amateur clubs used to relying upon men who, if they did not play entirely for fun, certainly gave their services free of charge. For a decade thereafter Somerset had no taste for professional cricket, and converted such paid cricketers as did play into characters, who, Ted Lewis apart, could be mistaken for true amateurs. And, in Somerset's opinion, no praise could be higher. Their ideal cricketer combined Palairet's style and gravitas, Newton's want of fuss, Vernon Hill's gung-ho spirit, and John Daniell's disregard for monetary reward. Their cricketers were expected to muck in, to make the best of a bad job. For some it was to be, more or less, a life's work.

Even before the war there were fewer gentlemen of the old sort, men who dressed for dinner, men who defended the code and were generous with their time and their money. At Somerset such sporting blood existed now, mainly amongst those older men who had survived, men who saw nothing in the bloodshed to lead them towards a different view. Newton, Palairet, Woods, Hill and Murray-Anderdon were amongst those who took responsibility for renewing Somerset County Cricket Club in the spring of 1919.

They fought tenaciously to protect what they knew and for a time their endeavours were rewarded, as a decent amateur team was fielded in the early 1920s. And then, from 1925 onwards the supplies began to run out, and it was only thanks to J. C. White that Somerset could collect a remotely competitive eleven. Reluctantly bowing to the inevitable, the executive committee began to employ professionals from London and elsewhere and it was these fellows, in so many ways reminiscent of Woods, Hill and Tyler, who guided Somerset safely through the 1930s, so that by 1939 the county could boast a team which had twice in the previous four summers finished in the top half of the championship – a boast denied them since 1893. It was a team, too, which included two England cricketers in Wellard and Gimblett, both of them professionals, and an attack consisting largely of home-grown talent, including Buse from Bath and Hazell from Bristol.

Domestic cricket after the war was dominated by northern professional clubs, Yorkshire, Lancashire, Nottinghamshire and Derbyshire. It was a harder game, not because the professionals were meaner, but simply because their world had been turned upon its head, and confidence had been lost.

These professionals respected the game, and followed its traditions, walking when they edged, never arguing with umpires and pitching up to tailenders, more even than the amateurs, amongst some of whom could be found traces of the unscrupulous. Inevitably after 1918 cricket lost some of its gaiety, not at first, perhaps, for everyone was relieved simply to be alive, but later, as batsmen took to building vast scores, their defence impregnable, on pitches cruel to bowlers. Remorseless accumulation by Ponsford, annihilating strokeplay by Bradman, found echoes in England as batsmen saw it as their task not to entertain, nor even to win a contest with the bowler (or to die in the attempt) but to construct huge innings. No doubt fielding improved too, and certainly cricket's new seriousness meant that few duffers were picked even by Somerset. Accordingly runs were scored at a gradually slower rate between the wars.

Somerset's run rate, incidently, rose and fell sharply depending upon the competence of their batsmen, most of whom were eager to hit out but few of whom were skilful enough to do so. They managed an especially fast rate from 1921 to 1924 when MacBryan, Johnson, Lyon and Earle were to the fore.

So dominant were batsmen that larger stumps and smaller balls were introduced, as batsmen were now prepared carefully to accumulate vast scores on chloroformed pitches, and bowlers toiled away practically without hope. Changes were needed.

Inevitably relations between amateur and professional changed as the years drifted by, as they did in society, for the division had been founded upon rules which no longer applied. It was a world, now, of trade unions and Labour governments and no longer could incompetent sons of the gentry play county games in their spare time as if by birthright. As the Jazz Age ended and Depression began, with professionals being paid an extra £1 for a 50 and £2 for a 100 or a 5-wicket haul, so cavalier treatment of paid players became less frequent, though it was not to disappear from Somerset cricket until the 1960s. And still some growl about 'mere players' as if Ypres, Normandy and universal suffrage were just a bad dream.

Somerset resumed its county programme in 1919 as a make-shift club with fond if somewhat distant memories. To encourage aggression, games were to be played over two days, a change which suited Somerset well for their matches seldom lasted beyond the second evening anyhow. Later finishes were also introduced, much to the disgruntlement of housewives used to cooking their evening meal before 7.30 p.m. Also the price of entry was doubled, and an entertainment tax imposed. Some lunatic laws such as abolishing left-handers, imposing penalties for maiden overs and limiting teams to three or four professionals were also contemplated but thankfully rejected. Plainly amateur imagination had run amok during long seasons of cricketing inactivity! All of these ideas, like so many since, were attempts to revive a golden age which, in cricket, is continually twenty years in the past, the age when current administrators and writers hit their off-drives and bowled their googlies.

John Daniell resumed the captaincy in 1919 though he did not play every game and was absent when the first drama of the new epoch occurred.

Sussex were to be Somerset's first opponents as this fresh start was made. Mr H. L. Wilson was the visiting captain and only George Cox of his pre-war regulars was able to play. Struggling to raise a team, Wilson summoned Harold Heygate to play his first county game for fourteen years.

119

Harold and his brother Reginald had batted aggressively for Epsom College nearly twenty years earlier and Reginald had become a county player. For his part Harold had played a few games in 1903 and 1905, to no great effect. Moreover he had injured a leg in the war and could now play only in dire emergency.

Somerset batted first and were bowled out for 243. Upon his team batting Heygate dropped down the list, the *Taunton Courier* reporting that he was lame. J. C. White promptly bowled him for a duck. Next morning Somerset provided their opponents with a 12th man but were dismissed for 103. Needing 105 to win Sussex subsided to 48/6 whereupon Wilson and Roberts took the score to 103 before Roberts was bowled by Dudley Rippon, whose next delivery dismissed Stannard. With one run added Miller was caught by Bridges off White.

The scores were level and 9 wickets had fallen. At the fall of the eighth wicket Heygate had sent out a message that he would be unable to bat. Accordingly upon Miller being dismissed umpire Street pulled up the stumps and declared the match a tie. Suddenly a shout arose from the pavilion that Heygate was padding up. Apparently Sammy Woods had urged him to do so and no one ever argued with Sam. Somerset's acting captain, White, raised no objection for there was none to raise. Minutes ticked by and finally Heygate emerged clad in his street clothes, clutching his bat and hobbling towards the middle. Exasperated Somerset players encouraged White to appeal, four minutes having elapsed, but he would not. It was Braund who appealed, cryptically saying, 'He's taking an awfully long time, isn't he?' With Heygate limping forlornly onwards Street declared the match a tie.

Woods thought Somerset's decision to be disgraceful, and certainly it lacked charity. Arthur Newton staunchly defended it, writing to newspapers to defend White and to say that no appeal had been made by him or with his approval. A terrific rumpus ensued, with the national newspapers divided between those accusing Somerset of sharp practice and those who blamed Heygate for his unpreparedness. (Heygate did not play first-class cricket again and died in 1937 at the age of fifty-two.)

A youngster called Maurice Tate was playing for Sussex in this match. If he was not a lugubrious chap at its commencement he was by its end.

120

MCC investigated the matter and concluded that:

> The actual facts are that the Umpires had every reason to believe that Sussex would bat only ten men, having been told so by the tenth Sussex batsman when he came in and so, Street reports, by the Sussex Captain. On the 9th wicket falling Street removed the bails, but on some intimation from the Pavilion that Mr Heygate who had been owing to rheumatism, unable to field was coming in, the Sussex Captain asked the Somerset Captain if he had any objection, some discussion took place amongst the Somerset Eleven whether Mr Heygate should be allowed to bat with the result that the Somerset Captain left it to the Umpires to decide what should be done. Meanwhile several minutes more than the legal two minutes had elapsed and the Umpires taking all these facts into consideration decided to terminate the match. The Committee agrees with the decision.

Wisden called it a 'very regrettable incident'. This historic scorecard bears reprinting.

SOMERSET

First Innings		Second Innings	
Mr. A.E.S. Rippon c Miller b Stannard	26	b Cox	8
Mr. A.D.E. Rippon c Miller b Vincett	60	b Cox	8
Mr. J.C.W. MacBryan lbw, b Cox	18	b Cox	0
E. Robson b Cox	14	b Roberts	11
L.C. Braund b Roberts	3	b Roberts	11
Mr. J.D. Harcombe c H Wilson b Cox	0	run out	5
Mr. P.P. Hope c Tate b Vincett	48	c Stannard b Vincett	6
J.F. Bridges c Miller b Vincett	34	st Miller b Vincett	14
Capt. Amor b Cox	14	c Cox b Tate	13
Mr. J.C. White b Cox	12	not out	11
H. Chidgey not out	1	c Vincett, b Cox	10
B 8, lb 4m w 1	13	B 5, w 1	6
Total	**243**	**Total**	**103**

SUSSEX

First Innings		Second Innings	
Mr. H.L. Wilson b Bridges	56	not out	42
Mr. A.K. Wilson c Braund b Bridges	4	c Braund b Robson	4
Mr. T.E. Bourdillon b Bridges	21	c Bridges b Robson	7
Mr A.C. Somerset b Robson	33	c Braund b Robson	0
Mr. R.A.T. Miller b Bridges	2	c Bridges b White	0
Mr. J.H. Vincett b Bridges	14	b Bridges	6
H.E. Roberts b Robson	5	n. D. Rippon	28
M.W. Tate c Braund b Robson	69	c Chidgey b Bridges	11
G. Stannard b A.D.E. Rippon	3	c McBryan b D. Rippon	0
G. Cox not out	24	b Bridges	0
Mr. H.J. Heygate b White	0	absent	0
B 5, lb 6	11	B 1, lb 5	6
Total	**242**	**Total**	**104**

SOMERSET

	O.	M.	R.	W.		O.	M.	R.	W.
Roberts	17	4	51	1		16	1	40	2
Vincett	31	4	69	3		9	0	20	2
Stannard	8	0	27	1					
Tate	12	3	32	0		6	1	11	1
Cox	15.4	4	51	5		18.4	6	26	4

SUSSEX

	O.	M.	R.	W.		O.	M.	R.	W.
White	18.4	1	76	1		33	0	14	1
Robson	15	3	49	3		14	2	51	3
Bridges	22	4	84	5		12	2	32	3
D. Rippon	9	2	22	1		2	1	1	2

Umpires – F.G. Roberts and A.E. Street

Histories must not concentrate solely upon triumph or incidents for to do so is to present an inaccurate picture. But, nor must the colourful be ignored. It is time to dwell upon Dudley and Sydney Rippon.

They were identical twins of sensitive, highly-strung and eccentric disposition. Their family had moved from London to Radstock and the boys were educated at King's College, Taunton, where they quickly showed their skill at cricket. Dudley began working on a Bath newspaper while Sydney scored umpteen runs in Bristol club cricket and, as David Foot relates, won praise from reporters, one writer saying:

> Rippon should achieve very high honours in the cricket world and when the Somerset executive tire of the many fruitless experiments with players of doubtful ability, they will awaken to the fact that in the Knowle batsman they have one of the very best brand.

It was not to be so easy. Dudley in particular started well in 1914, carrying his bat at Bath hitting a chanceless hundred, following which he was cheered all the way back to the pavilion.

But both the Rippon twins were scarred by war. Perhaps, too, they were too bright, too imaginative easily to accept the ups and downs of life as a regular county cricketer. 'Separated in the war,' writes Foot, 'one posted to France and the other Egypt, they corresponded regularly and looked forward with romantic, unrealistic optimism to a renewed playing career with Somerset.'

It was a life they had hitherto merely sampled, the hazards of which were not yet apparent. Good and popular men, they were by temperament unsuited to county cricket and, war or no war, it is hard to imagine that either could have been truly outstanding.

As it was, Dudley was to play just thirty-one games before sickness took him away from county cricket for ever in 1920. He had played reasonably well in 1919, scoring Somerset's only hundred, 134 at Leyton, but appeared strained and withdrawn as the new season began. No one was aware of his ill health until his antics in the field and at the wicket made it plain. Evidently he was sick and help was provided; everyone was pleased to hear that early disquieting rumours about his state had proved to be inaccurate. He was gentle and decent and, for the time being, needed to lead a less urgent life. At least Dudley had time to play beside Sydney against the Dentons of Northamptonshire, their contemporaries as cricketing identical twins.

Sydney led a happier life. Wounded at the Somme, he suffered badly from meningitis but was able to carry on playing for Somerset after the war, even reappearing occasionally in the 1930s. He was a curious batsman who could, if so inclined, adopt tactics of Jessopian vigour, as he did during one especially vivid assault in 1923, but who usually relied upon an orthodox approach, though in other parts of his life he was not a man restrained by undue reverence of the orthodox, or by any introspective desire to appear as others appeared.

For Sydney had a sense of the dramatic, and at the crease he was the centre of attention even when doing very little with the bowling. Between deliveries he indulged in a range of Swedish exercises, followed by a twirling of the bat greatly enjoyed by home supporters, who would wait upon it and cheer it to the echo if the mood took them. During an innings, too, his cap would move around his head, as did Ponsford's, and a new spectator could tell how long his innings had lasted by the rakishness of its angle. But Sydney knew something that few batsmen understand. Every ball is unique, every innings an opportunity to be taken seriously, for it is a part of life. He applied a penetrating and original brain to a game found easier by those whose minds are more conventionally placid.

Sydney was easily absorbed within Somerset cricket, of course, for this is a county expressive of character. He played 102 games, scoring nearly 4,000 runs at an average approaching 22. In retirement Rippon used to appear nattily dressed and still sporting horn-rimmed glasses at Somerset's London games. In the evenings he would entertain the players at the Civil Service Club, and his company was much appreciated.

But it is not possible to leave these brothers and to return to 1919 without relating a few of the anecdotes which are told whenever their names are mentioned in Somerset cricketing circles, to remind us that their seriousness and humour, tears and laughter are brothers too.

For a start both men thoroughly enjoyed adding to the confusion caused by their appearance, wearing a tie and a belt to help scorers, supporters and opponents with identification and then secretly swapping their labels. John Daniell called them 'a couple of bloody lunatics', but it was said with a smile, as of eccentric relations rather than dangerous underlings.

Once one brother batted for his sibling, a turn of events which escaped detection save by Somerset's scorer, who solemnly noted in his scorebook that 'last night one of the Rippon twins batted for an hour disguised as his brother'. Former colleagues such as Reggie Ingle and Horace Hazell tell many other tales, all of them playing upon Sydney's formidable seriousness. Ingle, for instance, tells of an incident at Pontypridd:

> Sydney hit the ball to cover and called for a run. It was a very risky one and I got in only because the wicket-keeper fumbled the ball. At the end of play I was changing and had only my shirt on, I turned to Sydney and recalled how I was almost run out. I suggested it was a damned silly run. He picked up his bat and chased me. Guy Earle followed. We ran out of the dressing room and down the steps of the pavilion. Then, I'm grateful to say, Sydney tripped and fell. Guy sat on top of him until he'd calmed down.

Sydney knocked on Ingle's hotel room at 3.00 a.m. the following morning. 'He couldn't sleep and only wanted a chat. He could be a perfectly charming and grand fellow.'

Others recalled Rippon running agitatedly round in circles on the field after being teased by the crowd, while Hazell remembered him standing in a position of some menace behind the professionals' door, waiting for George Hunt, who had just run him out. Hazell told Earle that Rippon was having a queer turn and he quietly led him away.

Finally there is the tale of Rippon being 99 not out at the end of a day's play. Hazell recollects:

> He had been wearing new pads and complained that they were too stiff for quick singles. Back in the hotel he put his pads on and ran up and down corridors for 2 hours, to widespread surprise. At last he was satisfied the stiffness was gone. He went to bed and was out first ball next morning!

Somerset has never had a more methodical or dedicated cricketer than Sydney Rippon. He rode to home games on his motorbike, kept a cricket ball in his office desk so that his fingers stayed supple, and gave sound advice to others.

> Don't chuck your wicket away by being chicken-hearted or thinking that instead of a bat you have a scythe in your hand . . . I often think that when it is a race against time the quickest rate is secured by methodical acceleration rather than by abandoned actions.

Returning to 1919, Sydney Rippon was on sick leave from the Civil Service and so could not play in the home fixture against Gloucestershire, L. H. Key taking his place; and then Key stood down and was replaced by a fellow called S. Trimnell. Scour such history books as have been written, scan columns of batting averages in search of this Mr Trimnell and you will do so without reward. Yet this Trimnell scored 92 and 58 not out as Somerset won handsomely. The *Western Daily Press* was not fooled, reporting that 'S. Trimnell, who is far better known facially to Somerset cricketers and supporters than he is to the general public . . . played in capital style. Although his name is new, he is by no means a stranger to county cricket.'

For Sydney had played after all. Using his grandmother's name as a disguise to hoodwink his employers, he batted with panache and to effect. Perhaps if others could borrow a name they too, freed of the shackles of reputation, might risk – and attain – more.

125

Eventually, of course, Sydney's boss found out and he was forgiving.

Somerset had begun 1919 fearing the worst, announcing that they would 'take part in the championship, but the immediate outlook is not very hopeful as it may be a hard matter to get together a team of adequate strength'. They were, in fact, about equally short of players and money. Only two professionals, Braund and Robson, could be employed, and the executive had begun a recruiting campaign at the universities, for they saw salvation only in the arrival of amateur talent.

In the event Somerset did better than even the most sanguine supporter could have expected, losing only three games and finishing fifth. Apart from Braund, who was steady with the bat, and the still energetic Robson, they depended heavily upon White, who took over 100 wickets as he was to do every year until 1932, only once paying more than 20 runs on average for his victims. Few have taken more than White's 2,167 wickets. With Robson he bowled unchanged throughout the away game at Derby as Somerset fought for victory. He might be a trifle aloof but he'd nag away all day and Somerset rarely won without him.

Credit was given to Daniell too, for Somerset, like England, cherishes the notion of manly leadership, of the rugged major first out of the trenches. Under Daniell's inspired leadership the Somerset team, whether winning or losing, always seemed to enjoy itself. No doubt surviving where millions fell had thrown cricket into a different perspective. Perhaps White, who had not fought, was least touched by this sense of release.

R. C. Robertson-Glasgow has caught the Daniell of this period:

> At the end of the 1920 season John Daniell, our captain, said to me: 'Well, come again next year and bowl some of your inswingers; and for God's sake burn that straw hat.' There was a good deal of laughing in the Somerset side, and not a little cursing. The captain excelled at this, and nobody minded. It was part of the show, and would have been missed. Besides, he had good reason, for he was shepherd of a strange flock.
>
> Like all men of character, he had strong prejudices. He believed that inswingers were heaven's gift for hitting, and, if assailed by them, he would have a terrific swat, whatever the state of the game. As often as not this would end in a skied catch to long-leg or deep square-leg; but that made no

126

difference to the theory. The same assault would be committed next time.

He believed also in Homburg hats, and my chief memory of these games is Daniell standing with such a hat on the back of his head, very close at silly-point to Jack White's bowling, scowling severely at the batsmen, making terrific stops, and sometimes wonderful catches; or, perhaps, once in a while having a half-volley driven straight through him, when he would look at White, and some fearful observation would stir unexpressed on his lips.

As a batsman he was best in an awkward situation, for his defence was very fine, and his attack was strong enough to look after itself. He excelled against the off-breakers on a difficult pitch. Forward play was the foundation of his method, and none that I remember showed better that these off-breaks can often be smothered and played dead with a half-forward stroke. At the same time he never missed a chance of hitting the over-pitched off-break. He had a great duel with Morton, of Derbyshire, one day on a wet pitch at Weston, all sawdust, and off-spinners, and about once in two overs he would hit hard to mid-wicket for four or six. It was the best century I saw that season. He had a strong contempt for the obsession of back-play on fast wickets. This habit was increasing in the early 1920s, and, together with exaggerated pad-play, was already beginning to injure batting as a spectacle. I think that in some respects his batting improved with years, as the ability to hit violently was retarded. At any rate, he made a century in each innings at the age of forty-six, which argues a bed-rock correctness of method.

His exhortations to bowlers were memorable. They would begin, as we walked on to the field: 'Can you bowl these beggars out?' After twenty minutes or so, if success were still but a dream, he'd say: '*Can't* you bowl these beggars out?' Still no change. And then: 'Oh, I believe *I* could bowl that beggar out.' There was a magnificent combativeness in his attitude to the opposing batsmen. If they played with what is known as 'commendable care', he would contemplate them from silly-point with a pitying gaze, as if the remainder of their sunless days could most suitably be passed in a wheelchair or rest-home for the stricken and palsied. I believe that he stared some self-conscious batsmen from the wicket. They felt that they were a false pretence, and that further tenure was useless.

He was a great leader. You bowled or batted or fielded your best for him. He praised by look more than word; and I have thought sometimes that we and our swerves must have seemed pretty dull stuff to one who had begun under Sam Woods and learnt batting against Tom Richardson and C. J. Kortright.

There was no really fast bowling in these years. Sometimes he told us so. But the young don't believe that sort of thing.

Sammy Woods was around too, also larger than life and in 1920 he took up appointment as Somerset Secretary, a promotion owing more to reputation than administrative skill. Sam did not much care for committees. Upon being berated by one chum with 'You're the boss here, why don't you get something done?' he replied: 'Me? What's the use? Whenever I make a suggestion on committee some deaf old so and so who was in charge in Delhi ups and downs it.' Bridgwater Cricket Club presented him with a cheque for £178 in recognition of services rendered, so possibly Woods was strapped for cash. He was living at the George Inn and magnificent and kindly as his manner continued to be, he was in pain only partly softened by the bottle of scotch it was his practice to drink each day.

Braund was near the end, and 1920 was his last season. He went off to coach at Cambridge and later to umpire, though gout, a product of years of heavy drinking, affected him in both callings. Even in these last seasons only fastest bowlers worried him and he could still catch scorchers at slip – though he was apt to drop sitters, whereupon he'd resume his calm conversational discourse with one of his chums. Some thought he was allowed to depart too early, and certainly little was done to stop him leaving. Yet he was forty-four and in decline. So much conflict in cricket clubs has begun with a committee and a player disagreeing by one summer when they should part company.

Somerset dropped to tenth place in 1920, winning seven games and losing ten: nothing to boast about, said *Wisden*; and yet a satisfactory season historically speaking. Rippon hit a dashing century against Sussex at Bath, his ailing brother's final game, and Daniell hit two match-winning hundreds. Somerset's only Chilean cricketer, J. A. S. Jackson (educated at Cheltenham), recorded his only century in his only season before returning to Santiago and cricketing obscurity.

Naturally it was not a season entirely without incident. Warwickshire players arrived at one third day so convinced of the futility of their efforts to avoid an innings defeat that those already dismissed did not bother to change. To their surprise tailenders dug in to leave Somerset to score 5 runs. Six Warwickshire fieldsmen took to the field in ordinary clothes an a laugh was raised by the bowling of Smith, though one member did object to this scurrilous conduct. And in the Leicester game at Weston, Robson and King scored one run between them in their four innings. Their combined ages were 99. King took a hat trick in the second innings.

Had fewer catches been dropped Somerset might have held a stronger position. It is an old lament.

Nevertheless a fine crop of young amateurs was being gathered. MacBryan, White, Considine from Bath, Robertson-Glasgow and 'Dar' Lyon from Bristol, a dashing fellow often photographed in the company of beautiful ladies. England was recovering its confidence, and Somerset was finding a new way along an old road which promised much but which was, ultimately, to prove to be a dead (if enjoyable) end.

Somerset's chief contemporary hero, by dint of longevity and personality if not entirely performance, was Ernest Robson who was still willingly working away to a length, just as he had when he started in 1895. R. C. Robertson-Glasgow wrote of him:

> Among more regular Somerset players I suppose that Ernest Robson was one of the best of *any* county who never won high honours. He began to play in the 'nineties, and his style of batting, with left shoulder towards mid-off and the full flow of the bat towards extra coverpoint, was as much a mirror of those quieter times as was his deportment on the field, which was Victorian, reserved, dignified. Whatever he may have thought no shadow or light of emotion passed over his features. So with his bowling. He excelled with very late outswing of the new ball; Hobbs admitted that no other of this kind troubled him so much; only if he did some remarkable feat would he permit himself a slight, a very slight, smile, and, with a smoothing of the moustache, a "thank you, sir. I was

129

lucky. He should have played that one – thus, or thus." He died in early middle age. I often wonder how he would have fared with the newer publicity that tends to disregard all but the stars.

For once the phrase 'salt of the earth' is appropriate. Robbie was a man of few words and somewhat melancholic appearance whose manner, in times good and bad, was of 'unequalled tranquillity'. Impassive of countenance, he had arrived as a medium-pacer respected for his unflagging determination and unfailing accuracy, and as a batsman liable occasionally to lift his perennial forward stroke into the pavilion. In 1921, at the age of fifty-one he sent down 839 overs for Somerset, skipping in off a few paces, and took 81 wickets; he also scored 682 runs. Overall he played 424 matches for his adopted county (for Ernest had been born a Yorkshireman) and scored 12,411 runs including five hundreds, and took 1,122 wickets at an economical rate despite having to bowl year after year in an attack notable for its want of penetration.

Besides bowling his outswingers and hitting his off-drives with a freedom and suppleness of elbow which was almost acrobatic – though he did not invariably choose the right ball for his shot – Robson also assisted on the grounds, eventually replacing Mettam. Often this massive and gentle person would be seen pushing his roller before play, or fitting leather shoes on to the white horse which was still kept in the stables over by the Coal Orchard Cottages, and behind which he would walk as the grass was cut.

Away from cricket Robson was a splendid soccer player, a full back for Derby County, a keen student of snooker and a singer with a pleasant tenor voice whom George Nichols, a rather more extrovert fellow, could sometimes prevail upon to perform at his concert parties.

In truth Robson bowled himself into his grave. For years he suffered badly from rheumatism yet he never stopped sweeping the pitch at tea-time and bowling his overs from noon till night fell. Game to the end, he smote a 6 in the final over of a match at Weston-super-Mare in 1922 to bring victory over Middlesex and a cheque for £50 from Lyon snr, not bad for a man of fifty-two. Appropriately a verse was written to celebrate this famous victory.

'How Robson Made the Winning Stroke'

When Middlesex came over
They felt they were in clover,
Having a score of 346
With wickets still to spare.
We thought with this beginning,
The Champions looked like winning;
At all events, they seemed to think
'Twas better to declare.
But Somerset undaunted,
With hope of vict'ry haunted,
Knew that a game may still be won
Until entirely lost.
With heart that failed them never,
Put forth their best endeavour,
Determined they would struggle through
Whatever was the cost.
Next day – it was the last one –
The wicket was a fast one;
Their score was just "one-fifty" up,
With but four wickets down.
When all their scoring ceasing,
And hope with us increasing
As fortune turned and smiled on us,
On whom she seemed to frown.
But though we now played cricket,
With smart men at the wicket,
To make a score, 244,
Was no small task, you bet.
In two hours and three-quarters,
'Twas quite a work for Tartars;
And so we thought, and likewise thought
The men of Somerset.
But steadily and surely,
Serenely and securely,
The score crept up – but steadily
The time past just the same.
Till 'mid the greatest tension
We think it best to mention,
Ere stroke of seven, with stroke of six,
Our Robson won the game.

They chaired him and they cheered him,
That stroke had so endeared him
To everyone who saw the game

They never can forget;
While to the county's glory,
We oft shall hear the story,
How Robson made the final stroke
That won for Somerset.

(G.D.C.)

Carrying on, he played in 1923, for Yorkshiremen do not give in easily and though he could barely run in the field he was still crafty enough to take wickets. Finally he was taken ill, brought down by cancer. Jack Hobbs and Phil Mead arrived in Bridport in 1923 to play a testimonial game for Robson, who was by then plainly extremely sick.

Ever optimistic, he joined the umpires list for the 1924 season but he never stood, dying in May following an operation to arrest the disease. Somerset's year book said of him: 'He was deservedly popular on any ground at which he appeared, and especially at Taunton where his seraphic walk to the wickets was always sure to evoke a rousing cheer.'

Somerset had taken this tenacious, lugubrious and peaceful man to its heart. After twenty-eight years' service Robson had not entirely lost his Yorkshire characteristic of absolute devotion to cricket, and yet he was a rounded Somerset man too and, as contemporaries said, his county were never beaten until he had been dismissed twice.

His wife continued to work in the ladies' pavilion and to stitch batting gloves upon a gentleman's request while Vic, her son, continued to run errands for the grand amateurs rushing in to town to send a telegram to their London bookmakers. Vic thought Johnson to be aloof, MacBryan, who despised Johnson, tense and yet approachable, and Sammy Woods hilarious if loud. He recalled his father in his days as Somerset's only professional, sitting alone in his fenced-off area, while his amateur team-mates sat in their viewing cubicle outside by the graveyard. They remembered seeing Robson take to the field through his own gate in 1919, and that Yorkshire stood for no such nonsense, walking smartly on to the field through the main gate no matter if they were paid or amateur. For years several wanted to field a team of amateurs against a team of Yorkshire pros, but they leant too heavily upon Ernie and could not afford to be without him. Nor did they consider him to be inferior in any way; to the contrary they sought his advice and friendship; they were all simply victims of conventions.

And so was Somerset for years afterwards. In 1938 two men strode to the crease upon a wicket falling, both entirely unaware of their colleague. One was a pro, the other an amateur and both thought their turn had come. Heads down they marched onwards, a situation resolved only when Jack Meyer bellowed to Wally Luckes that the order had changed and he had to return.

The county programme was extended to twenty-two games in 1921, and Somerset managed to win eight while also contriving to lose eleven. It was a dry summer and White once more showed his mastery on crumbling pitches, taking 139 wickets. Robson offered support but Bridges had been injured in a motor accident and Robertson-Glasgow was below his best. Somerset could not sustain a promising start, a pattern which was to continue for years – until White retired, in fact. While he was fresh matches were won; once he began to droop they were lost.

Arthur Sanders died in 1920. A Harrow man, he had played once for Somerset in 1919, as a late reserve, batting at number 9 and being bowled for a duck after the Rippon twins had added 144 for the first wicket. 'Sixteen months later,' according to David Frith, 'Sanders, a second Lieutenant in the Grenadier Guards, shot himself in the head with a revolver and died in Millbank Military Hospital.'

John Daniell was a Test selector by now and many thought White deserved more than one England cap that chaotic summer when Gregory and McDonald scythed down weak opponents. Daniell's name was mentioned as a candidate for the captaincy, for as usual England was blaming a difficult period upon poor leadership, but in the event Lord Tennyson was appointed.

Somerset won a fine game in Essex, reaching 163 on a pitch which, like Jezebel, was fast and unaccountable. In reply, Loveday endured Daniell's curses for three hours and, aided by dropped catches, Essex led by 83. Daniell hit out, Rippon dug in, continually rubbing his damp gloves upon his posterior, Johnson contributed an aristocratic 81, Tom Young (a new pro) a handy 63 and Essex were left to chase 222. Immediately a delivery rose to strike Freeman upon his chin upon which Loveday commented, 'I don't like that,' went off for a drink, returned

133

and was promptly bowled. Somerset won by 65.

Cricket in the county was perking up and interest was growing. Schoolboys would run through the back streets to the ground after their final lesson, entering at 4.00 p.m. when admission fell from sixpence to threepence, though a scorecard still cost twopence. Away matches were eagerly followed too, with the scoreboard still being posted in shop windows – Mettam and Lewis' outfitters were seldom more than an hour behind play in Taunton. Those who could not afford to see a home game could study play from Town Market Bridge and other vantage points in the vicinity. It was quite like old times.

Not that everyone was happy. A profit of 7s 6d was recorded in 1921 which the club considered 'very satisfactory' and which members considered disgraceful.

Evidently Somerset was undergoing a powerful metamorphosis from an amateur club run by a few friends of traditionalist persuasion into a club in which supporters and areas demanded a say. Life thereafter was to be less cosy, and less autocratic too. Henceforth Somerset committees were to be accountable, not a preserve of local gentry. Never again was the club to be a sea of calm buffeted only by defeat and inpecunity, for ahead lay two mutinies and countless meetings.

Profits rose to £83 10s 11d in 1922 and it was little wonder that Robson's application for a second benefit match was rejected. Somerset finished tenth for a third year running, winning six and losing eleven.

Greswell was back and taking wickets, while Robson, creaking bones and all, held his own. With White as effective as ever and Bridges playing regularly, Somerset could at least field a respectable attack.

Alas, Robertson-Glasgow, could play only one game and 'Dar' Lyon was rarely available; besides which, while Tom Young did play it was only as a batsman for it was to be eight years before anyone realized that he was also a splendid bowler. Bridges played for the Gentlemen, Rippon hit a century in Cardiff and MacBryan (who dislocated a shoulder at Edgbaston whereupon Woods shoved it back into place) was easily the best batsman.

Somerset's greatest victory of 1922 was at Weston, where Robson, as has been related, made the winning hit. *Wisden* tells the tale:

134

SOMERSET *v.* MIDDLESEX

Played at WESTON-SUPER-MARE, Wednesday, Thursday, Friday, July 26, 27, 28. – This match proved the event of the Somerset season. Steady rain cut the first day's play short at the tea interval, and when on Thursday Mann declared at lunch time, with six wickets down for 346, the defeat of his side seemed out of the question. However, Somerset played up finely, and in the second innings of Middlesex the last five wickets fell for 35 runs. It thus came about that Somerset had to get 241 against time. They just managed to beat the clock, winning the match at exactly seven o'clock by two wickets. The winning hit was a 6 by Robson clean out of the ground.

SOMERSET v. MIDDLESEX.

Played at Weston-super-Mare, July 26, 27 and 28, Somerset winning by two wickets. Score:

MIDDLESEX

First Innings		Second Innings	
H.L. Dales, b Robson	9	c Robson, b Bridges	9
Lee, run out	66	b Robson	24
Hearne c Lyon, b Bridges	84	c Lowry, b White	61
Hendren, not out	100	c White, b Greswell	12
F. T. Mann, c Daniell b White	45	b Greswell	49
N. Haig, c Young b White	45	b Greswell	10
G.T.S. Stevens, st Lyon b White	4	b Greswell	0
C.H.L. Skeet, not out	6	st Lyon, b White	3
Murrell		b White	0
G.O. Allen		lbw, b Bridges	0
Durston		not out	12
Extras b 6, lb 8, w 1	15	Extras b 3, lb 2	5
Total (6 wkts dec.)	346	Total	185

SOMERSET

First Innings		Second Innings	
P.R. Johnson, c Murrell, b Durston	74	b Haig	28
J.C.W. MacBryan, st Murrell, b Hearne	23	c Skeet, b Stevens	65
Young, hit wkt, b Hearne	34	c Hearne, b Haig	16
S.G.U. Considine, c Stevens, b Durston	0	c Stevens b Hearne	40
J. Daniell, b Allen	23	b Hearne	22
T.C. Lowry, st Murrell, b Hearne	40	c Murrell, b Haig	15
M.D. Lyon, b Allen	34	st Murrell, b Haig	11
J.C. White, lbw, b Stevens	8	st Murrell, b Hearne	13
W.T. Greswell, c Allen, b Durston	35	not out	20
Robson, c Murrell, b Stevens	9	not out	12
J. Bridges, not out	0		
Extras b 3, lb 5	8	Extras b 4, lb 2, w 1	7
Total	288	Total (8 wkts)	249

135

BOWLING ANALYSIS
MIDDLESEX

	O.	M.	R.	W.		O.	M.	R.	W.
Robson	22	7	44	1	Bridges	8	1	42	2
Bridges	25	3	76	1	Robson	8	3	15	1
White	38	10	89	3	Greswell	27	7	66	4
Greswell	22	6	70	0	White	26.4	7	57	3
Young	13	1	52	0					

SOMERSET

	O.	M.	R.	W.		O.	M.	R.	W.
Haig	13	3	24	0	Haig	22	6	54	4
Durston	17	3	73	3	Durston	8	0	44	0
Hearne	22	1	93	3	Allen	8	1	38	0
Stevens	15.4	1	71	2	Stevens	13	0	59	1
Allen	9	1	19	2	Hearne	9.2	0	47	3

Umpires – T. Brown and A.E. Street

Somerset's championship averages for 1922 tell a tale too:

SOMERSETSHIRE

Matches played, 24; won 6;
lost, 11; drawn, 7; won on first innings, 6; lost on first innings, 1.

BATTING

	No. of Inns.	Times not out	Total runs.	Most in an Innings	Aver.
J.C.W. MacBryan	43	1	1,428	164	34.00
A.E.S. Rippon	11	1	275	102*	27.50
S.G.U. Considine	40	3	973	91	26.29
M.D. Lyon	8	1	180	59	25.71
Young	39	4	881	71*	25.17
T.C. Lowry	25	2	572	77	24.86
J. Daniell	40	1	872*	78	22.35
W.T. Greswell	31	3	561	55	20.03
P.R. Johnson	24	1	401	74	17.43
A. Marshall	7	0	116	37	16.57
J.C. White	35	2	433	49	13.12
Hunt	15	0	142	48	9.46
Robson	37	5	298	39	9.31
M.L. Hambling	4	0	35	14	8.75
A.W. Burgess	4	0	35	22	8.75
S.L. Amor	15	9	52	12*	8.66
F.E. Spurway	6	1	43	17*	8.60
J.J. Bridges	35	14	177	25*	8.42
T.E.S. Francis	3	0	12	7	4.00
L.E. Wharton	4	0	11	6	2.75

The following also batted:- A.S. Bligh, 6 and 5; K.G. Blaikie, 19; M.L. Hill, 0; J. Jones, 2 and 0; L.H. Key, 0; R.C. Robertson-Glasgow, 4*; and C.A. Winter, 15 and 11.

BOWLING

	Overs	Maidens	Runs	Wickets	Aver.
J.C.White	1,091.2	375	2,207	146	15.11
W.T. Greswell	671.2	227	1,436	71	20.22
Robson............................	660.5	208	1,437	54	26.61
J.J. Bridges	675.4	135	1,925	66	29.16
Young..............................	148	22	442	13	34.00
Hunt...............................	40	6	122	3	41.00
A. Marshall	26	4	93	2	46.50

The following also bowled:– K.G. Blaikie, 52–13–109–3; L.H. Key, 17.1–2–50–2; M.D. Lyon, 2–0–9–0; A.E.S. Rippon, 2–1–6–0; R.C. Robertson-Glasgow, 5–2–14–1; and C.A. Winter, 27–3–86–1.

Some of these were minor characters. Algie Bligh was, a contemporary recalled, a tall, cantankerous Etonian wicket-keeper who played club cricket for Minehead and The Stragglers and whose fury at being adjudged leg before was a sight to behold. He played fourteen county games from 1922 to 1926.

Stanley Amor had been playing a game or two a year since 1908. Another wicket-keeper, he was a big noise in Bath cricket, which he was to captain for thirty-six years, earning the nickname 'The Skipper'; later he was elected chairman and president of this prestigious club.

Spurway, a wicket-keeper, and Burgess (a hitter from Minehead) were from local families of varying distinction, while Blaikie was an all-rounder from Johannesburg who, having won his Oxford blue in a competitive time, played several games for Somerset before returning to his native land. Wharton on the other hand was a Trinidadian who had been a Harlequin and whose chief merit as a cricketer was his athleticism in the field, though he was no worse a batsman than most colleagues, managing to average 21 in his eleven games.

Jones was a Welsh wicket-keeper; Key was a left-arm spinner educated at Taunton School and perhaps coached by Tyler; neither was to endure. Montague Hambling was another part-time cricketer, though in eighteen games spread over eight summers he did take his 24 wickets at an extremely respectable average, though he does not seem to have bowled in 1922. Winter was a Londoner who had been educated at Repton and who was to take

15 pricey wickets for Somerset with his fast deliveries. Several of these characters, and others who played a few games thereabouts, paid for the honour of representing their county. Somerset was hard up and hard pressed to raise a team and ever ready to fill a gap with a local notable willing to add a few pounds to their account. Important amateurs could do rather well out of playing, and lesser lights could bribe their way onto the team as if it were run not by Daniell but by Lloyd George.

Thomas Francis was another man of South African birth. He was educated at Tonbridge and Oxford where John Daniell, on one of his recruitment drives, asked him if he had anywhere to stay during the summer holidays. Francis said no, whereupon he was invited to stay with Daniell in Taunton. Tom Lowry, a New Zealander, was also resident. Both played for Somerset whenever time permitted. Francis settled in Rhodesia where he became prominent in cricket and rugby circles.

And, finally, Alan Marshall was one of two brothers born in Madras and educated at Taunton School, where both were to teach, who were to play occasional games for Somerset until 1931, though with a lack of success mystifying to their many admirers in the county town.

It was, in other words, a not untypical bunch of Somerset cricketers, a team with a backbone of seven or eight reasonably competent players, including three exceptional ones in MacBryan, White and Greswell (when home) and assorted others gathered hither and thither, men willing to lend their time or forlornly hoping to impress.

Finances dictated that only a small group of professionals be retained. Braund, Chidgey and Robson had departed, or were about to do so, leaving only Tom Young and George Hunt as paid players. It was a situation justified for the time being because funds were low but a situation which endured for longer than was necessary because Somerset meant to remain as an amateur club, come what might. Even when counties of similar mind had long since given up the quest Somerset continued to search for an amateur captain, approaching several men of significance in the 1950s before finally appointing Maurice Tremlett as the first professional skipper. Until 1956 an overwhelming majority of Somerset captains had attended Oxford or Cambridge University and every single one since entry into the championship had been to a public school. Much the same, of course, could be said of Somerset presidents, and indeed of the Somerset committee. In the formative years too, a large proportion of subscribers were soldiers or vicars of good birth and education. Somerset was a county of old money and rural conservatism; industrial attitudes and nouveaux riches were few and far between.

Meanwhile Harry Fernie had arrived to take care of the grounds. Fernie was to be second in line of distinguished Somerset grounds-men. A naval man who had been a stoker in Shearness, Fernie (*né* Fernando) was a Maltese cockney with an air of distinction. He arrived for his interview in breeches and leggings and upon his appointment took command at the ground in a manner which brooked no argument. With his powerful voice and imperious man-ner he'd bark at amateur and pro alike should they be so careless as to harm his precious turf. Children dared not trespass upon his outfield yet his assistants, including a youth called Cecil Buttle, regarded him as one of Nature's gentlemen, for he was a formidable fellow, notwithstanding his humble origins. In time Fernie took to directing affairs from Scarlett's pub, a hostelry on the main road where they served draught Bass so tasty that no traveller ever passed without sampling a pint. Fernie's great chum and drinking companion was Lord Portman, 6 feet 4 inches tall, wafer thin and wearing huge flat feet; this pair were often to be found sipping ale as the groundstaff happily carried out their instructions. In his early years Fernie rose at 4 a.m. every sum-mer morning and, accompanied by Buttle, his youthful assistant, walked to a local stables where a hundred or so horses were held. He chose one, took it to the ground, put leather shoes upon its hooves to protect the sacred few acres and began cutting or rolling the grass. Eventually a horse was bought for £10, otherwise habits did not change much until after the Second World War, when a motorized roller was purchased.

Fernie was paid £12 a week, a handsome wage, and Buttle 8s a week. Even in adulthood Buttle's pay rose to only £1 17s and only after Pearl Harbor and upon rich American soldiers arriving in Britain towards the end of the war was he reasonably paid. Buttle served as a fireman working from the County Ground and from Shire Hall: Harold Gimblett was in his squad, and a brave fireman he was. Gimblett, who used to drive a silver Rolls-Royce which had belonged to Murray-Anderdon to and from fires, saw the worst of the war in Bristol and some of his closest friends and colleagues were killed; this experience had a considerable effect upon Harold, according to Buttle, who remarked, 'He was never much use after that.' Yet war and suffering which took so terrible a toll on Gimblett's spirit left Buttle almost untouched. Fernie retired after the war, let down by his legs but struggled in every week to collect his £2 pension. Appropriately Buttle succeeded him, as one generation passed on its knowledge to another.

Thanks to Daniell's collection of local and imported amateur talent Somerset managed to finish ninth in 1923. It was a vintage year for amateur batsmen, as Lyon scored 1,109 championship runs and also struck a 120 for the Gentlemen at Lord's. Stevens also hit a hundred but *Wisden* reported:

> There could be no comparison as to the respective merits of their play. Except for a chance at short leg, Lyon, very brilliant and always master of the bowling played an innings worthy of the best traditions of the match.

Plainly he was pressing for a tour to Australia in 1924–5 yet the call never came, much to Woods's fury, for he believed that '2 or 3 redundant elders had been preferred'.

MacBryan's form was even better, as he hit 1,507 immaculate championship runs. Some said he was England's leading opening batsman and complained that he owed his obscurity to a 'lunatic theory' that he could not field. Perhaps it was not so daft. Contemporaries cannot recall having seen MacBryan chase a ball from his customary position at mid-on. With Lowry and Earle – 111 against Gloucestershire in 70 minutes, astonishingly fast for a maiden hundred – biffing away merrily, Somerset were, for once, seldom short of runs. Reggie Ingle, later to be captain, played his first games and so did Percy Ewens from Yeovil, a player whose career was to be brief. (His son now runs a pub in Taunton.)

Gloucestershire were beaten by an innings (besides Earle, Lyon hit a hundred and Robertson-Glasgow took 11 wickets), and Sussex were twice demolished. Somerset lost heavily to the more ruthless clubs, Yorkshire beating them for a record 25th time. Gaiety – such as it was for White and MacBryan in particular were singularly serious amateurs – could not combat class professionally used. Moreover Somerset, often fielding just one pro, still had a few weak links in its team. Nevertheless had Greswell been available much might have been achieved in 1923.

Off the field it was a difficult year. A deficit of £447 was recorded and to correct matters an attempt was made to raise subscriptions from one to one and a half guineas, the first rise since 1891. Members rose in fury and a special meeting was called at which this change was overturned by an overwhelming majority. Nor was that all. Such was the commotion and criticism at the AGM that Sammy Woods resigned as secretary, saying that those who doubted his business capacity had been right and that a 'new secretary with a business-like head' was needed. Somerset's auditor and treasurer also resigned.

W. G. Penny, an important servant of Somerset cricket, called Woods 'a beacon of light' and regretted his departure. Woods was asked to serve on the committee but declined to do so by letter after first appearing to agree.

In an effort to balance the books a shilling fund was started and statements made that subscriptions must rise from £1,500 to £3,000. Rumours that £250 had been spent in staging a single three-day game were hotly denied. Evidently Somerset cricket was full of bad blood and gossip. Meanwhile Daniell, committed amateur, contemptuous of criticism, continued raising his teams.

A. F. Davey, former secretary of the Somerset Agricultural Show, was picked to replace Woods and upon his arrival efforts were made to improve a ground which had not changed much since 1885. Within a year plans were made to erect a scoreboard near the river, a replica of the small board at The Oval being chosen. Arthur Newton, president in 1923, was asked to raise funds for it. Somerset Stragglers presented a clock and asked for a piece of land upon which to build their own pavilion. Newton himself lent money for the erection of hoarding to hide the ground from unpaying eyes upon the newly developed bridge and road at the River Tone end of the Rack Field.

Somerset's Executive Committee wanted more power to allow things to be run more efficiently – a cry often repeated in the ensuing sixty-seven summers. They banned tennis from the ground and, in 1925, contemplated knocking down the Old Pavilion and replacing it with a new stand. Architects reported that a pavilion seating 796 people would cost £7,000 while sacrificing 280 seats would reduce costs to £5,000. Press and scorers would also be freshly accommodated. This plan, strongly approved in principle, was shelved for financial reasons. Somerset decided to concentrate upon building a strong team – a poor decision, for nothing less than a massive change of structure and attitude could help to produce players. A new pavilion with its extra facilities might have promoted commerce and interest. As it is this relic continues to survive every attempt upon its life, for it is now protected by sentimentality which sees in its timbers Sammy Woods and Arthur Wellard rather than a futile and ultimately destructive impracticality.

But a new stand was built, replacing the Hen Coop, which was in decline and no longer a haven for the distinguished. Colonel Ridley paid for the stand and it was named in honour of him, resolutions being passed that seats should be reserved for the colonel and his friends. Alas, the stand was made of pre-fabricated material because the chosen surveyor had a pre-fab place of his own and strongly advocated it. Accordingly the new stand had to be painted every winter to prevent it falling apart.

Nor was Ridley's gift without controversy. Cynics noted that he was elected president in 1926 and they condemned this as a somewhat Lloyd-Georgian approach. Ridley stood down for the 1927 season so that he could donate new sightscreens and was re-elected for 1928.

Somerset lost its first encounter with the West Indians in 1923 and a year later they were beaten by the South Africans. No doubt Newton, Vernon Hill, Wickham, Poyntz, Daniell and Johnson (all committee men by now) shook their heads at this pusillanimous play. Daniell's men were dismissed twice in a day by Glamorgan despite MacBryan's highly skilled resistance as he scored 100 runs and batted like a master on each occasion. MacBryan was not taken to Australia – Herbert Sutcliffe and Sandham were, unsurprisingly, preferred – and this disappointment heralded an early end to MacBryan's career. Lyon was not taken either, and he too reacted bitterly, accusing Lord's of a prejudice against amateurs. His attack upon the game's rulers became heated and public, letters and articles being printed in the national press, but Somerset's executive decided not to interfere.

Lyon, MacBryan, Robertson-Glasgow and White were picked to play for Gentlemen v Players, only to lose heavily. MacBryan was criticized for not scoring enough runs in front of the wicket and certainly he was inclined to play back and cut, especially against

Maurice Tate, a method taught to him by Samuel Woods.

Somerset as usual depended heavily upon White, who bowled as many overs as any other two men combined, and once he tired Somerset faded, which was a characteristic of those years. White was not taken to Australia either, presumably because he did not spin the ball enough, though he was a wonderful bowler on hard pitches. There was always something wrong with Somerset cricketers; yet perhaps of them all White had most reason to feel disappointed, for he was a match for any contemporary.

And the unsung Tom Young, whose bowling still sheltered in the shadows, scored 198 against Hampshire at Bath, including 2 sixes and 26 boundaries, an innings during which Lord Tennyson, who had been stung by a wasp on the journey to Bath, sat grumpily in the pavilion and could do nothing to prevent.

Unfortunately Somerset's second period of dashing amateur cricket was approaching its end. Daniell's team finished eighth in 1924, but Lyon, MacBryan, Robertson-Glasgow and Lowry and Johnson, were, for differing reasons, fading from the scene and after them there was nothing. Perhaps 1923 had brought their greatest day, as they smote 532/9 against Gloucestershire, and filled North Street for the visit of Yorkshire. Somerset's record against other counties since entering the Championship was not, in fact, a proud one, for they were constantly overwhelmed by the mighty:

County Championships 1891–1924 (30 playing seasons)

Against	First Played	Won	Lost	Drawn	Abd	Total
Derbyshire	1912	13	2	3		18
Essex	1895	3	7	5	1	16
Glamorgan	1921	3	2	2	1	8
Gloucestershire	1891	25	22	43		60
Hampshire	1895	13	27	11	1	52
Kent	1891	8	37	9		54
Lancashire	1891	5	31	5	1	42
Leicestershire	1920	1	3	2		6
Middlesex	1891	7	32	13		52
Northamptonshire	1912	0	5	0	1	6
Nottinghamshire	1892	2	3	1		6
Surrey	1891	13	28	9		50
Sussex	1892	11	26	17*		54
Warwickshire	1905	9	5	4		18
Worcestershire	1901	10	15	12	1	38
Yorkshire	1891	6	36	10		52
* Includes a tie		129	281	116	6	532

143

All fixtures were arranged on a home and away basis.
Gloucestershire were the only opponents played twice every season.
Nottinghamshire were not played after 1894 until 1928.
Essex were played in 1895 then not until 1914.

But they had not finished lower than tenth since the war and this was something for which to be thankful.

So far due respect has not been paid to this collection of amateur talent. It is time to raise a hat.

15

A mixed bag

For once let us move from lesser towards greater men.

Guy Fife Earle was one of those batsmen adored by children who rushed from school in the hope of finding him still at the crease, for his innings were brief and brutish. Standing magnificently at 6 feet and 3 inches, he was as broad as a barn and had forearms as thick as many a man's thigh. As a boy he had been a fierce fast bowler but he grew heavier and took to bowling medium-pace supported by a vast and not unduly disguised googly. After the war he played a few times for Surrey and then, settling in Minehead, qualified for Somerset for whom he began to play regularly in 1923.

A buzz began as soon as he walked, cheerful and bluff in manner, out to bat. One of his techniques was to hit every ball as far as he could, using a bat heavy enough to satisfy later hitters of less rudimentary method. It helped that he paid little respect to any bowler. Robertson-Glasgow wrote of him:

> He had that rare and enviable spirit which sees no good in opponents. Technically, they were to him, about to bat, many miles below standard. Their fast bowlers had speed only in their own estimation; their spin-bowlers were mere fancy-work, farcical, Lilliputian, soon to become useful, if reluctant, accessories to acts of prodigious violence.
>
> I have known a few other batsmen of this outlook, but Guy Earle went further. To this contempt he added a strong, but, it must be added, quite temporary, dislike. From the moment that he strode from the pavilion, he really loathed the bowlers, and, when he was bowled or caught – rarely

145

stumped, for he hit firm-footed – he was not only out but insulted, and, as he unstrapped his pads, he would tell you, with fierce metaphor and dangerous gestures, all about the offending bowler.

Earle once hit Tich Freeman for several sixes in an innings, some of them landing in Luckes' yard beyond the river. As he took guard so younger members of the groundstaff took to a rowing boat ready to fish smitten balls from the Tone. Evidently Earle was a revered Somerset cricketer, for this is a club which loves nothing so much as a game hitter.

And yet Earle was not especially effective. His 4,627 runs were scored at an average of 18.9 and took 152 games to collect, figures less impressive than those, say, of Wellard, who had other matters to which to attend.

Not that Earle pretended to be more than a sportsman playing cricket because he was asked to do so. Sometimes he even went on tour and once he missed a season after injuring an ankle in a motor accident in Egypt where he was playing one winter, but generally he preferred to go fishing, for cricket was his second love. Earle missed many county games as he endeavoured to land salmon in Scotland.

One other point about Earle. According to reports, Malcolm Lyon, who was quite a ladies' man, ran off with his wife. By all accounts a considerable scandal developed, with shocked officials meeting in secret as appalled relations vented their spleen. Earle himself appeared unshaken by this turn of events, and his chumminess with Lyon was not impaired.

It may surprise Somerset's current young players to learn that, contrary to rumour, neither adultery nor alcohol are products of their fevered imaginations. Both were present at Somerset in 1925, in one case in considerable quantities, as were other modern vices and virtues. Somerset's amateur cricketers were as much a mixture as their professional brethren. Perhaps, though, it was just as well that, unthinkable as it might be, none of the professionals was involved in this particular affair. They had to settle for a new small tea-room by their tiny and public changing room into which a confused member might at any moment potter. Today it serves as the quarters for the groundstaff successors of Mettam, Fernie and Buttle.

Tom Lowry played for Somerset only while he was finishing

his studies at Cambridge. Not that studying is sufficiently broad a word to capture Lowry's range of activities, for he was a tough, gregarious, adventurous fellow. At university he was a member of the Hellfire Club, to qualify for which a man had to blow three smoke rings and spit through them. He was not inclined to take his degree too seriously, and was apt to wander off to Newmarket races, once departing with a £5 note and returning with a small motor car, thanks to a certain friend of his who was associated with a nearby trainer. A drinking man, he disdained anaesthetic at the dentist's and once, in his cups, referred to someone important at Lord's as 'an old faggot' – a remark happily forgotten by the time Lowry returned as captain of his country.

For Lowry was a New Zealander. He was born, it scarcely needs to be said, in Wellington and accordingly played as a thoroughbred man of Somerset. His rise to captain his country was no surprise for he was a formidable man, one who admired courage above all else, one who loathed unpunctuality. He did not win a blue in his first two seasons at Cambridge, for light blue cricket was extremely strong, and Lowry was a skipper as much as a competitor. Strong, versatile, courageous, and original, he was a leader in a thousand. His comments on the run of play, had they reached the spectators, would alone have justified the entertainment tax. He was a man first and a cricketer second, but it was a close finish.

Lowry scored 1,820 runs for Somerset, none of them dull, and he would walk out to bat in an old Homburg hat and gripping a bat as he growled darkly about the incompetents who had lost their wicket so feebly before. Returning to New Zealand, he matured into a distinguished sporting administrator, captaining his country on two tours, on one tour saying nothing to reporters – 'I'm saving it all for my speeches' – and later, in 1937, as a manager – 'they couldn't find anybody else'. Without him Somerset would have been a duller club.

Raymond Robertson-Glasgow (universally 'Crusoe') was not a Somerset man born and bred either. Crusoe's links with Somerset did not at first appear strong. Undeterred, Daniell found that he had cousins in Hinton Charterhouse, one of whom was MP for Bath, a High Tory of the utmost spirit and pugnacity. It was enough. And so arrived at Somerset a warm, marvellous cricket writer, a good county cricketer and a man once described

147

as 'that old charmer who hides his scholarship and private pain with a classless smile'.

Born in Scotland, he was instructed in cricket by a Mr Plumb (who was given to coaching in gaiters) because his father took no interest in cricket, limiting his remarks to 'I see you got a few wickets at Weston-super-Mare. I caught two fish yesterday', Crusoe was a swing bowler good enough to take 238 wickets (26.81) in seventy-seven games and a batsman capable of adding 160 and 139 in successive county games in an opening partnership with Tom Young. He used to joke about his batting, as about so much else, tossing with Jim Bridges for the right to go in last, and occasionally emerging from behind a sightscreen with his bat and an ice-cream, proclaiming that 'this should do the trick'. He played for the Gentlemen and yet only fitfully for Somerset; for he was a sensitive man, one who felt the sorrows of the world and bore them upon his shoulders.

Crusoe was popular with his colleagues, notwithstanding the straw hat and pumps in which he was apt to arrive. His habit of dampening one side of the ball to encourage swing provoked comment, though it is now accepted practice. Plainly Crusoe had a good heart, and his company was sought, yet though his constitution appeared robust he was at intervals profoundly discouraged and overwhelmingly sad. Sometimes his pessimism grew so deep that his nerves required treatment and often he was away from the game, recuperating, teaching prep school boys or writing with eloquent humour upon a game which constantly drew him back, a game of beauty, compassion and betrayal. It was no sort of a game for a man prone to severe depression which returned, wrote E. W. Swanton, 'in black, inevitable cycles'.

In 1965 Crusoe took his own life. Trapped by snow in his house, feeling desperately claustrophobic, he could face life no more and swallowed some pills. He told his wife what he had done and she called an ambulance but drifts prevented its arrival until too late. He was, groundstaff and colleagues agreed, a proper gentleman.

To remember Crusoe in sorrow is to miss the smile he brought to the world. Perhaps two stories to prompt that smile can be repeated.

He arrived once at Old Trafford to find two posters, one bellowing 'READ ROBERTSON-GLASGOW IN THE MORNING POST', its partner replying 'READ THE TIMES AND SEE WHAT REALLY HAPPENED'.

Inside the old press box at Old Trafford Crusoe was given a seat for the 1934 Test close to the right-hand wall in the third row. The box faced the pavilion more than the pitch, cutting out much of the field from his view. Instead of moving to the press annex in the old Hornby Stand opposite, Crusoe chose to stay where he had been put. His second paragraph of the first day story began 'McCabe, they tell me, bowled the second over'. He then proceeded to explain his situation and the players he could see, ending with '. . . five players – hardly a quorum'.

Finally, a cricketing tale . . .

Somerset *v.* Surrey

R. C. Robertson-Glasgow and his partner through smart fielding were left in the middle of the pitch and both dashed for the same end, beating the ball. Then they raced for the other end, again beating the ball. By now, fielders were almost in hysterics. Stumps lay uprooted at both ends, but as the batsmen prepared for their fourth sortie, one fielder, calmer than the rest, picked up the ball and downed a solitary stump. Then, as no one knew who was really out, the batsmen tossed up. Robertson-Glasgow lost and was one of the few men ever to lose his wicket on the spin of a coin.

Malcolm Lyon had no business playing for Somerset either, for he was born in a part of Bristol recognized as beyond our boundaries. Daniell, of course, knew this, and when he approached Lyon Snr with a view to capturing the services of his eminent sons Bev and Malcolm, known as Dar, he suspected a compromise was his best chance. Accordingly he proposed that, since both clubs might stake claims (though only one could do so with justice) it would only be fair for one son to play for Gloucestershire and one for Somerset. A coin was tossed and Bev went north to bat and to captain his team with drive and imagination while Dar took to playing with the Cidermen. Even by Daniell's standards it was quite a coup.

Handsome and nonchalant, Lyon was as bold a driver as anyone in England save Hammond and Woolley. His talent for hitting good-length deliveries back over the bowler's head so impressed Australia's captain Herbie Collins that he praised Lyon's 136 against the 1926 tourists as one of the finest innings he had ever seen. When concentrating properly Lyon could be brilliant and for Somerset he scored over 6,000 runs, hit two double-hundreds and

149

averaged over 30, not bad for his day. Sometimes he kept wicket too, though his penchant for ignoring anything down the leg-side with the word 'Whoops, there goes another couple of geraniums' (flowers decorated the front of the Old Pavilion in those days) rather exasperated his captains.

And yet Lyon, like MacBryan, had something in his character which discouraged selection into higher circles. Perhaps he was simply too debonair, and too disrespectful, for Lyon was his own man. In 1921 he stood for Parliament as Liberal candidate for the constituency of Bury St Edmunds, though judging by the way he asked Somerset to wait upon his return, he was not sanguine about his chances of election. Besides this he was suspected of sundry flirtations, wrote a humorous novel and an instructional book on cricket which advocated taking half a glass of beer before going in to bat and which suggested wearing a tin hat, a chest protector, a fencing mask and carrying a revolver in order to face a fast bowler. He was a man of independent opinion and considerable imagination. Possibly Lord's frowned upon him and, as has been related, he certainly frowned upon them, saying that at Lord's 'great players of advancing years rule the roost', and adding: 'I've never been asked to luncheon by any of them.' He thought cricket was losing its hold because as played by pros the game was a dull and wearisome business. He had hurt a hand during a Gentlemen v. Players match and believed his poor form in this contest had been held against him, his injury not being taken into account. Wilfulness, impudence and a hint at the reckless were not the combinations for which solemn authority was searching as it picked its Test team all those years ago.

Lyon resigned from MCC but changed his mind. Yet he declined an invitation to tour South Africa. Eventually he did leave English cricket to concentrate upon his career in law, and in 1931 he went to Gambia as a magistrate, explaining that 'the Empire is greatly in need of administration'. As a barrister Lyon had defended Robinson in the trunk murder case, and he later served as magistrate in Kenya (1945–8), as Chief Justice in the Seychelles and as a judge in Uganda. Apparently some bewigged lawyers found his humour too strong and his career fell victim to it. Lyon could never see a balloon without wanting to pop it, and sometimes those balloons contained water, so that he was drenched. In short he was on occasions a fool who rushed in and his life was more diverting if less fulfilled because of it. He returned occasionally to England in the 1930s and even played a couple of games for Somerset, when, sadly, he was just a shadow of his former self. Perhaps he was rather like another lawyer, Nigel Popplewell, full of laughter, and yet serious too, and inclined towards exasperation. Few were surprised on one occasion when, Lyon finding himself bowling to his brother immediately after tea, a struggle usually in deadly earnest, delivered a doughnut.

Jack MacBryan was by no means as popular a cricketer as Earle, Lyon or Crusoe, for he was a cantankerous man, apt to drink whisky, even before going in to bat, and to complain loudly about Somerset cricket. At heart MacBryan, a dapper man of chilling disposition, was a professional who wanted to play the game properly and found some colleagues unduly frivolous. Wilfred Rhodes said of him, 'He's a right fine bat and looks to me more like a Yorkshire pro than a Somerset amateur.' Cecil Buttle, working on the grounds, thought him 'toffee-nosed' yet regarded him as 'the best player I've seen'.

He played for Somerset reluctantly. His father owned some property in Bath, and he had attended school in Exeter when, being ambitious, he felt Eton was his due. David Foot relates that these frustrations embittered Jack, especially as his father was at the heart of them. MacBryan Snr, who ran a mental asylum, discouraged his son from his chosen career as a doctor. When Jack was taken prisoner in the Great War (in which his brother served in the Somerset Light Infantry, and was killed at the age of twenty-two) his father did nothing to advance his release.

In time Jack learned to live by his wits, and to make a dollar. He married a Gaiety Girl, an arrangement which ended badly when her eye strayed elsewhere, and he lost his money on the stock market where he worked. Let down, he thought, by an envious father, let down by life, he was a difficult man, a would-be socialite prevented from mixing with the best. He was not popular in Somerset, especially with Randall Johnson who was influential with the Test selectors and considered him too bad tempered. He was out of place, a player of science, footwork and application in a world of inspiration and gung-ho spirit. Nor did he hide his contempt for colleagues who, never learning from their mistakes – 'still played like schoolboys. They were, or at least some of them were, dull and unsophisticated. I'd been a prisoner-of-war.'

151

To his dying day, as he completed the *Mirror* crossword and finished his embroidery, he felt he could have amounted to so much more had luck been on his side. Certainly he had the intelligence that turns the good into the very good, besides which he was a fighter and unafraid. For Somerset he propped up the batting, scoring 8,372 runs at an average over 30. Arguably his war service – he was wounded in 1914 and a prisoner for four years, though he did manage to play some cricket in Holland during his internment – affected his temper. Plainly he was a grumpy man unprepared to muck in, in the way of Daniell and his chums, a man who did not bother to conceal his contempt for plumed aristocrats such as Johnson, so popular at Lord's, or rustic swipers such as Earle. He was a grafter, a man with little money, not much native talent and a manner calculated to disturb those in charge, but one determined to score runs and to make his way in the world. In the end he did neither to his satisfaction and for this his temperament may in part be blamed. In truth, though, he pinpointed weakness in Somerset cricket, for cheeriness is not – save in fantasy – a convincing substitute for conviction. Many at Somerset would have been happier without MacBryan, though they wanted his runs, yet really if another two of his equal could have been found . . . But 'twas ever thus at Somerset, a club which has chosen its course, and seldom has it been the way of MacBryan or others of his ilk.

Jack White rarely inspired warmth in his team mates either, for he was a farming type, kindly and impassive. White was a poker-player, a man of reserve, incapable of the remark or deed which would inspire affection, a quality which he did not appear to seek. He was, in short, a plain chap, a cold fish even and a person accordingly about whom colleagues were liable to imagine the worst, especially those who arrived upon the scene when White was approaching retirement, and no doubt still more enigmatic and silent after decades of skilful donkey-work willingly undertaken even when surrounded by incompetents.

Apparently unfathomable, probably shallow, White has not been well served by history. Contemporaries thought him selfish and remote. Bill Andrews refused even to attend his funeral. Lyon said he was the best fielder off his own bowling in the world, a compliment and yet a comment. Others remember that he picked the seam so much that their hands were cut as they stopped a drive at cover. White never admitted to raising the stitches but was prepared to admit stopping them from getting depressed. And yet he often went racing with Arthur Wellard and assorted friends, drinking scotch and putting his shirt on horses selected, as often as not, by chums in the business. Nor did he so much as flicker an eyelash upon their winning or losing.

Easily Somerset's best cricketer of the period, he suffered from being far from its leading character. Too often he seemed to have things his own way, and too often he neglected popular opinion in the dressing-room. Being a farmer excused him from war service and yet, afterwards, he sometimes went on winter tours. His father too was a farmer, one who had the status of a village squire, and accordingly White was an amateur. Both his father, who took care of his son's farm whenever he was away, and Somerset officials helped him. It was Sir Dennis Boles (president 1934–5) who presented White with his farm, for Boles had acres to spare. Evidently White was an important figure in the club, a friend of the old families of the county set, whose importance had been diminished rather than extinguished. No doubt this, too, provoked resentment.

If his personality was not universally appreciated, no one in Somerset ever doubted White's calibre as a cricketer. Wheeling away over after over, to a tight line and length, with a carefully placed off-set field, with Daniell crouching at silly point, scarcely spinning a ball and yet constantly curving it, constantly probing, White was a formidable, even bewitching bowler capable of sustaining long spells and seldom mastered even by the best. Economical of emotion, he was niggardly as a bowler, and as a batsman he seldom went beyond his strict limitations. Epochs may end but White simply endured, impressing team mates such as Lyon who thought he was the best slow bowler in county cricket for a decade. Lean of beam, ruddy of countenance, fierce of concentration, White could pin a batsman down and intimidate youngsters with his accuracy. On hard tracks, where guile and deception mattered, he was deadly, on soft pitches he had his masters, for he did not truly spin the ball, rather he used it, and this fault was obvious on a pitch receptive to break.

He feared no batsmen, rather plotting, even predicting their downfall, though sometimes blundering fieldsmen betrayed him. He was a craftsman of high standards, a player who took 2,167

153

wickets for Somerset at an average of 18, and still found time to strike 11,000 runs and to collect 6 hundreds. In terms of Somerset cricket he was a giant.

Eventually he did play for England, even rising to be a temporary captain and a Test selector. His hour of greatest glory arrived in 1928–9 when, for the first but not the last time, a Somerset all-rounder played a vital part in winning an Ashes series. Curiously he had not really wanted to go on tour that winter, preferring to hunt with his friends (a pastime which was to cost him an eye in his retirement). Upon being persuaded he cast a spell over Australians old and emerging, just as he did over schoolboys when he returned to play at his Alma Mater, Taunton School. When he arrived back in Somerset as a hero, his car was pulled by ropes to his village in the Quantocks, a collection was made and a dinner given in his honour. Appropriately when new gates were erected at the ground they were named after him, for no one, not even Woods, Tyler or Daniell gave greater service.

It is odd, perhaps, that two of these amateurs – White and MacBryan – were so little loved. Earle and Lowry, plainly, were men cast in Daniell's light, the sort of men about whom stories are told as beers are sunk. Yet they were lightweights and the heavy work was left to MacBryan, White, Greswell when he was around, Lyon if in the mood and the solitary professional Tom Young, himself a cussed fellow who was not yet bowling, partly because White dominated the crease (too much, some thought), partly because he was inclined to be lazy.

On reflection it is not, perhaps, a tale of glorious amateurism, though Robertson-Glasgow was often persuaded to remember it as such. Rather it is a matter of identity, as Somerset stumbled along, caught midway between the rationalists whom it despised and the hearties, whom it embraced and whom led it into defeat. It is a tale which was to be repeated.

16

Last gasp of a dying world

Fielding, a critic said, 'one class player and 10 others of uncertain quality', Somerset fortunes began to decline in 1925. Thanks to the stringency of the imperturbable Davey, now secretary, profits were now being recorded and efforts made to remove old seats and to build a 'Hill' by laying 400 lorry-loads of earth in one corner, a revival for the Rack Field had provided hills from the start. Alas, with Lyon and MacBryan only sporadically available, though in form when they did play, Somerset returned to its old ways of scratching around for a few amateurs to complete their side, and now appeared men such as Charles Barlow from South Africa, Montague Hambling, Esme Haywood, Edward Collings, and Percy Ewens.

Percy Ewens was typical of this number. He owned a glove factory in Yeovil until it went bankrupt and in Taunton he played for The Stragglers and was great friends with Sydney Rippon and John Daniell who used to ring him up whenever Somserset were one short, which was usually for away games. Ewens, to whom cricket was life, made his début as a forty-one-year-old and played seven games in four years, scoring 114 runs in his 11 innings. So broke was he that in Huddersfield Daniell arranged a race between 'Box' Case and Ewens for a purse of £5. Ewens won. It was a way of giving him money without turning any heads.

Two other men, Mervyn Robert Howard Molyneux Herbert, an Etonian, and Phillip Hope, from Sherborne School, were playing their final matches hereabouts. Between them these imported public schoolboys had played seventy-two games in umpteen seasons and scored under 2,000 runs at an average modest enough to be an embarrassment. Between them they took one wicket. Herbert, who died in Rome in 1929, played until he was 42 and Hope until he was 36. Plainly they were friends of Somerset men who invited them to play a few games in their holidays. Besides Hope, Daniell might as well have called upon Faith and Charity.

1925 was a sorry season containing three victories and fifteen defeats as Somerset sank to fifteenth place in the Championship. Naturally there were murmurings, for Somerset's affairs were a matter of public debate and no longer could it be pretended that followers should attend to their own affairs. Dismissing a call for more professionals – only Young, Hunt (a moderate cricketer) and new wicket-keeper, Wally Luckes, were being paid – one committee man said, 'We don't want Somerset to be a team of pros. It's a pity schoolboys are going straight to work. Somerset is the last hope of amateurism.'

But schoolboys were going to work, for old money could no longer be found to support them. Quite simply, the supply of distinguished amateur talent was running dry. Lyon, MacBryan, Johnson and Greswell had been distracted by the need to raise a regular income, and they were men from a previous, easier generation, talented men eager to play cricket. Percy Ewens was more typical of his period.

Nevertheless Somerset did field some relatively new amateurs, notably Edmund Longrigg, Reggie Ingle (whose form was no more than satisfactory) and Cecil Charles Coles Case, a heavy, thickset man of 39 who hailed from Frome, dressed smartly, backed horses, was notoriously tight with money, of which he had plenty, lived as a bachelor, and played with the enthusiasm of a sixteen-year-old. Case had made runs in club cricket so Daniell tried him, an experiment not especially successful (340 runs in twenty-seven innings) though, in his early years, he was a fast runner in the outfield, a characteristic he was not to sustain. This trio was to represent Somerset more or less until war broke, a constancy which owed as much to their preparedness to play as to their skill.

Only White, cunning and cool, maintained his form throughout. Nevertheless 1925 had its moments. The Prophet, Daniell, scored 174 not out and 108 against Essex at Taunton, this at the age of 46. Ageing cricketers do not die, they just get run out. Not that his efforts escaped censure, for Somerset did not enforce the follow-on and did not win; moreover in his second innings Daniell, 'playing with a peculiar nonchalance', was dropped five times.

And against Derbyshire at Clarence Park, Mervyn Hill, Etonian son of Vernon, hobbled to the wicket on a couple of sticks when Somerset was in trouble in its second innings. He scored 9 but Derbyshire won by 3 wickets in the dying minutes.

Mervyn Hill, by the way, was a chip off the old block, a man of easy temperament, as strong as a Suffolk punch and, said Robertson-Glasgow, an artist at working, sleeping and eating; epicurean by taste, he could be a mighty hitter but was inclined towards idiosyncratic conduct, once allowing five balls from Charlie Parker to pass by without so much as raising his bat and then swiping the sixth into the grandstand.

Vernon had another Etonian son who played for a while. Evelyn was explosively fast for 4 overs, following which he was a spent force. Accordingly he did not play as often as Mervyn, who was a fair cricketer. Beyond doubt both men brightened Daniell's team whenever they were around, which is not to say it was stronger for their presence. They ought, perhaps, to have played twenty years earlier.

Lyon, returning to the field after his dispute with Lord's, ended with a bang, a sizzling hundred against Warwickshire; and Earle occasionally clouted to good effect, which cheered everyone up. But Somerset, by and large, were pushovers for those who built powerful sides founded upon the calibre of a player rather than his availability and generosity.

One day of glory did occur, late in August, though this belonged entirely to a visiting batsman. For an eternity, apparently, Jack Hobbs had been trying to score his 126th hundred, to equal the record of W. G. Grace. Time and again he fell short, as press, photographers, commentators and public followed his every twitch. Upon Surrey arriving at Taunton, Somerset were dismissed for 167 and Hobbs at once began nervously, running out his partner, D. J. Knight, who sacrificed himself with what degree of willingness cannot, at this distance, safely be said, for reports vary. Hobbs was caught at cover off a no ball but cobbled his way in charming style to 91 not out at the close

157

of Saturday's play. Could he do it at last? Hobbs takes up the tale:

> From the dining-room window I was greatly amused to see a shoal of reporters and photographers who had come off the train from London.
>
> I slept well that night and awoke fresh and fit. When I arrived at the ground there was a huge crowd waiting at the gates. But, evidently, the authorities had not sufficient entrances or gatemen, for the crowd was not all inside when the time came for me to continue my innings. John Daniell, the Somerset captain, asked if I would mind waiting until those outside had been admitted.
>
> As soon as I reached the wicket I was all right. A few minutes later I had hit up the nine.

In fact it took Hobbs until 11.50 to reach his hundred, with a push to leg through Jim Bridges who was bowling as usual, to an on-side field. At once the crowd cheered and sang as players shook the Master's hand and Percy Fender brought out a glass of champagne. Hobbs drank a little and was soon dismissed, caught behind off Bridges by Mervyn Hill, who was wearing a bowler hat and sundry other accoutrements, many of which he left behind in a blazing trail whenever he chased the ball. Within minutes Hobbs's wife received a telegram saying 'GOT IT AT LAST – JACK'. Apparently it had been dispatched before play resumed! Apparently, too, Hobbs changed bats just before reaching his century because he was not using a product of the company with which he was contracted but rather an old favourite. Hundreds of messages were sent to Hobbs, including one from E. M. Grace of Thornbury, W. G.'s nephew. Others were addressed to 'Greatest cricketer in the world' and 'Superman, Taunton'.

Hobbs broke W.G.'s record in the second innings, though no one bothered much about that for he was already amongst the immortals. Meanwhile MacBryan recorded a flawless hundred of his own and no one, sadly, worried about that either.

Nor did Somerset's performance improve in the year of the General Strike. Takings from membership had risen from £951 in 1922 to £3,032 in 1926, and a further £870 was spent on improving accommodation. But the team was weakening.

It was to be another summer remembered, with the kindness of cricketing history, for its moments.

Somerset had a wonderful game at The Oval. A collapse and some inhospitable Surrey batting left Somerset to chase 402 to win, a target which moved far into the distance when Daniell, Lyon and Young were quickly removed. Robertson-Glasgow takes up the tale:

> Guy Earle was smacking about lustily when the imperturbable Shepherd bowled him with a ball that was neither better nor worse than the others. Jack White, George Hunt, in and out they went. Jim Bridges remarking, according to wont, that the sun was shining and the bowling 'not so good as yours and mine, Glasgy,' proved his point to the limit of 23. Mervyn Hill, stout left-hander, was cursed with no emotions beyond defiance, but he was at once caught and bowled by that lazy-looking leg-breaker Stan Fenley, and so strung himself a pair of noughts and returned to arrange more hospitable processes than batting. On the morrow, Somerset were receiving Middlesex at Bath, and some of the side were already moving Bath-ward when it fell to No. 11, me, to join Peter Randall Johnson, whose score stood at 38, made in the old and classic style.

Somerset still needed 217 to win and Johnson and Crusoe felt free to indulge their most adventurous strokes. Johnson drove fiercely and Crusoe slogged so effectively that Percy Fender changed from leg-spin to his faster range of deliveries. Soon a waggish crowd was cheering Somerset's 250 and 300. Tempers slipped somewhat upon the field. Only 80 runs were needed and Crusoe had advanced to 49, when Jardine, whose peremptory manner was apt to upset his opponents, took the ball, whereupon Crusoe had a rush of blood, a noted characteristic amongst lower-order batsmen, and was caught behind. It left Johnson on 117 not out, his greatest innings and his final hundred. Small wonder that a local reporter, midway through the season, summed up Somerset's efforts to date with the words 'Not many games won but sporting spirit maintained'.

Tens of thousands of people flocked to Taunton to see the 1926 Australians. People queued from 8 a.m., trains were crowded and traffic in town was described as 'phenomenal'. Garage accommodation was unequal to the task for seldom had Taunton bustled so, long rows of cars blocking every road. For a time it looked as if these eager spectators would be rewarded, for Australia collapsed to 127/9 and had a run out been properly executed Ellis

159

and Everett could not have added 98 for the last wicket. Despite lusty hitting from Earle, whose contests with Clarrie Grimnett were not for the faint of heart, Somerset ended 72 behind and eventually were asked to chase 302 in 220 minutes to be the only side apart from England to defeat Collins's Australians. Lyon batted nobly and at tea Somerset were a mere 106 adrift. Alas, Lyon fell for 136 scored in 165 minutes and the rest went meekly as Australia won by 56 runs. Lyon's fine innings won universal praise.

With no trains running in 1926, for a time anyhow, Somerset players were forced to travel by charabanc as they did to Worcester, having left at 9 a.m. the previous morning. No matches were cancelled.

By 1927 it was evident that Somerset urgently needed to supplement its resources with some solid professional cricketers. In the event they found a couple of good ones in Jack Lee, brother of Harry from Middlesex, and Arthur Wellard, whose arrival owed much to praise from Archie Heywood, a Kent man lately coaching at Taunton School. Lee scored consistently and learnt to take wickets with his flighted spinners, for Somerset professionals filled the role of paid player at league clubs, batting and bowling even if their skills hitherto had not been so broad. Wellard, aged twenty-five, was signed somewhat to the chagrin of Kent and quickly proved to be a dangerous purveyor of outswingers, a willing cricketer, a hard hitter and a cheery if crafty fellow. Fred Lee was tried for a few games too. A left-arm spinner from Chard, Fred was also a hard-tackling professional footballer with Taunton Town and he was just as fiery and argumentative upon the cricket field. Alas, he was picked to play only when Jack White was on Test duty and unlike Hazell, later, he could not wait upon his chance.

Archibald Young was Somerset's best batsman in 1927, an eminence he was to sustain for five years until bowling took him up, more or less (for Young was an exception, a gifted professional inclined towards laziness). Despite Greswell's reappearance Somerset finished fourteenth, though they were harder to beat, losing only nine times. MacBryan, dismayed by failure, did not play and Bridges was injured. Still Rippon was back and plundering a dashing 133 at Knowle (86 in boundaries) where, at a dinner, Mr Barrow, a local committee-man, spoke for the soul of Somerset cricket when he said that Somerset played

160

Cricket as it should be played because they hadn't won the championship and never would. They did not want them to either . . . It is the finest game in the world and I'd be sorry if it ever took second place to bowls.

In reply a taciturn White said: 'I can't speak but I'll bowl to anyone in the room.'

Barrow's words, besides being prophetic, merit contemplation. Somerset is trapped between a yearning to win a first championship (many say they would die happily if this day ever dawned) and a certain reaction against such means as may be necessary to achieve it. It is a confused, warm club which attracts high emotion and those who depart unwillingly feel a terrible, unforgiving bitterness. People play for Somerset best who play with their hearts.

Daniell had made his last judgement, as a player anyhow, and Jack White was captain. Defying at least one committee man he was prepared to pick Lyon, whose outbursts against Lord's had not been forgotten, and managed once again to be the first amateur to take 100 wickets. 'What a pity', they exclaimed, 'he isn't fifteen years younger!' . . . Soon enough the Australians were to wish him fifteen years older.

Earle hit merrily (which is practically a tautology), Case defended stubbornly (ditto), rarely using his shoulder or wrists to drive, and in general each man followed his personal dictates, in true Somerset fashion.

Wellard could play only against the tourists, for he was qualifying and while doing so he lived with Bill Andrews, an extrovert youngster then serving as a professional for East Coker but a man with ambitions of his own.

Glamorgan, fielding imported professionals from Yorkshire, Surrey and Hampshire, followed a route disdained in Taunton though to no avail. Meanwhile Somerset contemplated building a practice shed and squash courts but instead decided to patch up existing buildings and to concentrate upon their team. A new bottle storeroom and new latrines, a splendid partnership, were erected. Otherwise, plans rather exceeded achievements.

Unfortunately a damp summer brought a loss of £1,515 in 1927, and discouraged further signings of professional cricketers. This deficit led Somerset to reduce its fixture list in 1928, and they stopped playing their most distant opponent, geographically

161

and technically, Yorkshire. Games played numbered twenty-four, of which four were won and eleven lost.

Owing to his law practice Lyon hardly played and MacBryan played only two championship matches and against the West Indians at Bath, where he scored a neat 84. Robertson-Glasgow averaged 41 as a batsman, while Rippon and Longrigg also had satisfactory summers, Rippon playing for The Gentlemen but, to his profound disappointment, being bowled for a duck. (Thirty years later, five years after his retirement from the Civil Service, he passed his law finals and became a barrister, remarking, 'I am content to have scored a victory for the old.')

Sadly Jack Lee had a poor summer (376 runs at an average of 14). For a time he returned to club cricket in Bath and it was only with perseverance and high scoring that he was able to renew his county career.

As usual all sorts of curious coves appeared in Somerset colours in 1928, including Charles Mayo, an Etonian born in British Columbia and killed in action in 1943, and John Madden-Gaskell from Haileybury and via Glamorgan, a military man and an OBE who was also a fine rugby player. Once when facing Bill Voce, Madden-Gaskell, who batted in glasses, was much put out to find one ball whistling past his nose, whereupon he called to the opposing captain that Voce was dangerous and should be taken off. Madden-Gaskell played a good deal of Straggler cricket.

Other new amateurs included Laurie Hawkins, a pleasant leg-spinning all-rounder from Wellington (Somerset), and Geoffrey Bennett from Wincanton by way of King's Bruton School. Hawkins was to represent Somerset on forty-six occasions in the pre-war years, before concentrating upon his trade in jewellery and knick-knacks. Charming off the field, he was fiercely competitive – even unscrupulous – upon it, especially in club cricket, where his rows with his colleague, Jim Priddy, who also bowled his spinners a few times for Somerset in the 1930s, were legendary. Priddy, by the way, later owned a TV shop. Backgrounds were changing. Bennett, Michael to his friends, played 109 matches, scored 2,330 runs and took just 14 wickets with bowling which had seemed fast at school. Bennett, rather like Chris Greetham, made his mark as an attractive batsman whose best moments were memorable, as a brilliant fieldsman, and as an immaculately dressed and invariably debonair fellow whose wavy hair and sporting eye bowled more maidens over than could be managed at the popping-crease.

A team ever changing, a team cobbled together from amateurs local and distant, a team increasingly dependent upon its professionals, who had increased in number from 2 to 6, could not with any regularity compete with powerful clubs who enjoyed a steady supply of men from working backgrounds eager to play cricket for a living. Moreover, since Somerset had no indigenous supply of professional league cricketers, their paid men were either especially gifted youngsters from a background humble enough to allow them to play for money without losing social status, or failures from elsewhere such as Wellard and numerous others of lower achievement.

Continually Somerset tried to turn this tide of professionals. Realizing that a growing fixture list was the death-knell of amateurism, failing to see how many other factors were involved, Somerset proposed a reduction in the fixture list, complaining that every additional game cost them £250. Nevertheless county matches increased to twenty-eight in 1930 for professionalism was rife and accordingly the game was turned into an industry with men working from 9 a.m. until close of play and then often packed into trains to fulfil another engagement. Ever since this final defeat of the amateur, English cricket has demanded more and more of its body of professional players. In part this was due to economic necessity, for the wage bill is considerable, and in part it was due to an attitude which held cricketers to be workers rather than artists. Economics apart, it was a question of officer and infantryman, of gentry and tradesman. It is a peculiarly English view of games and those who play them best, and a view held strongest and longest in Somerset. In the handbook for 1930 officials proclaimed that it was 'most desirable and in keeping with the traditions of Somerset cricket that Amateurs should predominate – modern cricket makes this hard'.

In fact it made it impossible, especially as the Depression set in so that sons born into previously wealthy families felt an urgent need to earn their keep. Soon enough talented cricketers such as Mitchell-Innes and Woodhouse would appear at Somerset, only to be lost to service in Sudan, a plum job reserved for those with brains, background and sporting prowess.

Somerset's new professionals changed, as the old ones had done, in a small room to which privacy was lent only by the

163

erection of a blanket. Every morning they were expected to bowl to the amateurs and on rest days to the offspring of members, duties which they carried out, for the most part, in good humour for professional cricketers are trained to take the rough with the smooth; besides, it was not so bad a job in these grim times. When play began they took to the field through separate gates, so that if MacBryan and Tom Young, for example, were opening they met for the first time in the middle. Away from home they stayed in different hotels and travelled in different parts of the train, a circumstance which provoked less offence than it would in more egalitarian times, for being out of sight and hearing of the captain and his chums had its advantages, and the interests of university men and professionals did not always overlap.

Playing as a professional for Somerset had its compensations. Since these men were regarded as retainers, once established they were rarely dismissed. In Somerset's amateur period the professionals tended to play until their legs could carry them no more, for they were few in number and regarded as part of the furniture. Only when a determined move was made towards gathering a professional staff were judgements made and insecurity began. Only in the 1930s did Somerset begin to sack important professional players – notably Bill Andrews and George Hunt.

To a degree Somerset's preference for amateurism was understandable. In 1870 just 1.8 per cent of all batsmen were dismissed leg before, because paid play was considered unfair and to hit to leg was *infra dig*. By 1890, with Arthur Shrewsbury shamelessly using his pads as a second line of defence, the figure had risen to 4.3 per cent. In 1930 it was 11.2 per cent and in 1935, with professionalism and depression rife, 16 per cent of batsmen lost their wickets to leg before decisions. In conception, if not execution, 1870 offered a better game in a different world. In both cricket and elsewhere something had been lost, and something gained.

Money was lost in 1928 and talent money for professional players was scrapped at Somerset, an economy measure. Somerset finished fourteenth, fielded badly, and could be proud only of Reggie Ingle's two splendid hundreds in a game against Middlesex at Taunton, of George Hunt's first and solitary century (whereupon a collection of 20 guineas was raised around the Clarence Park ground) and of Bill Greswell's 9/62 against Hampshire at

Weston-super-Mare, five of these batsmen being caught by Hunt at short leg.

Still, it was a poor and a worrying season. Thankfully Somerset supporters were immensely cheered by events during the winter, cheered by the efforts of one of their sons, a local farmer who helped to bring back the Ashes.

17

Jack White downunder

Seldom has a Somerset cricketer played an influencial part in an Ashes series. Until Ian Botham did so in 1981 only John Cornish White could claim such an honour. For years White had been delivering his slow, apparently innocuous and yet cunning offerings, taking hundreds of wickets and yet hardly ever being called upon to serve his country. Robertson-Glasgow wrote that the secret of his bowling could be grasped only from very close, and lay in the precision of his length, his ability to move the ball a little either way and in his understanding of his opponents. He

> was a yeoman, four-square . . . Whether it was cows or batsmen he had the treatment for the trouble; and in those days he never seemed to tire. In cricket he was serene, but not merely placid, for the artist in him could resent too much luck in an opponent or too little attention in a fielder. As to the latter, he would often say 'the trouble about that cock is that he's fast asleep'.

Perhaps he did not much miss playing for England, and even in the winter of 1928–9 he was reluctant to leave his farm and his stag-hunting season. Then his father said he would take care of the cattle, sheep and crops and White was free to go.

It was an inspired selection, for White was a master on hard pitches, and, moreover, was too fast to permit easy assault by Australia's ageing and heavy-footed batsmen, and too wily for newcomers such as Archie Jackson and Donald Bradman. By the time he returned he had captained England in a Test, ignoring a badly injured shoulder to play, had dropped a laughably simple catch off his own bowling at a vital moment and had won respect and matches.

White's role in Australia was to bowl with economy while Larwood, Tate and George Geary were resting. He did rather more than that, taking 4 wickets for 7 runs in 6 overs in the first engagement in Brisbane, as Larwood bowled England to a huge victory. Soon enough Joe Darling, a former Australian captain, was writing that he would have 'revelled in having such a bowler, he'd never have been left out of my XI'.

England won again in Sydney, White bowling with economy, and took an invincible 3/0 lead in Melbourne, chasing 332 and winning by 3 wickets as Sutcliffe struck 135. In this absorbing contest White bowled 113.5 overs and took 6 wickets for 171 runs, a performance of epic proportions which was to be surpassed when the teams moved to Adelaide.

Once again the teams scrapped at close quarters, Hammond's two majestic hundreds being matched by Archie Jackson's brave 164, so that a cigarette paper could not have been slipped between the teams on any of the seven days of cricket played in scorching heat. White bowled 124.5 overs, took 13 wickets for 256 runs and outshone Clarrie Grimmett (no less), so that England won a desperate contest by 12 runs. *Wisden* described White as 'really wonderful in stamina, clever flighting and remarkable accuracy of pitch'.

Astonishingly White took the last 2 wickets with long hops, deliberately bowled according to reports, deliveries which led to catches being offered to and superbly taken by Tate and Larwood on the leg boundary; truly the work of a poker player. Adelaide lurched between hysteria and deathly silence as White led his victims to their doom. Blackie was Australia's last man, and he took a draught of the right stuff before daring to go in. Patsy Hendren related that when Blackie came in to face White, he, that guileful Patsy, standing close to the wicket, said: 'My word; I wouldn't be in *your* shoes for all the money in the world.' 'I shall never forget,' said Hendren, 'the look of pitiable horror that came over Blackie's face when I said this.' Bravely Blackie defended for a few balls, then was caught by Larwood at deep mid-wicket.

Jack Ryder, opposing captain, called White's bowling a decisive factor and Somerset was proud of its conquering hero. Later

White revealed that at one stage he was so angry at the umpires that he asked his team to sit down for five minutes in protest, a gesture acknowledged in eye-witness accounts. He also brought home a piece of Australian turf to show to boys at Taunton School, who expressed amazement at its hardness and brownness.

Upon his return to Somerset White was given a royal welcome. His train arrived at 1 p.m. and was greeted by a vast crowd. He made a modest speech, shook hands with dignitaries including a mayor, a High Sheriff, magistrates, Lionel Palairet, Sammy Woods, Arthur Newton and all his relations, whereupon the company proceeded to the Town Hall to partake of a magnificent banquet following which the thousands of supporters who still waited upon him sent White on his way towards his Combe Florey farm. 'Just see what Jack can do when he is properly supported in the field,' they told each other.

White's luggage was sent on a farm cart and 'Farmer's' car was stopped in traditional manner a few miles short of his home by a veritable army of relations, supporters and workers who attached ropes to it and pulled it from Bishops Lydeard to his property, where a convivial party awaited. Jack told this congregation that he had got through lots of shirts and a fair few whisky-and-sodas in Adelaide. Then he returned to work amongst his hay, his renowned flock of sheep and his Devonian cattle.

Naturally a poem was written to mark the occasion. Constructed by a Taunton School boy it was published in *The Tauntonian*:

'VOWER VOR ZEBEM'

Wull done, then, Farmer! We be proud o' you
To Zomerzet; an' zoo's all England, too;
You, what can pitch zoo wull a pook o' haay,
Can pitch a ball, too, in a cannen waay;
D' sim to I that you d' mean to vill yer
Girt bag wi' wickets out in vur Austrilyer.
    But 'pon me soul, now, fancy vower vor zebem,
    An' all agen Austrilyer's crack elebem!

When o' the fust daay's plaay we got the news
Zome volk wur turble down wi' fits o' blues;
But we zaid "Wait, we han't a-done wi'm 'eet,

168

They hadn't a-got to Jack o' Zomerzet;
An' don't 'ee know that our good Farmer Jack,
Meade up his mind to bring they ashes back?"
    But 'pon me soul, now, fancy vower vor zebem,
    Au' all agen Austrilyer's crack elebem!

They mid be proud o' Ponsford, Woodfull, Ryder,
But we've a-got our Jack to gi'e 'em cider;
An' he can plaay the stiddy geame, or het like vlashes,
Or bowl their hottest batters all to ashes.
Zoo Jack, me sonny, don't 'ee please vorget
That we be looken on vrom Zomerzet.
    But lard o' mussy, fancy vower vor zebem,
    An' all agen Austrilyer's crack elebem!

169

18

Professional times

Somerset's cricketing performances did not improve in 1929, as they sank to fifteenth place despite Arthur Wellard's marking his first full season by taking 131 wickets with outswingers and breakbacks so sharp that sixty-nine men were clean bowled. Eager to make up for lost years, over six foot tall, sunburnt, capless, black hair parted in the centre as was the fashion, Wellard was muscular, fit and capable of bowling for hour upon hour with seam rigidly upright, every ball an examination. Moreover with hitting as prodigious as Earle's he made 130 runs against Gloucestershire and took 11 wickets too. Not to be outdone Earle swiped 50 in 15 minutes, hitting 2 over the press box, one of which dented a car belonging to a senior Somerset official.

White trapped his annual one hundred victims too, as if he were potting clay pigeons. He scored 192 against Nottinghamshire at Taunton, dealing with Voce's leg theory by placing the ball between four short-legs. During the luncheon adjournment he was presented by the Marquess of Bath with a silver salver and a cheque for £958, some war stock for himself, and a pair of silver hairbrushes for his daughter, gifts raised by donations from supporters in recognition of his winter of triumph. During this game the pavilion caught fire and everyone rushed on to the field. Cecil Buttle helped to extinguish the flames, not for the last time for it was a service he contributed every decade or so, and often with regret, for it was the aged not the young who found sentiment in those decrepit rafters.

White also captained England in three Test matches against South Africa, only to be dropped after taking a 1/0 lead. Plainly he was not a born leader.

Unfortunately Wellard and White could not carry their county team, and though Young, Longrigg and Case were dependable none rose to great heights. Unsurprisingly defeats outweighed victories by a margin of more than 5 to 1. Somerset's generally indifferent batting let down wholehearted efforts by Wellard and White.

At least efforts were being made to improve. Jack Lee's brother Frank had been signed as a steadfast batsman destined to play for Somerset 338 times before donning an umpire's coat, and two local men, Horace Hazell from Bristol and Bertie Buse from Bath appeared, capable fellows both and bowlers to boot. Somerset had not produced many distinguished cricketers and bowlers were as few and far between as pubs in an Islamic state. A year later another, Bill Andrews, was to appear so that, having embraced Wellard (who was not so foolish as entirely to adopt the club as his family, though he caught many of its characteristics) Somerset could soon hope to field an overwhelmingly local attack. Between them White, Wellard, Buse, Hazell, and Andrews took 6,047 first-class wickets, while representing Somerset.

Membership was stable at 2,347 but a deficit of £607 was recorded in 1929 which led to further agitation by such as Vernon Hill (president in 1930) on behalf of amateur players and to a questioning of the accounts by suspicious members.

All was not well amongst the players. Wally Luckes was sick with heart trouble, Robertson-Glasgow suffered a series of breakdowns and Rippon was absent for similar reasons. MacBryan was hardly playing and Lyon was electioneering once more. Recruitment wasn't easy and Somerset still relied upon amateurs generously giving of their time. William Baldock played a few games as a batsman from Wellington who had attended Winchester. He was soon off to the Far East and then to Tanganyika, in pursuit of business interests (tea planting) and a Civil Service career. Baldock died in 1941 after being taken prisoner by the Japanese while serving his country in Malaya.

Dickie Burrough played too, as he was to do with some regularity until 1947, fitting in 161 matches and managing to score four hundreds, though his average was modest. Burrough, from Wedmore, had been educated at King's Bruton, a reliable source of good cricketers in those days. His father had played

171

for Somerset on four occasions. Dickie had to wait until 1937 for his greatest game, scoring 90 and 133 in a match against Kent. Burrough was, in some respects, typical of the sort of amateur now playing for Somerset. A noted sportsman, a man with a profession, and a man from Bath, he could combine work and play in a manner echoed by Ingle and Longrigg. Fortunately he was a popular fellow whose appearances caused little resentment amongst his paid colleagues, partly because he was a gregarious type with a fondness for playing spoof in bars, partly because his skills were respected. Longrigg was a partner in their law firm, and apparently Burrough did the work and Longrigg was the playboy. Amateurs of the period, and especially these Bath amateurs, were a lively, sociable lot who enjoyed their drink, their snooker, and their ladies, who were, sometimes, wives of good and hospitable friends.

Cecil Case, also from King's Bruton, was a different sort entirely. It was said of him that he could score at a slow pace in a more entertaining manner than anyone else. 'Case', wrote Crusoe, 'was a batsman who invariably appeared to be in a terrific hurry during his stay at the crease but never getting anywhere in the process' . . .

> After carefully playing a defensive stroke he would walk around and around in ever widening circles, bend down stiffly to play the next ball, and then proceed to do it all over again. He was a determined player who waited for the bad ball before dealing safely with it. He was an enthusiastic member of the side and once he was set he was extremely difficult to dislodge. Prone to become very suspicious while playing cards or at some unusual occurrence, Case received much good-humoured leg-pulling both by friend and foe alike. While playing in a match at Taunton against Surrey, Jack Hobbs (with his dry sense of humour) and his partner Andy Sandham were batting, and after a whispered consultation, a few balls were cut down to third man where Case was fielding. The batsmen, after running several quick singles, turned and started as if on another run, only to return to their respective creases. Case who could throw hard but with poor direction, duly obliged each time by throwing the ball to midwicket, with Jack White, our skipper, despairingly shouting, 'Back up.' With another ball played to Case, the batsmen were this time near to completing a

172

second run when we heard Case call out, 'You don't kid me this time.' What J. C. White said cannot, I'm afraid, be repeated here.

Case also executed a famous stroke in Old Trafford where, assembling his defences, he fell flat forwards on the pitch and nevertheless managed to play the ball in front of his forehead.

He was, in other words, a cricketer of so serious a conviction that funny things were bound to happen to him. Fast bowling was not to his taste and once he was so confounded by Voce that, upon diving to avoid what he took to be a bouncer, he found his stumps shattered and, arising, picked up a stump instead of his cast-off bat and proceeded to leave the field in its company. For a time hushed spectators wondered if Case meant to thump Voce with this stump; was he walking towards him with intent or merely in a daze? No one will ever know, for he returned and collected his cricket bat with as much dignity as he could muster. At the crease hours of rigid defence were suddenly followed by bouts of aggression, following which he'd return to his customary approach. Prodding with a crooked bat, never hitting freely, he was regularly barracked at Taunton and elsewhere, especially in the Orchard Cottage corner of the ground where the public bar was to be found, and where Taunton's more disreputable citizens could accordingly purchase a pint of cider when other avenues were closed.

Case was a curious fellow, rather selfish, some thought, who before turning to golf managed to acquire 8,515 runs at an average just over 20 in his 255 county appearances. He caught only 47 chances in his career for, as locals were wont to exclaim towards the end of his career, when bow legs limited mobility, milk turned quicker.

This batting average is by no means untypical of respected Somerset batsmen for Earle, Daniell, Considine (now playing), Gerald Fowler, Ingle, Jack Lee and other famous men could not improve upon it and yet held in place at the top of Somerset's order for years. Case's chief merit as a cricketer was his readiness to play, for he had started late and meant to make up for lost time. Perhaps a phrase of his own best captures his view of cricket, and of life. Scoring astonishingly well against Tim Goddard on a turning Bristol pitch – it was his finest hour – he peered at a nearby fieldsman and said: 'You may laugh, but laughing doesn't

173

take wickets.'

As a season 1930 was marginally better than most of its predecessors though only an optimist could find in it sufficient evidence that a rise to thirteenth position heralded a revival. Membership slipped fractionally to 2,317, of whom 549 were to be found in Taunton and 362 in Bath. By finishing thirteenth Somerset did at least confound those critics who, in July, by which time White's team had lost ten and drawn four of its fourteen fixtures, announced that Somerset were 'strong favourites to take the Wooden Spoon'. It was Bunty Longrigg, son of a martinet major, a public schoolboy whose airy off-side shots unnerved those awaiting their turn at the crease, who renewed spirits by hitting 205 against Leicestershire, following which Somerset hurried to victory as the clock ticked by, Young and Ingle hitting the winning runs with two minutes to spare. Only one more game was lost, nine being drawn and three won.

Lyon, who played in just four games, struck a crushing 210 against Gloucestershire, an innings which could not prevent defeat, so feeble were his colleagues. Unfortunately Somerset's professionals did not contribute much, especially George Hunt, who was fading, and the Lee brothers, who were still struggling to survive.

But Tom Young had a marvellous season, as men of cussed temperament sometimes do in their benefit years. To date in his career Young had been a dashing opening batsman with a taste for lifting drives over cover-point. A small man with a weak constitution, Tom played from 1911 to 1933, scoring 13,081 runs (25.49) many of them with cuts of a savagery surprising in one so frail. His game was all adventure, an attitude betokened by his bright blue eyes, and yet his temperament was somewhat downcast for, as Robertson-Glasgow wrote, he looked generally as if he had lent someone threepence without the remotest chance of its being repaid.

Honest and downright, Young was a man of firm opinion and strong character. Bowling to Jardine once he took a caught-and-bowled and tossed the ball into the air. Jardine barked, 'Did you catch it, Young?' to which Tom replied, 'Sir, when I throw it up you are out.' In the nets at Taunton he would coach Somerset's younger players in a forthright way, insisting that they apply themselves with rigour. Many later praised his contributions.

174

Given better health Young might have been even more effective, though Somerset cricket history is littered with 'might-have-beens'. A sickly child, he had been gassed while serving in France during the war and though he bore this affliction with courage it slowly wore him down. Poor lungs, scarcely helped by living next to the gasworks in Bath, made him vulnerable to fast bowlers, for a bad blow upon the chest could have been fatal, a handicap upon which men such as Larwood and Voce traded. None the less Young stood his ground in his quixotic way, pretending lack of enjoyment and carrying on regardless.

No doubt his pessimism was confirmed when his benefit game against Sussex at Bath in 1930 finished in two days and raised less than £100. Fortunately subscribers donated £750 in the year, a tidy sum to help Young in his retirement which, alas, was to be brief for he fell sick in 1934 and had to abandon an intended career as an umpire. He died two years later.

For Tom Young 1930 was to be an extraordinary season. Hitherto he had never been seriously considered as a bowler though he might break a partnership from time to time, with a straight delivery in the opinion of watching small boys. Suddenly against Australia, Young was asked to bowl his off-spinners, a brand of delivery scarcely taken seriously in the years of amateur cricket, and he responded by taking 5 wickets, including those of Bradman (caught and bowled), Archie Jackson, and Vic Richardson, at a cost of 70 runs. Australia won, of course, Bradman and Jackson scoring hundreds, but Somerset took £1,407 on the gate of which £478 was given to the Tourists and £219 paid in entertainment tax, leaving a profit of £677.

Against Derbyshire Young took 11 wickets for 77 runs, and scored 63 and 70. In his career he was to take 388 wickets at an average of 25.48, respectable figures for one who only really bowled in his last four seasons, supposedly years of decline, and certainly so in his case for he was at death's door.

Greswell played his last few county games in 1930 – too late he had returned to settle in England – and George Hunt distinguished himself chiefly by deciding to bat left-handed when facing Voce, whose dangerous bowling was roundly barracked by a noisy Taunton crowd. Reginald Northway (aged twenty-three) carried his bat against Yorkshire, scoring 21 not out as Somerset were dismissed for 43 to lose by an innings and 328 runs; possibly they regretted resuming relations with this tough northern foe. Northway, who was born in Ceylon, bagged a pair against Leicestershire and was to play seventeen games for Somerset before moving to Northampton. A steady batsman and an alert fielder, he died in a car crash at the age of thirty, his sports car jumping over a humpback bridge, missing a telegraph pole, crashing into a kerb and then turning on its side on a hedge. Colleagues said he was a marvellous driver and must have nodded off to sleep. His friend, Bakewell, was badly hurt and never played county cricket again.

Reginald's older brother, Edward, also born in Ceylon, had also played a few games for Somerset as a useful batsman.

Dr Poynton, whose observations proved so useful earlier, died in 1930 and left £100 to the club, which Vernon Hill said was a splendid example to everyone; people took it that he meant leaving money rather than merely dying. Hill said that Somerset were playing too many games, which was ruining amateur cricket. No doubt he enjoyed Arthur Wellard's batting, for it was of the old school, an unbending pursuance of sixes, a pursuance which relied upon a golf swing with just a hint of a draw. He scored 673 championship runs and wondered if he ought not to take batting more seriously. Young constantly nagged at him to hit straight.

Sadly Wally Luckes was sick again in 1930 and with Lyon absent, Somerset urgently needed a substitute wicket-keeper. After taking soundings they summoned Seymour Clark, an engine driver from Weston-super-Mare who was to play five games and to keep stumps so well that he was offered a contract – which he declined, saying that, in these hard times, regular jobs were precious.

Clark had not taken up cricket until he was twenty-five, when fellow railwaymen started a team which played on rough rural pitches. Since he could not bowl, Seymour kept wicket and, knowing no better, he stood up to everyone's bowling, which proved to be splendid training. So skilful was he that people wondered if he might not have played Test cricket had circumstances been different.

And yet it is not for these humble five games that Clark is remembered, for in his brief career he achieved something unique, a record which will probably never be beaten. On nine occasions Clark went out to bat. On nine occasions he took guard, surveyed the field, essayed a shot and returned to the pavilion without having added a notch to his team's tally.

David Foot found Seymour alive and well a few years ago and inquired about his experiences. Clark recalled White's coldness, recollected dropping his bat twice on the pavilion steps as, with some reluctance, he walked out to face Bill Bowes. Team-mates tried to instruct him in the mysteries of batting, Hunt advising him to hold his bat still and allow the ball to strike it. Soon opponents joined the fun, Peter Smith, Essex's leg-spinner, offering double bouncers in an effort to provide a run. Unfortunately Clark still continued to miss. He thought it wise not to confess that he had bought a new bat to honour these county experiences.

Somerset's batting averages for that summer merit reproduction . . .

COUNTY CHAMPIONSHIP

	Inns.	N.O.	Runs	Highest score	Aver.
M.D. Lyon	7	0	407	210	58.14
E.F. Longrigg	44	1	1351	205	31.41
J.C. White	36	1	958	97	27.37
Young	49	4	1198	70	26.62
S.G.U. Considine	5	0	112	77	22.40
R.C. Robertson-Glasgow	8	0	179	80	22.37
Wellard	36	5	673	75	21.71
C.C.C. Case	46	6	826	108	20.65
R.A. Ingle	43	2	795	73	19.39
Lee (J.W.)	36	13	378	50*	16.43
Hunt	37	10	398	80*	14.74
Lee (F.S.)	35	1	498	79	14.64
R.P. Northway	20	2	236	42	13.11
A.G. Marshall	15	4	141	36	12.81
W.T. Greswell	3	0	37	21	12.33
P.H.F. Mermagen	10	0	114	35	11.40
H.D. Burrough	4	0	40	15	10.00
E.J.H. Hart	6	1	45	16	9.00
J. Madden-Gaskell	4	0	34	29	8.50
L. Hawkins	9	0	69	18	7.66
Luckes	11	5	41	13	6.83
Andrews	17	7	47	9	4.70
Clark	9	2	0	0*	—

Clark was asked to play a sixth game but dared not take any more time off and Lyon returned.

Patrick Mermagen added 81 with Robertson-Glasgow for the eighth wicket against Hampshire. He was another amateur passing through, a nineteen-year-old educated at Sherborne. A vigorous batsman, an accurate schoolboy seamer and a superb cover point, he represented The Public Schools at Lord's and played for Somerset before going to Pembroke College, Cambridge as an open scholar in mathematics. Mermagen pursued an academic career at Radley and in time won appointment as headmaster of Ipswich School.

Longrigg and Wellard apart, Somerset's outlook seemed bleak. White was playing only because Daniell had persuaded his father to pay even closer attention to his farm. Only at Bath was the crowd satisfactory, this because many had entered under the impression that a Rose Show was being held upon the Recreation Ground.

Money was tight once more and wages were reduced, Bill Andrews's falling from £3 to £2. Membership sank by 200 in 1931 and a loss of £743 was recorded, raising the overdraft to £2,437. Times were hard and entrance for the unemployed fell from one shilling to sixpence. Nevertheless rows began over the accounts and, rather discouraged, Secretary A. F. Davey left to accept a position at Surrey, an efficient and professional club which showed up Somerset's numerous failings of constitution, administration and, sharpest of all, attitude.

Players and paid officials volunteered to take a 5 per cent cut in wages, which saved £100. More was needed and an appeal was launched by Major Barrett, the new president. Somerset, he said, was in danger of extinction and £3,000 was urgently needed. Newspapers supported the appeal and donations were listed in their pages, as cricket clubs gave £10 or a raffle raised £20. A dance at Downside School brought a profit of £132, and this dance, encouraged by Father Trafford, the headmaster, and organized by Reggie Ingle, became a regular event. Somerset could be thankful that it owned its own ground and that it had so many friends in society, for it could not rely upon local businesses, which were already in parlous trouble, not being robust enough easily to survive the Depression.

Nor was finance Somerset's only problem in 1931. A dispute arose over the appointment of a secretary to follow Davey. Jack

Sam Woods.

Khartoum 1916

Sammy Woods, a fine cricketer but above all a great character, jovial, colourful and informal. Indeed, in many ways he epitomized the Somerset cricketing ideal

Ernest Robson had an outstanding game against Australia in 1896. Leading by 90, Somerset collapsed to 49/6 then rain intervened with the game delicately balanced

SOMERSET COUNTY CRICKET GROUND,

TAUNTON, AUGUST 24th, 25th & 26th, 1896.

SOMERSET v. AUSTRALIANS.

DRAWN—RAIN.

SOMERSET.	First Innings.		Second Innings.	
1 L. C. H. Palairet	b Jones	6	b M'Kibbin	0
2 Capt. Hedley	b Jones	40	b M'Kibbin	0
3 R. C. N. Palairet	c Kelly b Trumble	31	c Hill b Trumble	1
4 S. M. J. Woods	c Iredale b Jones	35	c Iredale b Giffen	16
5 W. N. Roe	c Hill b Trumble	46	run out	0
6 Robson	c Trott b Trumble	2	b Giffen	10
7 J. B. Challen	b M'Kibbin	23	not out	12
8 V. T. Hill	b M'Kibbin	4	not out	10
9 Nichols	st Kelly b Trumble	6		
10 Tyler	c Jones b M'Kibbin	13		
11 A. E. Newton	not out	0		
	B 4, l-b 9	13		
	Total....219		Total.... 49	

1-37 2-64 3-118 4-126 5-137 6-183 7-200 8-202 9-219 10-219
1-0 2-1 3-1 4-1 5-27 6-27 7- 8- 9- 10-

AUSTRALIANS.	First Innings.		Second Innings.	
1 F. A. Iredale	c and b Hedley	9		
2 J. Darling	b Hedley	0		
3 G. Giffen	c Tyler b Robson	40		
4 H. Donnan	run out	41		
5 S. E. Gregory	c Newton b Robson	4		
6 C. Hill	b Robson	1		
7 G. H. S. Trott	c and b Hedley	1		
8 J. J. Kelly	st Newton b Robson	14		
9 H. Trumble	c Newton b Robson	8		
10 E. Jones	c Challen b Robson	9		
11 T. R. M'Kibbin	not out	0		
	B 2	2		
	Total....129		Total....	

1-0 2-17 3-88 4-92 5-96 6-98 7-98 8-117 9-127 10-129
1- 2- 3- 4- 5- 6- 7- 8- 9- 10-

Umpires—J. Lillywhite & J. Phillips.   Scorers—W. T. Webb & F. A. Lemon.

Interval at 2.   Stumps Drawn at 6.

"ON WOODS-MAN SPARE THAT TREE"

BY PERMISSION FROM THE ATHLETIC NEWS

A contemporary cartoonist illustrates the latest Somerset triumph over Yorkshire in 1903

Hewett and Palairet after their record opening partnership of 346 against
Yorkshire at Taunton in 1892

George Nichols, one of Somerset's early professionals, whose contribution to Somerset was vital at a time when the county was trying to establish its cricketing reputation

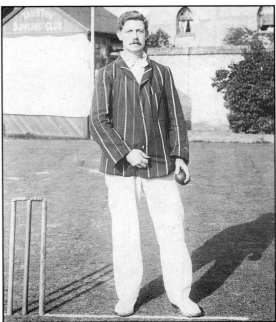

Edwin Tyler, another professional and Nichols' business and bowling partner

The Reverend Archdale Wickham. A respected wicket-keeper, he played for Somerset in eighty-two games over seventeen summers, during which he stumped 48 men and caught 81

Wisden said that Vernon Hill hit the ball with 'a power which was absolutely amazing'. Not just a hard hitter, he was a cheerful man who helped Somerset cricket on and off the field for decades

Bill Greswell was a central figure in Somerset cricket in the early part of this century. A talented bowler, he had, according to Robertson-Glasgow, 'an exaggeratedly side-on action, throwing his head back almost at forty-five degrees from his body and continuing the swerve of the ball entirely by the way he held it.'

Dudley (left) and Sydney (right) Rippon, walking out to bat in 1914. Identical
twins, they delighted in the confusion caused by their appearance and were apt to
swap clothing to fool opponents, scorers and the public

White wanted the job and leaked this to the press, or so his critics said, a manoeuvre which greatly annoyed John Daniell, who thought it discourteous. Daniell, much more of an insider than White if rather less qualified to attend to administration details, applied for the position himself and offered to do it for nothing, a most sporting offer in the opinion of Somerset's executive committee, and one they could scarcely reject.

Daniell was to be secretary from 1932 to 1936 and his influence continued thereafter until he served as president from 1947 to 1949. Somerset loved domineering men, admired courage and vigour, and accordingly took Woods, Daniell and others to its heart, encouraging them to build teams in their own light. Yet perhaps it unduly underestimated the merit of men such as Murray-Anderdon and Davey, people who went quietly about the business of building up lasting strength in Somerset cricket. Warm and intimate, putting ''ave a go at 'em' above all else, Somerset set personality above achievement. Valour was to the fore, and possibly this was right. Perhaps they understood Somerset cricket best who believed it could not match powerful rivals save in the heat of a few glorious moments, a good cup run or an occasional cluster of brilliant years. Failing the latter, supporters might settle for plucky fightbacks and irregular conquests. After all, Somerset folk were tolerant, patient and suspicious of committee rule, so that if chaos and failure did not surprise them nor did it, by and large, galvanize them into action. Many have tried to reform this club and several of them advanced it far enough for it to be no more than ten years behind the times, but all have been ultimately frustrated. Decades afterwards Peter Roebuck was rebuked by a senior commentator for criticizing club management. 'Somerset has always been badly run,' said this sage, as if that were an end of the matter. Certainly Somerset has resisted and mistrusted reform, and has never happily embraced business principles. This is a ramshackle club to which bits have been added, here and there, and some removed too. There has never been a grand design. Vested interests and, arguably, a native docility, have prevented a drive towards excellence.

Daniell was no reformer, rather he was an unapologetic reactionary. Since Somerset was facing yet another difficult period he was perhaps the right man, for it was a time for digging in, a time for stirring the spirit of defiance rather than planning a careful advance.

179

Despite this troubled background Somerset enjoyed a reasonable season in 1931, winning six games and rising to thirteenth place, their best result in seven years. It was Jack White's final season as captain and certainly his players were not unduly sorry about that, for they found his manner somewhat grudging.

Somerset's victories owed nothing to their fielding, and so poor was their catching that local newspapers felt called upon to include in their columns a list of those who had most recently allowed chances to elude them. In the pavilion Daniell, The Prophet, muttered that 'You cannot ruddy well win matches if you drop catches'. Five early games were lost although 'Box' Case (who, fielding abominably, had been giving away to sprightlier men) hit two hundreds in three games, and then, despite Young's being too ill to play, a revival began, as Longrigg hit a splendid hundred against Yorkshire, Frank Lee had his best season so far, and Wellard, after a dismal 1930, took a swagful of wickets.

Spectators enjoyed most of all a rousing win over The Saucemen – Worcestershire – for it was a dramatic victory snatched with minutes to spare as Longrigg and Wellard, opening the innings, launched a violent assault. Both men emerged half-dressed to acknowledge the cheers of an enthusiastic crowd.

Such moments apart, Somerset cricket was largely humdrum and (as ever) heavily dependent upon a few truly competitive players. Cricket was a profession now and at night players and umpires would sip beer and chat, unless it had been a final day, which meant piling into trains and wiling away hours playing brag, a dangerous occupation when in the company of Wellard or White. Apart from Luckes, they drank a lot and, in September, by which time most had concluded that cricket was 'a ruddy silly game anyhow', they would sleep, and wonder if their contracts were to be renewed and if their friends in the real world still had a job and a living wage.

Somerset bade farewell to two men of differing dispositions in September 1931. Guy Earle was forty years of age and increasingly susceptible to the lure of fishing. He scored just one hundred for Somerset but no man in England provided richer entertainment, no man better represented an age when individuals did not count for much, when results and figures were less important, when cricket, like battle, was a challenge to the spirit of those who had not yet heard of trench warfare.

George Hunt departed too, sacked by his employers with

much regret and as an economy measure. For years he had been a struggling professional, taking a few rather expensive wickets with his steady outswingers and collecting a few runs with his careful batting. In 233 games he took 386 wickets and scored 4,952 runs, respectable figures which hide a gradual decline. Sadly Hunt, who was a quiet man at a gregarious club, did not survive long enough to be awarded a benefit, but a collection was taken for him in 1932 so his efforts were not entirely unrewarded. A good fellow, he had been a fine soccer player and now found a second career as a carpet salesman. Five years later his brother, Bert, played eleven times for Somerset, taking 7/49 against Derbyshire in Ilkeston. Bert was an amiable fellow disinclined to complain when catches were missed off his bowling. Perhaps it was just as well he did not try to pursue a career with Somerset. As it was he played long enough to share one of cricket's most improbable partnerships, hitting 2 sixes and 2 fours and watching Horace Hazell, no less, smite 28 in an over off Hedley Verity, whose figures were somewhat alarming – 9 overs 2/89!

Depression gripped England. Queues of unemployed men curled around factory gates where work might be found at a pittance. No longer could Somerset depend upon men born into money, for they too had bills to pay; besides which, public school cricket had fallen far behind the professional game so that only outstanding boys could move directly from school to county cricket. And since ever more fixtures were being organized, Somerset could not rely upon schoolmasters or students either, for they were available for too few games. Somerset was in a cleft stick. Thanks to world-wide economic decline they could not afford to employ many professionals and this at the very time amateurs of any merit were fewest and farthest between.

For once it was not a matter of poor management at Somerset. Hunt was released because income at 20 shillings and expenditure at 20 shillings and 6 pence entails misery. All Somerset could do was sit tight and hope this grim period would pass.

19

Led by lawyers

At heart 'Farmer' White had been a professional for he thought as a professional, led as a professional and his life revolved around cricket. No matter that he was also a farmer: only arbitrary factors such as background and education set him apart from his paid colleagues, turned him into a village squire and as much lord of all he surveyed as ever was Lionel Palairet. Being a professional in approach, he must have viewed his fellow players, especially those incompetent amateurs who cavorted across his stage with a quizzical eye.

Somerset has always taken much from its top players and yet expected them to be as free and easy in their ways as an August amateur (not that the best of them were remotely free or easy). Hardened by his early experiences under Daniell, White had become ever more distant from his players and his severe manner had a dampening effect upon their boisterous enthusiasm. Eager for praise, they found themselves subjected to silence and rebuke. White, no doubt, meant to force them to do better, for he had seen so many of early promise wither and fade. Possibly he was reluctant to give premature credit to talented fellows such as Wellard, Andrews and Frank Lee. Experience had brought scepticism, and if White was not reserved at first he certainly withdrew his emotions towards the end of his period as captain. Somerset boys, professional and amateur, shed no tears when, at the end of 1931, he stood down as captain and was succeeded by Reggie Ingle.

Born in Cornwall, educated at Oundle and Cambridge (where, to his dismay, he had not won a blue in cricket, for the university

182

team was powerful and his performances inadequate), Ingle had been playing for his county since 1923 and had won a reputation as a fearless, mercurial player of jolly temperament whose streak of impetuosity had led him to hook Larwood for 6 at Trent Bridge (a feat matched only by Leslie Ames), to take 70 off a roused Ted McDonald, to hit two hundreds in a county game and to throw away his wicket countless times as following dark whisperings in his head, he tried to clear boundary fieldsmen.

Ingle was a popular rather than an astute captain. Unlike White he could communicate enjoyment and build spirit, and his men raised their games and helped to lift Somerset to seventh in the table. In particular the professionals liked him, especially once he relaxed, for captains in 1932 were supposed to be apart and this did not really suit Ingle. Robertson-Glasgow wrote of Somerset's new captain:

> Ingle needed to catch his proper mood, and could be casual in its pursuit. Far from the field of supposed and immediate play his heart would sometimes conduct his eye on tours of preferable enjoyment. His necessary spur was wrath, no matter whether justified or manufactured on the premises. He was inspired by those scenes of stress and argument that unhook the sensitive, alarm the virtuous, and employ the conversational. For then he could persuade himself that what other batsmen would regard as a routine attempt on the stumps was nothing less than a conspiracy against his existence, and, ripped from a pleasing suggestion of stylishness to the very suburbs of greatness, he would hook Larwood from his eyebrows, shatter the designs of Yorkshiremen, and loudly ask for a fresh guard, as if there had been something rotten about that which the umpire had just given him. Next day, he would be opening telegrams at cover-point, and distantly inquiring of his bowlers whether they would be agreeable to temporary relief.

Like Burrough and Longrigg, who were partners, Ingle was a solicitor working in Bath and its surrounds. He was from a family of lawyers and could find time to play cricket because of the graciousness of his father. He was not an outstanding player, for he lacked the discipline of collecting runs any old how so that his career figures – 9,601 runs at an average hovering around 20 – bear testimony to limitations and to a refusal to live safely within

183

them. A creature of the moment, a player of inspiration, and yet otherwise a solicitor of conservative if not autocratic opinions, it was typical of Ingle that during one of cricket's sporadic calls for brighter play he continued to be caught at long-off nine times before June had turned to July! As captain he believed he must set an example to his men, and his methods if not imaginative were none the less intrepid.

His fellow amateurs were rather more wary of Ingle, whom they suspected had suffered from a sense of inferiority to them ever since failing to win his blue. They thought him an odd cove and a fellow mistrustful of old school ties and inner circles. It was as if he felt he did not belong, that he was standing in for men of supposedly higher calibre, such as Longrigg and Burrough, men with an inside run. Ingle was something of a maverick and felt certain that sooner or later the Establishment would nobble him. Perhaps the thought was father to the deed.

For a time Somerset blossomed under Ingle, as a team is apt to when its shackles are removed. Eight games were won and seven lost in 1932, and this despite Wellard having a dreadful season as a bowler, a season during which he took just 37 expensive wickets. Though White and Hazell, ever improving as a left-arm spinner, took wickets, Somerset's rise owed much to a team effort, for no batsman stood out, no one scoring 1,000 runs in county games, or averaging over 26. Ingle had a group of professionals regularly at his command – notably Wellard, the Lee brothers, Young, Luckes when he was well and Hazell when he was picked, which was usually for away fixtures, White preferring to play at home. Prince Nayudu hit a brutal 130 not out at Weston-super-Mare, defying Ingle's field placements, with a powerful array of shots. Ingle had told Hazell that Nayudu hit hard and straight, and men were positioned accordingly. Hazell's first delivery was a pearler and Nayadu smote it into the cottages at deep mid-wicket. Ingle could field a reasonably consistent if not especially brilliant team and this undoubtedly helped. Lancashire were beaten for the first time since 1903, Essex were beaten by an innings, Jack and Frank Lee adding 234 for the first wicket, and Somerset drew with Gloucestershire and Hampshire. Spirits high, Somerset also managed to record three narrow victories in August to round off a season in which achievement for once exceeded expectation.

Not that 1932 was all sunshine and roses, for at Cowbridge in

July Somerset managed to be bowled out for 88 and 40 by Mercer and Clay, exploiting a drying pitch, and this despite sterling batting by White (24) and Wellard (27).

Somerset's financial position was still parlous, membership having slipped to 1,931, and Ingle was asked to play as many amateurs as possible, a request he seems to have ignored. Tasmanian-born Keith Linney played a few games as a professional though in six summers of occasional appearances he was unable to establish himself. Luckily, and much to the satisfaction of Newton, White, Palairet, Poyntz and Daniell, all still on the committee, two promising amateurs did appear in the persons of Norman 'Mandy' Mitchell-Innes, who had played as a sixteen-year-old from Sedbergh in 1931, and Jake Seamer (nineteen) from Marlborough, who was also to win a blue at Oxford and to captain Somerset but whose cricket career was otherwise to be rather less distinguished. Ken Kinnersley, a nineteen-year-old from Clifton was tried too and found wanting. Born in Samoa, Kinnersley had a solid defence, and bowled his spinners well enough to take 3/40 and 2/53 against India at Clarence Park. In the end it was not to be, for he played only seven matches after 1932 and then moved to Devon.

Nevertheless Somerset was fortunate to be able to include such schoolboy promise in its ranks, for Mitchell-Innes was immensely gifted and Seamer was proud of his Cider County origins. Alas neither could find time to play much county cricket for they had to earn a living and after university they were off to Sudan where the blues governed the browns, and where Mitchell-Innes once scored a hundred before breakfast, games beginning early in that hot part of the world. Thirty years earlier both men could have expected to assist Somerset so long as they had the talent to do so, and probably a few seasons longer too. Times had changed.

Arthur Wellard was nearly sacked at the end of the 1932 season, and Somerset were to be grateful that no such hasty decision was reached for in 1933 he became the second Somerset cricketer after Jack White (1929 and 1930) to complete the double of 1,000 runs and 100 wickets, a combination within reach now that county fixtures had increased to twenty-eight. Previously Len Braund had done so in all first-class contests as distinct from Somerset games alone. Only three other men – Bill Andrews, Ken Palmer and Bill Alley – were to reach this celebrated target for their county.

Ingle depended upon Wellard, for White (forty-two), playing

185

when he chose, failed to take 100 wickets for the first time before the Great War, trapping 44 men at 31 runs apiece, and Hazell was just as expensive. Thankfully Luckes was back from his debilitating illness and both Lees were in form so that Somerset, without ever matching their efforts of 1932, could at least hold up their heads in proper company.

Jack Lee scored 193 not out against Worcester at Clarence Park. Frank took 5/53 against Warwickshire and was given the new ball in the following game – which must have surprised him for his bowling singularly lacked venom. In his final summer Tom Young took 90 wickets, 29 catches and scored 951 runs, and this despite tiring in August and in a season when his start had been delayed by an attack of bronchitis.

A small profit had been recorded in 1932 but Somerset was still hanging by a financial thread. This persuaded the committee to take county games out into their county, reasoning that if Mohammed would not go to the mountain it was surely time for the mountain to move.

A game was played at Downside, partly because the head-master, Father Trafford, was well disposed towards cricket in general and Somerset in particular, and partly because the chosen opposition, Glamorgan, were led by Maurice Turnbull, a splendid fellow, a dashing captain and a former pupil of that Benedictine establishment. Turnbull was a brilliant player whose life was cut tragically short by war.

Besides Downside, where every expense was borne by the school, Somerset also spread its wings to Yeovil (in 1935) to Frome and to Wells. Commonly conditions were somewhat primitive. Horace Hazell, who had bowled 61 successive overs from the same end against Warwickshire at Chilvers Coton in particular objected to having to find a penny in order to relieve himself in Wells. Since Somerset were invariably entertaining, if scarcely less often infuriating, this mobility added to their popularity even if it did not substantially improve their books. Somerset continued to play on various grounds dotted around the county until the 1970s, when county fixtures were reduced and costs rose.

Relations between player and club changed significantly as a result of the spread of professionalism and thus a need for a tight financial regime. Somerset's proudest boast was that 'after 39 seasons of first class cricket we remain, in spite of vicissitudes,

186

the most amateur team in the championship'. It was a heartfelt cry. Now they had five or six professionals, not one or two, and were forced, at times, to choose between them. In 1929 Frank Lee had received an extremely terse note from the secretary (Davey) to say that his contract had been terminated. No such treatment had ever been contemplated in regard to such old faithfuls as Tyler, Braund or Robson, and inevitably it changed everything, for Somerset could no longer present itself as a family club but as a club which hired and fired men like any other. It was not a world Somerset officials inhabited easily, for, being somewhat high-handed of manner, they tended to treat their professionals as if they were servants rather than men with a stake in their club, about which many of them felt no less passionately than did those in charge. Fellows such as Harold Gimblett, Bill Andrews and Horace Hazell were to take Somerset cricket with them to their graves. They deserved more consideration than they sometimes received.

In truth from around 1930 the barricades were up between player and committee, barricades which have seldom been moved for long, for, notoriously, players and committee have a want of mutual understanding; whilst, inevitably, a club and an employee are bound, from time to time, to differ, because if they have much in common they also have much over which to argue. Immature management, determined to assert itself, has often reacted too strongly against what it has called player power but what is usually merely an expression of opinion rather in advance of that held at committee level.

George Hunt was quite rightly dismissed at the end of 1931 and Bill Andrews was sacked in 1932. Andrews promptly took up a position in Forfar and, being a consummate publicist and a considerable politician, he telephoned his friends on the staff of Somerset newspapers so that his exploits did not escape the attention of his erstwhile employers.

To suppose that such shifts in relationship did not change everything is an idle fancy and it is a tribute to Somerset that it managed to hold its position as England's best-loved county, a position which owed something to those occasional valorous victories, something to the broad expression of personality to be found in its players, and something to the spirit of usually doomed adventurism which prevailed. People could see that

Somerset, without being especially good at cricket, was full of splendid fellows who did their best, for even the professionals were inclined to live for today and tomorrow be blowed. Nor was this romantic image entirely undeserved. For to concentrate upon internal squabbles and professional insecurities, to underline outdated management techniques, is to miss Somerset cricket as outsiders saw it. Ingle's men were popular throughout the land, and Somerset was everyone's second favourite team.

Stumbling onwards, Somerset sank to fifteenth place in 1934, losing ten games and winning three. Too many catches were dropped, especially off Wellard, who must have yearned for a Braund to hold his snicks. Both brothers Lee had satisfying seasons, scoring seven hundreds between them and thrice adding over 100 in four days of sun-blessed cricket in August. Apart from this pair only Case, whom no one could get out and who could not score runs at respectable pace, reached 1,000 runs for the season. Wellard hit his first hundred, at The Oval, striking one six on to the roof of the East Stand, and Jack White played for MCC against Australia but otherwise local supporters had little of which to boast. Hazell did not do much, and Buse was dropped, a shade prematurely, some thought.

With Bill O'Reilly taking 9/38 Australia was far too strong at Taunton, though Frank Lee carried his bat for 59 out of a total of 116 on a damp pitch. Still Somerset could reflect upon one glorious victory, and settle into winter with the remembrance that it was inflicted upon their nearest neighbour, against whom matches were played to an intensity worthy of Test cricket. At Bristol Somerset had been bowled out for 225 and, trailing by 50 on first innings, they slipped dismally to 37/7, their notoriously long tail exposed once more. And then Case – 'a batsman of unusual style' said *Wisden* – and Michael Bennett joined forces. Launching an improbable counter-attack they added 119 in 90 minutes before Bennett fell, leaving Somerset 100 in front overnight with 2 wickets left to fall. Next morning 'Box' added 35 of the 36 runs scored and reached a meritorious unbeaten 106, much the best innings of his career. Left to chase 143, Gloucestershire collapsed to 30/5 and promptly promoted Tom Goddard to have a go. White told his boundary fieldsman Frank Lee that he would bowl his first two balls down the leg-side and flight his third temptingly wide of off-stump, enticing Goddard to lift a

188

catch straight to him, which is precisely what happened, though umpires had to confer before acknowledging that Lee had taken the catch inside the boundary. Somerset won by 39 runs which cheered everyone up for they had not, of late, been in the habit of beating this foe.

White scored a hundred and took 9/153 as Hampshire were beaten but otherwise Ingle, his own form variable, could not galvanize his weak team.

No one but a fool approached 1935 with any optimism. Somerset was hard up. The old amateurs were gone and new ones kept going to Khartoum, of all places. To hope for much was to live in a land of fantasy populated by those capable of imagining that a farmer's son might suddenly appear on the horizon to demoralize fierce enemies with the cheek of a David confronting Goliath.

But time enough for such nonsense. Meanwhile let us contemplate the new professionals who had appeared at Somerset in the last few summers and thanks to whom Somerset's executive could at least field a team which could give rival counties a game.

20

Professionals

Arthur Wellard deserves a chapter to himself but he would be happy enough to sit beside his fellow professionals who did their best to defy formidable odds during those years of economic destitution, the fraught thirties. Nevertheless he was one of a handful of giants to grace Somerset cricket.

As a boy Wellard did not play any organized cricket, for his school in Bexley lacked the facilities. Boys played pick-up matches of course but until happening by Bexley Club ground at eighteen years of age Wellard had seen little serious cricket. Finding men practising, he took to chasing and retrieving balls for them and, invited to turn over his arm, made a mark as one with a natural affinity for the game. Alas, Kent were not so easily impressed and took no interest in Wellard, whose aspirations were thwarted by this disregard for one who could play only as a professional. And then came a three-day trial at Somerset in 1926, a chance which he took. Lord Harris raised a fearful row about Wellard's going to Somerset but Daniell and his cronies absorbed that easily enough.

While he was qualifying Wellard stayed in Weston-super-Mare with one Bill Andrews, himself a cricket professional with East Coker (much to the horror of his parents who, like thousands before and after, wanted him to find a steady job). With his smart suits, in which loose change endlessly jangled, his honest and yet crafty air, and his capable and independent manner, Wellard greatly impressed Andrews. He could drink with the best and yet was always one pint behind his accomplices. As a cricketer he would bowl all day, with strains duly strapped, his huge hands and high action sending the ball swinging away off an unerring length towards his fallible slip cordon. He learnt to bowl spin as he aged, and to play straight too, so that his sixes, with which he scored 25 per cent of his 12,500 runs, were made with correct swings rather than wild swipes.

Wellard was an uncomplaining man who took life as he found it without ever entirely trusting it to direct his affairs. As Eric Hill has written:

> He was a countryman at heart, relishing the hunting, shooting and fishing people and chatter that often came his way, and he surely had the countryman's appreciation of what was right, wrong, prudent and profitable. What he did not know about horse-racing, poker, gambling generally, snooker, skittles and social drinking was not really worth knowing. With his sharp cockney accent softened by long observant contact with the West Country burr, he spoke with a quiet courteous manner that frequently belied the pointed content of it all . . . A real gentleman doing a job he loved.

Never giving himself away, Wellard did not quite embrace Somerset. Reluctant to give up his sweet-shop in Sutton, he did not move to the county but stayed in hotels in Taunton instead. Whenever Somerset played in his neck of the woods colleagues, and especially Bill Andrews, would stay with him, saving on expenses, though risking finding Wellard's false teeth in their bed, a risk undertaken on northern away matches with equanimity and generally considered to be worth a few pounds.

Beside those activities chronicled by Eric Hill, Wellard was also reported to be the best poacher in Somerset, and certainly he often took Horace Hazell shooting on the flats east of Taunton, a foray which commonly ended with a few drinks at the Prince Alfred pub.

For Somerset Wellard took 1,517 wickets at 24 apiece and scored 11,462 runs at an average approaching 20. Despite intense competition and slipshod catching he won selection for England in 1937 and once against Australia in 1938, when he took the wickets of Hassett, Badcock and Fingleton at some cost, and struck 42 runs too. It was not, apparently, enough. Twice in county cricket he struck five consecutive sixes – off T. R. Armstrong and Woolley, a feat easier to accomplish on the small grounds of that period.

He played until 1950, a longevity owing much to his fitness and adaptability, for he took up off-spin bowling and he was devastated when, finally, Somerset released him, wandering around in shock and with his shoelaces hanging loose by way of protest. He swore never to return to the club, as others have done since, but time healed the wound and he was back eventually and still as popular as ever. Later he played for the Gaieties eleven beside such as Harold Pinter, who has written warmly of Arthur and his ways. He died in 1980 as a man who had never betrayed himself.

Frank and Jack Lee were Londoners too. They were well-brought-up lads with the politeness to be found in those days, trained to respect their elders and yet with a cockney wit which helped them to detect humour in banality, hope in absurdity and fast horses in a slow race. Both served on the groundstaff at Lord's, where their elder brother, Harry, played county cricket and in whose footsteps they were quietly keen to follow. Frustrated in this ambition, Frank began to qualify for Somerset, and made his debut in 1929.

Then in 1930 Frank appeared to fail. So miserable were his efforts that year that Somerset sent him back to Bath, where he prepared pitches, bowled to members and scored hundreds. With no contract for 1931 he concentrated upon improving his game and did so well that two Bath amateurs with county experience, Sidney Considine and Stanley Amor, urged Somerset to give him another chance. Slowly Frank built a career as a steadfast, unfussy opening batsman who would wear down the attack with staunch defence so that others, lesser men by and large, might score freely down the order. Typically when he scored his first county hundred and received an award of £50 he gave a third of it to Arthur Wellard, who had started at the same time and whose support had been important.

Frank was also helped, more vigorously it must be said, by Tom Young, who once spent a morning telling Frank on no account to play back to Tate and who, upon seeing his charge duly fooled into retreat and comprehensively bowled, so berated Lee that he never ventured back to Tate again. Determined to earn a living in cricket, Frank was a learner and a survivor. He played 328 games for Somerset and scored 15,000 runs including twenty-three hundreds at an average just below 30: respectable considering the disasters usually occurring around him. Somewhat to his surprise (for he was not educated in the ways of Somerset cricket) he also found himself summoned to the bowling crease from time to time and quite often he stood in for Luckes behind the stumps, two assignments he carried out with characteristic simplicity and effectiveness. He ended his cricketing days as a famous umpire, regularly joining Frank Chester at Test matches, and retired to his beloved London as one who had with phlegmatic temperament managed to absorb those sudden changes of fortune which Somerset cricket thrusts at a man with a frequency matched only by the experiences of a member of a government in Italy.

Jack Lee, by three years the elder, arrived in Somerset and began playing in 1925. He was not quite so secure a batsman as his brother and depended upon his inviting and hitherto unsuspected bowling skills as he forged a career for himself in county cricket. He had been a fine soccer player for Arsenal, had qualified for Somerset by residence (the club paying part of his wages as he tended to Lansdown's ground) and survived year by year at Somerset until, following his benefit in 1935, he accepted a job as coach at Mill Hill. Lee asked Daniell if he should take the position and was told he would be a fool not to. Fellow professionals suspected that Daniell wanted to be rid of Lee, who was a handy rather than commanding cricketer, because Jack had once refused to follow Daniell's instructions to hit out, returning to the professional changing room, slamming the door and growling, '*That*'s what I think of John Daniell'.

This story may be apocryphal and the professional interpretation of Lee's departure may have been unfairly hostile to Daniell. It was, though, a significant and unsurprising reaction, given the change in relations between player and committee and the varying views of cricket held by professional cricketers and a rich amateur administrator used to a different sort of game.

Daniell's advice to Lee was sound. Mill Hill were offering a job for life and a house to go with it; here was a rare chance for a moderate professional cricketer to secure his future and Jack Lee took it. Perhaps Somerset were not eager to keep him, and certainly Daniell was a disciplinarian, none the less it is hard to avoid the conclusion that Somerset professionals read too much into Jack Lee's departure. No doubt it was not managed with especial sensitivity. Far too often amateurs fail to understand that professionals want to belong to the family, feel as if they do, and upon being cast out, are overwhelmed by a sense of rejection. Able to promise Lee nothing, Daniell should have told him how much he would be missed and advised him on no account to forsake this opportunity of retiring while he was ahead.

Daniell can be blamed on one score. Until Longrigg assumed the captaincy in 1938 Somerset professionals were retained on shamefully short contracts, few lasting more than a year. This was a bone of contention with Jack Lee, Wellard and others who rightly objected to being given so little support even when their performances were strong. Daniell's failure to offer enduring contracts to distinguished players smacks of a high-handed attitude calculated to provoke unease between player and club. It was, perhaps, symptomatic of the club that in 1935 professionals were forbidden to sign autographs on the ground and amateurs were asked not to do so.

Jack Lee scored 8,000 runs for Somerset in 241 games and took nearly 500 wickets, a notable record for a determined cricketer. He died on the beaches of Normandy in 1944 and a benefit match was played in Bath for his widow.

Wally Luckes, born in London, settled in Bridgwater, defied bad health to play for Somerset from 1924 until Harold Stephenson arrived to replace him in 1949. Luckes played in 365 games, scored 5,640 runs (average 16) and claimed 827 victims, a tally surpassed only by Stephenson amongst Somerset wicket-keepers. A non-drinker, and blessed with a gentle temperament, Luckes was an unobtrusive guardian of the stumps and a typically inventive keeper–batsman who made a noble 90 batting at number 10 in 1938 in a famous game at Leicester. He had also scored a hundred against Kent the year before, a hundred hastened by Les Ames who, finding Luckes had never reached three figures, introduced weak bowlers to help him through the nineties.

Had his heart been better Luckes could have scored more runs. As it was, doctors insisted he drop down the order after his sickness in 1930. He was never entirely well and John Barnwell, a dashing amateur colleague, remembers calling for a quick single, following which 'Wally turned green and they had to cart him off to hospital'. Undeterred, Luckes played hockey during the winter, though he was constantly penalized for raising his stick like a cricket bat, worked for the electric light people in Bridgwater and lived to see his eighty-first birthday! A faithful servant, he absorbed Somerset cricket and was dreadfully disappointed when Stephenson arrived to take his place. A dependable man, he adopted Somerset as his home and never went back to London.

21

A bright day dawns

Membership dropped steeply in 1935 and yet Somerset was solvent for the first time in many years. A profit of £1,519 was recorded and the overdraft dramatically reduced, good news for a club which owned its own ground.

Nor were those members disappointed by the entertainment provided. Arthur Wellard was now a formidable hitter, having forsaken his somewhat erratic 9 iron for a skimming, thunderous wooden club. In 1935 he struck 72 sixes and four times in these pre-war summers he broke 50, a total passed by no other batsman until Ian Botham, returning refreshed from a winter's break from cricket if not notoriety, smashed every record in 1985. Wellard was helped by short boundaries but in Manchester he smote 112 in 90 minutes of calculated violence, an innings C. L. R. James described as extraordinary.

And yet it was not a satisfactory season, save for Wellard and a certain local débutant soon to be mentioned. Supporters bemoaned a lack of spirit, complained about the passing of the 'old devil – have a go at 'em.' Faces were long, spirits damp. It was not entirely Ingle's fault. Trying to set an example of selfless and dashing play, he repeatedly lost his wicket to bold shots. On the greensward he continued to field well, off it he could curse, his team noted, for five minutes without ever repeating himself. He was doing his best but slowly his task was wearing him down, for every Somerset captain begins determined to sort it all out and most usually grow weary of the struggle, find themselves fighting on too many fronts; for a county captain is not a senior man in his cricket club, rather his position resembles that of a

195

head prefect, someone to marshal the troops while decisions are taken elsewhere.

Moreover, with so little talent at his disposal, especially in the batting department, and with no depth whatsoever (for club cricket was as weak then as it was always to be), Ingle's energies were inevitably spent upon trying to shore up what existed rather than creating a braver, newer world. Slowly his own form was to betray him, so that he was scarcely worth his place in the team, a vulnerable position for any leader whose team is not powerful enough to accommodate a player out of sorts. Predictably, too, people began to blame the captain for Somerset's endless struggles, for Englishmen are trained to believe in a class bred to lead. For what else has it all been about?

As usual a few rays of sunshine could be detected amidst the gloom. At twenty years of age and just four summers after first appearing for Somerset, Norman Stewart Mitchell-Innes was picked to play for England against H. F. Wade's South Africans in Nottingham. Born in Calcutta, educated at Sedbergh, 'Mandy' was already a considerable sportsman, having captained Scottish boys at golf and won blues at golf and cricket while at Brasenose College, where he was currently a second-year undergraduate. In May of this season he hit a typically sparkling 168 against South Africa for his university, an innings which convinced watching sages that he was made of the right stuff.

Mandy's Test début was unremarkable. Batting at second wicket down he scored 5 before falling leg before to Mitchell. South Africa followed on but a match spoilt by rain petered out into a draw. Naturally he was picked to play in the second Test at Lord's. Unfortunately Mandy suffered from hay fever which restricted his cricketing activities at the height of summer and as the Lord's Test approached he thought it wise to contact Sir Pelham Warner to warn that he might be a risk. Warner told him to stand down and E. R. T. Holmes was summoned in his place. In the event Mitchell-Innes felt fully fit and on the Saturday of the Test he scored an outstanding hundred at The Oval. Holmes scored 10 and 8 and was pictured next morning being introduced to his King. Mitchell-Innes stayed with Holmes, a great chum, at his London house during that momentous week in both their careers.

Mitchell-Innes never played for England again. In truth he did not play all that much first-class cricket, though his career stretched

196

from 1931 to 1949. Appearing sporadically his performances for Somerset paled beside those given at university, when he was at his peak and playing regularly. Two things defeated him: first, no cure could be found for his ailment, though large rewards were offered by Somerset and though he went on a long sea voyage to New Zealand, where he thought of settling; second, he had to earn a living and accordingly took a position in the Sudan, where his quiet authority helped to settle numerous tribal disputes. With his friend Jake Seamer he did play some idiosyncratic cricket in the ferocious heat of Khartoum but service insisted that games be but idle pastimes in a hurried world.

As a cricketer Mitchell-Innes was a simple, elegant player with a hint of hauteur about his batting and manner in the field. While respecting his skills some thought him aloof but probably it was merely reticence with strangers, for Seamer was a democratic sort with little time for pretension and he took to Mitchell-Innes as a dolphin takes to a breaking wave.

Years later as Somerset scrummaged desperately around for an appropriate man to be their captain and secretary, a position created by the faith held in amateur captains by the executive committee, Mitchell-Innes offered to return to county cricket. By now an elder statesman, in cricket at any rate, he said he expected to be paid £1,000 a year, rather more than Somerset were prepared to offer. No compromise could be found and the chance slipped away. Charlie Palmer (from Worcestershire), Trevor Bailey and Richie Benaud were all sounded out at various times but none of them ever agreed terms so that, eventually, Somerset were forced to appoint professional captains. But this is to jump far ahead.

Other amateurs were appearing in 1935 and playing a few games with various degrees of naïvety and competence. John Barnwell, educated like the Palairets at Repton, and settled in Somerset, was summoned by telegraph for the local derby game in Bristol. Lightning fast at cover, and always nattily dressed and wearing a cap speaking of broad experiences in amateur cricket, Barnwell began his career with a handsome drive to the boundary. Attempting to repeat this glorious shot he was bowled – 'my first lesson', he later admitted. No doubt Somerset's professionals, who had seen a bit, were rather wary of this cheerful, innocent, rather inadequate cricketer who had joined them in their rough-and-tumble world. For his part Barnwell, now

197

on Somerset's cricket committee, found the professionals to be 'a grand lot' ready to help if asked. He discovered too, that several of them could drink on the grand scale, especially those willing opening bowlers Wellard and Andrews, who had now returned as a vastly improved cricketer.

In time Barnwell too was to be asked if he would consider leading Somerset. Regretfully he replied that he was too busy 'breeding silver foxes' and could not spare the time. Once again a living had to be earned by a man who, in previous eras, might have expected to play for years. Not that Barnwell was so serious a loss as Mitchell-Innes, or Greswell for that matter, for his technique was not tight enough to score consistently in the county game.

Ronald Gerrard played three games in 1935 too. A boy from Taunton School, he died during the Second World War, in the Middle East, at the age of thirty.

And Dar Lyon was back, briefly. He had played some cricket on matting in Africa but was now a shadow of his former self and scored a sad pair at Lord's on a bad pitch. Soon he too was to volunteer his services as an amateur captain of Somerset and to be rejected. He wanted to succeed Ingle when he resigned in 1937 but his path was blocked by Longrigg who, in some opinions, had set his eyes upon the position and did not intend to let so doubtful an outsider frustrate his ambitions.

None of these men, not even Mitchell-Innes or mighty Wellard, was remotely Somerset's most famous cricketer in 1935. It was not much of a season – Ingle's team finished fourteenth – yet it contained one of cricket's most extraordinary events. A star was, apparently, born.

During April a youngster called Harold Gimblett had been employed as a 'ground bowler' for three weeks at thirty shillings a week. Somerset officials noted his talent, having heard rumours of intrepid performances for Somerset Stragglers and others in local cricket. In 1932, batting as a schoolboy in a red-and-black cap, Gimblett hit 142 in 75 minutes for the Stragglers against Wellington School. A year later he smote a respectable Straggler attack for an astonishing and audacious hundred, whereupon, hinting at wilfulness, he promptly walked off the field and had to be persuaded to return which, eventually, he did . . . lobbing a gentle catch next ball to end an innings of 80 minutes in which 168 runs were scored. Gimblett was by no means unknown amongst cognoscenti in West Somerset.

Still his trial was not a success and, with no money to spare, Daniell sent him back to his farm, pausing to tell his committee that Gimblett had 'possibilities' of developing into a useful cricketer.

With a constantly changing batting order and with too little talent, Somerset did not begin well in 1935. By May their spirits were languishing and, as he prepared to face Essex at Frome, Ingle found that he could scarcely raise a side. Hawkins was injured and he was a man short. And then he remembered Gimblett. Somerset's fielding was woeful, and this sprightly youth might at least buck it up. Accordingly messages were sent to Harold and arrangements made that he should meet Wally Luckes in Bridgwater.

It is a famous tale. Gimblett missed his bus from his small farm under the Quantocks and had to hitch a lift to his meeting point. Reggie Ingle, expecting little of this rustic youth with a fresh face and a curiously resigned air, asked him to bat at number 8. Nichols, bowling fast, took early wickets and though Frank Lee reached 41 and Box Case 35, Somerset sank in its customary way on a doubtful pitch to a precarious 107/6. Enter Gimblett bearing a bat borrowed from Arthur Wellard and with a head full of dire warnings about 'googlies' (a term he had not hitherto encountered). Uninhibited, unabashed, Gimblett, perhaps feeling at home on that unpretentious pitch, set about himself and commenced belting Essex's respected bowling all over the field, and all with the detached air of one plucking apples from a tree.

Nothing could be more simple. Gimblett hated fuss, hated show, sought anonymity and yet notoriety too. He wanted to be noticed and yet to be private, a dichotomy which led to a tension enduring throughout his troubled life.

Later Gimblett said that 'except for the atmosphere being different I felt no more concern than if I'd been playing for my club'. It was an unduly precocious statement and a significant one, for this was ever to be Gimblett's view of cricket, an uncompromising view which brought him countless runs brilliantly made and led to an abbreviation of his Test career.

Gimblett rushed to 50 in 28 minutes and to 99 in 55 minutes of chanceless, nerveless batting. Losing the bowling, he did not score for three overs but at last he was there after a mere 63 minutes at the crease. Unbelievably it was the fastest debut hundred recorded to date in cricket history. Emerging from the beer tent, farmers cheered and locals stood to give a rousing reception. Hands were shaken. It had all happened so quickly. He scored 123 out of 175 in 80 minutes, his principal strokes being three sixes and seventeen fours. *Wisden* said, 'possessing a very upright stance, Gimblett cut, drove, pulled and hooked in a manner that set cricket circles talking for weeks'.

So it did, one critic writing that 'a new star of phenomenal brilliance' had arrived. Gimblett, of course, detested the ensuing rumpus (or thought he did) yet as Somerset recorded a notable victory, Bill Andrews thrashing a barely less vigorous 71 and Wellard, Hazell and Jack Lee finishing the job, Harold greeted photographers who dashed to the scene in vast numbers with the news that a guinea must be paid for his portrait. At heart he did not trust the 'buggers', or life for that matter. Apropriately a verse was written to celebrate this famous victory:

'*Harold Gimblett's Hundred*' by John Arlott

Bicknoller was his village, Harold Gimblett was his name,
Farming was his working day, but cricket was his game.
When he was but twenty, and first played for Somerset,
He played the mighty innings, that we remember yet

Chorus

Oh! he struck them with skill, and he struck them with power
Times out of number
He gave them Stogumber
And he knocked up a century in just on the hour

Stogumber is the village where Jack White used to live;
But for cricketers in Somerset, that's the name they give
To the fierce cross-batted stroke they will use forever more
Swinging it right off the stumps, and past long leg for four

Young Gimblett went to Taunton to have a county trial.
John Daniell broke the news to him, they did not like his style;
Then a man cried off and he was called back to the room:

200

'You'll play for us tomorrow, against Essex, down at Frome'.

On May 18th, '35 at six he left the farm
On the way to catch the bus, his cricket bag under his arm,
Soon to drink pavilion tea, though he felt a little grim
With cricketers, who up till then, had been but names to him.

Somerset had Ingle, the two Lees, Frank and Jack,
The famous Farmer White and Arthur Wellard in attack.
For Essex – Pearce, O'Connor, the Smiths, Peter and Ray,
Eastman, Wade and Cutmore – they all were there that day.

There was Nichols of England too – the mighty 'Maurice Nick' –
His arms were long, his shoulders wide, his pace was mighty
    quick.
When Somerset went in to bat, his slips held all the snicks;
The score, when Gimblett's turn came round, was 107 for six.

The crowd had never heard of him, they did not know his name,
But since he was from Somerset, they clapped him just the same.
They saw him miss the spin off Smith, but very quickly then
For a single, pushed off Nichols, they clapped him once again.

In with Arthur Wellard, biggest hitter of them all,
Young Gimblett soon outscored him – he was middling the ball
When Smith tossed up his googly – that ball of mystery
He landed it Stogumber, on top of the old marquee!

Wellard went and Luckes came – Gimblett reached his fifty –
Luckes went, Bill Andrews then, played it cool and thrifty.
Nichols took the bright new ball, and Gimblett drove him
    straight;
When he dropped it short, he hooked him, and cut him
    neat and late.

The chilly crowd had watched him while he had changed
    the game,
And now they felt they knew him and they shouted out
    his name.
For one fine savage over, Nichols checked his score
But then the young man cracked him through the old
    pavilion door.

201

A different situation fell on the Frome ground then,
Because the tins there only marked the score up ten by ten;
Of tension in the dressing room, the team could give no sign –
There was no way of telling him his score was ninety-nine!

But Nichols bowled and Gimblett then drove him clean for
   four.
He'd done it – scored a century – the crowd let out a roar.
And to this day you may read it, it's in the record book,
An hour and just three minutes is all the time he took.

That night, all through Somerset from Minehead 'cross to
   Street,
Bristol down to Wellington, they talked of this great feat.
And thousands ever since have claimed that they were there
   to see
Harold Gimblett, from Bicknoller, make cricket history.

Nonchalant, even cussed, Gimblett struck R. W. V. Robins
for 6 into the professionals' enclosure at Lord's in his second
game, but already he was complaining of an injury. Nor did his
wonderful form continue, for soon enough his scores dwindled, a
dismal sequence of 2, 10, 0, 6, 5, 0, 11*, 0, 4, 18, 11, 2, 61, 8, 4, 7,
being recorded. No one was surprised, of course, by this failure and
it was widely supposed that this youngster had been found out, that
cricket was demanding its dues. Probably it was not so simple, for
Gimblett's batting belied his character. Uncomfortable on stages
and yet feeling he deserved to be a leading actor, Gimblett had
a streak of self-destruction, a part of his temperament which was
determined to defy prediction, and blow the consequences.

At Barber's Hall in the City of London that December Gimblett
was presented with the Lawrence Trophy and a token for 100
guineas, a reward instigated by Sir Walter Lawrence in 1934 to
discourage stonewallers. A distinguished congregation gathered
in their dinner jackets and speeches were made by politicians and
rear admirals. In such company Gimblett must have felt like a child
creeping on to a dark stage only for a spotlight to be turned upon
him.

And so began a remarkable, often brilliant career which was
to bestow upon Somerset 49 centuries and 21,142 runs, most of
them gloriously made. Too early perhaps, he was compared to

Jack Hobbs, too early men such as Plum Warner spoke of his 'authentic genius'. *Punch* went so far as to celebrate his achievements in verse:

> How come is that this agricultural youth
> Can meet the wickedest ball and neatly scotch it
> Simple and elementary is the truth
> His Gimblett eyes enable him to Watchet!

Ever after Gimblett's career was to advance fitfully, threatening to touch greatness only to retreat. He played in just three Tests, the first of these against India at Lord's when he finished a low-scoring match by belting an unbeaten 67 off bowlers as consummately skilled as Nissar and Amar Singh. And yet he fielded badly for England, dropping catches and appearing lazy, entirely contrary to the opinion widely held of him at Somerset that he was the greatest fielder since Hammond, whose majestic walk to the crease was recalled by Gimblett's scarcely less proud approach. A picture of an uneasy man emerges from sundry almost wilful failures in Test trials and in representative games. Criticisms were deeply felt and deeply resented, as with one remark made by Warner when he lost his wicket to an early hook in an important game: 'it was both the wrong ball and the wrong time to hook'.

In truth Gimblett had flaws of personality which prevented his acknowledged greatness finding expression. Arms like tree trunks helped him to hit the ball formidably hard and hinted at a village blacksmith born to orthodoxy, but Gimblett was not so straightforward a man. Inclined to bottle up his emotions, given to worrying terribly about his cricket, insecure in his talent, in his relationships and his position, he could explode in sudden anger or hide away suffering from some imagined slight. An independent streak led him to speak his mind – 'putting his cards on the table', Cecil Buttle called it – which upset diehards who expected professionals to be subservient. In short he could be moody, especially later in his career, and few felt easy in his company after the war.

Gimblett may sound a prickly character. If he sounds difficult or unpleasant then a disservice has been done. He was a marvellous player, especially for his native county, whose hopes he so often carried and which he served so nobly. Gimblett was a man whose faults were obvious and important because he was a powerful presence in a dressing-room and the atmosphere changed with his moods. Moreover he carried such a burden for so long that colleagues and captains felt dreadfully let down whenever he disappointed.

Plainly this was a troubled man. He had attended a minor public school and felt the divide between amateur and professional keenly, for the divide was great and yet small. He could have been an amateur himself, for was not Jack White also a farmer? He could not see why he should respect fools in office or colleagues of indifferent standard who owed their selection to their breeding. In time, especially after the war, during which he was in the fire service and saw many dreadful things, Gimblett began to feel even more an outcast, a man beloved by his public and misunderstood by those around him. Pessimistic, tense, Gimblett eventually broke down and was given shock treatment in a mental hospital. He left Somerset in painful circumstances and his attitude to the club thereafter surged between bitterness and profound affection. To the sorrowful end he was independent, wilful, separated from the Establishment, for whose chilly embrace he yearned, a fundamentally pleasant man who found in cricket the best and worst of times, and who gave to cricket much joy, laughter and consternation.

Two other events of 1935 must be remarked upon. Somerset's games at Yeovil and at Wells ended in two days, partly because county batsmen were at sixes and sevens with the LBW rule, partly because the pitches crumbled as pitches did before so much Surrey loam was used. At Wells a Yorkshireman, Ernest Falck, scored 28 out of Somerset's 56. It was to be his highest score. And Somerset arrived at Cambridge and found themselves four men short and promptly asked four undergraduates to play. Even for Somerset it was a bit much for it was after all 1935 not 1895.

By 1936 Gimblett was opening the innings for Somerset, a course advocated by Arthur Newton, and playing against Mitchell-Innes for The Players, failing dismally and apparently disdainfully. Gimblett scored a hundred in Somerset's first game against India, and with Horace Hazell taking 87 wickets and Arthur Wellard snaring wickets and clouting sixes Somerset had an exciting season, one which revived the fighting qualities of yesteryear much to the delight of large and enthusiastic crowds, particularly at Weston-super-Mare where all three games ended in victory, Hazell taking 20 wickets.

Rising seven places to finish seventh, Somerset won nine games and lost ten. Only one county was beaten more often and none played cricket of such drama. For once Somerset could field a fine pair of openers with bat and ball, and though Ingle was forced to pick thirty-four men at least he had a core of regular players of good quality. This talent was supplemented in August by the arrival of several amateurs of reputations and skill, notably R. J. O. Meyer, a Cambridge graduate lately in India and now founding a school in Somerset, Mitchell-Innes and Bunty Longrigg. With Jack Lee available for a few games too Somerset managed to win five of its final nine fixtures.

It was a splendid summer. Reggie Ingle chased around the field to catch Phil Mead's cap which had been blown off by a gust of wind, and he promptly caught Mead next ball.

Gimblett scored 84 runs in 18 scoring shots during an innings against Northamptonshire and Wellard hit 5 sixes in an over off Derbyshire's Armstrong as Ingle's men completed a double over that year's champion club. Chasing 271 in a low-scoring game at Wells, where there was no sightscreen and where the scoreboard was deficient (to put it mildly), Wellard entered at 140/5 and proceeded to thunder his way to 86 out of 102 runs scored in 62 minutes. He collected 74 runs in 15 strokes and older inhabitants of Wells still recall jumping over fences into gardens to recapture blackened cricket balls. Meanwhile Arthur, in Robertson-Glasgow's words, appeared as 'unruffled as the West front of Wells Cathedral'.

Horace Hazell, Somerset's rotund and amiable spinner, was not quite so calm, being of the opinion that number 11 was no place for a notorious bunny, for was not every close game decided with this rabbit at the crease? As crises arose he was apt to stride around muttering 'it's coming, I can feel it coming, it's going to be close'. This time he was right, and he joined Peter McRae, a new amateur with 6 still needed. Hazell, who was not a man impressed by half-measures, duly belted two boundaries off Townsend whereupon he and McRae were carried from the field by cheering spectators. Derbyshire, let it be said, were evidently displeased to lose a game they had contested with the utmost

205

intensity.

A profit of £475 was recorded and the appeal to raise £3,000 launched years earlier was now only £460 shy of its target. Membership was falling still, but a few more seasons such as this would certainly provoke a revival. Repairs were made to the roof of the Shilling Stand – later to be called the Two Bob Stand as prices rose after the war – and there was talk of the Weston festival moving away from Clarence Park to a bigger ground better suited to staging cricket matches, a change staunchly resisted by J. C. White, who thought Clarence Park to be lovely.

Besides these famous amateurs already mentioned, two others first appeared in 1936. George Rowdon was a splendid cricketer who scored umpteen hundreds for Midsomer Norton. An elegant batsman, his solitary chance in county cricket took him to a green Colchester wicket upon which he defied Farnes and Nichols for an hour. But Somerset could not afford to offer terms and though Essex expressed an interest, Rowdon returned to his family plumbing business and was heard of no more. He scored 11 runs for Somerset.

Peter McRae, born in Argentina, was to play twenty-five games for Somerset until war broke in 1939. A dashing centre-threequarter, one dangerous enough to earn an England trial, McRae was an immensely popular, gregarious and brave man who played county cricket whenever his medical commitments allowed, for he was trained as a doctor. One chum, Hugh Watts, played with him in 1939 and recalled being joined at breakfast by a dishevelled Peter McRae, 'one of the gentlest and most charming men I ever met'. Finding two breakfasts on Watts's bill, puzzled Somerset officials asked him to cough up an extra 7s 6d, which he duly did, Watts not having 'the heart to tell the Brigadier [Lancaster] that it was Peter after a night out'.

McRae scored 972 runs in his 45 innings and he recorded Somerset's last hundred before the war. It was to be his last innings of substance for he lost his life while serving as a ship's doctor in Russian waters in 1944. R. C. Robertson-Glasgow has written touchingly and tellingly of McRae:

In February 1944, Surgeon Lieutenant F. M. McRae, at the age of twenty-eight, was lost at sea after the *Mahratta* had been twice hit by torpedoes on a Northern convoy to Russia, and very many who knew and admired him would, perhaps, like to know the little, yet so much, which could later be added to the official story.

The first torpedo struck soon after dusk, doing enough damage for the captain to order 'abandon ship.' While the boats were being lowered the second hit midships, smashing all the boats and killing most of the crew. Seventeen survivors scrambled on to a crowded Carley Float with their doctor, McRae. Suddenly the doctor said: 'I appear to be in the way here,' and as if he were interrupting some private matter, slipped into the water. Rescue craft soon arrived, but McRae was not seen again.

To all games, including life, 'Peter' McRae had the easy approach of the all-rounder. Coming from Christ's Hospital to St Mary's, he early made a name as a Rugby centre three-quarter, and was a member of the St Mary's team when they won the Hospitals Cup for six consecutive seasons.

Sure of hand, and a strong tackler, he had an acute sense in attack and a baffling swerve. He played in one International Trial match, and would surely have won his England cap but for injury. Considering how often he was ill at school and later, it was remarkable that he should have played Rugby at all.

At cricket he played for Somerset, for whom he was qualified by residence. He was worth 30 or 40 runs before he ever took guard, being a superb fielder at cover or extra-cover point. His batting was graceful and correct, but lively; and his form in the season 1939 showed that, granted opportunity, he was heading for an established excellence. He played twenty innings for Somerset in 1939, scoring 608 runs for an average of 30.40, including 107 at his home town, Taunton, against Hampshire, and he finished third to H. Gimblett and F. S. Lee in the County averages.

In Squash Rackets, which he took to last of all his games, he quickly reached the first rank, captaining Scotland in international matches, and being highly reckoned by the then world champion, F. D. Amr Bey.

Praise of those who, in life, stand far beyond the need of it must have a sadly formal ring when they are gone; but, in the case of 'Peter' McRae, his friends will remember and agree that none who knew him could resist him, with his charm, his modesty, and the gentle humour that goes with the bravest hearts.

Hazell hit 28 off a Verity over in 1936. Somerset had decided that Verity could not be countered on a bad pitch and adopted a policy of reckless attack, an original tactic warmly advocated by those amateurs capable of seeing in cricket a battle of wits.

And Tom Young died, leaving a wife and three children. Reggie Ingle was at his bedside and Frank and Jack Lee arrived from London to pay their respects.

Weary of his efforts, John Daniell resigned as honorary secretary in 1936 but was persuaded to carry out his duties for one more year. He was not, in truth, a distinguished administrator, having no taste for detail, but he was brusque, autocratic, passionate and cheap, which were characteristics associated with the position of Somerset secretary by his executive committee. With his departure the old guard of university amateur sportsmen lost more of its influence, though Richard Palairet was to be president from 1937 to '46 and Daniell himself from 1947 to '49. And, of course, Daniell could not be around Somerset cricket without, more or less, directing operations.

Four applicants were considered to replace Daniell as secretary, a brigadier, a lieutenant-colonel, a major and a humble citizen. After a ballot Brigadier Lancaster was appointed at a wage of £150 a year with £50 expenses, a modest sum supported by Lancaster's army pension.

Lancaster, of course, was from the old school, for Somerset was not in the habit of appointing radical thinkers. He had begun serving in India with the Queen's Royals in 1900 and left India in 1936 having been mentioned twice in dispatches. During his time on the subcontinent he had helped to win the Punjab Commission Cricket Cup from 1900 to 1903, had been a captain in the Royal Indian Army Service Corps and had been elected president of the Punjab Wanderers, a cricket team which included British and Indian players. By temperament he was a martinet and as secretary he saw it as his task to stand firm against change, supporting the amateur code by maintaining separate dressing-rooms and gates on to the field.

But Lancaster was a keen cricketer and a competitor too. He was on tenterhooks throughout every home game and wished only that he could stride on to the field to sort things out himself. Perhaps he was frustrated by the intractability of professional cricketers. Certainly on occasion he treated players and members as if they were recalcitrant privates condemned to extra drill on the parade ground. Trained to lead by force of personality he lacked diplomacy yet was an admirable figurehead for a club which set great store by enthusiasm.

To Lancaster this appointment provided a congenial hobby for his declining years and he carried out his duties well if without paying much heed to minor matters of administration. Brooking no argument in weighty affairs, he scarcely bothered to attend to letters or check gate-money. An honest and trusting man, his inattention to detail proved an embarrassment when, in 1939, Somerset finally realized that one of its employees was pinching money and had been doing so for years. War began and the culprit escaped prosecution.

Lancaster was not, of course, unusual in his autocracy. Somerset's groundsman, Harry Fernie, himself cut a fine figure, as he issued his orders before returning to his beloved Clarke's Tap, leaving his chief lieutenant, Cecil Buttle, to carry out his orders, and this for a wage of £1 17s a week.

For Somerset 1937 was a year of change. Richard Palairet was president now and Major Longrigg an important figure behind the scenes. Reggie Ingle's period as captain was drawing to a close, for moves were afoot to replace him with Bunty Longrigg, the Major's son. Somerset amateurs were nowadays mostly professional men – lawyers and land agents – yet they were divided into two camps, one led by Ingle and one by Longrigg. To concentrate too keenly upon divisions is to distort history for this was, overall, a happy time, not least because so many Somerset cricketers of that era all played for fun; but to ignore such matters is to falsify the record.

It was a battle for supremacy between Longrigg, an ambitious, even arrogant man and Ingle who, he believed, had no gift either for leadership or for cricket. Longrigg was a man of style, and a throwback to an earlier time when Somerset, and cricket, and England, were led by well-bred and formidable blues. Longrigg was supported, in some cases, by Dickie Burrough, R. J. O. Meyer and John Barnwell, amongst other distinguished amateurs.

209

By contrast Ingle was an earthier man who had failed to win a blue. He felt this disappointment heavily and could be uneasy with men whose paths were paved with gold. He could sense that his rival was the sort of man for whom the Somerset executive yearned – a leader with style. Ever since the fixture list had grown, finding an amateur captain had been difficult, for few could spare the time to play regularly. Now with the Longriggs pressing Bunty's claim Somerset had a choice.

Perhaps Reggie Ingle was more disappointed by the manner of his going at the end of 1937 than in the event, for he had been captain for six long, hard summers and could reflect, no doubt, upon the wise words of one bishop upon the subject of a team's view of its leader:

> The first year I go into a new circuit I use this text
>> 'The gods are come down to us in the likeness of men'
>> Acts 14:11
> The second year the text reads
>> 'We also are men of like passions with you'
>> Acts 14:15
> The third year the text reads
>> 'Who made thee a prince and a judge over us?'
>> Exodus 2:14
> The fourth year the text reads
>> 'He hath a devil'
>> John 10:20
> If he was invited to stay a fifth year the text read
>> 'By this time he stinketh'
>> John 11:39

Ingle had made his contribution and was weary. Somerset slipped to thirteenth position in 1937 and he was held responsible. Much praise was bestowed upon the new amateurs, amongst whom Meyer and Cameron hit hundreds, but in truth it was Wellard and Andrews who carried the bowling, and sometimes the batting, while Frank Lee and Luckes were also at their best. Andrews and Wellard were amongst eight cricketers who did the double in 1937, and Andrews even rose to bat at number 4, too high really for a player of his mercurial spirit, too high for a man expected to bowl morning, noon and night. Hitching up his trouser leg before running in to bowl once more, Wellard took 140 wickets, while Frank Lee scored 1,836 runs, Somerset's highest tally since Lionel Palairet was in his prime, and Lee's best by 600 runs. Wally Luckes scored a hundred too, and claimed seventy-four victims, a Somerset record, a splendid way to celebrate his benefit year.

Only Gimblett of the senior professionals had a mixed summer. At Wells he hit 9 sixes and 141 runs, and he took runs off Voce too; but generally his batting was deemed unduly reckless and he was criticized for hooking too early, and reacted by hooking with still more dangerous disdain. No wonder opponents and colleagues found him unfathomable. Perhaps he too was inclined to feel too sharply the world's barbs.

Highlights of the season were Somerset's first championship win at Taunton since 1933 – Northants were beaten by a whisker – and Bill Andrews's astonishing spell of 8/12 at The Oval in June. Andrews was hobbling and didn't want to bowl upon a flat pitch, and yet, despite Wellard bowling with his customary skill, Andrews managed to trap eight victims, three of them as part of a hat-trick, and left the field reflecting that if a boundary catch had been taken his figures really would have been remarkable – for the ball went for 6! Unfortunately Somerset lost this game and the match report merits contemplation. A storm had broken on the second night.

. . . The hard and fast conditions to which batsmen had become accustomed for weeks past had suddenly changed, and the ball began to lift at a disconcerting angle.

With a lead of 140 runs, Surrey's second innings began just before 12 o'clock. In less than an hour the whole team – including four batsmen who, at one time or another, have played for England – collapsed before the fast medium bowling of Wellard and Andrews for a paltry 35 runs, Surrey's lowest score since 1893. In six overs and four balls Andrews took eight wickets for 12 runs, and achieved a hat trick.

Somerset were thus faced with the task of scoring 178 runs to win in ample time; but – in the absence of Gimblett – they had a weak batting side. Also, unfortunately, having to bat a quarter of an hour before lunch, they then lost their most dependable batsman – F. Lee. The sole factor in their favour now, was the steadily improving wicket. After lunch, however, with Gover bowling at the top of his form, Somerset's chances rapidly slipped away, and when the seventh wicket fell at 43 Surrey looked to be certain winners with plenty to spare. With only tail enders left to bat, and 135 runs still to get, the game seemed as good as over. But there was still Wellard to be reckoned with. He began shakily, giving chances in the slip and in the long field; but then settled down to hit in his best form, driving F. R. Brown for two fine sixes, one of them out of the Oval and across the road. Both Luckes and Hazell defended at the other end, and the score mounted rapidly.

The ninth wicket added 67 runs before Gover beat Hazell with a fine ball, and the last man came in with 29 runs wanted. P. S. M. Molyneux defended skilfully, but Wellard, who so far had attacked the bowling with great resource, now slowed down and missed several chances of scoring. Watts sent him a number of balls outside the off stump which failed to tempt him, but runs nevertheless were coming slowly, and Somerset's hopes were rising every over. Then, just when everyone felt that Wellard's great effort would gain a glorious victory for his side, he seemed to lose confidence in his partner's ability to face Gover. It was agreed that, whatever happened, a run must be got off the last ball of Watts' over. The ball was sent down wide, Wellard let it go by and ran – a wild single. Brooks threw the wicket down, and Surrey won by 7 runs.

Dropped catches were a perennial problem in this Somerset team, so much so that local newspapers continued to publish a list of culprits every week. What might Andrews, Wellard, Buse and Hazell have achieved with reliable men to seize upon the edges?

Sydney Rippon reappeared briefly in 1937, wearing horn-rimmed glasses now but still an interesting enough presence at the crease to cause the onlookers, transfixed by his exercises and his habit of sinking to one knee in fervent relief at surviving another ball, to fall off their bench and flat upon their backs.

It was Jack White's last year too, for he was forty-six years of age and had bowled tens of thousands of unerring overs. He confined his activities thereafter to life as a gentleman farmer and to occasional games during which schoolboys were lured into traps much as those Australians had been in 1928/9.

Scoring 543 runs at 38 and taking 26 wickets, at 27 apiece, R. J. O. Meyer was a tower of strength when his school holidays arrived and permitted him the leisure to play a few games. Ten years later, still in charge at Millfield, and now suffering from lumbago and various other ailments Meyer was persuaded, in the absence of other candidates, to captain Somerset, which he did with an originality which puzzled colleagues while interesting them enough to ensure that no one dozed off.

John Hemsley Cameron's career was to be less extraordinary but his two worthy hundreds scored in 1937 provoked delight as well as surprise, for 'Snowball' Cameron was a cheerful West Indian whose chief contribution to cricket lay in the flighted leg-spinners he bowled as a Taunton schoolboy, deliveries with which he took 10/49 for the Rest against The Public Schools at Lord's in 1931. Cameron was the son of a West Indian doctor who had toured England with the 1906 team, and he was a fine bowler until his fingers thickened. Short, sturdy and jolly, he took 45 expensive wickets for Somerset in his forty-eight games but scored three hundreds and was regarded as a useful all-rounder.

Sensitive to his colour, and suffering depressions, Cameron lost himself after leaving Cambridge with a blue and was found destitute by a friend in London. Brought back to Somerset and in need of a wage, he found himself as a teacher and courageously repaired his life. For a time he worked for Meyer at Millfield, only leaving because his boss was apt to interfere with his coaching methods. Nevertheless he had been happy to find work, for, pessimistically, he believed his colour barred him from most jobs. Cameron returned to England with the West Indies in 1939 as Grant's vice-captain, a position he owed as much to his experience and stature as to his ability. Nevertheless Cameron played in two Tests, taking 3 wickets in the first, including that of Harold Gimblett, whom he clean bowled with his second offering.

Cameron faded after this, as a cricketer anyhow, but he missed the game and in 1950 vainly offered his services to Somerset as a secretary-captain.

Scarcely to his surprise, though much to his disappointment, Ingle was manoeuvred out of the captaincy once stumps were drawn upon the 1937 season. Ingle had wanted a coach to be appointed but found that he knew one candidate well and so withdrew from the appointing panel. No reasons were given in the minutes for this withdrawal and upon hearing of it Major Longrigg, seeing his chance, demanded an apology. Ingle refused to oblige and resigned in anger, walking out and vowing never to return.

He played a few more matches and then concentrated upon his work. He has seldom been back since.

Invigorated by Longrigg and with just nineteen men picked to play, the lowest since 1892 (thirty-eight played in 1910), Somerset enjoyed a fine season in 1938, winning ten matches and coming seventh. Longrigg himself hit an unbeaten 187 on the bank holiday fixture in Bristol, adding 143 with John Barnwell, who finished on 49 not out. Their record was not broken until Viv Richards and Colin Dredge added 153 for Somerset's 8th wicket against Pakistan in 1982.

Arthur Wellard was in marvellous form, taking 169 wickets and hitting sixes far and wide. Having seen him smite 27 off one Woolley over, Alec Skelding said: 'You can go home now, lads, they've run out of balls.' A year earlier this idiosyncratic umpire awarded a hat-trick of leg befores in a Somerset game, greeting the third appeal with 'As God's my judge, that's out too!'

Wellard played for England against Australia in 1938 and with his perennial partner Bill Andrews, who did the double, formed a game and dangerous new-ball attack. Somerset had found a third pace bowler too in Bertie Buse, whose outswingers claimed sixty-one victims, and it might have been more if slip catches had been taken and if he had used the new ball. Buse scored over 1,000 runs too and quickly emerged as a typical Somerset professional cricketer, capable with bat and ball, long-suffering and somewhat underestimated, partly because of the company he kept.

Besides these men, Frank Lee scored 2,000 runs and struck seven hundreds, both records for Somerset. Harold Gimblett adopted defensive tactics, a strategy he applied too strenuously, and he had a frustrating year judged by the high standards now expected of him. Sages say it takes four years to turn a colt into a professional batsman, and this was Gimblett's fourth season of county cricket. So often a youngster starts brilliantly, is forced to reconsider his game and then emerges as a harder, better player. If he survives those terrible years of having his game pulled to pieces, that is. Certainly it was too early to abandon hope of Gimblett becoming a major batsman.

Dar Lyon played in 1938 too. Outspoken as ever, Lyon argued for eight-ball overs and fought for amateur cricketers against the supposedly deadening spirit of professional players

– not that such a label could be attached to Wellard, Andrews, Hazell or Gimblett. Lyon had a moderate season, 779 runs at an average of 20, and was plainly past his best. He gave one piece of advice to youngsters seeking counsel. 'Never hook till you've scored 49.' A singular man.

Despite Lyon's opinions, and thanks to a healthy bank balance, Somerset fielded seven professionals in 1938. They still changed in a back room, took to the field through a different gate, travelled in different train compartments, stayed in different hotels and were expected to bowl to the amateurs before play began and to members' children on free days. Their lives were by no means unhappy but they were exhausting and almost entirely lacking in security.

It was to Longrigg's credit that he persuaded Somerset's executive committee to award contracts lasting longer than one season to senior players. It was to his credit, too, that he insisted upon going for victory whenever possible, with no holding back. He had enough of the common touch to buy pints for his fast bowlers and it helped too that he was a gifted sportsman, being a noted player of rugby, hockey and golf. And he needed these qualities, for Longrigg was not a particularly good cricketer. On occasion he could bat with panache but generally his team regarded him as a public school batsman. For their part, opposing bowlers were irritated by his knack, so frequently found in left-handers, of playing and missing without ever losing his wicket or even appearing embarrassed – 'just leading them on,' he would say, and then he'd head off for an evening's snooker with his circle of friends, for he was a noted social climber.

Longrigg was a public school batsman and a public school captain; in both respects he fulfilled Somerset's idea of how cricket should be played. It was as if the Great War had not happened, had not turned the Western world upon its head. In 219 games for Somerset between 1925 and 1947, Bunty hit 8,339 runs, including ten hundreds, and averaged around 25 an innings. Upon retiring he served on several important committees at Lord's and was chairman of Somerset from 1960 to 1969 and president from 1968 to 1971, periods which if not exactly blessed with triumph were at least more fruitful than his father's miserable years as president from 1950 to 1953.

Thanks to Wellard, ever at his best against the county which had rejected him, Somerset beat Kent at Wells. Wellard took 13/115, mainly with his spinners, and made 57 in 37 minutes, an innings including 7 sixes, and 31 in one Woolley over, the single being off a dropped boundary catch.

Somerset's two best victories of 1938 were won against Gloucestershire and Leicestershire. At Taunton Hazell helped to dismiss the local rivals for 221, whereupon Somerset took a lead of 55, Gimblett, Lee and Lyon contributing. Wally Hammond rescued the visitors with an unbeaten hundred and Somerset were left to chase 284. An early collapse left Somerset needing 112 in 65 minutes with 3 wickets to fall, an apparently hopeless task. Now Wellard entered and struck 68 in 40 minutes, one shot cannoning between two ladies gently knitting in the Ridley stand, the ball ricocheting off concrete and back to the middle without either lady blinking. With Buse, calm and obtuse, on 66, Somerset needed 30 in 25 minutes. Luckes scurried helpfully but Buse fell for 79 and 7 were needed off Sinfield's last over. Failing to score off two deliveries, Luckes dispatched the third to the straight boundary. Gambling, Sinfield tossed one up, Luckes smote hugely and Jack Crapp ran, dived and could neither catch the ball nor prevent it crossing the boundary. Hundreds of people rushed on to the field and, though Horace Hazell had scarpered, they carried Luckes shoulder high to the pavilion where this tee-totaller with a dicky heart partook of some brandy and soon all was well.

Trevor Jones, barely eighteen years of age and born in Wells, where his father ran a garage, was the hero at Leicester. Suffering a first-innings deficit of 168, Somerset collapsed lamentably to 108/8 with 60 minutes left for play on the second day. Bags were being packed and train timetables studied as Wally Luckes joined his youthful partner, whose greatest hour this was to be. In the event this pair lasted until tea next day, adding 146, as Luckes fought his way to an unbeaten 90 and Jones reached 106, to deny Leicestershire victory. Horace Hazell chipped in with 18 not out and Somerset cheekily declared. It was a noble rearguard action speaking of sterling team spirit.

Sadly Jones, a shy and engaging boy, was never able to

216

approach such heights again and in his 34 other innings for Somerset he collected just 293 runs. War interrupted his development, of course, but cricket is so often a simple game until you start to think about it. Jones had a chance to turn pro after the war but his mother forbade it and he went to work for Imperial Tobacco instead. War took away his best years, the years of education, for he did not pass it in northern leagues but on horseback in Palestine. He might have played more in 1938, had not Longrigg preferred to pick Barnwell, a lesser player but a friend. After 1945 Jones did not do much, for he was rusty. Here was one who, in different circumstances, might have amounted to more.

And in 1938 Louis St Vincent Powell played the last of ten county games spread over twelve summers. Born in the West Indies, he ended up in Taunton where he was articled to a firm of auctioneers. He faced McDonald without a 'box' and Larwood bowled a few hostile overs to him to see if he really was a 'Saint' so his experiences cannot be counted dull even if his record was undistinguished.

Harold Gimblett enjoyed a glorious resurgence in 1939, scoring 905 runs in his first 13 innings, and five times reaching his hundred. By September he had hit 1,922 runs and played in a Test match, striking 20 and 22 and showing, said Plum Warner, 'some brilliant attacking strokes'. He also fielded 'extremely well'. Warner found in his play a 'certain uncommonness which looked the forerunner of something akin to greatness'.

Despite Gimblett's form, Somerset slipped back to fourteenth place, for Andrews and Wellard were injured and their absences were keenly felt. As usual, though, Somerset's season had its moments. At Kidderminster they played in one of cricket's closest ever matches. Having bowled out Worcestershire for 130 (Wellard 7/45), Somerset eked out 131 runs on a dubious pitch, whereupon, with Hazell snaring 5/6, Worcester were dismissed for 142. Needing 142 to win Hazell found himself joining Sam Weaver (aged thirty) a noted footballer who had played in a Cup Final and now found himself involved in exchanges of enormous tension in one of his two county matches.

With 1 over left and 5 needed Hazell swung hugely at Dick Howarth and scored a boundary, the ball landing just inside the fence. Hazell takes up the tale:

217

We arrived at the fourth ball and I couldn't believe it – the Worcester skipper had kept most of his fielders in the deep. We were actually level now and I calculated that a push for a single was all that was needed. Howarth was bowling over the wicket and I felt that he would field himself if I hit to mid-off. I decided to be cleverer and aimed for deepish cover point. Oh dear! I should have known better. I left a gap and my stumps were over.

Opposing players, imagining they had won, rushed over and carried Howarth from the field. Hazell remembered his mistake for fifty years, and so did his chums, denied their £5 win bonus!

Arthur Wellard enjoyed a record benefit of £1,413 and with Bill Andrews he bowled out a strong West Indian batting team, including George Headley and Learie Constantine, for 84 on a sticky Taunton morning. Somerset reached 345 with Bennett, Meyer and Luckes scoring half-centuries and the visitors were beaten by an innings. Already the year before R. J. O. Meyer had played for the Gentlemen of England against Australia, and played well enough for authorities to regret that he had not played more cricket in his younger days.

But Europe was in turmoil and cricket merely a game. T. R. Garnett, born in Stockport, educated at Charterhouse, later headmaster at Marlborough, added 101 against Northants with Peter McRae. Pretty soon brave young men such as these would be engaged in war. Hugh Watts, aged seventeen, from Downside and, in time, Cambridge University, made his first county appearances in the closing weeks of the 1939 season. He was a splendid all-rounder until shrapnel stopped him bowling, though nothing save his schoolmastering duties could prevent him playing. Writing fifty years later, Watts recalled staying, as amateurs did, in posh hotels and travelling first class. He remembered Horace Hazell as a 'devastatingly good slow left-arm bowler on a worn wicket and Arthur Wellard was very quick to change from bowling his away-swingers to off-spin as soon as the ball started to turn. Jack Meyer supplied any known variety required to suit the wicket and Bill Andrews was there with his banana inswingers.'

Peter McRae made a marvellous hundred, Somerset's last before the war, against Hampshire's attack and Northants were easily

218

beaten in an eery atmosphere as the news became hourly more depressing. After the game Longrigg drove Watts home to Stratton-on-the-Fosse and said, 'Hugh, we have played our last game of cricket together.'

Thankfully he was wrong. They played together in 1946. They were amongst the lucky ones.

Since 1919 Somerset had played fewer matches than most other counties because their bank account was so often in the red, and matches were expensive. Of the 526 played, 123 games were won, 180 drawn and 218 lost, a poor but not disgraceful record, for the plight of Glamorgan, Worcestershire and Northamptonshire was worse. There had been moments of joy and, on the field anyhow, a gradual and inevitable move towards professionalism had been undertaken, if not painlessly at least without undue bitterness. Somerset had not wanted to be a professional club and resistance was still strong, yet to outsiders it was astonishing that the amateur code had so long survived the First World War. In Russia they had a revolution, in England they had cricket matches between Gentlemen and Players.

County Championship 1919–1939
Results by County

	Played	Won	Drawn	Lost	Tied	Aban'd
Yorkshire	616	330	230	49	–	7
Lancashire	619	255	282	77	–	5
Nottinghamshire	565	216	255	90	–	4
Kent	579	264	162	150	–	3
Surrey	550	189	269	87	–	5
Middlesex	505	197	187	120	–	1
Sussex	616	227	199	183	1	6
Gloucestershire	577	200	161	213	–	3
Derbyshire	526	159	187	173	–	7
Essex	572	158	218	193	1	2
Warwickshire	540	120	238	179	–	3
Hampshire	584	142	231	209	–	2
Leicestershire	535	112	215	206	–	2
Somerset	526	123	180	218	3	2
Glamorgan	480	71	185	221	–	3
Worcestershire	550	87	186	275	1	1
Northamptonshire	506	67	161	274	–	4
Total	9446	2917	3546	2917	6	60

Results by Year

Season	Derby	Essex	Glam.	Glos.	Hants.	Kent	Lancs.	Leics.	Middlesex	Northants.	Notts.	Somerset	Surrey	Sussex	Warwicks.	Worcs.	Yorks.
1919	9	14	–	8	7	2	5	9	13	12	3	5	4	11	15	–	1
1920	16	9	–	8	11	5	2	13	1	14	7	10	3	6	12	15	4
1921	12	15	17	7	6	4	5	11	1	13	8	10	2	9	16	14	3
1922	11	8	16	13	6	4	5	14	7	15	2	10	3	9	12	17	1
1923	10	13	16	11	7	5	3	14	8	17	2	9	4	6	12	15	1
1924	17	15	13	6	12	5	4	11	2	16	6	8	3	10	9	14	1
1925	14	7	17	10	9	5	3	12	6	11	4	15	2	13	8	16	1
1926	11	9	8	15	7	3	1	13	6	16	4	14	5	10	12	17	2
1927	5	8	15	12	13	4	1	7	9	16	2	14	6	10	11	17	3
1928	10	16	15	5	12	2	1	9	8	13	3	14	6	7	11	17	4
1929	7	12	17	4	11	8	2	9	6	13	1	15	10	4	14	16	2
1930	9	6	11	2	13	5	1	12	16	17	4	13	8	7	15	10	3
1931	7	10	15	2	12	3	6	16	11	17	5	13	8	4	9	14	1
1932	10	14	15	13	8	3	6	12	10	16	4	7	5	2	9	17	1
1933	6	4	16	10	14	3	5	17	12	13	8	11	9	2	7	15	1
1934	3	8	13	7	14	5	1	12	10	17	9	15	11	2	4	16	5
1935	2	9	13	15	16	10	4	6	3	17	5	14	11	7	8	12	1
1936	1	9	16	4	10	8	11	15	2	17	5	7	6	14	13	12	3
1937	3	6	7	4	14	12	9	16	2	17	10	13	8	5	11	15	1
1938	5	6	16	10	14	9	4	15	2	17	12	7	3	8	13	11	1
1939	9	4	13	3	15	5	6	17	2	16	12	14	8	10	11	7	1

22

War years

During the war Somerset's cricket ground was lent to the military and used by soldiers at the local barracks, and by the fire service. Harry Fernie saw to it that his sacred turf was not spoilt by infidel invaders, and often his voice, as it bellowed at transgressing soldiers, resembled that of a sergeant-major.

As in the Great War the great bulk of Somerset cricketers volunteered to fight, Longrigg, Andrews and Horace Hazell joining the RAF, Hazell serving for a time in Iraq, while Lyon, Wellard and Hugh Watts joined the army. Mitchell-Innes and Seamer were in Sudan, and Gimblett served as a fireman, seeing sights which took a toll.

Several Somerset cricketers lost their lives – notably Peter McRae, Jack Lee, Charles Mayo, Geoffrey Fletcher (one game in 1939), Ronald Gerrard of Taunton School, and William Baldock. Gerrard won a DSO.

Others, including Watts, were badly injured and many were deprived of their greatest years as cricketers. Somerset did its best to take care of its cricketers, paying professionals £3 a week for the first two years of war, £1 a week in 1941 and, as funds ran out and contracts ended, nothing thereafter. In 1940 the professionals cost £1,000, a bill which could not long be sustained for, inevitably, membership was dwindling and by 1944 it had dropped to 570. Money was tight, and an old cash register was sold for £40 in 1943 to improve the bank balance. Thanks to careful housekeeping Somerset ended the war with £1,000 in the bank which drew comments that the club was only financially viable when no cricket was being played.

And very little cricket was played in the area in those years. Schoolboy practices continued but Somerset's executive committee had no taste for cricket in this time of battle. Elsewhere, and especially in the North where many professionals played in the leagues, cricket was played with some regularity.

It was R. J. O. Meyer, headmaster of Millfield, who arranged such significant matches as were played. His eleven met a team representing Southern Command, and other representative matches were played in Glastonbury. As usual Somerset men played with a good deal of vim in these contests, for only Gloucestershire and Kent had continued to draw a lower proportion of fixtures since 1873.

Besides McRae and Gerrard, one other Somerset cricketer was decorated for his bravery. Eric Hill had not yet played for Somerset, was only sixteen years of age at the outbreak of hostilities, but he was to become part of the fabric of a club to which he was already deeply attached. Guided by Arthur Wellard, who took a none-too-reluctant boy under his wing in a variety of ways, he was to play seventy-two matches for Somerset from 1947 to 1951, fighting valiantly to protect his wicket, to build a career, and yet constantly betrayed by luck. Disappointed but never embittered by failures, he served variously as a 2nd XI captain, as a committee man, as a father figure to promising players, as a constant supporter and adviser to captains and, later, even as a rebel leader in the troubles of the 1950s. For the present, though, it is sufficient to record that this cricket-mad youngster joined the RAF as soon as he could, and served as an observer in a photographic reconnaissance unit attached to 544 squadron in Oxfordshire, whose task it was to take intelligence photographs on sorties into France, Scandinavia, East Germany and Poland. Hill's pilot was Flight-Lieutenant F. C. Dodd, later an Air Vice-Marshal, and their work was so precise, so demanding of courage, that both were decorated, Hill first being given a DFM and later a DFC for gallantry in the execution of an operation. Today perched in his press-box, which has not noticeably changed since 1890, Hill continues to record Somerset's contests and never talks about his own valour. Charlie Sedgebeer was decorated for gallantry too. Charlie sold scorecards at the county ground, scorecards scarcely dry from being printed near the scoreboard, an area which almost smelt of ink. Charlie, who was, Buttle recalled, 'a right handful', for years afterwards sold his cards and wore his white uniform and his medals.

For some the war was their finest hour, for most their greatest tragedy.

23

Post-war blues

War, of course, changed everything. For a time, as men returned happy in victory, happy to be alive, happy to be playing cricket against old chums once again, these changes remained hidden. And cricket, ruled by its rich, aged conservative oligarchy, resisted change as best it could. As Robertson-Glasgow wrote of C. B. Fry's omission from service on an MCC Committee, 'birth and convention have always ranked higher than originality and knowledge'. In 1933 the average age of the MCC Committee was 65, and all twenty-one men had been to public school, eighteen of them also attending one of the great universities.

Somerset, of course, was a conservative country cousin, a club run by a rural petty aristocracy gradually losing its ties with the county set. Only three counties were not occasionally led by a professional player during the 1920s and 1930s: Essex, Kent and Somerset. Accordingly, as cricket resumed its place in the sporting consciousness of England, nothing was further from the executive committee's mind than to appoint a paid captain. Since Bunty Longrigg was still available – if feeling, at forty, rather stiff and somewhat reluctant – the choice fell upon him. No obvious alternative candidate could be found, for amateurism was now as dead as its world, and its continued existence owed more to fond hope than to objective reality. Men from all backgrounds had to earn a living, and county teams could no longer carry incompetents. It was as simple as that.

For ten summers Somerset was to continue its desperate search for amateur captains, a search which led it down numerous improbable culs-de-sac and eventually into deep trouble. Yet all was well in this first year of peace, for Somerset enjoyed a happy, successful, if delusory summer. Over the next ten years they were to be easily the worst side in the championship, as the following figures indicate.

County Championship 1946–1956

Results by County	Played	Won	Drawn	Lost	Tie	Aban'd	Points
Surrey	300	149	84	65	–	2	2036
Yorkshire	300	140	117	42	1	–	1982
Lancashire	300	116	140	39	2	3	1766
Middlesex	300	130	91	77	1	1	1750
Gloucestershire	300	102	110	86	–	2	1496
Warwickshire	300	97	113	88	1	1	1428
Derbyshire	300	93	111	92	–	4	1416
Glamorgan	300	90	135	74	–	1	1358
Hampshire	300	80	111	106	3	–	1228
Sussex	300	81	117	100	2	–	1222
Worcestershire	300	79	110	110	–	1	1220
Northamptonshire	300	66	146	86	2	–	1168
Nottinghamshire	300	66	145	88	1	–	1090
Essex	300	65	135	96	3	1	1082
Kent	300	70	99	130	1	–	1068
Leicestershire	300	65	113	119	1	2	1032
Somerset	300	60	89	151	–	–	914
Total	5100	1549	1966	1549	18	18	23256

Such a calamity could not be imagined in those cheerful if still rigorous months of 1946 as, with Gimblett, Wellard, Hazell and Buse to the foremost, Somerset emerged from war apparently stronger than in 1939. After losing their first four matches the team had a run of success almost uninterrupted till the last weeks of August. In those early defeats they were twice bowled out for 55 but thereafter the batsmen found their form, with Gimblett in particular proving a tower of strength. He made seven centuries and struck 231 against Middlesex, the highest score of his career to date. Frank Lee was less productive but he made his 1,000 runs and struck 169 against Nottinghamshire. With Bertie Buse and Johnny Lawrence also averaging around 24, Somerset was seldom short of a total at which to bowl.

And they had a decent quintet of bowlers too, in Arthur Wellard, Buse, Hazell, Andrews and Johnny Lawrence, a polite, dedicated leg-spinner from Yorkshire, who had engaged to play for Somerset in 1940 and had kept his promise by representing

225

them in 1946, though so much had changed at his home county that they earnestly if correctly sought his services. Luckily Lawrence, diminutive and balding, was a sportsman of the highest principles and he acknowledged Somerset's claims upon him.

It was these men who, after Gimblett had launched his merciless 231-run onslaught against Middlesex at Taunton, bowled Somerset to victory. By September Wellard had taken 106 wickets, Hazell 52, Lawrence 60 and Buse 69, none of them paying more than 20 runs a victim. Only Bill Andrews, his arm decidedly lower, was obviously showing the strain of his 38 years. Buse (36), Hazell (36), Wellard (44) and Lawrence (32) seemed ready for seasons more of toil. Perhaps their advancing years were too easily ignored. Certainly Somerset's bowling quickly began to decline, for which those struggling amateur captains could not be blamed.

Wally Luckes (45) had an Indian summer too, catching 51 men and stumping 26, to commemorate which R. J. O. Meyer opened a fund.

Altogether it was a happy season. Three times in a short space of time Somerset reached 500, against Middlesex, Yorkshire and India, a distinguished trinity. At Taunton Hammond reached a hundred awesome in its power by striking Wellard for 2 sixes, one of them into the churchyard, taking 20 off one over. It was Sam Cook's début derby game for Gloucestershire and he could scarcely believe his eyes. Colleague George Lambert told him, 'Don't worry, Sam, he didn't get hold of that one properly!'

No wonder crowds flocked to the cricket, though players at Taunton were, on one third day, surprised at the fall of a wicket to see a lady with an umbrella and a huge picnic basket walk down the pavilion steps, straight across the field and into the crowd. Later it emerged that she had not realized that tea was taken at a different hour on the final day.

Besides their solid if ageing professionals, amongst whom the improvement in Horace Hazell was particularly remarked upon, Somerset could also boast an enterprising and gifted group of amateurs.

George Langdale was a thirty-year-old left-handed batsman from Yorkshire who astonished the world, and probably himself too, by striking 146 brilliant runs on his début against Yorkshire. Langdale had moved to Somerset and upon being asked about him his former captain Brian Sellers observed that he might be good enough for so weak a county, a comment which Sellers may temporarily have regretted but which ultimately proved accurate. Langdale scored 357 runs, won his cap, and thereafter began to fade.

Fred Castle from Kent was another amateur to begin playing in 1946. A skilful footballer, he had played for Crystal Palace as an inside forward, and had also won honours at hockey. Apparently too, he had a mellifluous baritone voice and was an accomplished magician. Having moved to Somerset in 1942, working as a schoolmaster, he found himself playing for Bath and was in time summoned by Longrigg to assist the county. When Longrigg was injured Castle even took over as captain, and Longrigg, as Fred later recalled, 'gave me a long list of instructions starting with how to call at the toss. It was to be heads if the coin landed on the wicket and tails anywhere else. I wrote all his instructions down and still have the list in my desk.' Castle played twenty-three games and though he contributed usefully his highest score was 60 not out.

R. J. O. Meyer had a splendid year as a batsman, as courageous and inventive as of old, though really cricket was to him merely an occasional if beloved activity. He was forty-one years of age now, his best years long since behind him. Nevertheless he managed to score 477 runs in 11 innings and to be his usual irascible, unpredictable self.

One other amateur began to play in 1946 and he was beyond doubt the finest batsman of them all, probably one of the best ever to play for Somerset. Michael Moore Walford, educated at Rugby and Oxford University, was a schoolmaster at Sherborne and could play only during the holidays. Had time permitted a greater concentration upon cricket he might have played for England, for Walford was a superb sportsman; by all accounts an outstanding wing three-quarter (he was an England trialist) he also played hockey for his country in wartime internationals and at the 1948 Olympics in London.

Fiercely competitive and blessed with a sharp, analytical mind, Walford found in cricket a source of challenge and satisfaction. A reserved, brisk man, he may have contemplated Somerset's breezy approach to cricket with a distant eye, for at heart he was as tough as any professional and as competent as Jack MacBryan. Warmer contemporaries, to whom cricket was a game to be enjoyed rather than an intellectual exercise demanding ruthless application, thought Walford to be unduly narrow-minded, a mite pompous and certainly too fussy. Those whose abilities were lower felt themselves scorned when they yearned for reassurance.

But no one doubted that Walford was a superb batsman, a player capable of appearing in August and immediately taking command at the crease. In fifty-two games for Somerset from 1946 to 1953 he scored 3,395 runs at an average over 40, a figure rarely beaten at the county, and never by an Englishman. He could have played longer and was prepared to do so, yet Somerset asked him to relinquish his special registration as they needed it for another. Too easily a splendid player was lost. And once again Somerset were left to rue the unavailability of one of their outstanding cricketers. Still it was schoolmastering which had brought Walford into the area in the first place.

Bill Caesar played three games too. Twenty-four years earlier he had played one game for Surrey and now here he was, at forty-six years of age, still a regular club cricketer, appearing in Somerset's colours. He scored 14 runs in his 4 innings and took 10 wickets too, his best being 4/59. Nevertheless he took to the field with an air of faint surprise which in no way rivalled in its power the emotion felt by his colleagues at seeing him by their side. Truly Somerset had not lost its old ways. Professionals and amateurs were sharing one dressing-room, and taking to the field through one gate and yet the heart had not been moved by the communality of war. A Labour government was in office, a welfare state was being introduced, and Bill Caesar was playing for Somerset under an amateur captain.

Nor did Somerset's ageing professionals feel more at ease after the war. Rather to the contrary they were more inclined to argue for their quarter, be it in expenses or influence, especially Bill Andrews, who to some seemed a warrior for justice and to others a barrack-room lawyer. Andrews and his paid colleagues were more prepared to fight for themselves because they could see that workers now had rights, that relations between boss and employee had changed. Somerset, reflecting its world, could no longer be a paternalistic club in which a professional might expect to play out his time no matter how his form fell away. Certainly this position had been lost in the 1930s but now players felt a still sharper fragility of situation. If they failed they were out, and

228

they knew it. Moreover, since they were collectively somewhat long in the tooth, these professionals – men such as Andrews, Luckes, Hazell and Wellard, all of them destined to depart with a measure of acrimony – felt insecure. Inevitably Somerset was a less warm, comfortable club than previously, though its reputation never changed, for these things are relative.

One splendid professional arrived in this vintage summer of 1946 and Somerset's rise to fourth place owed much to his skills. As mentioned earlier, the balding, diminutive John Miles Lawrence was a gentleman. Later, during his benefit year, he was to refuse to organize the traditional Sunday games with village teams because any such frivolity offended against his strict religious convictions. Many sympathizers sent money to reward him for putting his principles first; so much so, that – thankfully – his benefit gave satisfactory recognition to his service.

But it must not be imagined that this Yorkshireman was a grim, solemn fellow. To the contrary, his company was light rather than burdensome, his conversation humorous rather than hectoring. His companions, a rumbustious crew, liked him. As a cricketer Lawrence was a batsman good enough to score over 9,000 runs in his 281 county games, and to average 20. A nimble short-leg, he also took 259 catches to add to his 791 wickets at 25 apiece – impressive economy for a leg-spinner whose googly was thought by some to be too obvious.

With Wellard taking most of his wickets with off-spin, and Hazell proving a handful on doubtful August pitches, Somerset had a wily trio of spinners to add to their forthright and long batting list. For a time Longrigg's team appeared capable of winning the championship, losing just once from 24 May to 23 August, a state of affairs which alarmed certain professionals, notably Horace Hazell who liked to turn a drama into a crisis, that they protested about pressures to which they were not accustomed and vowed never again to win so many games!

Somerset failed in the end but it was a memorable if wet summer. John Barnwell and J. C. Clay, captain of Glamorgan, were reprimanded by Lord's for arranging their declarations to set up a last-day run-chase after rain had interfered with Pontypridd's annual fixture. Somerset collapsed to 53 all out, and Glamorgan's victory was held to be unfair to other competitors. Thirty years later such agreements were all the rage.

229

Crowds and membership reached new heights as spectators filled grounds previously starved of cricket. And yet it was a more difficult land to govern too. Even in Somerset supporters were prepared to challenge their rulers. Disgruntlement led to the creation of a supporters club by such notables as Leonard Boothman and G. O. Boundy, local figures of some importance. Somerset, and J. Daniell in particular, was appalled at this effrontery. Finding himself accused of being an embodiment of the old school tie, Daniell retorted that Somerset's committee had never been approached and had merely read about this club and its complaints in the newspapers, for which Daniell had as little time as he did for whingers. Finding his committee condemned as inefficient and unbusinesslike, he replied that such supposed supporters had been notable by their absence in the hard times from 1919 to 1939 'when no cricketers could be found on village greens.' Hearing about complaints that it was not right to 'expect members to sit on planks', Daniell retorted that he had done so in his time.

It was not an argument likely to inspire Somerset to greater deeds, rather it was a first shot across the bows. Daniell and his committee must abandon its autocratic ways and listen to its membership and even to its employees. Perhaps it was too large a leap for old men, used to a different world and yet absolutely dedicated to Somerset cricket. In any event no heed was taken and as the supporters club crumpled so its points were lost. Thereafter rebellion was inevitable.

Bunty Longrigg decided to retire as captain at the end of 1946. It was time, he felt, to return to his legal practice. 'God help my successor,' were his last gloomy words, for Longrigg knew that his vital men were creaking, for all had been subjected to the wear and tear of war, and to a decade of gruelling cricket too.

As Somerset contemplated a replacement (a contemplation which embraced only the ranks of amateur 'gentlemen') they paused to appoint Cecil Buttle, already a servant for twenty years, as head groundsman to replace Fernie, whose legs had betrayed him. Buttle had insisted upon his appointment, 'put his cards on the table', as he phrased it; and Somerset's hesitation had been ended by Longrigg, who told all and sundry that Buttle was the right man, a judgement triumphantly vindicated.

Cecil was, in fact, a remarkable fellow, entirely devoted to Somerset cricket though he had an eye for a lady, a thirst for a beer and a relish for a game of skittles. Handsome, and with a distinct twinkle in both eyes, Buttle took to his task with a will, carrying on lessons he had learnt under Fernie. In the winter he painted hoardings on the ground, after play he wandered around collecting loose papers, and at night he lived on the ground in a caravan with Edie, his wife, who laundered the towels for a penny each, drying them on a line in the Ridley Stand. And on the last day of February, year after year, come hail or shine, he rolled the outfield. Cecil was a creature of habit.

He had seen a lot: saw Williams of Gloucestershire bowl underarm, saw horses used on the ground and remembered, later, having to go to the labour exchange to find men to pull the roller. Every Friday night, regular as clockwork, he took his weekly bath in the dressing-room and always he was spruce. As a groundsman he had an unbreakable faith in marl and worms. Marl he fetched from a brickworks in Wellington, crushing the bricks with his roller and rolling fine, powdery dust into his pitches so that they shone. Worms, he argued, gave the wickets air and pace. Once he took a bucket of worms from Taunton to Bath to help the pitches. ('They wouldn't believe me at Lord's when I told them that.') He would take the worms out of a wicket three weeks before it was to be used. And, just like Sammy Woods, he relied upon mustard powder to tempt them to the surface. Meanwhile the beloved if long-suffering Edie tilled her garden behind the decrepit club offices.

Buttle was a Taunton man and a batsman's friend. It helped, no doubt, that captains and amateurs were mostly batsmen, for Cecil knew upon which side his bread was buttered. Away from Taunton he was less happy. Condemned to erecting scoreboards and tents in haste he scarcely had time to prepare pitches. Once, in Bath, he arrived to find knee-high grass and the festival two days away. He used a scythe and soon batsmen were recalling the road sign 'Drive carefully, loose chippings'. In the year of Bertie Buse's benefit match at Bath, which ended in one day, he desperately rolled bull's blood into his pitches to help them last, for in them were to be found sufficient varieties of moss to interest David Bellamy. Those were the days of idiosyncratic festival pitches.

231

All of it Buttle took in his stride, reflecting only that his 'captains always seemed to have so much on their minds – they were moody buggers'.

Rollo John Oliver Meyer was to be Somerset's captain for 1947. It was a position he accepted with some reluctance, for his sight had deteriorated and his lumbago demanded a morning diet of six aspirins before he could move at all. Save that Meyer had been a splendid cricketer, an all-rounder good enough to challenge for Test selection if time and finances had permitted, it was an astonishing appointment. But then Meyer was an astonishing man.

Son of a parson, educated at Haileybury and Cambridge, Meyer had from the start lived on his not inconsiderable wits. His boyhood had coincided with a potato famine so that he was never robust in youth. His mother had killed off all the family hens by feeding them with rhubarb leaves so Meyer learned to shoot sparrows with an air rifle, though slugs were hard to find. At his school, a tough place, where precociousness was discouraged, not least by punishment upon the part of the anatomy specifically ordained by God for this purpose (or so Meyer's masters alleged), Meyer revealed his talent, his intelligence and his originality, things best left hidden.

At Cambridge he won his cricketing blue from Tom Lowry, who admired his fortitude, and played well enough for his name to be mentioned in the highest circles. Alas, he had to earn a living so, like many others, he went off to India to pursue a career in cotton-broking in which, they said, a fellow could make his fortune in nine years. Naturally he played cricket too (and other games, for he was a most gifted sportsman), once scoring 275 in 100°F and also hitting 211 against the Prince of Lindi's XI, an innings during which he ruined three pairs of gym shoes.

Alas, the Depression ruined his prospects in cotton, though for a time Meyer defied economics by using his skills at snooker, golf and predicting horse-races to win orders. About to leave and entirely bankrupt, Meyer bumped into Ranjitsinhji, who provided an opportunity in education. Meyer found himself working for a man of somewhat languid disposition who had a contraption built to lift him from his bed into his morning bath. This gentleman, upon hearing that his son had scored 50 for Eton, reportedly sent a telegram of delight informing his offspring of his intention to

232

sacrifice fifty slaves in honour of the event, a consummation narrowly avoided (so it was believed) thanks to an insistent Etonian headmaster. Meyer taught children of all ages, and coached cricket too, passing on his insight into its unique skills to brilliant pupils such as Amar Singh, soon to be one of cricket's greatest bowlers.

Meyer returned to England in 1935 and founded a school, Millfield, on an army camp in Somerset. His students were a mixture of Indian princes and the ragtag and bobtail of other schools in the area. An outstanding educator, his school was co-educational, informed about dyslexia, strict and yet individualistic. Millfield was to thrive and to contribute much towards Somerset cricket. Meyer himself had found time to play occasionally, and with distinction, before the war, and now he answered Somerset's call in its hour of need.

As a cricketer he was an original. 'He'd have been a great batsman save for one flaw,' recalled one colleague: 'he never stayed in longer than five minutes'; which is a trifle harsh for he had scored a double hundred against Lancashire (and, apparently, paid some occasional bowlers operating in a dead game to help him on his way). As a bowler he was superb, a student of cut, spin and swing who would have risen to be a master had time and temperament allowed it. As it was Meyer, bored by the dullness of routine cricket, tried to take wickets with every delivery, searching always for the key to this door, for the ball this batsman could not play. Accordingly he might be expensive but was never banal.

Somerset's professional cricketers did not see their new captain until the afternoon before their season was due to start at Lord's. Meyer arrived, apologized, and asked for a net, which led to certain rumblings which were silenced when heavy rain began to fall. Instead Meyer held a meeting at which field placements were arranged for each bowler – a move which led to immense efficiency at Lord's until the arrival of number 5, a left-hander, a great thing that Meyer forgot, and one which led to considerable confusion.

Meyer was a man of decisive opinion and he was to show it in this first game. Somerset were fielding a local youngster called Maurice Tremlett who, it was rumoured, was a bit hasty, and this in a land crying out for a fast bowler. Meyer had captained Tremlett as a boy, during the war and in Germany, and he did not think he could bowl. To the contrary he thought Tremlett to be a splendid batsman, an opinion which was to be proved correct but which contemporary thought dismissed as eccentric.

Tremlett took 8 wickets in that first game, a performance trumpeted as if a new dawn had arrived. Fair-haired and athletic, with a sweeping run and a high, natural action, Tremlett caught Middlesex napping, for it was only May and players were still finding their form. He took 5 wickets for 8 runs in 5 overs and one famous critic called it 'as exciting a spell of fast bowling as I have ever watched' and spoke of this 'heady promise of resurgent greatness in English cricket'.

Moreover Tremlett emerged as a hero, showing, said *Wisden*, 'confidence and rashness' as he hit a straight six to take Somerset, with their last pair in, to the verge of a famous victory. Upon the winning runs being hit, Tremlett and Hazell were cheered to the pavilion, not least by their opponents.

No one suffered more for those two days than Tremlett himself. Quite simply he was not ready for such responsibility, and not capable of carrying it either. Meyer found him reluctant to bowl at times, and often did not give him the new ball, no matter how the masses cried. Perhaps Meyer was too protective of his youthful charge, for Tremlett did take 65 wickets that summer, though he paid on average 30 runs for each of them. Nevertheless his instincts were right and those of the selectors who chastised Meyer in private, urging him to use Tremlett solely as a fast bowler and to bat him at 11, wrong. Tremlett was taken on tour the following winter and efforts made to change his action and to turn him into a consistent bowler of high pace. It was to no avail, for it was not in Tremlett's pleasant, gregarious and perturbed nature to be a fast bowler. In time he emerged as a fastish medium-pacer with a dangerous breakback who, to his relief, bowled less as his batting developed, and by the end scarcely at all, and certainly not with the new ball. Tremlett lacked confidence in his bowling, and when he lost control he felt keenly the jeers of those who, not so long before, had been shouting for his appearance at the crease.

Apart from the arrival of Tremlett, 1947 was memorable chiefly as a somewhat incalculable year, for Middlesex were beaten twice and yet finished as champions, and Lancashire once, their only defeat. Meanwhile Meyer developed some remarkable strategies, playing on scarcely cut pitches at Weston, because his men were too old to play three days in a row; also he instructed one opener, Hugh Watts, to swipe at the first ball of a game, which Watts did under protest, slogging a boundary, provoking substantial invective and some fast and wild overs which were severely punished, not least by Watts himself. Meyer also told Hazell to bowl a leg-side full-toss first ball after tea, which ball Meyer duly caught as he emerged stealthily and late from the pavilion, a vital wicket taken.

And he gambled. Somerset were bowled out for 25 by Gloucestershire and, stung, Meyer bet his opposing captain £100 that his men would score 400 in their next innings which, craftily, he knew was to be played at placid Trent Bridge. He won his bet, but only after a valiant last-ditch partnership with Hazell, whose defiance was won with a bribe of £1, which was increased to £5 when Voce was recalled.

It was an interesting year. Not every professional appreciated Meyer's use of his players, or his opinion that any move could be made so long as it was lawful. They did, though, like the way he stopped trains and returned with pounds of horse steak for his fast bowlers, a rare feast won by a man who had learnt, perforce, to scrounge in his cradle. And players now stayed at the same hotels and were not parted on trains either.

Hazell and Wellard took their usual quota of wickets but only Gimblett and, in the holidays, Walford, showed any form with the bat. Meyer himself defied his various ailments to secure 853 runs and 43 wickets and to remind many of what might have been had his life taken a different course.

Apart from Tremlett only Miles Coope, a Yorkshireman and yet a delicacy, made much of an impact amongst those of fresh blood. Coope won his cap but he was a passing star capable, in Meyer's opinion at any rate, of scoring runs only when ordered to slash out. He lasted three seasons, scored two hundreds and then went the way of batsmen who score too few runs.

Poor batting doomed Somerset to eleventh place in the championship in 1947, though they could rejoice in Wellard's 15 wickets against Worcestershire at Bath, and in Walford's run of 96, 52 not out, 90, 101 and 264, this last against Hampshire at Weston. Had Mitchell-Innes and Watts been available more often it might have been different. As it was the professionals, and especially Frank Lee and Bill Andrews, could no longer carry the side.

In fact Lee and Andrews were released at the end of the season, Lee to a distinguished career as an umpire, Andrews to a variety of roles sometimes loosely, sometimes closely connected with Somerset cricket, which was dear to his heart and which he never really left.

Having had a dreadful season, Lee wasted little time in lamentation for he was not surprised to be rejected. Andrews, who had taken only 24 wickets, believed he had been badly used by Meyer, and was devastated to be so summarily sent into the world beyond, a blow for which he was utterly unprepared. Eventually if painfully, he realized that his career was over and set about building a life as a journalist, as a coach, and as a committee man, in which latter roles he was to serve Somerset, carrying out his tasks with his customary loquacity, his irresistible charm and the air of a man of great enthusiasm who found much hilarity in the world and yet, every now and then, intense sadness too; for Andrews had the personality of a Lear, massive, bluff and cunning. A glorious companion, he was also troubled, for beneath his colossal embrace of life lay a loneliness, a kindliness and a fear.

So much mention has been made of Andrews, Buse and Hazell and yet no study of them has been offered. It is time to fill this gap.

24

More professionals

Around Bill Andrews legends grew, for though he never played for England, he was a splendid cricketer and, more to the point here, the very embodiment of Somerset cricket.

A man of Pickwickian appetite, Andrews was a popular figure with the public both during and after his career, so much so that in his regular difference of opinion with authority, amongst whom John Daniell in particular thought him to be a Bolshevik, he could count on public support. Twice Somerset sacked him as a player, in 1932 and 1947, twice as a coach and umpteen times he resigned from committees, on each occasion orchestrating a wave of sympathy which not infrequently forced his erstwhile opponents to embrace this well-meaning, humanitarian and garrulous man.

As a teenager Andrews worked in a solicitor's office, a position far too dreary for a person of his exuberant if uneven temperament. Against his parents' wishes, but guided by Arthur Wellard, Bill sought and found work as a professional cricketer and groundsman with East Coker for a fee of £3 a week. In time he caught Somerset's eye, but their affair did not last, Andrews being released after some moderate seasons. He went to the Northern Leagues to learn his trade properly, using his contacts in Somerset to broadcast his performances, and duly returned to fight another day. Bowling into the wind – Arthur used to say there was nothing in the ends even when a gale was blowing – he swung the ball back late enough to take 750 wickets for Somerset at a rate of 23 runs each. He believed that Wally Hammond had blocked his route to higher honours but perhaps this was mere suspicion, for Hammond was the sort of fellow about whom such things were often said. Probably Andrews, willing and skilled as he was, was not quite up to it.

He could bat a bit too and was apt at times to win promotion in the order to a place so respectful as to flatter his more ambitious notions. Nonetheless he gambolled away effectively, scoring 5,000 runs at an average approaching 16. Year after year he toiled away for Somerset and occasionally found controversy, as when Daniell bit through his pipe upon hearing a demand for higher expenses which he considered outrageous – a demand delivered in person by Andrews, ever one to rush in where angels feared to tread. Yet he was a humble fellow decidedly on the side of the ordinary man. His dad had run a pub in the railway town of Swindon and what he had served his son was later to drink in copious quantities, as he moved from one libellous and hilarious tale to another. In time he helped his local Labour Party candidate, and once he painted white lines on roads as a way of earning a winter wage. Never short of friends or a lively opinion he was ill at ease with those he considered to be stuffed shirts, and was apt to attack them somewhat surreptitiously through his newspaper chums. At forty-nine he was called upon to captain the 2nd XI and in 1957, when he was coach, Somerset had its best season in eleven years, notwithstanding which he was sacked as coach while on a scouting trip to London. After that he helped Somerset cricket at all levels, regularly discovering a new Fred Trueman or Eddie Paynter, and many local youngsters valued his help while being wary of his ability to sell wicket-keeping gloves to off-spinners. At times he took charge of the 2nd XI, and in the 1960s he worked closely with Colin Atkinson. Eventually, and inevitably, it ended in tears for Andrews was too large and unpredictable a man easily to be absorbed in a cricket club, especially one so conservative at heart. Nor did his prickly character and plain popularity lend themselves to gentle compromise. When he went it was usually with a bang.

Towards the end, which came in 1989, he loved life and even Somerset cricket no more, for he had been touched by the tragedy of sudden, willed deaths within his own family and he simply wanted to be alone with his memories. He was a wonderful companion, a fine cricketer and an artful man whose best epitaph lies with Cecil Buttle: 'D'you know, he opened his mouth too much but he meant well. And he was often right.'

Bertie Buse was a different character entirely. Robertson-Glasgow pictured him as an Edwardian butler, immaculate, polite, neat and

> unobtrusively medium in height and build. His moustache is meticulously trimmed and his brown eyes twinkle only decorously. His run, apparently, recalled a butler anxious not to awake echoes from a stone floor, and his pace was strictly military. Upon completing his over he would collect his cap, no matter what rough treatment he had endured. Buse bowled his outswingers with accuracy and as a late-order batsman he collected his runs off the front foot with tidy brain and carefully marshalled powers.

Buse's manner was in some measure misleading for he was a gifted enough sportsman to have played full-back for Bath Rugby Club, and for Somerset too. None the less he was a cricketer who relied upon astute use of limited resources and a man of considerable parsimony so that colleagues thought him to be a dry old fish. He took life at a steady amble and rarely gave much away with ball, bat or hand. In his 304 games he scored 10,623 usually important runs at 22 an innings and with his curling deliveries he took 657 wickets at 29 apiece – a trifle expensive, perhaps, but he bowled in long spells often into a breeze and without the assistance of alert slip fieldsmen.

Buse had played occasionally before being accepted as a professional in 1937 and he continued playing regularly until 1953, by which time he was forty-three and suffering from strains induced by *anno Domini*. Apart from his cricket, all craft and perseverance, he is best remembered as the man whose benefit game ended in one day. Somerset were playing Lancashire at Bath in 1953 and players arrived to find a pitch which had gravel and acorns upon it. Cecil Buttle had expected Bath to prepare the pitch, and Bath had depended upon Buttle. Buse took 6/41 but Roy Tattersall claimed 13/69 and it was all over by 6 p.m. *Wisden* said it was 'a financial disaster for Buse', which was not quite the case. Closer inspection reveals that Somerset waived Buse's duty to pay expenses for the return game and that Buse was constantly stopped in the street by well-wishers who, hearing of his plight, pressed a pound note into his hand. Typically Buse said nothing throughout, and few guessed that he had managed to emerge not so far behind the

239

game. So it is until ripe old age as Buse wiles away his hours in Bath.

For his part Horace Hazell was the stuff of legend, so much so that his considerable skills as a bowler are easily forgotten. Tubby, jocular, philosophical, Hazell was much beloved and yet contemporaries constantly remind observers that he was a splendid bowler of left-arm spin.

Behind his round figure and cheerful manner lay a man more complex than he cared to pretend. To the world Horace was a bluff fellow who could not bat, could not field and who had pints of beer ordered at every stop on his train journey home from Taunton to Bristol. Yet Hazell had never been educated (a deficiency he felt keenly), because he had suffered from double pneumonia and pleurisy as a child. Only rarely did he allow himself to be photographed and seldom did he sign autographs. Quite simply he suffered from a sense of his own inferiority, and felt at ease only with other professional cricketers, or amongst his chums, with whom he was a great character.

He was, beyond argument, an outstanding bowler. Ken Palmer recalls joining Somerset during Hazell's brief period as a coach. Hazell took him into the indoor school, put a saucer on a length and hit it four times out of six. 'There,' he said: 'that's what I mean by accuracy.' Palmer collected the broken saucers and absorbed this lesson.

Hazell hailed from Brislington which, said John Daniell, was in Somerset, which was not quite the case, Hazell's street being just within Gloucestershire's boundary. Upon joining Somerset he was groomed as Jack White's successor and usually found himself playing in away games. Probably White lingered too long, and it is a tribute to Hazell's patience that he waited from 1929 to 1937 to be Somerset's first-choice spinner. Mind you, the wages were higher – £14 for an away game and £12 for a home match, expenses to be paid out of your own pocket – than could be found in blue collar or clerical jobs.

Four times between 1946 and 1952 Hazell topped Somerset's bowling averages. In 1949 he bowled 105 successive deliveries to Gloucestershire's batsmen, including Tom Graveney, without conceding a run. Economical on good pitches, he could be deadly on a wet one. In the field he usually held his catches at slip, though R. J. O. Meyer did for a while place him at cover; and as a confirmed number 11, though Meyer did temporarily promote him to 4, Hazell was adept at pinching vital runs in the tight finishes he always thought to be looming. Off the field he sang songs with Bill Andrews, did rain dances when Somerset were in trouble, and by August grumbled that it was, in his opinion, a 'ruddy silly game anyhow!'

It was his roly-poly tummy which persuaded Somerset to release him in 1952, ending a career in which Hazell took 957 wickets at 24 each. For years he had been bowling behind an ineffectual pace attack, and within months Somerset were scouring the land for likely spinners and signing men rejected elsewhere. Perhaps Hazell was dismissed too early – he certainly thought so – but he forgave and forgot, which was his way.

Wally Luckes's career was just as long – he played 365 games to Hazell's 350 – and scarcely less distinguished. Luckes too, was replaced in time and he too bore no grudges, though he took it hard; at least his replacement was a splendid cricketer and a likeable fellow, Harold Stephenson. A Londoner, Luckes moved to Bridgwater and spent his winters working for the Electric Light people. Behind the stumps he was unflappable, a craftsman rather than an entertainer, a player respected by fellow professionals rather than one who wins public acclaim.

He played from 1924 to 1949 and might have broken all records had his heart been reliable. As it was, illness too often brought long periods of absence, and even when playing Luckes had to bat down the order and avoid undue excitement (Hazell did not believe these two characteristics sat beside each other). Efficiency was his trademark, and not one bye was conceded as Surrey scored 512 in 1936 and Glamorgan 574/4 in 1939. Small, squat and gentle, Luckes never won Test honours and never lost the respect of colleagues and opponents. He trapped 827 victims for Somerset; only Stephenson (1,007) has taken more. And he lived to be eighty-one, for such solid men are not easily beaten.

25

Captains courageous

Replacing Meyer was no easy task, for where was an amateur to be found with the time, money and inclination to captain a rural county side? Committees met, sages were consulted and finally a solution was found. As the *Manchester Guardian* recorded in its county prospects for 1948:

> . . . Somersetshire will be captained by three amateurs in rotation, N. S. Mitchell-Innes in May, J. W. Seamer in June and part of July and G. E. S. Woodhouse for the rest of the season. The first two are Oxford Blues and civil servants in the Sudan, who will spend their summer leaves in playing cricket. Woodhouse is a Cambridge war-time player. Three newcomers, K. G. Harvey and I. A. C. McLennan, both wicket-keepers, and K. H. R. Johnson, a batsman, are among other amateurs who may play.

None of the other amateurs did, in fact, play under any of the captains appointed for the year. Mitchell-Innes and Seamer were, of course, great chums both at Oxford and in the Sudan. Woodhouse had been to Marlborough, as had Seamer, and he was plainly a good fellow. He was, moreover, available to continue as captain in 1949.

None the less it was a remarkable state of affairs. Only Mitchell-Innes of this trio was really good enough to play on his merits, and even he had not played much in recent years. Jake Seamer was thirty-five years old and though he had played occasionally since 1932 he did not pretend to be a batsman of high calibre even in his prime. Fortunately he was a fine fellow, a sportsman capable of winning a hockey blue, a dasher who dressed the part and a proud Somerset man who liked to adopt a broad accent when in London and to observe, on the Underground, how odd it was that 'this yere lot looks loik rabbits – goin' round below ground'. Something of an eccentric, he carried around in his cricket bag an old train board saying 'To Tonbridge' which, he thought, improved his team's chances of victory. Had his batting been stronger Seamer would have made an admirable captain.

Woodhouse was a stripling of twenty-four who owed his elevation to background as much as skill. To him cricket was an interlude between study and a career in a brewery company for which Harold Stephenson was also to work. Born and bred in the West Country, he was a brave rugby player and an orthodox batsman who, like so many other public schoolboys, flattered to deceive. As captain he managed to lift Somerset to ninth place in 1949, a fine effort considering his age (he remains Somerset's youngest official captain) and his decrepit team.

Somerset started badly in 1948, failing to win a single point in Mitchell-Innes's five games at the helm. Walford was at the Olympics and hardly played, and no replacement had been found for Andrews. Gently treated, Tremlett took 83 wickets and Hazell snared 105. Wellard, in decline, could trap only 62 at 28.5 apiece and his batting was a shadow of its former self. And Somerset had sorely needed his runs.

Somerset scored only four hundreds in 1948. Harold Gimblett hit all of them. If he was at times testy it was hardly surprising, for his burden was heavy. He excelled himself against Sussex at picturesque Eastbourne, scoring 310 in 465 minutes of powerful and varied stroke-play. Upon passing Lionel Palairet's previous record of 292 he told John Langridge, 'Well, that's got rid of one amateur from the record books.' Even in his moment of glory Gimblett could not silence his resentments. Sadly they were reinforced when, returning to Taunton, Wellard's request for a collection in recognition of this feat was denied because 'he's paid to score 300'. Lancaster, as secretary, and Daniell as *éminence grise* were not men sensitive to the insecurity and commitment demanded of a professional cricketer in a long, torturous season. It is not all beer and off-drive.

Gimblett carried Somerset's batting. Facing Len Muncer on a dodgy Swansea pitch he hit 6 sixes in 13 balls, all with hard straight blows. Somerset won a few games, and lost plenty. At Taunton they drew, failing by 11 runs against Yorkshire as Johnny Lawrence bamboozled his erstwhile colleagues, taking 6/36, and Miles Coope struck 53 against his native county. 'Twas ever thus with Yorkshiremen.

Otherwise Somerset appeared to be treading water. Hardly anything had changed at the club, even at the ground since 1900. Money was not as tight as formerly yet the hand-to-mouth mentality was not easily shaken off. Subscriptions were raised, at last, from 1 guinea to 2 guineas and a new roller was bought for £78 which Brigadier Lancaster 'found from somewhere' as Buttle put it. Entry to the stands had increased too, and the open Sixpenny Stand was now called the Bob Stand. Buttle had just one tarpaulin cover at his disposal and he spent his winters repairing the ground, for no one had sufficient imagination or funds to contemplate building anything new. If this defeatism was unsurprising, for rationing was still in force, it frustrated those of more adventurous mind who felt Daniell and his friends were preserving themselves in power rather than providing leadership. Somerset had three captains, an ageing and losing team, old men on committees, ancient wooden seats upon which to sit and 2,169 members.

They could at least enjoy the Australians, who arrived in style and left in victory, having routed Somerset by an innings and 374 runs. Spectators remembered Keith Miller borrowing a tennis ball to bounce Walford, and they remembered too rough treatment meted out to Walford and pondered upon the cause of it. Perhaps this amateur reminded his visitors, a democratic lot, of an England they loved not. Certainly Walford appeared ruffled by this bombardment, for Miller, when moved, could recall Larwood in his prime.

Bill Andrews was given a testimonial in 1948 and £3,000 or so was raised. He could have made more, he thought, with a proper benefit. It was Horace Hazell's turn in 1949. Alas, the Lord's Day Observance Society took against some of his events and he suffered, though £2,324 was a satisfactory reward.

For Somerset 1949 was another year of struggle. Thanks to Gimblett scoring two hundreds in a game for the first time, Somerset players gained their first £5 win bonus by beating Hampshire towards the end of May, redeeming a dreadful start in which five matches in a row were lost. This victory was followed almost at

244

once by ten successive defeats as time after time the batting failed. At last the schoolmasters, Walford and Watts, arrived to bring fighting spirit and Somerset won all three games at Weston-super-Mare, beating Glamorgan, champions of 1948, Hugh Watts scoring his maiden hundred and Hazell taking wickets, as he did (12/66) in the following contest with Worcestershire.

Hazell took his 100 wickets and finished fourth in the national bowling averages. Harold Gimblett scored 2,003 runs, a new county record, his 184 against Kent being the masterpiece, an innings of a refinement far removed from the rough rural batting which had so offended the selectors a decade earlier.

No one expected Gimblett to be picked by England – for had not a cross been written against his name? And then, out of the blue, he was summoned to Trent Bridge to attack the West Indian spinners. Gimblett was astonished, for he had long since distanced himself from the high and mighty. Suddenly he was in a big pool again. Troubled, he did not play. During a county game a carbuncle developed on the back of his neck. Huge doses of penicillin were used, and reporters followed his fortunes. Would he play? He did not. Perhaps he did not really want to.

Only five games out of twenty-nine ended in a draw and plainly Somerset was in urgent need of fresh professional talent to sustain it until those amateurs were free to play. Apart from Harold Stephenson and John Lawrence, no cricketer of real quality had been signed since the war, though one or two locals had emerged. Nor, in truth, was anyone of importance to arrive for another five years.

Too much faith was put in young hopefuls such as Jim Redman, an honest seamer from Bath who played against the 1948 Australians and took 117 rather expensive wickets in his sixty-five games. Eric Hill, too, was struggling away, playing in a poor side, consistently under pressure and fearful of playing his shots.

As a boy Hill had been coached by Arthur Wellard, who also took Tremlett and Stephenson under his wing, calling them his colts. Hill did well enough to earn a three-year contract but to his intense disappointment he never quite broke through. It did not help, no doubt, that the war denied him vital, formative years of cricketing education. For a local lad to fail, a fellow with his heart set on Somerset cricket, a man whose father ran up a Somerset flag in his shop whenever Somerset won, was, as ever, a cause of particular sorrow. Nevertheless Hill continued to serve

Somerset after being released in 1951, captaining the 2nd XI with great acumen. Later he may have pondered upon his fate and wondered what might have been if circumstance and temperament had allowed him to play his shots a little more freely.

It is, incidentally, significant that Hill was playing as a professional after the war, for he was a public schoolboy from a background which, in the pre-war years, would have frowned upon a fellow playing for money. To have done so, before 1939, would have been costly in social terms. Now it was tolerated, if scarcely encouraged in men of 'pedigree'.

Wellard was not able to finish his work, for at the end of 1949 his contract was not renewed. A wise club might have offered him terms as a coach, but Somerset had managed without one since time immemorial and was not yet prepared to change, even though for the first time they now had a 2nd XI playing occasionally. Wellard was devastated by his release and, according to Bill Andrews, walked around with his shoelaces undone during the Weston Festival, at which time these decisions were made by a committee increasingly ignorant of cricketing matters and hostile to professionalism in games. Wellard had taken 87 wickets in 1949. Such men are not easily replaced and certainly Somerset had not trained a player to fill his position, a neglect for which they were to pay dearly. Playing in a weak side had been a disadvantage to Wellard, as to Hill, for at a time when he could contribute less he carried a greater burden. Wellard vowed never to return to Somerset and it was years before he softened. Somerset were not to find a satisfactory off-spinner until the sudden emergence of Brian Langford. Still, sad as it was, no tears need be shed over Wellard's retirement save in the apparent failure to discuss the whys and wherefores with him, for his career had been long and outstanding.

Beyond doubt Somerset should have been concentrating upon signing players rather than releasing them, upon building a 2nd XI and a strong professional staff, rather than dismissing ageing professionals still capable of stout service. As it was, with Woodhouse going into business they found themselves in need of a new captain, and a new secretary.

To date captains had been appointed, nominally at least, by the Annual General Meeting. Now rule changes were made to give this power to the executive committee. Having scoured the

land for a likely amateur, having closed their minds to the professional ranks, they summoned Stuart Scott Rogers, a dashing,
handsome fellow who had been a major in the Chindits during
the war. Bold and optimistic, cheerful and gregarious, Rogers's
chief faults as captain of Somerset were that he was a moderate
batsman and had no profound grasp of tactics. Once he bowled
Bertie Buse for 90 minutes at the end of which he approached
Buse and said, 'You'd better bowl now, Bertie!'

Rogers did not, in fact, do so badly, especially at first. Wily old
professionals enjoyed his gung-ho approach to life and absorbed
his weaknesses. But in time, he was found out, and so was his
team. Somerset's executive had been trying to conjure genius out
of nowhere, and were appointing captains with sufficient panache
to camouflage an absence of skill on their part, and a want of class
in their team. Plainly a far more radical approach was urgently
needed. Meanwhile Somerset's executive was content to play its
fiddle.

Brigadier Lancaster's retirement was marked by the presentation of a cheque for £308 19s 0d, a gift from members. After
twelve years of service he was tired, worn down by years of battles
with committees and members. Life had been simpler in the Army,
with its authoritarian structure. It had been easier at Somerset too,
in the early years, when it was more or less a private club run by a
handful of distinguished locals. Now it was a member's club with
a tangled web of committees and interested parties.

Nigel Daniell – 'the salmon' – was chosen as Somerset's new
secretary. In appearance it was a decision which recalled the
early years of family rule, for Nigel was John's son, biologically
if not in terms of personality. But Nigel had one serious fault –
he was, at thirty-five, a young man. Lancaster had been able to
bluster his way through, ordering everyone about in his clipped
way, for all the world a military man. Nigel Daniell had been
a soldier too, and a very good one, commanding 400 men and
100 vehicles in the Western Desert. A capable man of mild
disposition, he was unhappy in his new post, being constantly
hounded by bickering factions, especially those from Taunton
and Weston-super-Mare who had opposed his appointment.
G. O. Boundy, who had played two county games in 1926 and
1930 and who was now an autocratic, crusty, difficult figure at
Taunton Cricket Club, was a particular enemy. Boundy belonged

247

to an old school and was evidently bent upon pouring scorn upon Somerset's secretary. Daniell found himself doing all sorts of menial and administrative tasks, as if he were a junior officer in a mess. In truth his employers wanted a figurehead, a loud, charismatic figure with a manner sufficiently peremptory to instil enough fear to keep warring parties and argumentative servants in their place. Daniell was not such a man and he left at the end of the year to be replaced by another military man, Air Vice-Marshal Taylor, who suited Somerset well by recalling a past of confidence, vigour and empire. Taylor stayed for six years and when he left Somerset's more reasonable supporters, most of whom found themselves cast as rebels, asked Daniell to return but he would have none of it. Once bitten, twice shy.

Harold Gimblett scored 2,000 runs in 1949. For years he had carried the batting and now his old chums, including Bill Andrews and Arthur Wellard, were slipping away. His responsibilities and his insecurity were playing ever more tricks upon his nerves. As a player ages so bad form is mistaken for permanent decline. Gimblett had seen friends from a happy past depart before their time and he began moodily to ponder upon his own fate.

In 1950 he played, he thought, his finest innings, taking 87 off a strong Middlesex attack on a difficult Clarence Park pitch. Compton and Edrich professed themselves astonished by this skilful effort, and Gimblett enjoyed their praise for he was in need of it. That winter he toured India with a Commonwealth team and lost 2 stone in weight, having failed to eat properly. A season later he was ordered to rest by doctors after a poor start. It was the beginning of the end.

Some new men had arrived, none of them entirely satisfactory, though Ellis Robinson in particular was a dangerous bowler. Robinson had played a good deal for Yorkshire since 1934 as an off-spinner who could find turn on any track. In three years he took 256 wickets for Somerset and his departure owed more to a certain intransigence of character than to any flaw as a cricketer. Something in the spirit of the club affronted his ruggedly northern ways and even as he took 107 wickets in 1951 he continued to ruffle feathers, within the team and without. In a charity game, once, he told Michael Parkinson, perched unenthusiastically and ineffectively at short leg, 'Eh, thee, Leaden Legs: tha stands thir as if thy knickers were starched.' Upon his release people spoke diplomatically of the need to build a new younger team.

Roy Smith did, at least, have youth on his side. A local boy, he had bowled his left-arm spinners on a few occasions since 1949 and he was to last until 1955. Alas, he took only 19 wickets. Tiny and determined, Smith did score a first-class hundred before giving up the unequal struggle. Certainly he was no threat to Horace Hazell, still taking wickets and, after his benefit in 1949, able as well as willing to buy his round.

Sadly Maurice Tremlett could offer little help with the ball, his bowling now full of doubt, his manner apologetic as the ball flew around out of control, sending Somerset's new wicket-keeper Harold Stephenson diving cheerfully to collect it. Nearly £1,800 had been given to Wally Luckes as a testimonial to work his retirement.

Without Wellard, and with Tremlett losing all confidence, Rogers did well to take his men to seventh position in 1950. Setting a challenging example, he struck his first county hundred in Frome and reached his 1,000 runs, the first Somerset captain to do so in years. Apart from his attacking batting and the forthright contribution of Gimblett and Tremlett, Somerset owed its surprisingly respectable position to a wet summer, for Rogers had experienced and capable spinners at his disposal in Lawrence, Hazell and Robinson and they took their chances well, especially Lawrence, who trapped 115 men and was prevented only by rain from scoring 1,000 runs too.

Suffering from a wonky knee, Bertie Buse took few wickets but, being a good cricketer, he made himself indispensable by crafting some careful runs for his team. Nevertheless his decline was worrying to those who gazed at the horizon, for Somerset's bowlers were slipping one by one, so much so that Wellard was recalled from club cricket to play a few games. Somerset urgently needed to find some dangerous bowlers, for they had no pace attack and could scarcely compete if the sun shone.

As usual several marginal cricketers fluttered across the firmament, mixing with the stars and occasionally sparkling. A Devon player, Frank Irish, signed as a professional batsman, started promisingly and then fell away. Dropped in July, hastily some thought for he was averaging 25 (enough to pop corks were he an amateur), he returned to his business in Sidmouth and rejected offers of another contract. He was thirty-two and there was no future in it.

And Jack Conibere, twenty-seven, from Wellington (in Somerset), played four games, scored 16 runs and took 7 wickets at a reasonable price (31 each) before returning to club cricket with Wiveliscombe. Such honest club cricketers played odd games, odd in both senses of the word on occasion, before returning to swim in their own depth. Somerset cricket is full of optimists who recommend a local man who had, of late, been flummoxing village opponents or carting sixes into haystacks. These fellows are usually too untutored to last, for a Gimblett is found but once in a blue moon. Nevertheless captains, and supporters, live in hope, for which they cannot be blamed.

John Daniell had resigned as president at the end of 1949, lest his son's appointment as secretary appear in a poor light. Major Longrigg, Bunty's father and another fierce traditionalist, was president and with Air Vice-Marshal Taylor he set about restoring morale in the club as one might in a battalion, by providing vigorous leadership and frowning upon malingerers such as are commonly found amongst the ranks of ageing and sceptical foot-soldiers and professional cricketers.

If their manner was abrupt they did, at least, try to rebuild. They employed Harry Parks, a distinguished Sussex cricketer from a family of Sussex cricketers, as coach and he worked hard in the nets behind the Old Pavilion, especially with youngsters such as Derek Virgin (a leg-spinner) and Tony Davies a local batsman, who had been signed as members of the groundstaff. Parks used to sit with his boys in their little back room and ask each in turn about his efforts in club cricket the previous Saturday, reminding them that in professional cricket it is ends not means which count. Alas, Parks was not to stay long, for committees expect quick results from their coaches, results Parks could not produce, not least because of the uneasy relationships within the club between professionals and officials, nor least because youth and club cricket had been so weakened after years of neglect.

Air Vice-Marshal Taylor had not, in fact, been Somerset's first choice as secretary, for an idea had developed of finding a respected amateur cricketer to be a captain/secretary, a method used by other counties to appoint as leaders men of their choice

250

who could not otherwise afford to play cricket all summer. Sammy Woods had served as a notional secretary decades earlier and now this idea had been revived. In years to come Charlie Palmer, Trevor Bailey and Richie Benaud were all approached at various times, but too little money was on offer. Other men, including Mitchell-Innes and Jack Cameron, sought such a position, combining as it did lots of cricket, a little tiresome administration, a wage and yet no loss of social face. Such a position was a device by which a cherished illusion was maintained, that only amateurs were fit to rule. A captain/secretary, had one been found, would have allowed Somerset to delay the appointment of a professional captain still longer.

Not that captain/secretaries were entirely a bad idea: Somerset has worked best when there has been little division between captain and administration, when, in fact, a 'captain' and 'secretary' were not so far apart; in the era of Hewett, of Atkinson, and of Rose.

Besides changes of personnel, lots of changes were made to the constitution, as men such as Rex Frost, a local accountant with an active, legalistic mind and an attitude intolerant of pomposity, sought to revitalize Somerset's conservative cabal. For a decade Frost was to be a creative influence at Somerset, but in time, it being the way of all flesh, his radicalism grew rigid in a world which slowly passed it by.

Somerset finished fourteenth in 1951, a position more accurately reflecting current strength. Having served as sheet anchor for ten years, Harold Gimblett was no longer as dependable. With no regular opening partner to help him (Eric Hill, Hugh Watts, and Leslie Angell, a youngster from Bath, took turns), Gimblett suffered bouts of bad form and was rested in July. Returning refreshed, he hit three hundreds in August. His batting against Sussex on a turning Weston-super-Mare pitch, *Wisden* thought, 'infused new life into the Somerset team'. Gimblett followed his dashing 103 with a bright 58 and Somerset won handsomely as Robinson took 15/78 in this his outstanding season.

Gimblett's hundred against Worcestershire was scarcely less impressive, his unbeaten 174 following a first innings duck, and lasting nearly six hours during which, says *Wisden*, 'Gimblett rose to great heights'. Somerset lost the game as Worcestershire, chasing 214 in 36 overs, won off the final ball delivered by Buse

251

to Wyatt who hit it into the pavilion.

It was time for Gimblett to choose his games, to play perhaps twenty a year, for he lacked the nervous energy and the support to survive on this treadmill from April to September. No such accommodation was arranged nor even suggested, for a professional was a worker expected to clock in and out, irrespective of emotional ravaging.

Harold finished with 1,453 runs at 33 per innings. Micky Walford was touring Canada with MCC and so it was as well that Maurice Tremlett batted in commanding style as he scored 2,071 runs, top scoring on 15 occasions. He decided to play in New Zealand, with Napier Club, that winter, and rumours began that emigration was being contemplated, a rumour never entirely stilled even during his years as captain. By now, of course, he hardly bowled at all, though every spring he knocked stumps over in the nets. Being a batsman pure and simple – nearly, anyhow – Tremlett played his lofted straight drive less frequently but still caught the eye with handsomely executed cover-drives and cuts.

None of which could save a side so weak in bowling. Khan Mohammad, who had met Harold Gimblett when MCC were in Pakistan, arrived at Bristol University to continue his studies, took digs in Taunton and played for Somerset against South Africa. Watched by 2,000 people he took 5 wickets for 104 runs as Somerset sank to a narrow defeat despite a characteristically bold century from Stuart Rogers. Alas Khan did not stay, the call of the native land proving too strong. Apparently England was a trifle chilly for his taste.

Khan's departure was a disappointment for, despite playing ten professionals on occasion, Somerset began many games with slim hopes of victory. So many failed to break through. Against India in 1952 Somerset fielded four Yorkshiremen in Lawrence, Robinson, Malcolm Walker, who was to play twenty-nine games in seven years and take 28 wickets with his off-breaks, and William Dean, whose only first-class game it was. And David Kitson from Batley was twelfth man. Kitson played thirty-two games in three summers without raising many eyebrows.

Both Dean and Walker were protégés of Johnny Lawrence, who brought them down in the understandable hope that they might provide help in dismissing entrenched batsmen. Neither was

252

up to it. As it turned out, Somerset had a youngster of its own, a lad playing as a batsman for Bridgwater, who soon enough would arrive to cheer everyone up.

Probably Somerset were signing the wrong sort of men, rejects rather than gifted youngsters eager for opportunity or sage professionals prepared to help for a season or two. Yet these things are in part a matter of trial and error and at least an effort was being made. Nevertheless a more adventurous approach was needed and, in time, adopted, though not before battles had raged.

From 1946 to 1952 Somerset earned only three Test caps, Leicestershire (0) alone winning fewer. Nor were any in prospect, for Harold Stephenson, the most likely candidate, was suffering from having to stand up to the stumps practically all day every day. Jim Redman bowled with some pace and less accuracy, and his day of glory, 7/23 against Derbyshire at Frome in 1951, proved as frustrating as Khan Mohammad's solitary appearance, for neither brought any results of consequence.

Evidently Somerset could not approach 1952 with any relish, and their worst fears were confirmed. Somerset lost twelve games and drew fifteen. Just two matches were won, both of them because Rogers, now a beleaguered captain, managed to win critical tosses on dubious pitches in Bath. None the less these victories were celebrated by a chorus of 'The Three Black Crows', with Harold and Buse leading the singers as in days of yore. It was Harold Gimblett's benefit year and he responded with 2,000 runs, including two hundreds in a game against Derbyshire as he drove, cut and hooked in brilliant style.

Gimblett had hoped to be given the Gloucestershire match for his benefit but officials, agitated no doubt by his cantankerous manner (which they, being new to the club, and under no pressure themselves, easily condemned), merely allowed him a fixture against Northants at Glastonbury. His profit from the gate was £8, or so he said, but luckily supporters organized a raffle which raised £500. Gimblett duly hit a glorious hundred, and Rogers was scarcely less fluent as Somerset drew.

Its champion batsman apart, Somerset had little reason to recall 1952 with any joy. Fielding was poor and while new men were tried, including Gerry Tordoff, a Yorkshire amateur who had played twice in 1950 and who batted left-handed in vigorous style, and John Harris, a Tauntonian, so promising that he played as a

253

sixteen-year-old, no one fulfilled expectations for, notoriously, it is hard for new men to rise when their team is in decline.

As defeat followed defeat so Somerset supporters began to demand action. At its Annual General Meeting they were assured that the club was 'taking steps to increase the professional staff'. Significantly they said 'increase' rather than 'improve'. Still more significantly a rider was added 'but in doing so they did not wish in any way to lose the spirit of Somerset cricket which has been such a feature in the past and was due mainly to the Amateurs who had always been available'. So much for Tyler, Nichols, Braund, Gimblett, Wellard and Andrews.

And so much for Horace Hazell, released at the end of 1952, a season during which he had been Somerset's leading bowler. Major Longrigg told him that Somerset was implementing a youth policy and so the old spinners, Hazell and Robinson (now regarded as undesirable) were to be replaced. Alas, Roy Smith never did improve, bowling too slowly for county cricket, and with terrible speed Somerset resorted to signing spinners rejected elsewhere, while Hazell, ageing and decidedly rotund, sat and wondered in his Brislington home. Evidently something had to be done, not least to appease members; but to split Lawrence and Hazell, and with no satisfactory replacement in mind, was to court disaster.

Unquestionably Hazell was less effective than previously, as was Lawrence. Both were victims of being called upon time and time again to bowl to batsmen established at the crease. Somerset lacked penetration with the new ball and this left their spinners with too difficult a task.

In any event Hazell was released as Somerset finished bottom in 1952, a position it was to occupy, with rare consistency, for the ensuing three summers. With Hazell, Robinson, and Redman departing, the cupboard was nearly bare of bowlers. Colin Mitchell, a young medium-pacer from Brislington, was tried and thought to be promising, a view not confirmed by events as Mitchell took 53 rather expensive wickets in his thirty games.

Really only one ray of hope could be found in the darkness. Rex Frost and others had re-formed the Supporters Club, this time with a brief to be constructive rather than critical. Partly by luck, partly by judgement, they caught the rush towards football pools as it began and within two years were running one of their

254

own. In its first week this pool produced a membership of 1,163 and eventually 55,000 Somerset people paid their weekly shilling into it. Administered by enthusiasts at first, but soon professionally run, this pool in turn enabled the Supporters Club to buy houses, ten of them all told, which were rented and eventually sold to players at an attractive price after the benefit money had been collected. These houses helped to bring players to Somerset, for housing was expensive and in short supply after the war. To be able to offer cheap accommodation to a wavering cricketer was an immense advantage.

Besides housing, the Supporters Club used its money to pay expenses for a 2nd XI when it entered the Minor County Championship, to build in 1955 a 650-seat stand on the river side of the ground and to cover such unforeseen costs as might arise during a season. Naturally they did not want their money to be relied upon in the accounts, and no less naturally Rex Frost used this thriving club as his power base.

In time the Supporters Club went into decline, selling off its property at a generous price and then missing the lottery boom. As their pools business, with its agents in factories and shops, fell away so the club lost importance, for it lacked young ideas and business energy. Nevertheless it played a vital part in the revival of the 1950s, in the consolidation and periodic excellence in the 1960s, and in the 1980s its leading lights were still busy, raising funds and gathering items for a cricket museum in the ancient priory barn at the County Ground, a museum duly opened by Jeffrey Archer, athlete, politician, novelist and supporter, who had been a particularly generous benefactor.

Frost and his cohorts bestowed around £120,000 upon Somerset, mostly in difficult times.

By September 1952 Stuart Rogers had endured quite enough difficult times of his own and he left to concentrate upon his career in business. Finding a successor was no easy matter, for not everyone rejoiced at the prospect of leading a team nearly devoid of bowling, whose leading batsman was suffering, physically and mentally, whose supporters were up in arms, whose management was resolutely out of touch and whose treasurer was downcast.

History will not smile upon Ben Brocklehurst, the Berkshire farmer who was chosen to lead Somerset in 1953. At home he had a pedigree herd of cattle but he had wanted to play cricket, especially as a county captain, and had qualified by residence in 1952 so that he could assist Somerset. Brocklehurst was to lead Somerset for two summers, in both of which they finished last; he was to endure a members' rebellion and to lose his best, if most troublesome, batsman. And certainly Brocklehurst, being merely an adequate batsman and a solid rather than intuitive captain, was not trained for his task. In April 1953 Somerset needed a cricketer as great as W. G. Grace, a warrior as formidable as Horatio and a spirit as generous as Marshall. Brocklehurst failed, but he was as much a victim of circumstance as an architect of disappointment.

And yet one rare talent did emerge in Peter Wight, a slim, wristy batsman of Indian extraction who had played once for British Guyana before life brought him to Bath. Wight was qualifying for Somerset and was allowed to play against Australia. He had been playing league cricket in Burnley and needed to seize this opportunity to make his mark. Having failed in the first innings he was downhearted until at a skittles evening he was consoled by Richie Benaud, who predicted he would score a hundred in the second innings – which Wight promptly did, becoming Somerset's fourth man, after Bisgood, Gimblett and Walford, to hit a hundred on his county début.

Later Eric Hill, wise chronicler, wrote of Wight that

> despite all the snags inherent in a hypochondriac of occasionally heroic proportions (he once made a brilliant century when allegedly suffering from flu, double pneumonia, piles and double vision) he was a joy to watch. Despite what a lot of fast bowlers thought, he made many runs against all but Trueman.

Wight was to be a splendid Somerset cricketer, and later a respected coach and umpire but this, for the time being, was of little comfort to Rogers or his advisers.

Naturally 1953 was not without incident. It was the year of Bertie Buse's famous benefit match in Bath. Cecil Buttle had been unlucky in his preparation of the Recreation Ground. Cold winds and a lack of winter rain had slowed the knitting together of pitches relaid in October. Also fresh turf had been unavailable and work had been stopped because of Coronation festivities on the ground. Buttle still remembered all this thirty-six years later, his eyes filling with horror, his body shaking with laughter. As

Lancashire arrived so Buttle found his pitch devoid of grass and covered with dry moss.

Somerset batted first and were dismissed for 55, Roy Tattersall taking 7/25. In reply Lancashire slumped to 46/5, whereupon Marner and Wharton, using the long handle, added 70 in 25 minutes, taking 15 off one Lawrence over, and 18 off Buse and Redman. Though Buse took 6/41 he had little support and the visitors led by 103. Lancashire had hit merrily and 140 minutes remained as Gimblett and Lawrence walked out a second time. Every ball, now, removed a clod of earth as it pitched, and Somerset were soon 7/4. Harold Stephenson managed to clout a 4 and a 6 off Tattersall but at 5.15 p.m. Somerset were 44/9. Redman and a new blond débutant from Bridgwater, Brian Langford, added 35 but the game was over with nearly an hour left on the first day.

Poor Bertie Buse, they all said, as they pressed pound notes into his hand! Poor Somerset, too. What can Langford have made of it all? He saw Captain Deshon, a soldier educated at Sherborne who played very occasional games for no apparent reason, smite hugely at every ball he faced, scoring 0 and 9. He saw Somerset's feeble batting list, with so many batting far above their station and their dubious spin attack too. Perhaps he heard Air Vice-Marshal Taylor ask Buttle what he meant to do, and Buttle's reply: 'Hang myself, sir.'

Victory must have seemed far away. It was, in fact, two days away. Helped by Johnnie Lawrence, who lived in a caravan by the ground, Buttle decided he had to 'take drastic action' about his wickets. He brushed off the acorns and gravel, raked off the moss and mixed up bull's blood and cow manure, and spread it across his pitches with a watering can. 'The problem was how to camouflage what we had done. Then I hit on the idea of spreading grass cuttings and rolling them in. Johnny and I worked till 10 at night and we sorted it out.'

Buttle's wicket was as red as a farmer's face and as barren of grass as the Sahara. Somerset batted first against Kent and scored 123. In their turn Kent were dismissed for 178 by this seventeen-year-old novice, Langford, who had joined the staff only after his mother had consulted her neighbour Wally Luckes. Beginning as a batsman who could bowl medium-pace, Langford had been changed into an off-spinner and was already challenging Malcolm Walker for a place.

Gimblett rallied Somerset with a fighting 146, Bertie Buse collected a characteristically careful 102, and Somerset left Kent to chase 361 to win. After a bright start they were skittled by Langford who, in a burst of 15 overs took 6/27 as Somerset won by 153 runs.

If Langford had begun to regard cricket as a pretty good game, he must have thought it incomparable a few days later as he routed Leicestershire, following his 14/156 against Kent with 11/134. Cheers echoed around the tents whenever he was brought on, and in the excitement a small boy upset two urns of tea. Fielding at backward short leg Harold Gimblett helped his young team-mate, telling him how to bowl to each batsman. Off the field he stared at Langford's blue suede shoes, and they duly disappeared. Langford had not owned any cricket boots but Air Vice-Marshal Taylor had bought him a pair – 'ruddy great heavy things they were'.

For his 26 wickets and nine days of work, reduced to seven by events beyond his control, Langford was paid a sum of £9, which he considered princely. He had found a way of life which suited him.

Sadly Bath produced moments of genuine sorrow in 1953. Maurice Tremlett was fielding at short cover as Woollett, a modest opening batsman for Kent, protected his wicket. Suddenly Woollett hit out a thumping off-drive which smashed into Tremlett's forehead, a sickening blow which left an indent frightening in its depth. Tremlett was rushed to hospital for emergency treatment. Luckily his skull was found to be unusually thick and no splinters penetrated his brain. Even so it was a dreadful injury, and one which affected Tremlett's eyesight ever afterwards. He was to die, too early, of cerebral cancer and surgeons blamed this injury.

Nor is this the only hint of tragedy connected with Somerset cricketers of the 1953 vintage. Tom Hall was playing then. He had represented Derbyshire as an amateur since 1949 but his county had a plentiful supply of seam bowlers so he moved to Somerset, for whom he was to play twenty-three matches in two years, taking 63 wickets at a respectable cost. Popular and gregarious, he also helped Gimblett to add 130 for the ninth wicket against Northamptonshire to give Somerset a first innings lead.

Hall, says David Foot, had started his working life on the

railways in Derby, shovelling coal into the locomotives as an engineering apprentice, and surprising his friends by arriving at a hunt ball a few hours later resplendent in white tie and tails. At Somerset he married Air Vice-Marshal Taylor's daughter, but was not much called upon in 1954 and so took his wife to Norfolk, where they settled. Hall began a boat-building business which, by 1984, had hit hard times. He fell from a fast-moving train and was killed at the age of fifty-three. Two inquests were held and cause of death given as 'multiple injury' and 'hypertension'. Hall is remembered by friends as the nicest, staunchest, most honest of men and his loss was widely mourned.

Despite Bath, despite Langford, it was a depressing year and by the end of it Somerset supporters were up in arms. Walford was finished, Gimblett in decline, Buse the only reasonable pace bowler, and he was ageing, and no one seemed to be doing anything about it, save to sign men who had failed elsewhere.

26

Rebellion and rebirth

Ever since its formation Somerset's various governing bodies had had a firm and constant idea of what sort of club it was to be. As years passed and generations died so it became increasingly diffi-cult to fulfil this ideal. And yet fondness lingered for an amateur past, for a differently ordered world, a world of unquestioned authority.

By 1933, let alone 1953, it is apparent, especially from this distance, that such a club was beyond attainment. Romanticism would be appreciated by supporters so long as their team could compete. Once grim years arrived a cussedly rebellious streak emerged, for Somerset people loved their cricket and felt betrayed by sustained failure. Naturally those in charge were blamed, and rightly so for they had been bickering amongst themselves, and had provided leadership which was extraordinary only for its want of imagination. Their efforts to arrest the slide had been feeble, as they appointed incompetent and inadequate amateur captains and signed professionals singularly lacking in class.

Small wonder then, that in the autumn of 1953 a bridgehead of supporters formed themselves into a rebel group and challenged the authority of their club committee. Perhaps it was unfortu-nate that this challenge was issued by three men who worked on provincial newspapers, Ron Roberts, Bob Moore and Eric Hill, for this allowed them to be dismissed as trouble-makers in search of a headline when, in fact, each in his own way felt warm affection for Somerset cricket. In any case rebellion was on its way; these men simply had the passion, energy and time to lead it.

Argument raged. Petitions were signed, articles written, friendships broken, and slanders uttered until, eventually, a special meeting was called and held at Corfield Hall in Taunton. Proceedings began at 3 p.m. on a Saturday afternoon, a time carefully chosen because many supporters were working men who could not attend during the week. To widespread surprise the hall was packed, as 360 angry members sat and listened to a debate.

And quite a debate it was. Speakers were subjected to shouts and boos, to catcalls and interjections. Bob Moore and Ron Roberts argued their case, called for a revival, condemned the sacking of Horace Hazell and expressed astonishment that only eight professionals had been retained for 1954. They acknowledged that some improvements had been made in the last couple of seasons but said they were mostly cosmetic, designed to placate the mob. No one could feel any confidence in a committee which had to be goaded into action.

A Taunton member asked why Harry Parks had been sacked after one year, Eric Hill repeated criticism of Hazell's release, and a Mr Gill said 'what we need now is not an inquest but major surgery'. Voices called out 'Sack the lot', meaning the committee.

In reply Rex Frost observed how difficult it was to sign new players, and Mr Southwood, who was to be chairman from 1954 to 1959, said new members were needed to which a man called out 'Get a winning team', – a remark which brought tumultuous applause.

It was a fiery, emotional meeting, one from which club officials emerged with little credit. Inevitably ranks closed, for no establishment cares to see its foolishness so brazenly exposed. And by a bunch of newspapermen!

Sadly Somerset's reaction was not to reform but to counter-attack. Plainly this rebellion could not be dismissed as a few hotheads letting off steam. Polite assurances were not enough. Authority was being challenged. It was time to develop a strategy, time to condemn these rude aggressors.

Somerset's embattled committee fought for its life, and Brocklehurst, to the dismay of Hill, Roberts and Moore, rallied to the cause, reasoning that though his committee were undoubtedly hopeless the rebels had nothing constructive to say, which was unfair. Other players took a different view; Maurice Tremlett,

261

who was being paid half a crown an hour to help the club send out its defence document, helped the rebels in his spare time.

Seeking to silence this turbulent trinity and its thousands of supporters, the club launched an aggressive campaign and one businessman tried to persuade newspapers to sack Roberts, Moore and Hill forthwith. Such attitudes were regrettably predictable from men who saw themselves as protecting their club from an opportunist invader with no respect for hierarchies.

Soon, as in all civil wars, reason was lost, right neglected, and all energy concentrated upon winning. Nor is it remotely surprising that the committee was clever enough to reject a demand for a meeting at the ground and instead called for a vote of confidence at an emergency meeting held at a time and place of its own choosing. Had these men been as subtle and as determined in building Somerset cricket as they were in defending their position, no such dispute would have arisen. As Eric Hill recalled:

> Their choice of venue was a cheat in our opinion. We met at the Town Hall in Weston-super-Mare at 5.30 p.m. on a Friday night in November. There weren't so many cars about in those days and many working people had great difficulty getting there.

So it turned out. Moreover Weston was a far more conservative town than Taunton, and most members living there were old and traditionalist. Also Somerset invited the Bishop of Bath and Wells to chair the meeting, therefore forcing everyone to behave and using the silent voice of the Church to protect the status quo. Machiavelli would have been impressed.

Brocklehurst spoke out, dismissing the reporters as Faith, Hope and Charity. Major Longrigg, the president, complained that his committee were being blamed for mistakes made before they took office, and he spoke of team-building and of opening an indoor school, a project which was to cost £5,000. Damagingly, he pointed out that Moore and Roberts had refused to attend an emergency committee meeting called to iron out problems. Quite rightly Moore and Roberts had felt that the vote of no-confidence should be taken first, but they understood the cleverness of Longrigg's manoeuvre.

262

Only a small proportion of members was able to attend. Somerset's vast committee sat in all its glory upon the stage. Colonel Grey, later a successor as president to Longrigg father and son, rallied to the flag and the vote of confidence was carried by 157 votes to 107, a majority reinforced by a postal ballot.

Much good came of the rebellion. Complacency was shattered, frustration given expression, ideas aired. It was a family argument, if a particularly venomous one. Longrigg, realizing how hollow his victory had been, seeing that the vote had been won and the debate lost, consulted Bob Moore, Eric Hill and Ron Roberts, gave them parts to play in the club, on committee and, in Hill's case, on the field. They argued for a player-secretary, and Hill approached Mitchell-Innes, who had just returned with his family from Sudan. Alas, Mitchell-Innes was offered only £500, not enough on which to educate his sons, and he shook his head. Sub-committees were formed to bring fresh membership and to strengthen cricket. At least the old closed shop had been partially broken, though sadly some of the old faces and old ideas continued.

At first nothing improved in 1954, on the field at any rate. Bill Greswell and Bill Andrews were elected by postal ballot to the committee, Eric Hill captained the 2nd XI very well and Horace Hazell was appointed as coach, a position he was not for long considered fit to hold. Nevertheless these were steps forward, and thanks to them Somerset cricket began to improve quickly during the decade, so that within four seasons Somerset had at last appointed a professional captain, had found two Australian cricketers of outstanding quality and had finished third in the championship.

None of this was in sight as the 1954 season began. Indeed things very rapidly deteriorated. By April Harold Gimblett found himself in a nervous state beyond his own control. On occasions in 1953 Somerset was finding Gimblett absent as play was due to begin, and had been forced to send someone in to town to bring him back. He was usually wandering around the shops with a glazed look in his eye and was surprised to discover time had slipped by so quickly. For a year he had been taking endless pills, seeing psychiatrists and enduring electric shock treatment; for sixteen weeks he had stayed in Tone Vale mental hospital and he was still weak in April.

Failing in Nottingham, where he could scarcely concentrate,

he was in poor form in every respect as Yorkshire arrived in Taunton, losing his wicket with a reckless shot against Trueman on the first morning. After the second innings he said he had had enough, and promptly packed his bags and went home.

Brocklehurst asked reporters to say nothing, to give Gimblett a chance, and they complied. But inevitably Somerset's committee, already impatient with their ailing star, heard of this erratic conduct and called Gimblett to account. Brocklehurst, who had not grown up beside Gimblett and saw only his worst years, condemned him. Quite simply Gimblett's employers, his captain and many of his colleagues could no longer tolerate his sudden changes of mood.

Gimblett never played for Somerset again, a sad end to a wonderful career. Somerset honoured his contract but, despite the efforts of R. J. O. Meyer, Bill Andrews and others this fine batsman and his beloved county were never reconciled. Three years later Gimblett offered his services again and Somerset turned him away. They took too little care of him.

In his heart Gimblett never left Somerset, though for decades he believed he had been treated unsympathetically. He told David Foot that Air Vice-Marshal Taylor had thrown him out of the ground when he returned to see his old friend Tom Tout in the scorers' box. Sometimes in newspapers and in speeches, he told his 'woeful' tale and said how much love he had needed and how little he had received. Clubs are apt to regard their players as machines, as run-scorers or wicket-takers, rather than as men who might hold their county in just as deep an affection as these unpaid servants who sit in judgement.

And yet Harold was, perhaps, not so harshly treated at the end, for Somerset had taken medical advice and learnt that Gimblett could no longer endure the sustained pressure of first-class cricket and that to ask him to do so was to put him in mortal danger. Gimblett had finally been worn down by a game which delighted and tormented him. A difficult, private man capable of great kindness, he could not provide the leadership expected of him because he was himself constantly in need of reassurance. Admiring his play, people sought stability and strength in his character and were disappointed to discover only flawed humanity.

As this mighty batsman departed, so other cricketers arrived, for Somerset scouts had been hard at work, picking up scraps from rich tables to the north.

Jim Hilton arrived from Lancashire, and stayed for four years, bowling good, honest off-spinners and taking 133 wickets at a respectable rate, holding the fort until Langford matured. Jim's brother, Malcolm, was a distinguished cricketer, one capable of dismissing Bradman twice in a game, and of playing for England too. Rumours that Somerset went north to sign Malcolm and returned with the wrong brother cannot at this distance be confirmed, though contemporaries swear by them. A lesser talent, Jim was a gregarious fellow and an amusing companion, a typical Lancastrian in fact. He gave decent service to Somerset before returning to his native county.

Geoff Lomax was from Lancashire too, and he filled a breach for nine years, playing 211 games, scoring 7,516 runs at an average of 20, and taking 235 rather expensive wickets with his seamers. Relaxed, even naïve, Lomax was a handy cricketer whose chief characteristic was his steadfastness. A pleasant, popular fellow he was moved up and down the batting order, collecting brave runs as an opener and fighting hard on bad pitches. He was, too, a reliable slip fieldsman, a rare commodity at Somerset since Braund's retirement.

Lomax had many fine days, taking a hundred off Tyson, completing a hat-trick at Weston-super-Mare, scoring 60 with a broken wrist at Gillingham. He failed too, of course, and with some frequency, yet whichever difficulty arose he met it with a ready smile, a pint or two (or several) and a twinkle in his eye suggesting that, fun as cricket could be it was not quite so attractive as a day's fishing over at Lyme Regis where, in time, he kept a boat. Deservedly he was given a benefit in 1961 and a year later he departed, without an enemy, not even amongst those critics who mourned his want of aggression, but without truly leaving his mark either.

Life was not quite so simple for John McMahon, an Australian who had played for Queensland and for Surrey, and who now joined Somerset as a left-arm spinner at the age of thirty-four. McMahon stayed four years, replacing Horace Hazell, played 115 games and took 349 wickets at an average of 26, most of them with his orthodox spinners though occasionally, if quick wickets were needed irrespective of cost he delivered a few overs from the back of his hand. Given an equable temperament McMahon could have stayed longer, for he was a splendid bowler. Alas, he was something of a Jekyll and Hyde, a likeable fellow sober and a cussed, threatening one in his cups. A man without peace of mind, a man who hurt himself more than his family or friends, he was released at the end of 1957 because Somerset had heard too much about his private life and cared to hear no more. Realizing his essential harmlessness, McMahon's colleagues protested publicly about his dismissal but they were powerless to prevent it. They signed a petition begging forgiveness for McMahon and pointing out that he had secured eighty-four victims at an average of 20 that season. Club members began a petition too but the anger died and McMahon was gone.

Nor were these the only débutants of 1954. Phillip Fussell, from a family of brewers in Frome, played one of his two games. A regular with Eric Hill in the 2nd XI, Fussell is remembered as a true amateur, as a fellow who could sink a pint in eight seconds and did so for bets, a fellow willing to bowl all day regardless of reward or prospects unless, that is, he had been harvesting since dawn in which case noon found him exhausted. He was a throwback to a different era, a time when a public-school education and a robust manner would have brought more than one game a summer.

A polite, correct, thoughtful sixteen-year-old Yorkshireman first appeared in this year of change too. Despite his tender age Graham Atkinson had served an apprenticeship at Somerset, and had worked his way through the ranks. As with Langford, Palmer, Virgin, and Kitchen, he joined Somerset at an early age, knocking on the senior dressing-room door, asking if anyone might want him to run an errand, be it to back a horse or repair a bat. Thanks to Eric Hill and to other men of ideas Somerset had a system in which these youngsters could be tested, one through which they could emerge.

Atkinson was to have an outstanding career – he still appears regularly at Somerset Old Players dinners organized by John Barnwell – and there is no need to dwell upon him here except to remark upon the hope that he brought to a gloomy period.

By now Brocklehurst was the only amateur playing with any regularity. Somerset had its largest professional staff ever. Of course they were a hotchpotch of imports and discards, and since the team had not risen together spirits could sink with terrible speed as defeats piled upon each other. And even when Victory wiggled an alluring finger it could turn treacherously away just as Somerset arrived. Needing 72 to beat Essex at Clarence Park, Somerset had reached 10 without loss when a thunderstorm flooded the field. As Les Angell, who scored a neat maiden hundred against Pakistan in this season, recalled, 'eventually at one end the stumps gave up the ghost and keeled over in the water. Only then did skipper Ben Brocklehurst agree to the match being abandoned.'

At least the previous year Middlesex had been beaten, though Brocklehurst insisted upon the Lord's groundstaff rolling the pitch for a full seven minutes before allowing his men to chase their target of 8 runs! These moments had to be savoured for they were few and far between.

With precious little bowling at his disposal, and with limited experience and tactical acumen, those hard-won qualities, Brocklehurst could do little with his side, and few were surprised that eighteen games were lost. Nor were eyebrows raised when Brocklehurst decided at the end of the season to give up the unequal struggle and to return to his farm.

Seldom can any county have appeared in a worse state than Somerset in 1954, and yet, in truth, the corner had been turned. Besides Atkinson there was talk of Ken Palmer, a determined young all-rounder from Devizes, of Chris Greetham, a handsome cricketer born in Berkshire, and besides Langford would soon return from National Service. Moreover Somerset had begun to look beyond its boundaries for cricketers, and started to use its imagination.

Not that Somerset officials were yet ready to appoint a proper captain. Instead they searched once more for a born leader. Amateur captains are a splendid notion if an appropriate candidate can be found, but to appoint one irrespective of the calibre of professionals such as Tremlett and Stephenson was to go in hot pursuit of a principle in defiance of all evidence.

Somerset invited Trevor Bailey to be secretary captain but he declined. Apparently they offered him £2,000, a princely sum. Mitchell-Innes was offered much less and he too declined. Finally Somerset found Gerry Tordoff, a resilient, pugnacious Yorkshire left-hander presently serving in the navy, which generously released him for a summer. Fortunately Tordoff had two strengths as a captain: he could bat well enough to score 1,132 runs in his first full season and he was wise enough to listen to the sage advice of Johnny Lawrence, now in the final summer of a distinguished career.

Tordoff did his best to inspire his men – once encouraging Brian Lobb with the words, 'C'mon, Lobby, bowl him the one which leaves him in the air and comes back off the wicket' but to expect him to lift his team was hoping for too much. Quite simply they lacked authority with the bat and penetration with the ball. On spiteful Clarence Park pitches they were dismissed for 36, 91, 37 and 98, as Alec Bedser, Tony Lock and Derek Shackleton bombarded batsmen plainly out of their depth. For Somerset McMahon took wickets and Hilton his first hat trick but they were a beaten side and duly finished bottom.

Perhaps it was significant that this supposed spring of 1955 had begun with a public row over whether or not it was right to call players by their Christian names. Elders from Weston-super-Mare called this 'a serious breach of discipline', while Rex Frost, now serving as treasurer, dismissed such criticisms as scandalous. Editorials were written, pointing out that Somerset CCC was faced with serious financial difficulties and that discord over a side issue seemed to be out of place. It was, in fact, a battle between the old school tie and the new professionals (Frost was an accountant) in the club, a battle which was to move a stage further within a year.

Malcolm Walker, promoted to open at Romford, scored 100 in 3¼ hours despite suffering from appendicitis. He took 5/45 in Bristol but with Brian Langford soon to return from his soldiering duties his prospects were bleak.

Somerset was still trying hard to improve its staff, which considering its record in recent years was hardly surprising. In particular they were searching for bowlers, and found a couple in Ken Biddulph and Brian Lobb, who were to take 638 good, honest wickets between them.

Biddulph bowled inswing from wide of the crease and he was in the habit of stopping just before delivery. A willing bowler, one prepared to work all day, and one often condemned to doing so as a member of a usually toothless attack, Biddulph served chiefly as an understudy to Brian Lobb. A chirpy cockney, he surprised local Somerset players by using coathangers for his clothes, a custom hitherto presumed to be extinct outside Kent. He fancied he could bat too, and colleagues say he took guard with great style, though they draw a veil over what followed. Biddulph did once add 40 with Colin Atkinson to save an innings defeat at Essex, but even this was not universally acclaimed as his team mates had already showered, changed and packed their bags.

Biddulph took 270 wickets in his ninety-one games and stayed until 1961, by which time his bowling had been spoilt as efforts were made to quicken his pace now that Lobb was fading.

Brian Lobb was just as game and rather more skilled. He had been approached when acting as Warwickshire's twelfth man on Coronation Day, recalled Harold Gimblett pulling Eric Hollies for 6 last ball before lunch, and decided to join Somerset because his home county already had eight seamers. For a time he played for the 2nd XI under Eric Hill, driving to Seaton in Hill's old Morris Minor for club games, but once qualified he was seldom absent and usually Somerset's most dangerous pace bowler. An accurate inswinger, he developed an off-cutter which he was afraid to bowl since if it turned he was immediately removed from the attack and replaced by authentic spinners! Above all Lobb was a character, honest and earthy. As a batsman he played shots which, if they possessed a few too many arms and legs, were correct in conception and which none the less contrived to miss the ball by a distance. In his 116 games Lobb scored 624 runs at an average narrowly above 5, a figure more respectable than might have been expected. As a fieldsman, too, he was full of huff and puff, his legs pumping determinedly away entirely unperturbed by their lack of progress. His run-out of George Cox at Frome is recalled with hilarity largely because of its singularity. Cox saw Lobb chasing, ran a second, saw Stephenson shaping to catch the throw, was much amused by this bluff and realized too late that it was not a bluff at all.

Smoking his pipe, a smile seldom far from his face, Lobb gave Somerset fine service at a difficult time, becoming in 1957 the county's first fast bowler since the war to take 100 wickets in a season. He took 368 before decline demanded departure, a decline hastened by years of weary toil in a cause which was usually lost. Not that Lobb was one to grumble; like Tyler and Nichols before him, he took it all in his stride.

Others had appeared too, refugees from other counties or men simply happy to build a career in the West. Graham Tripp was

269

a local who played thirty-four games without scoring many runs, while Lewis Pickles was a Yorkshireman who was to score 1,000 runs in his first full season, 1956, after which little more was heard of him as a player, for he did not quite do enough to survive in a team which was gradually finding its feet, a team which by 1958 contained promising youth and brilliant overseas talent, always the two vital ingredients at Somerset.

One such youth appeared in 1955, and his arrival was by far the most significant of the season. More will be heard of Ken Palmer; for the time being suffice to say that he was signed on the advice of Harry Parks in his time as coach. After a trial lasting three days this sixteen-year-old had been about to return to his home in Devizes when Ben Brocklehurst's voice bellowed across the field. 'Palmer,' he roared, 'go and see Air Vice-Marshal Taylor.' Palmer signed for £4 a week, changed with other youngsters in the Stragglers Pavilion and, knowing his place, called his elders and betters Mr Tremlett and Mr Stephenson. His dad was a groundsman too and he used to provide Cecil Buttle with his witch's brooms. Occasionally, arriving in Taunton, he would discover that a sudden clutter of wickets had caught Buttle off guard, mid-pint in the Ring of Bells, whereupon he would brush and mark the wicket himself. His son played first in a pair of boots provided by Bill Greswell, now an esteemed figure in the club.

As an eighteen-year-old Ken took 2 important Middlesex wickets on his début, and managed to score 13 runs too. He bowled with Yawar Saeed, a striking-looking fellow who had appeared (no one quite knew how) to open Somerset's bowling in a few games. Yawar was apt to ask colleagues, 'Don't you think I'm quick?' but wisely he rarely waited for the answer. Palmer, who developed into a splendid, rugged all-rounder, was to play a major part in the strong Somerset XI formed in the 1960s, the origins of which are to be found in Eric Hill's 2nd XI, with its Palmers and its Langfords, in the nurturing of other youngsters and in two dramatic events during the winter of 1955.

One other advance was made in 1955. A Supporters Club now enriched by its football pools scheme built and paid for a stand by the River Tone. It was a stand not for members but for the general public and it proved popular. To this day particular men are adopted and cheered by the River Stand, men chosen without as much cricketing discrimination as is shown by members, men chosen by dint of their cheerfulness.

27

Australian revival

Somerset began 1956, the year of rude awakening over the Suez Canal, with a professional captain, in Maurice Tremlett, and a combative, skilful Australian cricketer in Colin McCool. Both events were of immense importance.

By proving himself to be a splendid captain Tremlett forced Somerset into a world for which it still did not much care, and by doing so he survives as a figure both beloved and significant.

Tordoff had been sacked as captain, Bunty Longrigg holding him largely responsible for Somerset's failure. An assistant secretary was sought too, a man who could play as well; few doubted that Longrigg was searching for another amateur captain. Nor, as Tordoff failed, did any official feel called upon to resign.

D. Heath from Hampshire and R. Dinnet from Leicester were considered as assistant secretaries but, in the end, Somerset plumped for Tremlett. McCool, who had been tipped in some quarters, later observed that Somerset had 'no feeling of being a cricket team. They'd had so many captains over the years the players just didn't know what was going on. They had lived and played in an atmosphere of uncertainty season after season. Tremlett was given the job. I wouldn't have taken it had there been a life pension to go with it.'

A press campaign had played its part in dragging Somerset into an age for which it did not care. Brian Chapman urged Somerset to 'swallow their patrician pride, stop hawking the job around and give Tremlett, in his prime at 32, a chance'; which, thankfully, they did. And they gave him a £150 pay rise too, this at a time when Brian Lobb, for example, was paid just £450 a year.

Tremlett's was to be a troubled regime for while his players respected him officials thought him much too lax. Throughout his four years as captain he was dogged by manoeuvres to oust him. He had not changed since his early days as a youngster with an eye for a fast horse, a pint of beer, a helping of fish and chips and a game of skittles. He liked his life to be simple and had no stomach for intrigue, which is so much a part of a county captain's experience. Nor was he one to butter up committee men, on the contrary he thought they spent too much time at lunch and too little watching cricket. Accordingly he was apt to withdraw into his own world, a fraction distant from colleagues and bosses. But it was a creative, optimistic world in which matches were played to be won or lost, in which Somerset had a chance of victory.

Tremlett was not much of a bowler now and instead concentrated upon batting, to which he brought considerable élan. His lofted straight drive and cut were much admired, as his leadership was to be. Under him Somerset learnt to chase a score, and to entice opponents not to abandon their chases. With Tremlett's easy personality running things, members noted an improvement in performance and enthusiasm, as is often the case under a new skipper. Tremlett was to sustain this change for three years before, feeling let down, he lost interest. Officials thought he lacked discipline, and lost faith in him, failing to see that he left such matters to Stephenson and McCool.

Somerset's new captain was lucky in his timing. Langford had returned and his bowling, fielding and batting caught the eye, which may surprise those who recall only his later years. They had found, too, in Dennis Raoul Whitehall Silk, born in Eureka, California, educated at Christ's Hospital and Cambridge University, where he won his blue, a gritty, brave amateur entirely capable of holding his place even though he could play only in the school holidays. Whether fielding at short leg or attacking with the bat, Silk brought much vitality to Somerset and his return from schoolmastering was welcomed rather than resented even though it might cost a pro his place. Sadly Silk was to play only thirty-three county games, in which he scored 1,543 runs at an average of 33.5 – impressive figures. Perhaps he was no Walford but how Somerset must have wished he could play longer than his five summers of occasional contribution.

Above all Tremlett had at his command one Colin McCool,

a gum-chewing digger from Sydney. Fielding at slip, bowling his leg-spinners as he had done under Bradman in 1948, or standing squat and square-jawed in front of his wicket, McCool was a tough and brilliant cricketer. He had trained himself to cricket by sheer hard work, practising as a boy by hitting a ball in a sock tied to a clothesline. He expected no quarter and gave none, and so brought to Somerset a competitive streak hitherto somewhat lacking.

McCool's own career had passed its peak, though it had been quite a peak as he hit a Test hundred and took important wickets, battling, as he saw it, against a captain bent upon a pace onslaught. After all he was forty years old and his spinning fingers were rather stiff and attached to an arm which was rather low. Accordingly McCool concentrated upon his batting and upon training Somerset's fresh youngsters, out of whom he scared the living daylights. When Ken Palmer played a bad shot once he growled, 'Do that again, son, and I'll kick your backside.' When bowling he'd roar at these fellows to let nothing through the covers, and they hardly dared to return the ball to him lest he should have to bend, which he was unwilling to do. In practise he'd dampen a roller and skid slip catches off it. Sometimes he would give a youngster a ball ten yards away and say, 'C'mon, chuck it at me, I know you don't like me.' He wanted to practise his back defence. In fact, of course, they respected him enormously, if from a distance, for he became something of a father figure.

In the slips he would say, 'Head down, backside up, here they come.' Preparing to bat, he would lie snoring in his corner and upon being told his turn had come he would pick up a piece of chewing gum off the ceiling and march out to bat. At the crease he cut ferociously, and often against the spin, much to the horror of off-spinners who thought such treatment impossible on turning tracks. Not that he was inflexible. Once, provoked by Wilfred Wooller's observation that 'you foreigners should go home', a comment made from silly point, McCool tore into Peter Walker, cutting his spin to ribbons, scoring a bristling hundred. Wooller had that effect upon certain opponents. Bill Alley, soon to arrive, once asked him, 'What's it to be, swords or rifles?'

McCool was a marvellous influence on men such as Palmer and Langford, telling them that 'when you walk out you must think you're the best player – better than any of these mugs'. McCool was paid more than any colleagues because, as he told

273

his employers, 'I'm better than any of 'em'. And so he was.

McCool only stayed for five summers before age and those cold winters which found him snuggled up under a blanket in his living-room, drove him back to his warm homeland. In those seasons he took 219 wickets and at a respectable cost (28/12) and scored 7,912 runs, most of them memorably cantankerous.

At first these changes made little difference to Somerset's position. Despite their eagerness Tremlett's men finished fifteenth, scarcely cause for celebration. Moreover though membership had risen from 1,998 to 2,575 a heavy loss, £4,789, was recorded. Upon the retirement from his honorary position of Air Vice-Marshal Taylor, it was to Richard Robinson that the secretaryship of Somerset was entrusted. Robinson, of course, could not waive his wage, but he held his appointment for fifteen years, not without controversy.

With McCool murdering anything short, and tiring as he reached 70 or so, and with Peter Wight as svelte and charming as ever, Somerset at least had some batting of quality around which to build. Determined efforts were being made to organize schoolboy coaching and with a powerful 2nd XI in the Minor County Championship it was plain that Somerset was moving forwards. Not since 1890 had they included in their ranks as promising a bunch of youngsters as Graham Atkinson, Palmer, Langford and, soon enough, Roy Virgin (début in 1957), Chris Greetham (1957) and Mervyn Kitchen (1960). It was a time of hope.

Langford took 8/23 against Kent at Bath after Wight, Pickles and Atkinson had given Somerset a good score. He took 6/25 to bowl Nottingham out for 86 a few days later on the same ground, and with McCool scoring 72 not out Somerset won in some comfort, a victory saluted with a rendition of 'The Three Black Crows'. The boys were singing again. Australia proved more formidable opposition, Jimmy Burke (138) and Slasher Mackay (71 not out) scoring well. Typically McCool, who struck 1,966 runs this summer, powered his way to 90 and 116 in this contest, every shot a message from a neglected cricketer to his national selectors. Five years later Alley was to score 134 and 95 against Benaud's tourists, a no-less-pointed effort.

In 1955 Somerset had beaten Kent at Johnson Park in Yeovil (a park named after Stanley Johnson, a glove manufacturer and benefactor who donated the field in 1945). McMahon took 8/46.

The Somerset professionals at Bath in the 1920's standing beside the entrance to their changing room. From left to right: Len Braund, Harry Chidgey, Ernest Robson, John Bridges, Archie Young

Jack MacBryan, one of Somerset's outstanding batsmen. At one stage, he was considered by some to be England's finest opening batsman

Jack White, certainly Somerset's leading cricketer of the twenties and thirties. A successful all-rounder, he took 2,167 wickets at an average of 18 and clocked up over 11,000 runs

Norman Stewart Mitchell-Innes was just twenty years old when he was picked in 1935 to play for England against South Africa at Nottingham. Sadly, hay fever curtailed his career, as did work, which took him to Khartoum where he once scored a hundred before breakfast

R.J.O. Meyer, another of Somerset's great characters, could play only occasionally, for he lived for a time in India and afterwards taught at Millfield, which was to produce many Somerset cricketers

The Somerset team, off duty, in the early thirties

Harold Gimblett opening the innings at Glastonbury in 1952. Begun in 1935, his was a brilliant career, during which he scored 49 centuries for Somerset and 21,142 runs. Yet his life was tinged with tragedy and ended wilfully

Three very different venues for Somerset cricket: Taunton at the end of last
century, Glastonbury (below) and Bath (below right), during festival week

Bill Andrews, an enduring and endearing character, did the double for Somerset, was sacked umpteen times and provoked a Secretary into biting through his pipe

Ken Palmer, the last Somerset man to do the double, clean bowls Phelan of Essex

A year later 3,000 people saw McMahon and Langford dismiss Derbyshire for 150 as Somerset won by 6 wickets. Langford, in particular, reaped a rich harvest from Somerset's custom of playing county matches on club grounds. Somerset nearly won on another new ground, at Moorlands at Glastonbury, where they played Middlesex in Maurice Tremlett's benefit match. With Edrich scoring 89 and Compton 110 and Lobb and McCool taking 7 wickets between them, the first day was full of engaging cricket. Thanks to Lomax, McCool and Stephenson, Somerset reached 286/9 – one behind – as Brian Lobb took guard. Players received a bonus of thirty shillings for a first innings lead, so Lobb, as he later recalled, was under considerable pressure. Meeting McMahon mid-pitch he decided to run wherever the ball went provided it was not to the keeper. Cannoning off a pad, the ball reached John Warr at short leg just as Lobb embarked upon a suicidal run. Incredibly Warr's throw missed and Somerset pinched a first innings lead. Eventually Middlesex invited Somerset to chase 208 and, after a hectic chase, they fell 5 runs short with 3 wickets left to end a bright county contest.

Still, fifteenth place and a heavy loss were scarcely the stuff of legend and, naturally, 1957 was approached with trepidation, for plainly Somerset was still a moderate side. And yet help was on the way in the form of a garrulous, cranky Australian who had been, as his features testified, a prize boxer as well as a cussedly effective cricketer.

William Edward Alley, also from Sydney, was to be a Somerset character in the great tradition of Sammy Woods, John Daniell and Arthur Wellard. He was a sportsman, a daring hitter, a drinker and a liver. His arrival was a remarkable coup, for Alley's fame had spread beyond his beloved Lancashire League, and also a gamble for he was at least thirty-eight years of age, his date of birth being the solitary part of his life about which he was coy.

In Australia Alley had led a merry dance, as a dance-hall bouncer, a blacksmith's stoker, a boilermaker's mate, and a prize-fighter, all intensely physical activities which suited his strength and his rough-and-ready manner. As a fighter he had been engaged in twenty-eight contests, winning them all and setting his sights on the world welterweight title. He had been a vivid cricketer too, a violent, dangerous batsman who had peppered grade bowlers all over Sydney. Ken Grieves, a colleague who

275

later played county cricket, used to say he was the best thing he ever saw on the field. And then, with Alley on the verge of Test selection, a dreadful accident occurred. When stooping to collect a ball in a net, Alley was hit by a fierce drive and his jaw was badly fractured. Accordingly he missed the 1948 tour and faced obscurity. Moreover his first wife died suddenly, and Bill was lost. It was Bill O'Reilly who urged him to try league cricket in England, and Sid Barnes, another colourful character, who helped to pay his expenses.

Alley was an immense success in the league, hitting grandly to leg and learning to bowl subtle swingers, trotting in on his toes so that he could not be heard, a rare moment of silence in a gregarious career. Counties tried to tempt him away but he stood firm, content with his lot. And then in 1956 Somerset issued its invitation and to widespread surprise Alley accepted. He liked the look of Somerset, with its rolling hills, genial ways and toleration of individual excess. He felt he would not be inhibited by too much mularky, and fancied he might enjoy stag-hunting and cider, in both of which guesses he was correct. Alley found within himself a streak of the countryman for, unlike his friend and rival McCool, he became a Somerset man, opening a chicken farm, sawing up logs and walking in the Quantocks. Yet he never stopped being an Aussie either, crafty in his bluntness, pessimistic in his certainty, evenhanded in his criticism. In time he became a legend amongst supporters who enjoyed his cricket and his scandalous repartee. Colleagues respected his cricket, laughed at his jokes, appreciated his relish for life, and found only one serious flaw in his character: Alley was a driven man. He wanted to be boss, to be Somerset's best player. If a fellow was down, Bill was his closest chum but, if he were in form, Alley could be distant, as if chiding a world which let so humdrum a cricketer do so well.

Alley's arrival made Greetham less important, for Somerset did not need two fast-hitting men capable of bowling crafty medium-pacers. Moreover, Alley was apt to pace himself, being too wily to burn himself out with fruitless spells on inhospitable pitches, for was he not already middle-aged? Greetham found himself bowling on flat pitches and fielding on green tops! None the less, Alley was to give twelve summers of outstanding service, scoring 16,644 runs mostly with irreverent clouts over mid-wicket or chops to third man (and all the while talking and cursing even if he had been sent to Coventry by opponents trying to unsettle him), and taking 738 wickets. Had he not suffered rotten luck as a batsman, had not umpires in his opinion been blind to the merits of so many of his appeals, he might have done even more, for Alley was inclined to believe that his aggressive methods were frowned upon and punished. And, never wearing a thigh pad, never apologizing, Alley was throughout his own man, come hell or high water (though he much preferred high water).

With McCool and Alley in their various and competing ways adding to Somerset's strength, Tremlett led his team to eighth in 1957, their highest since 1950. A depressing litany of failure had been interrupted and not until Alley's departure was Somerset to appear in the bottom three once more.

In his first five games Alley took 12 wickets and scored 365 runs. Against Middlesex at Lord's he opened the batting and bowling and also kept wicket. He was duly awarded his county cap.

Though taking only 67 wickets, Brian Langford won his cap too, and with Brian Lobb on top form and McMahon, a third Australian and one not so well blessed with humour, taking wickets in his last season, Somerset could field an attack which was, at least, competitive, if lacking a bowler of true pace.

Not that everyone was content. White, Greswell and Longrigg indulged in endless debates on committee, debates no doubt sustained by more litigious colleagues, debates largely about club rules, as Somerset contemplated its own navel in a manner which has survived, largely because no two men are able to agree upon the purpose of the club, let alone its organization. Nor did Tremlett's captaincy escape criticism, for he did appear so lackadaisical and this was a club in which a belief in dynamic leadership was deep-rooted.

Tremlett, Hill and various coaches, of which Bill Andrews was the latest, though on this occasion he did not last long, were meanwhile continuing to find young talent, and in 1957 Alan Whitehead, Chris Greetham and Roy Virgin embarked upon their careers. Whitehead was only sixteen when he made his début against Sussex as a fiery left-arm spinner but, like John Harris before him and Gary Palmer afterwards, his early promise was not to be fulfilled. Perhaps he was unlucky, for cricket is an especially difficult game for young spinners. With McCool ageing and McMahon being dismissed, Somerset needed someone to support Langford and must have hoped to nurture Whitehead. Had he appeared later in his career, as Hazell did, had he served an apprenticeship, his ambitions might not have been thwarted. As it was, 67 wickets and life as an umpire were for him.

Though playing 205 matches, Chris Greetham did not quite crack county cricket either. Handsome in his shots, bounteous in his talents, he was a glorious cricketer to watch and his innings, were they long or short, were recollected happily for weeks afterwards. And yet Greetham was an amiable, shy, even diffident man whose immaculate appearance and elegance of stroke belied a sense of inadequacy. In truth he was not tight enough, mentally or technically, to flourish against high-class bowling and accordingly he was a fitful cricketer. Had he played thirty years earlier perhaps the earth and stars would have been his, as it was, condemned to be a struggling professional, he found life too grim and eventually went off to play golf. A useful medium-pacer, if one thrown into the shadows by Bill Alley, Greetham took 195 wickets at a rate of 28 each, respectable figures, and scored 6,723 runs at a frustratingly low average of 22. A popular colleague and opponent, a cricketer who promised much, he was unsuited by temperament to the harsh and insecure world of pro cricket during the 1950s. He might have been kept longer, for he was only thirty when his contract was not renewed in 1966. Once Colin Atkinson was appointed captain, a position once promised to Greetham, his position was insecure, for Atkinson too was an all-rounder. Had he survived till the era of regular one-day games he might have found a niche. As it was he was eased away by harder men.

Roy Virgin was to be around rather longer, and to enjoy a solid, worthy career, forging with Graham Atkinson Somerset's most reliable opening pair since Palairet and Hewett, begging the forgiveness of MacBryan and Young, and even Gimblett and Lee. His hour will arrive; for the time being he is a determined youngster dipping his toe in the water and trying to avoid McCool's eye.

Tremlett's first year as skipper was not without controversy, for this was the year of the scandal at the Grand Hotel, Swansea. Details of what occurred remain murky, and suffice to say that letters were written from this hotel complaining about disrespectful conduct from senior Somerset cricketers. Somerset's executive committee met in emergency session that July and secretly decided to sack Tremlett, Stephenson, McMahon and Hilton, a decision which was leaked to certain reporters.

A full meeting was called and at this it was decided to sack McMahon and Hilton, who decided to retire anyhow, and to reprimand Stephenson and Tremlett, who was to be relieved of the captaincy. Had not Dennis Silk, schoolmastering at Marlborough and playing in his holidays, intervened, this calamity might have occurred. Silk told officials that a change in captaincy would have a bad effect upon morale, for Tremlett was admired by his men. While criticizing Tremlett for his handling of their team and his lack of interest in events after stumps were drawn, Somerset did reappoint him as captain. They were not prepared to forgive McMahon, no matter how his colleagues pleaded. Examples had to be made.

Plans had been afoot to replace Tremlett. Somerset signed Squadron Leader Shirreff (thirty-eight), who had taken 300 wickets for various counties, as assistant secretary on a five-year contract at a wage of £900 per annum. He was pencilled in as captain and upon Tremlett's unforeseen renewal Somerset found itself in a corner. Acting nimbly if without scruple they asked Shirreff to serve as coach and promptly summoned Andrews and sacked him!

Hearing all this Tremlett asked for a three-year contract and was refused. Officials said his position was secure and regretted they could not afford too long a financial commitment. Tremlett knew precisely how to interpret these words.

For Somerset 1958 was an *annus mirabilis*. In all probability it was the club's greatest year since 1892. So much work had been done off the field. A thriving Supporters Club provided cheap houses, Eric Hill was running a 2nd XI now playing twenty-five games a year (in 1954 only six fixtures had been arranged) and Maurice Tremlett, a professional and a local to boot, was captain. Promising youngsters, battle-hardened foreigners, a hint of dash with bat and ball and a captain born to gamble, all the ingredients were there for a competitive summer but to finish third, and to threaten a first championship victory, were beyond all expectations.

Certainly it was beyond the expectations of Tremlett's committee, upon which the old yen for an amateur captain had not yet died – as Dennis Silk and M. J. K. Smith were sounded out hereabouts. According to McCool Somerset's captain was sneered at, moaned at, sniped at, but he shrugged it all off and got on with doing what I shall always rate as a magnificent job . . . He had grown up with it, so he had no sloppy, sentimental illusions to be destroyed. He was never popular with those running the club because he treated them in the same off-handed manner that they treated their players.

Even allowing for McCool's democratic vitriol it is a heavy indictment and Tremlett was, in fact, to last only two more years as captain, losing interest in 1959, worn down by battles off the field, and wondering if he was to be replaced soon. As in later years, Somerset killed its golden goose.

Several factors combined to help Tremlett in 1958. For a start Peter Wight, so fine a player on hard pitches, so reluctant to adjust on wet ones, Colin McCool, Geoff Lomax, Alley, Tremlett and Langford played in every championship game. Alley and Lomax offered a solid opening partnership, for Atkinson and Virgin were wearing military clothes, and so learning a discipline absent in Somerset life save when McCool was around. But it was the spinners who were behind Somerset's greatest victories, and in particular Brian Langford, who took 116 wickets without so much as winning a mention in International circles. At twenty-two he was the youngest Somerset player ever to take 100 wickets in a season, a record he still holds.

Take two of Somerset's games at Weston-super-Mare as an example. Nottingham, with Simpson and Gammy Goonesena to the fore, arrived first and were promptly bowled out for 89, Langford taking 5/33 and Eric Bryant, a young local spinner with an action jerky enough already to be raising eyebrows, trapping three men. In reply Somerset reached 170/9, Lomax scoring 80 and adding 54 with Ken Palmer, so correct in defence, so unwilling to give anything away. Batting again Nottingham reached 211, Poole scoring 81 and Lomax taking 4/15, including his first hat trick, mopping up the tail, as Nottingham's counter-attack faded. Chasing 131 Somerset won in a canter, Lomax striking a rapid 53 and Alley and Peter Wight doing the rest.

When Lancashire appeared they found a pitch ruined by rain upon which, as *Wisden* reported in unusually intemperate language, 'spin bowlers ran riot'. First Statham and Tattersall bowled Somerset out for 60 and then Langford took 9/26, still a Somerset record, as Lancashire slumped from 37/0 to 89 all out. Somerset lost six men for 57 but then Silk and Palmer took charge, Silk attacking Malcolm Hilton, thumping 4 sixes and 8 fours, inspiring Palmer to hit 8 punishing boundaries of his own. Previously a poor player of spin, Palmer had learned much from hours of facing Langford in the nets. They added 112 and Lancashire were left to chase 144. Langford took 6/28, Wight chipped in with 3/13 turning his off-breaks hugely, and Somerset won by 89 runs, to the delight of supporters who shouted 'Here come Somerset' with a fervour seldom rivalled before or since.

Palmer was awarded his county cap for his brave efforts, but the championship was not to be, as Somerset failed to sustain their charge. In truth Tremlett's bowling resources were not quite good enough, and his team depended for victories too much upon playing on these seaside or club grounds. Once the Weston Festival was over points were predictably elusive.

No matter, it was a glorious effort, and its only problem was that hopes were raised so high, hopes which could not be fulfilled without a genuine fast bowler, especially as so much had relied upon the contribution of two ageing warriors, McCool and Alley, one near the end and the other presumed to be so.

Somerset's committee, and Shirreff in particular, regarded this exciting season as a mixed blessing. Shirreff was highly critical of Tremlett's captaincy, saying that he took no heed of youngsters, had no interest in running between the wickets or fielding standards, and cared not a jot about conduct. A sub-committee was formed to consider the captaincy, but events moved too fast and as victories heaped upon each other it was plain no change could be made. Though his committee did not care for his style they knew Tremlett could not be budged, not until he failed at any rate. Shirreff fell out with Richard Robinson, the secretary, and being reluctant to work with Tremlett, he resigned in some heat.

George Lambert, rather than Bill Andrews, was picked to replace Shirreff, and he too signed a five-year contract, which was not renewed, Somerset having decided, belatedly, that they could manage without this outside help.

By 1959 county cricket was in a state of decline. Over two million people had watched county games in 1947 and even in 1952 attendance reached 1.9 million. Now it had shrunk to barely one million and counties were struggling. Schemes for brightening

281

cricket were being aired and, within a few years, an explosion of one-day matches and imported talent was to transform the scene. In the meantime counties had to plunge on as best they could, paying their professional staffs from strictly limited budgets, and rarely undertaking any new capital costs. Somerset's executive must, in this dismal economic climate, have blessed their Supporters Club once more.

Somerset had a solid team in 1959, especially since Graham Atkinson was back from National Service. And yet they slipped to twelfth place and played some unsatisfactory cricket between occasional bursts of excellence. As usual the trouble stemmed from the top. Feeling unwanted, tired of fighting the same old battles, Maurice Tremlett appeared to have lost his desire to lead Somerset and was inclined to let things drift, even retreating to third man and allowing Harold Stephenson to provide the drive. Tremlett's eyesight was deteriorating and besides he missed the family atmosphere of his early years, a period about which he reminisced as he wandered around, his brow furrowed. Suspicious of his committee, he did not concentrate upon his task. Age brings insecurity and perhaps Tremlett played his part in those difficulties, for older cricketers are seldom quite so confident as younger brethren, who are certain of their own immortality. None the less, he was plainly lacking an elder statesman on the committee to provide him with straightforward support. Once again Somerset was betrayed by a massive and accordingly anonymous committee which contained few cricketers and few men able to talk easily with players. Still the division remained, not between amateur and pro these days, but between player and official.

Despite his edginess Tremlett did add 196 with Peter Wight against Middlesex at Bath, a record for the 6th wicket. This was to be Peter Wight's first truly great year. He missed seven games because he had double vision, probably simply the product of overwrought nerves, and yet managed to hit six hundreds, score 1,874 runs and strike 222 against Kent, carrying his bat. Nimble in his footwork, a player of finesse, he belied his reputation as being weak against fast bowlers by regularly scoring piles of runs against Surrey, whose fierce fast bowler Peter Loader never spared him. Wight did not move into line against the fast stuff and was therefore deemed to be frightened; but he did not move into line against anyone else either, relying upon eye and wristwork. Pitches were being covered now and it was this change which turned Wight from a regular county player who usually failed on wet surfaces into one of England's best batsmen. Certainly he was a delight to watch for several years, until his eyes and health began to trouble him.

Batting with intense determination, tucking the ball away to leg, and constructing his innings with care, as he had been taught to do in the Yorkshire cricket of his childhood, Graham Atkinson scored 1,717 runs in his first full season. He was to pass 1,000 runs in each of the next seven summers, twice topping 2,000 too. A dedicated, thorough player he might have played for England had his fielding yielded a higher reputation. As it was he scored heavily in Test trials, survived bombardments from cricket's fast bowlers, batted with great efficiency . . . but the call never came. A lesser Boycott, he did not have quite enough to offer.

With McCool scoring 1,697 runs, Alley 1,760 and Tremlett 1,056, Somerset were rarely short of runs. Alas, their bowling leaned too heavily upon Langford, for Alley was often troubled by a calf injury. It was Langford who helped Somerset to their finest victory of the year, as they beat Yorkshire by 16 runs at Bath, and this despite scores of 128 and 34 by a certain D. B. Close. Langford took 9/143. Bill Alley hit 56 not out and 45, and Lomax and Roy Virgin added 118 and 74 for the first wicket and, amidst scenes of high excitement, Somerset won a famous victory.

India were less accommodating, scoring 432 on a shaven, dun-coloured Taunton pitch which had neither pace, lift nor turn on that first day of June. Polly Umrigar batted for an hour in the nets and then scored 203 before presenting his wicket to Langford. Gaekwad scored a quiet 50 and then thrashed at Langford. In reply Atkinson showed his customary calm judgement in hitting 60 while McCool alone mastered Gupte's taunting leg-breaks. Certainly Ken Palmer could not fathom them, yet, utterly unprepared to surrender his wicket easily, he hung on to score 37. He was happier facing Desai, India's youthful pace bowler, who tipped the scales at under 9 stone and still managed to surprise batsmen with his nip. India collapsed in their second innings, slipping to 119/8 before declaring, whereupon Somerset lost 4 wickets cheaply before stumps were pulled and a draw accepted.

No season in which Yorkshire and six other counties were beaten could be deemed bad, and to finish twelfth, while disappointing, was no disgrace, especially as six players, Atkinson, Tripp, Keith, Langford, Palmer and Biddulph, had been developed on the ground staff. Neither Graham Tripp, a batsman from Clevedon, nor Geoff Keith, an all-rounder who was to play occasionally for Hampshire and Western Province before concentrating upon coaching, quite broke through; but, even so, Somerset was producing players. Nor had the supply run dry, for Roy Virgin, Haydn Sully and Terry Barwell had made their first appearances by now. Their birthplaces? Taunton, Watchet and Transvaal, a nice Somerset mixture.

All appeared set fair for a few years of solid cricket in the county. If a fast bowler could be found, and perhaps one more batsman too, a challenge might be issued to the high and mighty, for in Stephenson, Atkinson, Alley, Langford, Palmer, and Wight, Somerset had the backbone of a good side. But all was not well. Two names were missing from that litany of impressive cricketers, those of Maurice Tremlett and Colin McCool. For Somerset's captain this was the last hurrah. Throughout the season he had suspected, rightly, that officials were plotting against him. Though his team had played bright cricket it was plain his committee had expected more, and held the captain responsible. They could not see that 1958 had been an extraordinary effort, a rise of fourteen places from the terrible depths of 1955. Tremlett was blamed for failing to sustain this effort, and talk of his lack of evident discipline returned, and was heard. Somerset seemed to want a commander rather than a cricket captain. Feeling betrayed Tremlett withdrew during the season. His men, and particularly sergeant-major McCool, were sympathetic but Tremlett would not be saved. In September he was dispatched and though he carried on as a player in 1960 injury prevented him from contributing much. His disillusion was evident and he soon moved to Southampton, where he worked for Guinness, a company he had helped to keep in business on long evenings away from home.

His time was nearly up as a cricketer. Ever since his injury in Bath his eyesight had been deteriorating and his efforts to adjust to spectacles had proved painful. For a time his batting was propped up by memory and nerve but it was in decline. Nonetheless he was a splendid leader of men and he deserved a graceful and delayed departure. In truth Somerset had never cared for his style, and had accordingly treated him with an arrogance bordering on contempt – and this from men whose choices of captain had a decade earlier held Somerset up to ridicule, whose sister, calamity, had followed not far behind. As it was, Tremlett was offered an honorary life membership by Hampshire where his sons were to be seen regularly practising in the nets. Few had made as significant or as amiable a contribution to Somerset cricket as their father.

No wonder Somerset's professionals were constantly asking for more money. In such a club it was every man for himself. Determined to assert their authority, and with a tight budget to obey, Somerset officials usually dismissed these applications. Graham Atkinson asked for an increase from £525 to £600 and was denied, for this was merely 'his latest try-on'. Such negotiations recurred annually, and it was rare for Atkinson, Wight or their colleagues to have their wicked way.

That winter Rex Frost sought from members permission to increase subscriptions from 2 guineas to 3 guineas. Supporting his argument he produced a table showing that during the period 1946–59, while annual expenditure had more than doubled from £12,616 to £28,079, income from subscriptions had risen only 40 per cent from £3,763 to £6 360, while gate receipts had actually declined from £11,380 to £9,445.

During this period the rate of subscription has remained unchanged at £2 2s 0d p.a.

Year	Total Annual Expenditure	Professionals' Wages	Subscriptions	Gate Receipts
1946	12616	4411	3763	11380
1947	16485	4719	4719	11037
1948	18826	5309	5219	10610
1949	16350	6027	4987	10847
1950	17250	6258	5110	10897
1951	19037	6887	5112	10704
1952	17350	6148	5153	7908
1953	17848	6851	4931	8903
1954	21055	8357	4916	7137
1955	21206	9160	5684	8366
1956	19557	8405	5814	7697
1957	24082	11301	5802	7532
1958	25176	11646	6005	9432
1959	28079	14158	6360	9445

Colin McCool was near the end too. 1960 was to be his final season, for Brisbane beckoned. Supporters tried to raise a fund to underwrite his passage to and from Australia, a considerable tribute, but McCool thought Somerset should pay, which they refused to do. Perhaps McCool was not sorry to feel again the sun on his back. With Tremlett and Eric Hill he had done much to restore morale in Somerset cricket and he must have sighed with satisfaction when his county managed to finish in the top ten every year from 1962 to 1967, a performance matched only from 1976 to 1982.

Harold Stephenson was appointed captain for the 1960 season. It was not an easy time, for despite a donation of £3,000 from the Supporters Club, money was tight, so much so that a scheme was introduced whereby players' lunches would be sponsored. Undeterred the 124 members who attended the AGM refused any increase in subscriptions. For its part the club decided not to approach Tom Graveney, currently in dispute with Gloucestershire, and so presumably the sort of chap committees did not want. Instead they created a sixth area committee, in mid-Somerset, to appease those insisting upon a voice. In attempting to move towards democracy Somerset was, in fact, creating layers of officialdom, compromising the decision-making process but assuaging those who felt that all was not well.

Judging by the rapidity with which coaches came and went all was most certainly not well at Somerset even in 1960. Alan Shirreff had lasted twelve months and left after writing an accusing letter to his employers. George Lambert was appointed for 1959 but by 1963 Bill Andrews, committee man, journalist, scandal-monger, enthusiast, was back in harness. A few years earlier Horace Hazell had also served as coach. None of these men found their job remotely easy, largely because they were seldom given any power. Their position, more or less, was that of a professional player fifty years earlier, a servant of the club with no part to play in its management, a hopeless task for someone trying to shape a team.

Fortunately Stephenson was an affable, durable fellow who could absorb such arrows as fell upon him. He was, too, a superbly efficient wicket-keeper, as good as any in the country. A cheerful Teessider, he had been spotted in local league cricket by a friend of Micky Walford's and duly signed by Somerset to replace an ageing and ailing Wally Luckes. For ten years already his 'rolling gait and rueful humour' (John Arlott), his unobtrusive keeping and his dash for quick singles had won him popularity and recognition in cricket grounds everywhere. At first his wife had not been happy in the south, finding it less cosy, but the Supporters Club provided a house and in time Harold and his family embraced their new-found home, so much so that they live in Taunton still. Harold spent his winters working at the YMCA and for the electricity board, and he played good soccer too. Twice he had been close to selection for winter tours, and in 1954 he had claimed more victims than any other keeper. Had he played for a more fashionable club – it is an old Somerset cry – he might have won caps; as it was he had to be content with an outstanding county career. And he was a good captain, especially of players who needed chivvying along. Those of gentle disposition did not care for his drive and, of course, he could not match Tremlett's inspirational field placements, but Stevenson led with bags of energy. If Ken Palmer, whose moods swung between joy and despair (for out of sorts he was apt to panic), was not bowling at his fastest, he would march up to the stumps, challenging the youngster to drive him back. He was especially brilliant against spinners, reading turn and flight easily, removing bails without fuss, rarely missing a chance.

Stephenson's first year in charge was full of difficulties. Bill Alley suffered a string of injuries, muscle strains and a knee dodgy enough to demand a cartilage operation. He scored only 741 runs but he did manage 71 wickets between his rests. Even so he was considered to be in the twilight of his career, a prognosis he was to defy a summer later with a season as dazzling as any played for Somerset, no matter how illustrious the cricketer.

Nor was this Somerset's only injury. Lomax broke a bone in his wrist, and Palmer missed half the season, and this despite George Lambert's pre-season routine of training with rifles. Puzzled cricketers found it a change from the medicine balls of previous eras. Fitness work was to be ever more important in years ahead until coaches decided to return to the old verity of grafting in nets.

Considering these handicaps it was not such a poor year. Peter Wight scored 2,316 runs, a record for Somerset, while Roy Virgin scored 1,000 runs for the first time. Stronger on the off side these days, Graham Atkinson was even more prolific

287

(1,895) and with Brian Langford he was picked to play for MCC against Yorkshire, the champion county. Neither was ever picked to represent England, Langford because the competition was so stern, and perhaps because he lacked naked ambition.

Atkinson scored a magnificent 190 against Glamorgan at Bath, adding 300 with Peter Wight, breaking the third wicket record of 262 set by L. C. H. Palairet and C. A. Bernard in 1900. Thanks to rain, Glamorgan survived. Somerset did beat Lancashire at Taunton, but not before Higgs and Tattersall had made a bold effort to score 47 in 45 minutes for the final wicket, only for Tattersall to fall leg before to Biddulph with 9 needed. Earlier Wight had scored 100 and 90, and Colin McCool a typically forthright ton.

Somerset's leading wicket-taker in this match was Alan White-head, still struggling to break through as Somerset urgently sought a left-arm spinner, and not for the last time. Another local young-ster was being tried too, Eric Bryant from Weston-super-Mare. Alas, Bryant's action did not survive the scrutiny of Hugo Yarnold and he was called five times for throwing during the Bath Festival. Bryant had been called for throwing in 2nd XI cricket and few were surprised at this condemnation. Bryant had regarded Tony Lock as 'the bee's knees' of left-arm bowling and had copied his action. It was Arthur Milton who faced that traumatic over in Bath when Bryant was repeatedly called. He patted back every delivery, legal or otherwise, and finally said to Yarnold at square leg: 'Let's get this over finished with, Hugo.' For Bryant it was time to find another profession, and Somerset lost a man remembered for constantly having a half-burnt cigarette in his mouth and cards in his hand.

Fred Herting, a local lad presently working on the grounds at R. J. O. Meyer's school Millfield, played a few games too, bowling rather plodding left-arm seamers, as Somerset's search for bowling talent continued. He soon returned to less exacting pursuits.

More happily Abbas Ali Baig had been lured from Oxford to play for Somerset. Baig had stayed with Bill Andrews before going to university and he scored well for Somerset before returning to India. Baig, a neat player, hit a début Test hundred against England in 1959 but failed on his second tour in 1971. Possibly it was too late for him.

In any event it was an interesting season as the usual crop of faces fluttered across the screen. And it ended in high farce as, angered by Somerset's decision to bat on into the last morning, Hampshire's Roy Marshall decided to play for a draw, which he did in no uncertain terms by blocking such demon bowlers as Virgin and Atkinson. Five minutes from the close a spectator wandered in front of the sightscreen and replied to instructions to hurry up by pointing out that 'You've been taking your time all — day!' Upon retiring Marshall moved to a Taunton pub and gave his time to Somerset cricket, as opposed to cricket politics.

Money was still short as the 1961 season began. Nor were hopes high for triumph on the field, for McCool had retired and no one new had arrived. In fact it was a splendidly entertaining year, if not an especially rich one.

Somerset had only 2,800 members for county cricket was in the doldrums, a relic of a bygone age, an age when working men watched cricket and players were heroes in factories and schools, when cities and counties took pride in their traditions. Now it was too laboured, too lacking in glamour, too much a private conversation between craftsmen. Neither authority nor county clubs had any idea of publicity, for they lived in a world which did not turn, let alone dance, to the beat of Chuck Berry.

Naturally Somerset still lived hand-to-mouth. Their reaction to financial difficulty was to allow a local entrepreneur to build a greyhound track around the boundary, for an annual rent of around £500. Talk of greyhound racing in Taunton provoked a considerable scandal, for the Free Church Council and others strongly objected. In the end gambling was allowed and loudspeakers banned and for ten years dogs fit or fed with a sticky bun raced around this new track. Cecil Buttle, of course, was displeased with this intrusion upon his precious turf and every Friday he fought a cat-and-mouse battle with Pennington or Pipe, his successor, turning water hoses on and off, moving barriers, in a vain effort to avoid damage.

Somerset's campaign to raise membership to 8,000 was a failure too, for the product simply was not exciting enough. Only with the arrival of one-day cricket and overseas stars did county cricket revive, for they brought colour and heroics to a middle-aged game.

The summer of 1961 was a memorable season. Somerset did the double over Gloucestershire for the first time since 1923. Graham

Atkinson became, at twenty-three, the youngest-ever Somerset player to score 2,000 runs in a summer. Ken Palmer became the first Somerset man to do the double since Bill Andrews in 1938, and this with previous little fast-bowling support. He was nearly the first man in England to do the double, only for Trevor Bailey to beat him by 53 minutes. And Palmer was still only twenty-four.

But, beyond all else, it was Bill Alley's year. He had been granted a benefit and, cussed and combative as ever, produced his best. He was forty-two years of age, a battered old sportsman who cursed and smote to leg and tiptoed in to bowl an impeccable line and length, so much so that in 1960 he had bowled 14 maiden overs in a row to Trevor Bailey on a crusty Yeovil pitch, a spell broken when Bailey slashed out immediately after being dropped by Roy Virgin at short leg, the simplest of catches. In two games against mighty Surrey in 1961, Alley scored 396 runs without losing his wicket. At Taunton he hit 183 and then a match-winning 134 not out in under two hours against an attack including Peter Loader, Eric Bedser and Tony Lock. Somerset won with four minutes to spare. Twice in 1961 Alley hit the first ball of the day for 6 and in all matches he belted eleven hundreds and scored 3,019 runs. And yet he had three dreadful matches, scoring a pair against Glamorgan at Weston-super-Mare, 0 and 1 at Street against Warwickshire and 9 and 0 on a no-less appalling pitch at Frome, where Roy Marshall was bowled as he tried to pull a long hop delivered by Michael Latham, a new fast bowler from Birmingham who lingered for a while without troubling many batsmen.

Alley found time to take 62 wickets, though he was seldom inclined to bowl after a long innings, and he played in the Gentlemen v Players match (on the players' side). And yet none of this was the highlight of this *annus mirabilis*. Alley was just as stubborn a man as McCool and he steeled himself no less when Richie Benaud brought his tourists to Taunton. On nought he survived a shouted appeal for a catch behind, telling everyone within earshot (and he could be heard in Bridgwater) that it had glanced off his belly button. He proceeded to hit 2 sixes, a five and 22 fours and to bat for 3$\frac{1}{2}$ hours. A collection was made for his benefit fund that day and it raised £221, a princely sum.

Australia piled on the runs in their second innings, but Alley responded with 95, and a last-wicket stand between Langford and Biddulph saved the game, to the delight of a packed crowd. Alley had scored 939 runs in June, not bad for a cranky old pro!

Alley struck a robust hundred against Yorkshire too, one of eleven scored that summer as he took up the challenge of succeeding McCool as Somerset's senior cricketer, which is not to say he neglected 'my leg-side scythe'.

Palmer was superb too, hitting his maiden hundred as he added 265 with Alley in 230 minutes against Northamptonshire. Alley had been no less brilliant on the colliery ground in Nuneaton as Somerset chased 389 on a worn pitch. For once he had an early night and next morning he reached 100 in 29 shots and 103 minutes and finished unbeaten on 221 as Somerset lost by 47 runs. The murderous belting of Basil Bridges' off-breaks on that cruelly turning pitch is remembered by those who saw it, for he hit out against them and never seemed to miss. Everyone else scraped to survive.

It was a glorious year and yet Somerset could finish only tenth. Under Stephenson they attacked at every opportunity so that only three of their first nineteen games were drawn, one of them that tense finish against Australia. They lacked strength in depth in batting, and needed a fast bowler and a second spinner if they were to be a strong side. For the time being they could offer fighting performances capable of upsetting an applecart or two without ever appearing likely to challenge for the title. By September they had won ten games and lost fifteen.

And a Downside boy, Anthony Pearson, had played for them as a pace bowler who had taken wickets at Cambridge, mostly with outswingers. He did pretty well too, before moving on, in the words of one contemporary 'to become a vet or something'.

Another new face appeared in 1962, and it too did not stay. Ian Lomax had played for Wiltshire and had won something of a reputation as a batsman of aggressive persuasion. Nor was that all. At thirty-one he drove a Mercedes, owned a farm in Blagdon and trained racehorses, which, combined with his complexion, won him the nickname the White Horse. Somerset players, suspicious of the club's yearning for the halcyon days of amateur captains, thought he was being groomed for leadership; and perhaps he was, for certainly the yearning had been quietened rather than silenced. In fact Lomax found time to smite an 83 against Hampshire and to play six games before returning no less jovially to his farm.

Thanks to solid team-work Stephenson's men rose to sixth

place in 1962, winning twelve county matches and losing seven. With £2,700 in the bank from his benefit, Alley returned to do the double and to be elected as the County Cricketers Player of the Year – this a season after being one of *Wisden*'s five Cricketers of the Year. He failed by only 85 runs to score 2,000 and at The Oval he returned his best bowling figures of 8/65. And never stopped talking throughout.

Ken Palmer took over 90 wickets, while Atkinson and Wight both scored 2,000 runs.

Had a better start been made, Somerset might even have challenged for the championship. As it was, not a single point was taken from the first five games, and it was not until Harold Stephenson and Colin Atkinson, a new all-rounder, added 74 for the 9th wicket against Sussex at Taunton that this duck was broken. Even so, and despite Alley's 5/15, it needed two leg-byes for the last pair to secure a thrilling victory.

Hereafter Somerset marched on in style, beating Pakistan by an innings, Brian Langford taking 6 wickets, defeating Glamorgan twice and generally reaching a result in such of their thirty-two fixtures as were unaffected by rain. Peter Wight scored 215 against Yorkshire after Vic Wilson had dropped Fred Trueman for disciplinary reasons, which the loquacious Yorkshire fast bowler thought was 215 more than Wight could have hit off his bowling. Stephenson, who had a marvellous year behind the stumps and who scored 853 championship runs, also managed to strike a dashing 147 not out against Nottinghamshire, adding 110 for the 9th wicket with a characteristically stubborn Palmer. For Stephenson, too, it was a typical effort, all hectic running and brave cutting, as he led a fight back from the perils of 15/3. Somerset won this game, and were seldom easily beaten from May to September.

By now Somerset's batting was strong. Although Roy Virgin was absent peeling potatoes, Graham Atkinson had found a neat, efficient opening partner in Brian Roe, a diminutive, Puckish fellow with a boyish face and an enthusiasm which won the hearts of supporters as they sat munching corned-beef sandwiches on windy Taunton days. Roe scored 1,544 runs in 1962 in 60 innings and he was to play 131 matches before his lack of power told against him. Twenty years earlier, in the doldrums, Somerset would have cherished his determination; by 1966 they yearned for power and authority, not least because they were a good side bent upon winning a trophy, and most particularly the Gillette Cup.

Other new faces included Mervyn Kitchen, a lad from Flax Bourton who could punch merrily off the front foot and who was inclined to walk with a rolling, naval gait. Kitchen was to be one of Somerset's best left-handers, and he was to play with passion as Somerset moved towards its greatest period to date. His time had not yet truly arrived. Geoff Hall was around too, a swing bowler who wore horn-rimmed glasses, notwithstanding which he seldom delivered two balls on the same portion of the pitch. A great trier, he did take 111 wickets but is chiefly remembered now for his surprising habit of snaring a hatful of victims during Somerset's cup run of 1964. One year later Hall was off to find a field more sympathetic to his particular crop.

Colin Atkinson (no relation to Graham) was playing too. Searching for a leg-spinner to replace Colin McCool, Harold Stephenson had heard of a likely lad playing in the Northern Leagues. Ambitious, determined, combative, cunning, and pre-pared to graft at cricket and in life, Atkinson was willing to risk a few years in county cricket as an amateur for he knew he was not good enough to rely upon his cricketing skills as his chief source of income. Stephenson prevailed upon R. J. O. Meyer to appoint him to a position at Millfield School. Whenever Atkinson played for Somerset he did so as an amateur, the county paying Millfield £175 for his services in 1960, and Millfield serving as sole paymaster for this new employee. Later Meyer was to demand first £600 and, soon enough, £1,000 a year to release Atkinson for a full season.

Colin Atkinson was not, in truth, a cricketer of high class but he used every ounce of his talent to the utmost and never gave up without a fight. His leg-breaks were to be useful for a few years, until loss of confidence and injury caused him to turn to containing medium-pace; he batted gamely down the order and was never less than a tiger in the field. But it was as a captain, first of the 2nd XI and later of the county side, that he left his cricketing mark. For a time he left Millfield, because a promised sports hall had not been built, but he returned and eventually supplanted Meyer as headmaster. It is a curiosity that neither Stephenson nor Meyer, the two men who had promoted Colin Atkinson most zealously, would have anything to do with him after he had succeeded them as captain and headmaster. Perhaps they had not expected such ruthlessness or such drive. Colin Atkinson had far to go and he did not care for his path to be blocked. A shrewd brain and a resolute will drove his career onwards at club and school and those left by the wayside were not inclined to forgive him. He brought, too, energy, calculation and a fine grasp of business, from which characteristics his world was certain to benefit.

Atkinson was at his best against the old enemy, Gloucestershire, at Taunton, smiting a cheerful and unbeaten 54 and then taking 7/54 to give Somerset a handsome victory. Chris Greetham scored 41 and took 4/66 in this popular win.

It had been a wonderful season, far beyond expectations, and supporters, paying 3s 0d to enter before tea and 1s 6d afterwards (for children it was 1s 0d and 6d respectively) enjoyed it greatly. Somerset could not, though, hope to sustain this challenge unless a fast bowler could be found. Not since the heady days of Wellard and Andrews had Somerset taken early wickets with any regularity, and now with Alley ageing (actually he had been ageing for a decade, and was to continue ageing for another five years at least!) they relied too heavily upon Ken Palmer, below his best in 1962. Palmer was happiest in a supporting role, for he was too much of a worrier easily to carry a heavy burden. Somerset urgently needed a cutting edge. By great good fortune in that winter of 1962 they found one.

28

Our Fred

For a time it seemed as if all great fast bowlers were called Fred. Somerset's new man, Rumsey of that ilk, had been languishing at Worcestershire, hidden in shadows cast by Jack Flavell and Len Coldwell. Fred was not by temperament suited to shadows. In every respect he was a big man. As a bowler he could lumber rather and his face could grow so red as to bear comparison with a ripe plum; he appeared to be an honest yeoman, even a struggling simpleton, whereas in fact he was a man of ideas, of imagination, of style.

Contemporaries recall that it was never possible to tell whether Fred was in funds or temporarily out of pocket. Arriving at a bar, and it was an arrival, he would at once order drinks for the entire company, to pay for which he might fish a splendid £10 note from a wad kept in his pocket, or borrow a fiver from an impoverished colleague. Life was for living. In away games he would wine and dine in his hotel, and put the bill on the club's account, a measure designed to delay any call to settle it. In time he duly went bankrupt occasionally but also made his millions, and last reports find him decidedly on the black side of the ledger.

As a cricketer he could be somewhat enigmatic. Apt to sip pints on the boundary edge, liable to sleep off a night on a couch in the pavilion, he was too bright, too analytical to hurl down his fast left-arm deliveries day after day without an occasional protest from his spirit. Once, at Westcliff, preparing to bowl on a green pitch he announced to colleagues that he was suffering from a mental block and could not possibly bowl that day. By and large, though, he was a dangerous bowler, a man capable of beating opening batsmen, breaking the first line of resistance so that his chums might investigate those hiding in trenches far from the front.

Rumsey was used in short bursts, which annoyed Alley who thought it soft and accordingly dismissed Rumsey as 'that big Myrtle'. Grafting was for others, and apart from his late swing Fred's greatest strength was that every spell would be fast, and just as testing. Helped by the uncovering of pitches in 1963, Rumsey took 102 wickets, an astonishing effort for he had never previously captured more than 18 in a season.

Within a year he was playing for England, and bowling to Bob Simpson on a graveyard in Manchester. Simpson scored 311, Rumsey took 2/99 in 35.5 overs, the pick of Dexter's seamers, and upon returning to Taunton he slumped into a chair, still gasping, and asked colleagues if they 'had ever taken a third new ball'. Rumsey was promptly dropped and he did not tour Australia in 1965/66 under M. J. K. Smith, David Larter, a lesser bowler, being preferred. Bill Alley was less impressed than most by Rumsey's skill, sensitivity and rapid rise to stardom. Did he feel his mantle under threat? This scepticism reached the ears of selectors and Rumsey was ignored, which was less than he deserved.

It was a year of lower scoring, partly because only twenty-eight county games were played, partly because wickets were left open to the elements. Langford finished ninth in Somerset's bowling averages yet he took his wickets at a rate of 23.8 each. Only Graham Atkinson of the batsmen averaged over 30; for his chums it was a season of hard work on spicy pitches.

But it is bowlers who win matches and though Alley concentrated upon his batting, Somerset now had a balanced and incisive attack. Palmer took 121 championship wickets, Langford 65 and Greetham, who had another satisfactory year, snared 44. For his part Colin Atkinson found time to play in only two games, his services being used in the 2nd XI during the holidays. Peter Eele, too, was still on the books working away, taking his catches easily, his glovework unobtrusive yet precise, waiting for Stephenson to retire, hoping as local lads do for a chance to be number one, a chance that never came.

Right until the season ended on 3 September Somerset had a chance to taste their first title. Despite both games at Bath being ruined by rain, despite losing a thrilling match against Middlesex at Clarence Park by 1 wicket, John Murray adding 25 for the last wicket with his captain Moss, Somerset were never far behind Yorkshire. On few occasions at Glastonbury, did an opposing team score 300. If Rumsey did not get them Palmer usually did.

Take Trent Bridge as one example. *Wisden* recorded that 'some of the most amazing cricket seen at Trent Bridge for many years was crowded into the play on the first morning'. Ken Palmer did not drink much as a rule. Others could do as they pleased (and did) but so far as he was concerned drink and cricket did not mix. He trusted no one, least of all himself, and thought he could survive only by being at his sharpest all season, a fearful load for any player to carry. Just for once, though, he had dropped his guard and he arrived that morning with an admonishing headache. His first two overs cost 23 runs and his captain was not pleased. As if Fred Rumsey's idiosyncrasies were not enough! For Fred wind, footholds, pitch and field placements were rarely in accordance with his expectations. And now Palmer, dogged and reliable, was bowling his deliveries far and wide.

After 8 overs Nottinghamshire had shot to 59/0 and, despairing, Stephenson recalled Palmer, this time at Rumsey's end. Palmer proceeded to take 8/28 in 11.3 overs and to return figures of 9/57 as Nottinghamshire collapsed to 153 all out. It was the first time a Somerset player had taken 9 wickets in an innings since Langford in 1958, and the second since J. C. White in 1932.

White, by the way, had died two years earlier and some fine wrought-iron gates had been erected in his memory, gates which still stand protecting the entrance behind what is now the Old Pavilion. Dudley Rippon, who would have found in Rumsey and Alley colleagues of suitably interesting personality, played his last forward defensive in this year, and John Daniell cursed his last curse.

Only when they failed to win either of their last two games did Somerset concede the championship. Yorkshire made no such error, winning their final matches in style. They were the best side, beating Somerset by an innings at Harrogate and holding them to a draw at Taunton. Still it had been a wonderful and exciting challenge by Stephenson and his team, and to this day no Somerset side has finished higher. With a reliable second spinner they might even have pinched it, though it was a year for seamers by and large.

Frank Worrell's vibrant West Indians were the tourists in 1963 and Somerset played them at Bath. In the 1950s, as Kenneth Gregory has written, Bath was a delightful city if you wished to hear Beecham conduct Mozart, but not if you wished to see displayed the art of batting. Bath had not lost its eighteenth-century grandeur, but its wickets had improved and, taking advantage, Gary Sobers hit a hundred off 97 balls with batting which Gregory had never seen equalled. Basil Butcher hit 130 and Somerset lost by an innings, confounded by Charlie Griffith's terrifying change of pace.

Somerset's campaign in the new knock-out competition sponsored by Gillette was less successful. They lost to Glamorgan in the first round, their opponents scoring 207 in 65 overs and Somerset replying with 197, at which Langford hit 56 in a valiant last effort. Nevertheless this cup, and the visit of the West Indian team, helped to revive county cricket in 1963, ridding it of unnecessary solemnity, taking away some of its middle-aged crossness. Somerset had a side well suited to attacking batting and accurate bowling but, like Yorkshire, they were not inclined to think too seriously about their limited over games, frowning upon revolutionary tactics such as putting every fielder upon the boundary, used by Ted Dexter, whose county won the cup before an enchanted audience. Beyond doubt the Gillette Cup was a triumph of innovation and in time Somerset would learn to love it, to yearn for it and, eventually, to win it.

Nor should 1963 be left without some reference to the usual retinue of odd-bods who flitted across the scene like shadows across a cave. David Doughty first appeared in 1963. A spinner from Chiswick, he could turn the ball a considerable distance but he did not pay sufficient attention to its pitch. Accordingly his career was brief, and his 33 wickets in 1963 proved to be by far his greatest contribution. Soon enough his confidence had deserted him; so much so that he was condemned to 2nd XI cricket in 1964. In time Doughty, who had an eagle's face, won the nickname 'doubtful' and eventually he went off to find another way of earning a living, still clutching bottles of his beloved beer. Cricket, and in particular left-arm spin bowling, was to him as elusive as a mosquito whining in a darkened room.

Bill Andrews was back, appointed in November 1963 to take charge of the 2nd XI, and paid £400 a year for his trouble. Confusingly for those of traditional opinion, Andrews was also a committee man, for his Pickwickian characteristics were beloved by members. Somerset was not inclined to appoint him as coach, for many to date had been tried and all had failed, and instead used his abundant enthusiasm in this halfway-house position.

Andrews had managed the Pakistan Eaglets on their tour to England in 1953, spending most of his money buying them glasses of Guinness. Ten years later they returned and met Somerset in Taunton. Cleveland Vincent Lindo, a twenty-seven-year-old Jamaican bowler, played for Somerset. It was to be his only game. Possessed of a whippy action, he took 5 wickets for 1 run in 17 deliveries with the second new ball, finished with 8/88, and scored an unbeaten 23. Nor was the opposition weak, including as it did three Mohammed brothers and Intikhab Alam. Peter Eele scored his only first-class hundred in this contest, seizing upon a rare opportunity. Neither Lindo nor Eele was much heard of again.

But 1963 had been Rumsey's summer, and Palmer's. Palmer was included in the twelve for the 4th Test, and he won the National Single-Wicket competition, an event popular at the beginning of the nineteenth century, beating Tom Cartwright, Jackie Van Gloven, Ray Illingworth (after a replay), and Albert White of the West Indian tourists, on his way.

For Somerset all seemed set fair, for at last they had a balanced attack. Nor, in the event, did this team disappoint, never finishing below eighth before it began to break up, and returning to third place in 1966. It was a run which was to last until Alley's last season, in 1968, a year which, no less significantly, also marked the end of Fred Rumsey's captivating career. You do need a fast bowler.

With so much bright cricket being played, and with Somerset in such form, it is unsurprising that by 1964 membership had risen to 4,742, the highest in the history of the club. All told 4,636 people paid to watch Somerset play, and takings rose to £8,960, an increase of £356. Australia were touring, which helped, though their cricket was to be uninspiring beside that of Frank Worrell.

Somerset's professional staff also increased from fourteen to seventeen and this too was a sign of confidence and prosperity. No doubt Bill Greswell, now president, and Rex Frost as treasurer, and all of those dozens serving on Area committees, held high hopes of triumph in 1964. In the event the season was slightly disappointing as Somerset won eight games, lost eight and finished, appropriately, in eighth position.

For once it was the batting which failed, Graham Atkinson being first to reach his 1,000 runs, and this on 13 August and without hitting a hundred. Overall the batting was woolly, with Peter Wight out of sorts and Roe and Greetham fading. Only one game was won in the final six weeks, a handsome victory over Gloucestershire at Bath, where the festival was staged in the middle of May. Somerset were not victorious again for a month whereupon Roy Virgin hit a hundred in a low-scoring match against Nottinghamshire. A good patch in July, as Somerset won in Westcliff, Worcester, Hinckley and Glastonbury could not entirely redeem that somewhat lackadaisical beginning.

Bowling with his customary craft Langford enjoyed himself at Clarence Park, taking 6/27 against Glamorgan, which did not prevent a defeat, and 7/42 against Surrey, which heralded a victory, and generally the bowling was adequate. Bob Simpson's tourists thought Langford the best off-spinner they met all summer, a notable tribute for he did not take a wicket against them.

It was a year for spin, because Lord's had asked groundsmen to leave less grass upon the pitches, which did not please Palmer or Rumsey, neither of whom was quite so effective. For their part the spinners had for years been handicapped by short boundaries, introduced to encourage bold batting, a mistake because it simply led to niggardly bowling.

Far and away Somerset's happiest moments of a difficult season arrived during the Gillette Cup, which was now being taken seriously, not least because county players, most of them paid £600 or so for their services, found themselves roared on by big crowds and playing for decent prize-money, to boot. Neither was to be sniffed at. After a first round bye, Somerset won a great victory over Nottinghamshire, Langford pushing a single off the last ball to leave the scores level and Somerset triumphant by dint of losing fewer wickets, this amidst scenes of immense excitement at the County Ground. Earlier Palmer and Geoff Hall had reduced Notts to 17/3, from which position their innings advanced by fits and starts. Somerset were just as nervous, and they owed much to brave contributions from three lads trained on site, Graham

Atkinson (69), Roy Virgin (43) and Mervyn Kitchen (41). Even so, it took a nerve-racking last partnership before victory was secured.

Enjoying their first taste of knock-out cricket, Tauntonians packed the county ground for a quarter-final meeting with the champions, Sussex. Eight thousand people sat cheek by jowl in a heaving, vibrant ground which had not known the like since 1946.

Having elected to bat first on a humid morning, Sussex lost Langridge to the first ball of the match and Rumsey, 'all bulky hostility', according to one critic, quickly removed Suttle too. Geoff Hall, whose finest hour this was to be, caused Dexter to play on and he took 4 more wickets to end with 5/34. Somerset's reply was just as tentative, for the players were just as edgy as the crowd. Somerset slipped to 77/7 but then Peter Eele joined Roy Virgin and gradually, run by run, they crept towards their target of 141. By now Taunton was roaring and sighing as runs were collected or balls missed. Nowadays such an atmosphere is commonplace, in 1964 it was entirely new, a heady experience of dashed singles and calamitous errors. Which side would lose its nerve? Suddenly Virgin drove wildly, snicked and was caught by a jubilant Jim Parks. Dexter, not afraid to bounce Eele, dismissed him leg before, whereupon Lord Ted caught Rumsey one-handed and Somerset, to heartfelt disappointment, had fallen sixteen runs short.

Bill Alley led Somerset in this absorbing match, and for much of the season besides. Harold Stephenson had slipped in his bath and had not played since May. He saw a surgeon in London and was told that even at forty-four he was in good enough condition to continue his career, once his back healed. Nevertheless Somerset decided it was time to appoint another captain and to find a new wicket-keeper. Stephenson was saddened by this rejection and wondered if it was not the old yearning for an amateur skipper. He had, once, refused Bunty Longrigg's request to drop professionals to accommodate university boys at the end of their term, and certainly he was a man loyal to his colleagues. Medical reports confirmed Stephenson's fitness for 1965 and he was still a fine stumper. Would he be re-appointed? But his back was sore at times and others stood in for him some afternoons when he was playing. Moreover, he had rather too much fondness for beer in some opinions. Perhaps it was time to go. Notwithstanding, he kept wicket for Dorset in 1965 without losing any of his brilliance.

Plainly Somerset were bent upon change, and their choice of leader was significant, indicating as it did a high measure of politicking behind the scenes. As senior professional it had fallen to Bill Alley to captain Somerset most of the season but Alley was not a conventional thinker content to appease his senior players by picking them no matter what. As Alley saw it, if a fellow was out of sorts he should be dropped. Perhaps he was apt to condemn a man too quickly, and certainly his team was alarmed by the omission of Brian Langford (no less) from the eleven which played at Bournemouth in August 1964. His replacement, Roy Cosmo Kerslake, was a bright cricketer and he had been in form; even so, it was only a fortnight since Langford had taken 10/67 in the match to beat Surrey at Clarence Park.

In defence of Alley, Somerset did beat Hampshire, Palmer taking 7/34 and Langford did return beside Kerslake in the following games. Nevertheless the damage was done. If Langford could be dropped who was safe? Rumours spread that Alley had accused Langford of not trying hard enough. Articles were written 'deploring the fact that Langford had been absent from the side this week . . . Whatever else he may be he is no malicious troublemaker.' Langford, of course, was too crafty and too skilful a bowler long to be out of the team. Alley failed to carry his hard-bitten, financially insecure professional team mates with him in his move and cannot have been surprised by their campaign to obstruct his appointment as captain. Graham Atkinson, in particular, was upset at the treatment of Langford, who had already taken over 90 wickets that year, and with Palmer and Virgin he let his feelings be known. They thought Alley impetuous, and they were not prepared to play under him.

Unfortunately Alley was too long thinking he was to be captain and he was devastated upon another being appointed. At home on his chicken farm Alley had thought it was in the bag, believed Somerset had told him as much. And then club president Bill Greswell rang to say that his executive committee had voted for Colin Atkinson instead. Alley thought Somerset had played a dirty trick on him and he said so. Atkinson did his best to soften the blow, offering consoling words and taking care to consult the old warrior at every opportunity, while Alley for his part carried on playing, though it cannot have been easy. The committee had also considered Greetham's merits and he too thought that the job had been promised to him; probably he was thought to be not tough enough.

Atkinson's appointment was remarkable. He had played only two county games since 1962 and at his peak he had been an average player. Moreover a strange hand injury had stopped him bowling leg-spinners (nor can it have helped that his fingers were ageing and thickening, and that his back was often sore) though gamely he had learned to bowl some adequate seamers. Beyond argument Atkinson was the choice of a committee still searching for the ancient spirit, one reacting against bloody-minded professionalism, with its averages and its cussed selfishness. Atkinson was, in this view, distant from the players, belonged in the officers' mess. In meetings and in conversation he was calm and impressive, a man clear in his thoughts incisive in deed, a mixture of ruthlessness and perception. Evidently he had drive and enough determination to see a task through to its end.

Fortunately this choice was also popular with the players who, sorry to lose Stephenson, would contemplate anyone except Alley. No doubt they played their part in influencing the vote.

It was probably the right choice, if one had to be made. To promote Langford above his peers would have been to ask for trouble. Captaining a county is no sinecure, especially for a man taking charge of players of his own generation. Atkinson was an outsider who had, none the less, led the 2nd XI well and if he was an ordinary player he was, at least, a fighter.

Nevertheless it was an unhappy, messy business in which good men suffered in a struggle for power. A sour taste was left in some mouths.

Nor was Alley the only Somerset cricketer to endure a miserable winter. For so long thirstily waiting, Peter Eele now found his cup snatched away just as he was about to drink of it; for in Stephenson's place Somerset signed Geoff Clayton, a rough-and-tumble character from Lancashire, an agile and energetic stumper, as his nickname 'Chimp' indicated. He was no angel, and it had been some wantonly defensive batting in front of a large Old Trafford crowd in an important cup game which led to his parting with Lancashire. Somerset had signed a capable if cynical cricketer who did his job well, and not a jot more. For years he had an arrangement with Sam Cook whereby Clayton gave Cook his wicket while Cook contrived to be stumped by his collaborator.

For Eele, this signing heralded the end of his hopes. He felt let down, as if he had been used as a reserve by men never intending to give him a proper chance. He played his last game in 1965 and then left, later returning to cricket as an umpire. Probably he recognized in Clayton a better cricketer, but he must have wondered if he truly gave better service. After Clayton was dismissed, without much regret, Somerset fielded a number of scarcely competent keepers before finding Derek Taylor.

Whatever the rights and wrongs of signing Clayton, Somerset plainly needed a second spinner for 1965 because Kerslake, who had taken 39 wickets in 1964, was training to be a lawyer, while Doughty had lost all control, so much so that opposing 2nd XIs were anxious to discover if Bill Andrews had picked him to play against them.

In the event Somerset found a round-faced left-arm spinner, a nephew of Roly Jenkins, in Peter Robinson, who had been on the Worcester staff since boyhood, whose father had been a stonemason and whose mother had never allowed a heater in the family home – ideal preparation for life as a coach in Somerset's draughty indoor school. Robinson was an old-fashioned bowler, an alert and safe fieldsman around the bat, and a determined if restricted batsman whose fate it was to be moved up and down the order, filling breaches rather than asserting his own authority. More will be heard of him, as player and coach; for the time being it is enough that he has arrived to offer support to Langford and variety to a Somerset attack no longer blessed with Atkinson's leg-breaks.

A perusal of the accounts reveals that it was now costing Somerset £33,587 to run its affairs. Adminstrative wages and costs amounted to £5,129 while groundstaff were paid £2,206 all told. Players' wages and bonuses were listed as £12,271. A loss of £5,681 was recorded, this despite a record list of members. Not for the first time Somerset were thankful to their Supporters Club, which donated £2,000.

Since 1965 marked the seventy-fifth anniversary of Somerset's entry into the County Championship, it was deemed time to launch an appeal to provide funds for the rebuilding of the Old Pavilion. A tie was made, and donations requested to celebrate this anniversary. Appeals had occurred with some regularity over the years, upon flimsy pretexts. Appeals will continue to be made with regularity, for efforts to make county cricket pay for itself have seldom been successful. This one did not fulfil hopes, and nothing had changed a year later, save that Somerset was now asking its members to contribute to a loan scheme whereby in return for an interest-free loan of £90 the subscriber received a membership card. Treasurer Rex Frost was prepared to try all manner of schemes to reduce Somerset's losses (£9,142 in 1965) and its overdraft of £11,007.

Facing all these difficulties, and with a staff of players of independent disposition, Somerset officials may be forgiven if they recalled those far-off years when Robertson-Glasgow used to arrive in his straw hat and pumps, happy to play for nothing. Perhaps Crusoe shared a longing for this lost world too, for he took his own life in 1965.

Ever optimistic, and with as potent a bowling team as Somerset had fielded since Wellard, Andrews, White and friends thirty years earlier, Atkinson and his team approached 1965 with hopes of conquest. In the event Somerset won eight games, lost eleven and finished seventh, a rise of one place. They reached the quarter-finals of the Gillette Cup only to be bowled out for 63 by Fred Trueman. A satisfactory summer, rather than an exciting one.

This was the year of débâcle at Bath. Somerset had been playing well, winning home matches in style only to lose at Edgbaston, Canterbury and Northampton. As usual everyone arrived at Bath ready to enjoy nine days of festival cricket. Unfortunately communications between Bath and Taunton had not been at their best, which had led to one unforeseen difficulty: no one had prepared a pitch. Cecil Buttle was under the impression that Bath Council had undertaken to bear this responsibility. For their part Bath Council thought everything could safely be left to Mr Buttle. Moreover heavy winter floods had turned the Recreation Ground into a lake, from which rude invasion it had never satisfactorily recovered.

Buttle, arriving two days before the festival began, was alarmed to find an outfield sorely in need of a scythe, which it duly received, and a pitch with so many varieties of flora growing upon it that

305

sending for Percy Thrower was, for a time, contemplated. Apart from a flurry of watering, mowing and cutting it was too late and Worcestershire arrived to find a pitch as crusty as any retired rear-admiral. They were bowled out for 143 by Alley and Langford; Somerset led by 47 and won by an innings as Graveney and Kenyon were skittled by Rumsey, Headley and D'Oliveira by Alley. Hampshire arrived and were bowled out for 64 and 77, Rumsey following his 6/21 against Worcestershire with 8/26. Both games ended in two days. Somerset's luck ran out against Nottinghamshire and they were dismissed for 62, ending a winning streak built largely upon dreadful pitches. Clayton and Robinson, battening down their hatches, must have felt they were in for interesting careers at Somerset.

For a time, hereabouts, Somerset headed the championship but it did not last. With Palmer, Rumsey and Wight often injured they were too dependent upon Virgin and especially Graham Atkinson, who carried his burden with dogged determination. Alley's batting was not as effective as of yore, for he took no heed of age in his choice of shots, though he bowled tirelessly and took 73 wickets. With Clayton sharp behind the stumps, taking eighty-five victims, one short of Stephenson's record, Somerset were competitive in the field and could win if their batsmen were in form. Alas, only the openers, of those who played regularly, averaged over 21. It was not nearly enough.

Efforts were made to find fresh bowlers, Johnny Martin arriving from his duties as captain of Oxford University. Tall, blond, likeable, his seamers were seldom sufficiently accurate to trouble good batsmen and he was not to linger at Somerset, moving off to more promising fields. Within two years he was driving around Spain in a battered old car, still drinking bottles of his beloved cider. Besides being a cricketer Martin was a Welsh hockey international. He had caught Somerset's eye playing for Oxfordshire against the County 2nd XI in the Minor County Challenge match of 1961. Roy Palmer, Ken's brother, was signed to bowl his rangy, generous seamers and he was to make a mark, not least in the Gillette Cup run of 1967.

Having finished seventh, a frustration but by no means a disgrace, Somerset decided to release Peter Wight, who had, wrote John Mason, 'nearly but not quite become one of the greatest batsmen ever to play for the county'. Perhaps he was too

306

uncertain of himself to do full justice to his brilliant, fragile talent with its simplicity and its sense of dash. Wight was thirty-five and sorry to leave, though his season had been spoilt by sickness and injury. He had scored over 17,000 runs in first-class cricket, and had enchanted, irritated, yet never bored, Somerset supporters. He retired to coach in Bath and to umpire, a task 'Rajah' still carries out with distinction after a somewhat fussy start.

Having lost nearly £10,000 Somerset had to be prudent and this led to Wight's release. Already there were rumblings about poor financial management. Inevitably these whispers led to a sense of unease within the club, a mood which was to emerge only when Somerset's playing fortunes declined.

For Colin Atkinson it had been a promising first season as captain. He scored just 410 runs and took only 38 wickets, yet his contributions were often vital, as when he scored 9 tense runs in a last-wicket partnership with Geoff Hall to give Somerset a narrow victory over Warwickshire. His men enjoyed his abundant enthusiasm and were prepared, for the present, to ignore his limitations as a player, not least because injuries had left Somerset weak in a variety of positions. Atkinson had provided a spark, had helped to cajole a bunch of wilful men into something resembling a team. Considering his handicaps it was not a bad effort.

And Somerset did win one trophy in 1965, lifting the Minor County Championship, after beating Nottinghamshire in the Challenge Match. Young locals, including Roy Palmer, Graham Burgess, Terry Willetts and Richard Paull, a splendid fellow from Huish Episcopi who had attended Millfield, fought his way into Cambridge and was now trying his rather nervous hand at cricket, were to the fore.

By 1965 it was clear that county cricket was dying on its feet. Though membership was reasonably steady, crowds were dwindling, and only 513,578 people paid to watch county games that season. Advisory committees were set up at Lord's to investigate this slide. All sorts of recommendations were made in an effort to brighten up the game, including the introduction of a one-day league and a reduction in the number of county matches. By and large these ideas were rejected as too low church, but as turnstiles continued to tick too slowly they could not for long be resisted. County cricket then, as now, was cherished by some and followed by many, yet it was out of date and lacked imagination.

Cricket loves its traditions and protects them vigorously.

Financial gloom continued in 1966 as Somerset recorded another loss approaching £10,000. Gate receipts reached just £7,495 and expenses crept from £37,238 to £38,240, notwithstanding which slow rise they could not be matched by income.

Fortunately these worries, lessened as they were by Somerset's ownership of its ground, were the only bad news of an exciting season. Winning 13 games, a record, and losing only 7, Somerset rose to third position in the championship. Had not injury prevented Alley bowling against Yorkshire, the eventual champions, who won by 49 runs, had not last-wicket stands twice denied them victory, the title might have been brought to Taunton for the first time.

For Colin Atkinson it was a year of triumph. More confident now, he scored 1,000 runs at a respectable rate and his fielding was outstanding. With Graham Atkinson and Roy Virgin regularly providing solid starts, and young Mervyn Kitchen proving punchily effective at first wicket down, Somerset's batting was solid if rarely commanding. But it was the bowling which lifted Somerset upwards, as in the championship Langford took 111 wickets, Rumsey 95, Palmer 98, Alley 50 and Peter Robinson 70 with his accurate, seductive spinners.

By and large Somerset was a team of craftsmen. From top to tail these players knew their job and executed it with a grit which conceded nothing to romance. Times were hard and every September a committee met to ponder upon its list of cricketers, to see where economies might be made. Small wonder that players were inclined to protect their careers by carefully collecting appropriately impressive statistics. It is no easy task to lead a team of cricketers who have long since moved from naïvety and idealism towards an instinct for survival.

And yet the very idea of Somerset cricket still carried with it a notion of charming unpredictability, of a jolly country cousin mixing it with the smart set from London. To add to it Somerset could boast of very little else, for local sport was by no means strong. Accordingly cricket was followed with fervour, for it was our lads pitted against the rest, and no matter that some of our lads were from Lancashire and elsewhere. Every Somerset team which has so much as toyed with success has quickly found itself playing to a large and boisterous gallery. Every man who has given his heart to his cricket has been adopted as a son.

So it was with Colin Atkinson's men of 1966. New rules were in force allowing only 65 overs for the first innings in some games, and most contests brought a result. Twice Peter Robinson bowled them to victory, taking 5/28 to beat Leicester in May and an astonishing 7/10 in 17 overs on a blameless Trent Bridge pitch upon which Notts managed to collapse from 37/0 to 62 all out, losing a game hitherto within its grasp. Two victories at Bath, spinners again in the thick of it, a handsome win at Glastonbury (Langford 11/91 in 69 overs against Northants) and a conclusive victory at Southport took Somerset towards the top. Nor did they falter this time, Colin Atkinson hitting 88 in the last match to bring one final triumph. It was not enough because Yorkshire did not stumble either, rather they kept overpowering teams in a manner which brooked no argument as Illingworth, Nicholson, Wilson and Trueman proved too strong. Having lost twice to the White Rose County, Somerset had to concede second best, but did so after a terrific fight.

In one respect Colin Atkinson was lucky in 1966, for seven of his men, including all of his important batsmen, played in every game. And Virgin (42 catches) and Peter Robinson, alert close to the bat, missed very little, so that Somerset fielded a settled side which took its chances, a fair starting-point for any team.

To round off a year happy in performance if not entirely in relationships, Somerset enjoyed a gripping, pulsating run in the Gillette Cup, a run which ended in a sorrowful semi-final defeat at Edgbaston. Playing to packed houses rejoicing in these dynamic occasions, Somerset first beat Sussex, winners in 1963 and 1964, at Taunton, Alley taking 4/14. They followed this with a no less courageous victory over Yorkshire, Kitchen and Alley scoring fifties, and Ken Palmer contributing 35 as Somerset reached 190 in 60 overs, to which Yorkshire replied with 150, Alley taking 3 wickets and Roy Palmer 4. Players of this era, of course, had not mastered, or been compromised by, the skills of one-day cricket in conventional usage nowadays, so the scoring tended to be lower even if the action was just as compelling.

With all Somerset approaching fever pitch, Atkinson and his team met Lancashire at Taunton, a third successive home draw. Heavy rain delayed the start and Lancashire, invited to bat first, quickly lost Pullar, Green, Beddow and David Lloyd to a scintillating opening burst from Roy Palmer, all arms and legs and effort. Despite Jackie Bond's 29, Lancashire could reach only 103, and Somerset won by 4 wickets with 10 overs to spare. For his 5/18 Palmer was made man of the match.

It did not last quite long enough. Drawn to play at Edgbaston, Somerset were bowled out for 189, collapsing from 97/1 in 34 overs. Graham Atkinson made 72 and no one else reached 30. Alley did his best to contain Warwickshire, his 2/15 in 12 overs being a masterpiece of controlled bowling, but the game was lost when Roy Palmer's first 6 overs were thumped for 46 runs, mostly by Bob Barber. A Lord's final, a first trophy, these were still dreams. Within a year one had been fulfilled. It took a further twelve summers until the second duck was broken.

Rounding off a vintage season, spectators at Taunton were treated to a magnificent 206 by Conrad Hunte, while those who arrived late at Clarence Park on 29 July saw no cricket at all, for Somerset had already been bowled out for 43 in an hour. (Included amongst the disappointed supporters was a ten-year-old from Bath. Eight years later he was playing for Somerset in Weston-super-Mare and now he is writing this book.)

Off the field 1966 was a painful season, bringing about as it did the end of three notable careers, those of Brian 'Chico' Roe, Chris Greetham and Graham Atkinson. Neither Roe nor Greetham could complain unduly about their departures, though Greetham might have wondered if he were not a better cricketer than the captain who had replaced him. Shy and retiring away from cricket, he appeared debonair and imprudent upon the field. Perhaps his kindly, gentle temperament was unsuited to the hardheaded world of professional cricket, an unsuitedness hidden for years by his talent. Roe, in contrast, was a bubbly, cheerful fellow utterly unprepared to give his wicket away easily, no matter how witheringly a fast bowler might stare at his tiny frame. With Virgin in such form, and Kitchen emerging, he cannot have expected his contract to be renewed.

Graham Atkinson was another matter entirely. Though Terry Willetts, a determined left-hander from the Midlands who was not destined to shine in this company, was offered a two-year contract, Somerset decided to invite their senior batsman to stay just one more season. Word had it that his captain believed Graham scored too slowly and was too lackadaisical in the field. Certainly he had not been as authoritative as of yore, but still Graham regularly scored his 1,000 runs and had managed 1,307 in 1966. No doubt his approach was inhibited by insecurity, both his own and Somerset's, for he was twenty-eight years of age now and approaching a benefit, so that he could afford no mistakes. Moreover he had been batting at the sharp end of the order for ten years, itself a responsibility calculated to sap nerve and energy. And he must at times have wondered why it had not fallen to him to lead the team. Possibly he was regarded as too much of a Bolshevik – a label attached to many a cricketer who, like Oliver, brings back his plate and asks for more.

To offer this reliable opening batsman a one-year contract was to wound his pride. Unsurprisingly Atkinson was bitterly disappointed and asked Somerset for better terms on pain of his departure. Plainly the offer was not an oversight but a calculated move, for no improved offer followed and Atkinson departed after twelve years of service with nearly 15,000 runs under his belt and with no benefit to help him towards a second life. He played for Lancashire for a while, but his heart was never really in it again. It is not easy for a sensitive man to drive himself out there year after year, and always against the new ball.

To treat a solid opener so was surely a dreadful mistake, for such men are not easily replaced. Perhaps Colin Atkinson yearned for a team he could lead more easily; possibly Somerset intended to break up a group of senior professionals respected as cricketers rather than cherished as men.

By September those hardbitten pros who remained were complaining about their terms. Mervyn Kitchen had been capped and he demanded a pay rise in accordance with his new standing, while Brian Langford believed that too much was being paid to stars such as Bill Alley. Virgin and Ken Palmer were no less determined to win a rise and agitation continued most of the winter, arguments raging as to whether capped players should be treated alike. They wanted a pay rise of £15 a week and a common wage. Somerset, backbone stiffened by poverty, resisted firmly, reminding players of their place; and in the end it was the players who capitulated, Langford signing first and then his colleagues, realizing that their united front was broken, quickly following. It was an unhappy episode, if by no means unusual save in the publicity given to it, and it must have left officials at Somerset mourning still more for the old days when professionals were not so demanding. Of course, the 'old days' were largely a fantasy. Now secure in their numbers, professionals were more confident of their power, especially considering that there were no amateurs to replace them. So they did not need to bow and scrape for grace but could fight for what they were worth. Their weakness lay in internal divisions and jealousies, for these were a hardened crew who knew that in the end it was a dog-eat-dog world.

Such ingrained attitudes on both sides were understandable. Somerset loved its amateurs and it was broke. Players could barely pay their bills and were inclined to treasure every pound that entered their pockets and to wish that more did so. Lest it be forgotten: when Langford joined the Somerset staff from Dr Morgan's school in Bridgwater in 1952 he was paid £2 a week. He could be thankful that his benefit season in 1966 added £4,250 to his coffers. A second testimonial in 1973 was to raise £2,250.

Even as relations between committee and players, the old guard and the new, were breaking down, Somerset could, at least, console itself in the emergence of two fine local batsmen, Roy Virgin and Mervyn Kitchen. Neither was to play for England, though Virgin nearly did during 1970, his *annus mirabilis*, but both were to be regulars for years, Virgin collecting his runs at one end, cap perched on his head, every movement economical and neat; Kitchen, boisterous and competitive, hitting hard, running harder, if not always advisedly, chasing a total capably and willingly, as a man does who wants his £5 win bonus, as a man does with Somerset close to his heart. Virgin was calculating and unrepentant, Kitchen was impulsive and mean by persuasion rather than instinct.

Virgin, of course, was already established as an efficient scorer of runs. Born 200 yards from the County Ground, in King Street, long since demolished, Virgin played as a boy for Taunton British Rail, captained by his father, and for Huish's Grammar school, where he was coached by Peter Eele's dad. Rising through the ranks of Somerset youth cricket, he was taken in hand by Colin McCool and John McMahon and made his county début in 1957. After serving with the Somerset and Cornwall Light Infantry he returned in 1962 and had been a regular ever since. Most of his runs were scored through the covers, at least until a widening experience in one-day cricket introduced an unsuspected freedom into his game, so that a chip to leg and an efficient hook were added to his repertoire. For the present he was a tidy, under-stated batsman who scored his runs safely, deftly, and seldom felt inclined to risk a charge.

Mervyn Kitchen was a much brisker cricketer, especially later in his career, a flowering also encouraged by the aggressive demands of limited-over cricket. First appearing in Somerset's 2nd XI as a seventeen-year-old, Kitchen built his career painstakingly, as a player must who is fighting for his livelihood, and it was not until 1966, upon Peter Wight's departure, that he could count his place secure. Until then in 142 innings he had not scored a century, and had averaged under 20. It says much for his rumbustious promise that he was able to survive so long. Now, at last, he was beginning to emerge from a defensive shell which suited neither his temperament, for he was not a selfish man, nor his technique. Kitchen's best innings, and he was to be important for another eight summers, were played when he allowed himself to attack, cracking hard off front or back foot, chasing victory with the eagerness of a pirate after a swag. Because he bubbled and occasionally burst, Kitchen was popular with Somerset crowds which liked its characters and could sniff out honesty in emotion no matter in what garb of cynicism it was sometimes framed.

Great hopes were held for 1967, for were not Somerset now as strong a side as any in the championship? Alas, hopes were to be dashed, for they were once more too sanguine. With Fred Rumsey a pint or two overweight, with Ken Palmer worn down by worry, with Bill Alley's apparently ageless bones beginning to creak, and with precious little pace support in reserve, Somerset's bowling was not as potent in deed as on paper. Plainly, too, Colin Atkinson was feeling his responsibilities more heavily than previously and in an unhappy season he hardly bowled and had a thin time as a batsman. Since Langford and Robinson were not as effective as previously, though Bath and Weston-super-Mare were just as hospitable, Somerset found victories elusive and they slipped to eighth place, a signal for celebration rather than a gnashing of teeth in a weaker period, but a disappointment here. Perhaps, as ever, Somerset had underestimated its opponents, failed to see that they too would be trying to improve, and that victories must be won rather than commandeered.

After starting dismally, with eight points from the opening seven games, a start calculated to prick every airy hope, suffering three heavy defeats as the batting, shorn of Graham Atkinson, whose namesake took his opening berth in an experiment which did not last long, failed dismally. Somerset did fight back to trounce Yorkshire and Northamptonshire at Bath, where the old road sign 'Drive carefully, loose chippings' was erected upon the pitch. Every so often Somerset won again, notably by 10 wickets at Lord's, where Roy Palmer took 9 wickets and Peter Robinson hit 97, and they were seldom easy meat even for the highest and mightiest, but really the rush up the list never gathered steam and Somerset languished in mid-table, each cricketer playing a little below his best, in all matches, no batsman averaging 30, only one bowler under 20. And it was Alley who finished top of both averages, as he scored 1,244 runs and took 59 wickets. Within twelve months he was to be cast out.

Nor did Somerset's encounter with Pakistan illuminate a generally difficult year. To the contrary it was as forgettable a game of cricket as has ever been played. Winning the toss on a plumb pitch, Pakistan surprised their hosts by electing to field. Hereabouts they made their mistake. Enquiries by suspicious Somerset players, no novices these, revealed that Hanif and his men intended to field for one day and to bat for two. Pakistan fielded and bowled sloppily, and Somerset stretched its innings into Sunday, Kitchen scoring 189 and Virgin 162. Pakistan, replying to 502/6, duly batted till stumps were drawn on Monday evening. Langford bowled 70 overs and took 1/99. And then everyone went home.

Despite a steep rise in money received from the Gillette Cup, Somerset suffered a running deficit of £3,580 in 1967, and their overdraft stood at £11,884. Frost's scheme for borrowing interest-free money from supporters who took membership in lieu of interest raised nearly £10,000.

For their part county cricketers, affected by the prevailing economic gloom and doom, realizing they were virtually the only group of workers in Britain with no voice in their own affairs, formed a Cricketers Association. It was Fred Rumsey's idea and only forty people turned up to the inaugural meeting in October 1967. Not one of them, Rumsey apart, played for Somerset. Cider cricketers were used to Rumsey's bright ideas and took them with a mountain of salt. They were unprepared to advance £5 to his latest highfalutin notion which, they predicted, would go bankrupt within a twelvemonth. County officials, of course, were no less suspicious and it was an age before authority and tight-handed players learnt to respect Rumsey's brainchild.

Rumsey's enterprise knowing no limits – which was rather his colleagues' point – he was soon asked to serve as Somerset's public relations officer, one of those positions created from time to time with the best of intentions, positions which rarely survive when belts tighten. By the end of 1968 Somerset's fastest bowler and most imaginative thinker had left his berth on and off the field.

So far contemplation of Somerset's efforts in 1967 has been clothed in words of frustration, and yet it will be remembered as a wondrous season, for this was the summer of the great cup run, and of Somerset's most cherished cricket match since Yorkshire had been beaten all those years ago.

29

Up for the cup

Somerset's campaign had begun in chilly April with a victory over Leicestershire at Taunton. Mervyn Kitchen hit 72, and Graham Burgess, that gifted, bluff young man who had arrived a year earlier and was now blossoming, struck a heartfelt 73 as Somerset reached 251. In reply Leicestershire were undone by Rumsey and Roy Palmer, who was still showing a talent for taking a bagful of wickets in cup cricket, a talent he shared with Geoff Hall and, later, Bob Clapp.

After this first victory by 91 runs, Somerset returned to Edgbaston, scene of their disappointment a year earlier. It was now mid-May and Somerset battled to reach 206/8, play ending for the day with their opponents on 84/4, Alley having broken through. Heavy rain prevented cricket for two days and it was on sodden turf that a resumption was made at 5.15 p.m. on Tuesday evening. Warwickshire fought back but fell 25 runs short as Alley took 3/24, following his 45. Somerset, adept at this form of cricket, were in the quarter-finals.

And so to Northampton, and Colin Milburn. Once again Somerset's batting failed as they advanced by fits and starts to 184. Once again it was the pace bowlers, most particularly Rumsey, who dismissed Milburn for a duck, and Roy Palmer who took 3 good wickets, who pulled them through. Geoff Clayton, querulous, unapologetic, scored 35 and took 4 catches, 2 of them scorchers, and might have been saluted as man of the match had not Bill Alley hit 30 and taken 2/8 in 12 overs of remorseless, probing medium-pace. Not bad for a man of forty-eight.

Perhaps Somerset's attention was distracted by this cup run for only one of the following eight county games ended in victory. Certainly Taunton and surrounding districts were afire with talk of Alley and Fred, talk of a trip to London, as enchanting an idea then as a flight to Sydney is now. And if Atkinson and his lads, for they had all been adopted no matter how distant their origin, did reach the big smoke they could depend upon lots of distinctive Somerset support, because farmers were dusting their straw hats, polishing their pitchforks and filling barrels of cider for the great day. Adge Cutler and his splendid Wurzels were singing all manner of proud Somerset songs, including one which was embraced as an anthem by County supporters.

> Drink up thy Zider
> Drink up thy Zider
> Vor tonight we'll merry be
> We've knocked the milk churns over
> An rolled 'em in the clover
> The Corn's half cut and so be we.

Not quite Perceval Graves, save in spirit, but lots of fun and a hit to boot.

Somerset now faced a semi-final at Old Trafford where so many hopes had been crushed in years gone by. A home victory was confidently predicted on the sports pages, and by Lancastrians, packed as they were to the rafters of their citadel. Atkinson decided to leave out his spinner, Langford, and upon winning the toss he asked his senior advisers to inspect a damp pitch and to give their verdict. Acting upon it Atkinson chose to bat, a decision triumphantly vindicated. By 3 p.m., when Manchester recaptured its reputation for rain, Somerset had fought their way to 100/2 in 29.2 overs, an unusually promising start. Virgin had scored 20, and Clarkson, a Yorkshireman, correct and dour, contributed 35.

Play resumed on Thursday in an emptier ground, Somerset's 500 supporters having headed for home, one coachload having seen not one ball bowled after suffering a puncture en route. Somerset doggedly fought its way to 210 on a deteriorating pitch, Kitchen striking 40 and Terry Barwell 30. Barry Wood and, sweetest of ironies, Graham Atkinson took Lancashire to 40 but thereafter they collapsed, worn down by an accurate, determined attack. Alley was yet again a hero, taking 2/19 in his 12 overs, so that in 48 overs of Gillette Cup bowling he had dismissed 7 men at a cost of 81 runs. Ordered by his captain to partake of an early night after Wednesday's abbreviated play he had instead crept out to a night-club where, long after midnight, he was introduced by a compère who recognized a familiar figure in his darkened emporium. If Alley was embarrassed by this turn of events he did not show it, and he roared with laughter when he found Langford and Robinson no less surreptitiously sipping their ale in a distant corner! Alley was not a man for a silent night.

As soon as victory was secured, celebratory gin-and-tonics drunk, backs slapped and hands shaken, phones started ringing and letters arriving at county headquarters. Everyone, it emerged, wanted to make the pilgrimage to Lord's on 2 September.

It was, perhaps, the greatest of all cup finals, belonging as it did to an age when county identity was strong, before the gentrification of the provinces. Kent arrived as Saxons, with their hops and cottages. For Somerset folk it was a day out, a day in which to bring their cider, songs and laughter, a day upon which to be Somerset through and through.

A wonderful time was had by all as solemn Lord's was taken over by cheering country cousins. Nor did Somerset disgrace itself on the field. To the contrary after a nervous start they fought back manfully and could, at various times, have pinched the game. Finally they were beaten by the tension as much as by Kent, a fate also suffered in 1978 when a powerful eleven could not relax enough to climb its mountain. For any club the first trophy is the hardest to win.

Batting first, Kent were given a magnificent start as the Palmer brothers Ken and Roy lost their line and length. Possibly they felt shy, as county cricketers sometimes do upon playing in front of a vast crowd on so historic a ground. Rumsey, so temperamental on dull days, was master of himself as, of course, was Alley and this pair managed to stem the torrent of runs. Even so Kent had reached 129/1 after 34 overs and if Somerset's thousands upon thousands of followers were not in mourning, the cider having flowed freely, neither were they as full of cheer as at 11 a.m.

After lunch everything turned upon its head, first Denness was caught by Clayton, a character unlikely to be inhibited by Lord's, where he was prone to arrive in his scruffiest clothes, where he once helped coalmen unload their lorries, pulling off a

318

sack and emptying it himself. Then Virgin caught Shepherd, and Cowdrey, cheered all the way to the wicket, was splendidly caught by Robinson at mid-wicket, following which catch Robinson's face was observed to be as white as a sheet. Astonishingly Kent subsided to 193 all out, 2 wickets being lost to run outs. Somerset had a chance.

In a highly charged atmosphere they failed to take it. Despite a staunch effort by Peter Robinson, promoted to open the innings, they lost wickets in a hasty chase for runs. Kitchen and Virgin skied catches and it was not until Barwell and Burgess lashed 27 in 4 overs that hope was renewed. Alas, whenever Somerset appeared to be back in the game they made a mistake, as if they were afraid to win. Barwell was run out and Somerset went down, guns blazing, by 32 runs.

And so the buglers and those with rattles were silenced, but not for long. Recovering their voice, they cheered their men, waved rosettes and wore their smocks proudly. It had been a thrilling game and mere defeat was not going to dampen the ardour of those who had advanced upon Lord's, a pitchfork army to rival Monmouth's nearly 300 years earlier.

30

Low points

If 1967 had ended in a pitch of excitement on the field, matters had been rather more difficult off it. Colin Atkinson resigned in September, and was congratulated for his efforts by committee, supporters and players alike. He must have realized he had done his bit, for his own game was being hampered by injury and his team was ageing. To widespread surprise Roy Kerslake rather than Brian Langford was appointed captain in his place, a choice which may have owed something to pay disputes a year earlier. Somerset yearned for a leader and found a capable, idealistic Cambridge blue who had been an elusive fly-half and who was a purveyor of alluring off-spin, a hard-hitting batsman, a courageous and brilliant fielder and a man who put the team first. Only time would tell if he were strong enough, cussed and ruthless enough to impose his will upon a team used to trench warfare and sceptical of enthusiastic officers. On committee Eric Hill had suggested Somerset's cricketers be left to choose their own skipper, an idea altogether too radical for his colleagues.

Just as controversial, if less remarked upon, was the sacking of Geoff Clayton, who had offended too many with his 'bolshie streak', as John Daniell would have called it. His cynicism was thought an enemy to team spirit, a quality greatly valued in Somerset.

Without Graham Atkinson, Clayton, even Greetham, with Rumsey thickening and Alley rather immobile at gully and apt to pick his days to bowl, it was certain to be a tough year and so it proved. To add to his woes Kerslake was injured before the first game and not properly fit until June, whereupon he bowled hardly at all and batted down the order, as if he were an impostor. Topping it off, Ken Palmer was badly affected by sickness and injury during his benefit year and took only 19 wickets, leaving a gap which neither his willing brother nor Burgess could satisfactorily fill.

Though Kitchen had a fine summer, though Virgin was prolific, and though Somerset recorded two inspiring victories in early run-chases it was not a happy season. Winning five games and losing eleven, Somerset drifted to twelfth in the table, evidence that a strong side was on its last legs. Sadly, too, Somerset, led in Kerslake's absence by Virgin, lost its first Gillette Cup game to Leicestershire by 4 wickets.

More happily Somerset did sign a batsman of high pedigree, a player who was to grace Test cricket for a dozen summers. Seeking to brighten up the domestic game, counties sought to attract outstanding overseas players. Somerset's first thoughts fell upon Graeme Pollock, who rejected an offer of £3,000. There was also talk of David Holford, of Farookh Engineer, and even of Richie Benaud. None of these was available and finally Somerset's eye fell upon a young Australian. Picking brilliant overseas players was to be one of Somerset's strongest points and this time, too, they had picked the right man.

In 1968 Gregory Stephen Chappell was just nineteen years of age. He had played no Test cricket and only a handful of Sheffield Shield games. Signing him was a gamble. Tall, thin, upstanding and stylish, he proved to be a splendidly classical and yet never dull batsman with a game particularly strong on the leg side. At first he was puzzled by damp and crumbling English pitches but he realized this was part of his education, told his colleagues 'I'll work it out, mate,' and went to the nets so to do. Practising hard, learning quickly, he scored 1,108 championship runs at an average of 30 in his first season and impressed everyone as a batsman and man of the highest stature, so much so that it was hard to remember that he was but a teenager.

Arriving as a leg-spinner, he found English conditions discouraging and, upon seeing Bill Alley taking wickets with gentle medium-pacers, he is reported to have said, 'I reckon I could do that.' And, it was no sooner said than done. Chappell took to bowling swingers, dismissed twenty-six men and was economical in limited-over cricket. Plainly this was a fellow with whom to reckon.

He even managed to fit into a Somerset side noted for its insouciance off the field. Playing in a struggling team under a novice captain must have been a curious experience even for a tough Aussie but it was one he remembered with happiness some years later, as he recalled his fellow Australian, cantankerous Bill Alley, staggering into bed at a godless hour and promptly telling his protégé all about everything. No callow youth himself, Chappell could take rough and smooth alike, and did so for two seasons in county cricket.

Somerset's other new arrival was less illustrious but just as necessary: Dickie Brooks, an Oxford blue, replacing Clayton as wicket-keeper, a task he carried out with aplomb though a career in education called him away at the season's end. Perhaps in one summer he had realized what a hard life it could be as a county player in a club running out of steam.

Sadly there were departures too, some acrimonious, some inevitable. Terry Barwell had never quite established himself, though he was a fine player of spin, and he decided it was time for schoolmastering. Michael Barnwell, nephew of John, and also a Reptonian, had proved lightweight too and he went off to serve Derbyshire as a public-relations officer. Fred Rumsey retired after taking 72 wickets but his farewell was not the most dramatic of the season, not by a long chalk.

In September, Somerset decided to offer Bill Alley match terms embracing only Gillette Cup and Sunday Cricket. Alley was furious, for had he not performed creditably even in this dismal summer? He went to see Richard Robinson, an increasingly embattled secretary, and offered to carry on playing if he were paid match money for such championship games as he was picked to play. He could not, he said, survive on £300 a season. Alas, Somerset did not call a new meeting to discuss this compromise and Alley, complaining bitterly about lack of communication, went off to be an umpire, truly a poacher turned gamekeeper.

Suspicions lingered that Roy Kerslake did not want Alley in his team, finding him rather wilful. Then, to the astonishment of his committee, Kerslake himself resigned and retired, pleading that it was time to concentrate upon his legal work. He may have felt incapable of resolving Somerset's manifest problems on and off the field. Officials urged him not to despair but Kerslake had a stubborn streak and his mind was made up. Somerset had to find a third captain in three summers.

Brian Langford, wily, plausible, and very much the senior pro, was chosen, and paid £1,400 for his troubles, which were to be considerable. Efforts had been made to strengthen the team and John Inverarity was approached after word broke that he meant to spend a year teaching and playing in England. R. J. O. Meyer was prepared to employ him and release him provided Millfield was paid £1,000 a year. In the event Inverarity did not leave Australia, much to Somerset's regret.

Matters were scarcely any easier off the field for still those rumours of poor financial management continued. As treasurer Rex Frost had implemented one bold new scheme. In an effort to stimulate interest membership was reduced to £1, though a 5-guinea vice-president ticket stayed in place. Frost's hope was to attract 25,000 members so that income was guaranteed rather than dependent upon weather. And it worked, temporarily anyhow. Volunteers walked around Taunton selling membership cards as if they were raffle tickets, and if it was all rather chaotic, records of such random sales being somewhat unreliable, income from subscriptions did rise by £5,000 in 1967. A few unforeseen problems arose too, for how were those thousands of members to be accommodated at home and away grounds where their card won them special privileges? Somerset realized that handicaps attended its innovation and a return to traditional subscription rates was decided upon at the 1969 AGM, if not without a tinge of sorrow for the demise of a popular and exciting idea.

Nor was this Frost's only innovation. To save money Somerset and Gloucestershire combined their 2nd XI, for both had cut staffs to reduce bills. Also a car lottery was run with reasonable success, and Harold Gimblett appeared at the AGM to advocate more lotteries to raise more money. Gimblett, still beloved amongst Somerset supporters, was to emerge from time to time with desperate pleas issued on behalf of a club and an officialdom he had for so long held in contempt. Sadly his efforts were idealistic rather than practical and little came of them. Having ended 1968 in poor form, amidst rumbles about mismanagement, with two of their best seamers leaving and a third troubled by self-imposed pressures, Somerset could not approach 1969 with much hope.

In the event their worst fears were to be confirmed. It was as dark an hour as Somerset had ever endured, yet within it could be detected, by those with eyes to see, faint glimmerings of light.

Wisden, years ago, had seldom felt inclined to dwell upon feats of Sammy Woods's cheerful if incompetent crew, for to do so would be to depress. Suffice it to say, regarding Langford's not-so-merry men, that only one county game was won, that Somerset's pace attack was as friendly as any ever in its history, that Langford and Robinson suffered accordingly, and that morale plummeted. Len Creed, bookmaker and committee man, had told Langford that 'We don't expect you to win a game' and he was close to the mark.

Ken Palmer hardly played, and this season was to be his last. Carrying the attack was a burden, but really it was one-day cricket which finished him. Throwing his wicket away in a final slog, and being hit around the park were not to Ken's taste and he retired after scoring just 257 runs and taking 19 wickets in fifteen matches. Later, when Tom Cartwright arrived, he contemplated a comeback and was rejected because Somerset felt he had let them down when they needed him most.

Roy Palmer and Graham Burgess were simply not good enough to take the new ball in county cricket yet this was their allotted task in 1969. Nor could John Roberts, a left-arm seamer from Liverpool, convert his humour into wickets and in time he joined the police force, where victims might more easily be snared. Behind the stumps Charlie Carter, a delightful character who might, with more reward, have concentrated upon amateur cricket of the variety played by Hampshire Hogs and Devon Dumplings, proved an amusing companion, if one apt to drop as many catches as a cockney does aitches. Also his batting average did not rise above 3.4 – which hastened his move into the City, where he built an immensely successful career.

Inevitably it was a year of odds and ends. Trevor Holmes, a Yorkshireman, kept wicket against the West Indies and proved to be one of Bill Andrews's less inspired discoveries. Bill Buck did not shine either, on his solitary appearance, and nor did Roy Windsor from Wellington (Somerset), a bearded hitter who played against Tony Greig at Taunton, appearing, wrote one critic, 'like a pirate, and he was soon all at sea.' He was never given another chance.

Fortunately Mervyn Kitchen continued to bat brightly in his

new role as an opener, while Greg Chappell honed his batting and bowling skills further before announcing that he was not to return in 1970. Heaven alone knows what he made of Somerset C.C.C. during his two-year sentence.

If things were grim on the field they were even worse behind closed doors. At Morlands Club towards the end of July Somerset had one of its most fierce committee meetings.

Robinson and Frost had been under scrutiny for some time. Mistrusted by committee members, who wondered at their reliability, they could afford no further mistakes. In June Rex Frost announced that the £1 membership fees totalled £7,000 less than in 1968. Then Richard Robinson, long since dismissed by members as a merchant of gloom and doom, said it might be necessary to sell the Taunton ground. His Save Somerset Cricket Now! campaign had not worked.

At once a pent-up fury was unleashed. Bill Andrews attacked such an idea in the *Somerset County Gazette*, saying this club had not been so faint-hearted when whist drives had been held to pay wages in the 1930s. A cricket committee had been re-formed in 1968 and the management committee abolished, 'thank goodness', said Andrews. Things were looking up. Gimblett offered the critics support and a meeting was called. Before it Andrews said he would resign if Robinson did not.

It was a stormy affair, this meeting in Glastonbury. At it Andrews and Colin Atkinson resigned, and a motion of no-confidence in Longrigg (as chairman), Frost and Robinson, was put by Michael Hill and passed by a majority of 18 to 4, though only after a bitter debate. An immediate overhaul of the club's administration was ordered, and in view of this Atkinson and Andrews withdrew their resignations.

Longrigg resigned, and later realized sickness had caused him to neglect his duties and allow those he trusted too much sway. Frost did not seek re-election, and Robinson resigned. A painful period had reached a conclusion, and now at least Somerset could hope to forge ahead under imaginative, confident and financially sound leadership. Hard as it is to say, especially after their services, none of these men was to be missed. All ideas of leaving Taunton were abandoned. Had not receipts from the Sunday League been substantial matters would have been worse.

This heavy loss was softened by two factors. In 1962 Rex Frost had wrung from the Inland Revenue a repayment on pool betting duty amounting to £5,355. As this had at last been confirmed it was now entered into the accounts. Also £1,750 was received from the River Authority for the use of club property in connection with their river-improvement scheme. Every little helped. Talk arose of target golf at the ground and the club was grateful for a bequest of £500 from 'Box' Case's will. Alas, Premium Bond investments had not so far resulted in any money being won.

Somerset had also been left £10,000 in the will of Dr Heathcote, money which was used, against advice, to reduce their bank deficit, though since overdraft facilities were available at low interest it might have been better invested for profit. Meanwhile the Supporters Club continued to give £2,000 a year to pay 2nd XI costs.

These dramas and difficulties clouded a season which did have its happier moments. Somerset supporters enjoyed the new 40-over Sunday League and could rejoice that Greg Chappell scored the first Sunday League hundred ever recorded, at Brislington, watched by thousands on television whilst Tony Clarkson scored Somerset's second Sunday League hundred soon after.

And Somerset had found two bright youngsters too, in Peter Denning and Brian Rose. Blond, teenaged, left-handed and Somerset to the bottoms of their hearts they appeared as similar as crops of corn and barley, and were as different. Electrifying over a few yards, alert, grittily uncompromising, disdaining all airs and graces, Denning was a fighter from Chewton Mendip, where his dad, a butcher, was a popular figure. Scurrying between the wickets, cutting hard with a shot later celebrated as 'The Chewton Chop', pinching runs without caring if they were prettily made, he did not, at first, catch the eye of those searching for talented batsmen. From first to last he had to battle to survive.

Rose, in contrast, was a handsome stylist whose gifts were evident and whose chief fault lay in an apparent dreaminess. His off-drives could flow with rare elegance, and his straight drives were a joy for ever, yet people wondered if he had the stomach for it.

For both youngsters it was a difficult baptism, one they were never to forget. Condemned to playing their early years in a side full of demoralized men who, perforce, concentrated upon their own productivity, Rose and Denning yearned for a happier spirit, and vowed to build one if ever they were given a chance.

New men were needed, and urgently. Somerset could not afford to wait five years for youngsters to mature and so decided to recruit some experienced campaigners. They were in luck for by April 1970 their ranks had been swollen by several distinguished cricketers. By April 1971 three more fine players had been signed. Between them, and helped by a few local men, these fellows proved to be the backbone of Somerset cricket in the 1970s. Thanks to their arrival Somerset could introduce the brilliant youngsters who appeared in 1974 at a leisurely pace.

Derek Taylor, Allan Jones and Tom Cartwright took guard at Taunton in spring 1970, and at once their professionalism brought an atmosphere of competence to Langford's team. Taylor, whose twin brother played for Nottinghamshire, had been languishing in the Surrey 2nd XI, where his superb glovework was lost in anonymity. Jones, from Sussex, was a fast bowler, or he was when the mood so took him, who was signed to sharpen Langford's attack. Cartwright, of course, was a master of swing and cut, one of the greatest of all county bowlers. In the twilight of an extraordinary career in which he changed from batsman and net bowler to outstanding medium-pacer he was eager to join a club on the rise, and to leave disputatious Warwickshire.

Each man, and Cartwright in particular, did his bit. Cartwright took 86 wickets in 1970, 30 more than anyone else, and easily topped Somerset's bowling averages. Taylor's quiet methods impressed everyone, especially his taking of Cartwright up to the stumps; he quickly won a reputation as England's finest keeper standing up to medium-pacers. And he batted usefully, too, never straying too far from the pastures he knew, which was ever to be his way. Jones proved to be a somewhat wayward fieldsman, a batsman of snicks and heaves, and a bowler of sporadic fire. He took 46 wickets, lots of them good ones, but was apt at times to be expensive. His grunt at delivery – a grunt which once misled Illingworth into a missed slog and to a complaint that he thought the umpire had shouted 'no ball' – indicated an effort which was not always properly directed. Still, at least, he had pace, a blessed relief, not least in that it allowed Burgess to concentrate upon slow swing, his true *métier*.

But it was Roy Virgin's year. He scored nine hundreds and in fifteen days beginning on 30 May he scored hundreds in all three competitions. He was the first Englishman to score 1,500 runs and 2,000 runs and was saluted as one of *Wisden*'s five cricketers of the year. Nor was he blessed with luck, regularly losing his wicket to astonishing catches. As he blazed his shots through cover it was as if a duckling had turned into a swan. For a time he was mentioned as a candidate to tour Australia but it was not to be, and he returned instead to work in County Hall for an eighth consecutive winter.

Winning five games, three of them against the clock, Somerset rose four places, which was a start. Memorable events included Virgin's illuminating 108 in two hours as Somerset rushed to victory over Hampshire, his 103 in a chase against Derbyshire, and a Gillette Cup run which brought victory by 50 runs at Northampton, Virgin hitting a hundred, and a triumph at Trent Bridge where, slightly to his captain's surprise and distinctly against his advice, Burgess carried the day with a mighty six.

Somerset's run was stopped in front of a seething crowd of 10,000 at Taunton, a crowd which brought gate receipts of £4,600. Thanks to Virgin and Robinson, who shone in these knockout games more often than his stubborn play might predict, Somerset reached 117/1 in 34 overs at lunch. Sadly they collapsed afterwards, sinking to 207, and were beaten by 4 wickets.

Alas, after a scintillating start Somerset faded in the Sunday League too. Four marvellous wins were followed by controversial defeat at The Oval, where a certain Mickey Stewart instructed his bowlers to direct their final 5 overs down the leg-side. Despite heated exchanges both umpires, one being Bill Alley, signalled a wide only if the ball was decidedly out of reach, a judgement long since changed. Hereafter Somerset won only once more.

All told it was not a bad summer, even if it did provoke one of Somerset's oddest incidents. One sunny final day at Clarence Park Somerset's innings was allowed by Langford to meander on after tea, Worcestershire having batted too long and no opportunity arising to set a challenging declaration. This was not how spectators saw it. Upon Taylor and Maurice Hill continuing to bat meekly after tea, one gentleman, heartily upset, wandered out to the centre, took a large and juicy pear out of his bag and threw it upon the pitch, telling players to 'Get on with that!' as he did so.

Other disgruntled people walked to and fro in front of the sight-screen, and afterwards dressing-rooms and players were besieged.

Two senior committee members went to the press box to disassociate themselves from Langford's deed and to promise 'drastic action'.

Tempers cooled and Worcestershire's guilt was recognized. A little imagination on both sides would have allowed Somerset to set a target of 200 in two hours. As it was Langford survived, vowing never again to be manoeuvred into such a corner.

Jimmy James, hitherto a civil servant with African experience, proved to be a popular and efficient secretary, not least because he allowed cricket matters to be decided by cricketers. Somerset's fortunes were low, and after recent battles committee men thought it best to offer silent support. With Cartwright and Roy Kerslake, soon to be chairman of cricket, it was James's custom to repair to the Crown and Sceptre at lunchtime to sort everything out.

A lottery for a Ford Capri raised £700, and crowds rose in championship and Sunday cricket. After the departure of Robinson and Frost a healthier mood was discernible at Taunton, as if everyone was eager to begin afresh. Alas, one disappointment was keenly felt. This fellow Brian Rose had not made it, and he was sacked, beside Roy Palmer, whose wickets were proving too expensive. Rose was invited to play if required for a match fee, despite which sugar he had to swallow a bitter pill. No one expected to hear from him again.

Pay disputes persisted throughout the winter, and were finally settled in the club's favour once more, largely because cricketers such as Burgess and Robinson were living in supporters-club houses and had young children to raise. Having had so dazzling a season Virgin was now less inclined than previously to accept a principle for which he had fought, that capped players should be paid the same. This rankled with his team mates and Virgin was to leave within a year.

Otherwise Somerset had a vigorous winter in 1970–1, bringing three more capable cricketers to Taunton.

Hallam Moseley had a broad grin, flashing white teeth, time for anyone and everyone, and could swoop and throw in one flowing movement which at once endeared him to Somerset supporters. A kind, gentle man, he bowled his outswingers to a full, zippy length and was willing to hurtle in over after over if his captain asked. His batting, too, was captivating for it combined off-driving reminiscent of Seymour Nurse and slogs recollecting

329

Weston Sands. Hallam's name used to be chanted soulfully by thousands of supporters even in the hardest days because he was so plainly genuine. Fortune was not to smile upon him as repeatedly he was prevented from counting as an Englishman by a movement of the goalposts.

Moseley stayed fourteen years, Kerry O'Keeffe lasted just two. Brassy, apparently cocksure, he was a twenty-one-year-old Australian who bowled leg-spinners and googlies which few could tell apart. On the crusty early season pitches of 1971 he was devastating but his manner did not endear him to older hands, who were less inclined to offer help when rains brought slower pitches. A scallywag who had not yet mastered the art of discretion, O'Keeffe was to fade in 1972, his confidence draining away as batsmen countered his fast breaks with back foot play. Water, bringing sluggish pitches, extinguished his flame and he returned to pursue his Test career still loving cricket but much the wiser.

Somerset's third arrival was charismatic, controversial and courageous. In the winter of 1970 Brian Close was sacked by Yorkshire in one of their perennial bloodletting episodes. Hearing of this Bill Andrews, sacked as coach in 1969 largely at the behest of Brian Langford and senior team mates, approached Close and soon enough it was settled. Somerset had signed an aggressive batsman with a burning desire to show Yorkshire he was not past it yet, and a man used to winning. Close felt wanted in these mild parts, and foresaw a fresh career shaking a dozing club into life, and this without the constant fear of a knife in the back.

Stories about Close are legion and can wait. At Somerset his impact was immediate. Membership rose from 4,624 to 5,574, helping to reduce liabilities now stretching towards £30,000. Despite poor weather at Bath and Weston, gate receipts rose £4,000 to £13,000, and even the car lottery was thriving. Only £2,844 was lost in 1971, a reduction of £9,000. Evidently things were on the move.

Fortunately Somerset started their campaign in 1971 with home victories over Sussex and Worcestershire, thrillingly beaten by 2 runs. In these games O'Keeffe took 24/236 as batsmen floundered on crumbling pitches. Burgess was no less effective against Gloucestershire, taking 12 wickets, while Hallam Moseley, 'leading a charmed life', said *Wisden*, scored 58. Though Jones was disappointing and Burgess rather wanton with his swingers bowled in the style of Alley if without his extraordinary finesse, Somerset could field a respectable and varied attack in which, sadly, no place could usually be found for Peter Robinson, whose days were numbered.

Cartwright had a second excellent summer (96 wickets at 18 apiece) and with Close a driving force at short leg and first wicket down Somerset rose to seventh place, winning seven games, six of them at home and none of them in a run chase, for Close in particular was apt to rush headlong at a target. None the less the 'cussed old beggar' enjoyed scoring 102 against Yorkshire, and beating them by 10 wickets too.

Beyond doubt Cartwright, Close and Taylor brought an entirely different mood to Somerset cricket. Jones, Moseley, O'Keeffe and Cartwright had strengthened the bowling and officials could congratulate themselves that their county was on the right road. Had O'Keeffe not been curiously neglected mid-season, a neglect which led to a reminder of his skills from committee to captain, even more might have been achieved. Certainly Somerset had no reason to feel inferior, and they did not do so. To the contrary in May they embarked upon a run in the Sunday League and, for a time, they seemed bound to lift their first trophy. Somerset won their first home game, beating Sussex, Close taking Dexter's wicket with a long-hop, which surprised everyone except Close, who said he had expected some such turn of events. Thanks to Burgess's unbeaten 66 Gloucestershire were defeated by 2 wickets and soon Somerset scraped home against Northants.

Surrey arrived in Torquay to find Somerset riding high. Announcing that he meant to sweep every ball, which was on occasion his custom, Close edged Hooper into his mouth and was soon spitting blood and teeth. Next morning he arrived at Taunton clutching his jaw, agony on his face, only for Maurice Hill, absent on Sunday, to waltz in and complain that he had a fearful toothache. Close's pain was assuaged by a narrow league victory as Surrey failed to score 8 runs off 7 balls.

Sunday after Sunday Somerset squeaked home by a handful of runs as their batting failed. Essex were beaten by 11, Warwickshire by 15 and Close's men were top as Sobers brought his Nottinghamshire side to a packed Rack Field. This time there was no escape from poor batting and Somerset were trounced. Sobers took 4 wickets, caught a catch and, after defending carefully against Cartwright and Langford, cut loose memorably to reach 73 not out. It was here that Close and Cartwright met as Sobers walked familiarly out to bat. To young players around this was truly a meeting of mighty minds. What would old Closey cook up for this formidable foe? They rushed to hear. Upon reaching Cartwright, Close said, 'Now, Tom lad, this lad's a left-hander.' And then he returned to his position!

Somerset's bubble had burst and they lost their last two games narrowly, and sank to fifth position. Their supporters were left to mourn another captivating campaign which ended in nervous disarray. Would this wretched club ever dare to win a trophy? These falls at final fences were occurring often enough to appear wilful. And what might happen to supporters who awoke one morning to find their cupboard no longer empty? People yearned for a cup and yet followed their team in part because of the ever-fascinating lure of the beautiful and the damned.

Maurice Hill, John Roberts and Tony Clarkson, northern cricketers who had journeyed south to assist an ailing county, were released in September 1971. Like pre-fabricated buildings they had provided a shelter in an emergency. Now it was time to build a proper house.

Brian Langford stood down as captain at the end of 1971. Three summers in charge is enough for most county captains. In 1969 he was leading a demoralized team representing a club racked by dissension. Support had been dwindling, hope fading and his team walked naked into matches. Now Somerset had a team, a club administered by sound men, and crowds catching the scent of victory, be it distant or near. For this Langford can be congratulated, though he was perhaps lucky to inherit at a time when matters could scarcely worsen. Also he was fortunate to have around him, besides Jimmy James and Tom Cartwright, such experienced advisers as Colin Atkinson, elected club chairman in 1972, and Roy Kerslake. With such men in power, and with Ralph Showering now president, Somerset could step confidently onwards, and might even whistle a merry tune.

Naturally Brian Close was appointed captain for 1972. His task was to inspire, to curse, to goad his team until it embraced fame and glory. In this he failed, though not by much, and if his failure was due to flaws in an impetuous character he did, none the less – and simply by being so large a man – guide two young

332

cricketers, bursting with talent and in need of restraint, towards their greatness.

After fifty years' service Cecil Buttle retired at the end of 1971. A testimonial raised £4,000 but it had never been about money. To him Somerset cricket was a way of life, a passion, and he never counted the hours nor did he worry unduly about his wages, which was just as well for they were wretched. Spruce, handsome, twinkling and seldom surprised, for he had seen so much, Buttle was as familiar and archetypal a Somerset cricket character as Bill Andrews and John Daniell.

If Close's first year as captain was not especially successful nor was it without incident. On 12 June Wilfred Wooller, Glamorgan's secretary, took an unusual step. Agitated by Somerset's dawdling pace as they crept to 245/4 at lunch on the second day he suddenly announced over the tannoy that anyone who wanted his money back could have it. Close carried on batting and he did not declare until Somerset had reached 314/7. By the close Glamorgan had collapsed to 145 all out and were following on. Wooller said: 'The spectators are the people who matter in this. They pay the players' wages, and Somerset tactics seemed to be quite unreasonable. It's a pleasant afternoon but I doubt if we have collected £20.'

Close's reply was unprintable and he enjoyed the last and longest laugh, as Somerset won easily. Despite Cartwright's brilliance, and a vastly improved effort from Allan Jones, whose relationship with Close was diverting, as Close tried to cajole fiery bursts from an irreverent and sometimes irresolute fast bowler, victories were few and far between.

Jones was at his best (predictably) at Hove where he took 9/51 teasing his former employers. Tall, with a high arm and spindly body, he could be as lively as anyone in England. From Fred Rumsey to Allan Jones to Joel Garner and to Adrian Jones, Somerset's fast bowlers have been highly strung, as men can be who touch life's extremities.

Moseley was missing for six weeks with a back injury, while O'Keeffe and Robinson lost form entirely. Robinson was not at ease with Close's belligerent style and O'Keeffe lurched from abundant confidence into self-doubt, which may not entirely have saddened those seniors who had not cared for his initial brashness.

O'Keeffe chose not to return in 1973, breaking his contract and leaving Somerset unable to field an overseas cricketer for a year. Robinson, his playing days apparently over, found work as an assistant groundsman and assistant coach, though he continued occasionally to be summoned from the roller to play, usually when Close found himself a man short or detected a crumbling pitch. Like Buttle, Robinson was to show a talent for enduring these curious metamorphoses as he changed from groundsman to player to coach apparently on a whim.

With Virgin out of sorts, and soon off to Northamptonshire, Somerset did not bat well, though Close shored up many an innings in his combative way.

Rotund Richard Cooper was signed from Wiltshire to strengthen the batting. He played just one county game, at Trent Bridge, and was out first ball, a demise worthy of recall since it led to a favourite story about his captain. Upon Cooper being dismissed Close entered the scene, Somerset's innings in dire straits. Since Stead was on a hat trick Nottinghamshire fieldsmen crowded around, leaving only Nanan to protect the outfield. To widespread surprise Close took a heave at his first delivery. Here his luck let him down for his skied shot settled in Nanan's hands. Returning to a stunned dressing-room Close berated Cooper with, 'Ruddy hell, Coop lad, you told me it were swinging – but you never said it were seamin' too!'

Besides these mistakes, of course, Close played many brave innings and rarely retreated from short leg as he tried to harden his team. Sometimes his leadership was inspired, as when he asked an astonished Mervyn Kitchen to bowl in a cup game, whereupon Kitchen took a wicket. Richard Cooper, whose bowling skills had remained a secret for a decade, was also summoned and in his only over Mike Proctor was dropped as he swished at a high full toss. Playing under Close could be infuriating, for his gambles were not always shrewdly calculated, but it was never dull.

Money was still tight, especially as Somerset did not challenge in any of the three limited-over competitions now in force. Costs of running the club had risen in a few years from £30,000 to £70,000 and expenses of 6p a mile and £1.50 meal allowances were paid to players. Nevertheless with Virgin leaving and Langford retiring, though he was prepared to play a few matches in 1973 if required, and with a staff of only fourteen players, Somerset could, at least, afford to employ a coach and Tom Cartwright accepted a three-year contract to occupy a position for which his professionalism and analytical mind suited him, even if his distaste for cricket's hierarchy seemed bound, sooner or later, to lead to difficulties.

Despite working desperately hard in his legal practice, Roy Kerslake found time to captain a 2nd XI which included lots of promising local cricketers, notably Botham, Marks, Slocombe, Hook and Roebuck. It was a task he carried out with humour, patience and enthusiasm and those youngsters were helped by his kindness and by Cartwright's technical advice.

Thankfully, too, those flaxen-haired débutants of 1969, Brian Rose and Peter Denning, were beginning to shine too. Rose had completed his studies and at Glastonbury in 1972 had scored a memorable maiden hundred, those flowing off-drives back in evidence. Denning was his partner on that enterprising, optimistic afternoon and he too was emerging as young players can in a fresh atmosphere. Denning was called 'Dasher', a sobriquet saluting his flashing fielding and audacious running.

Apparently treading water, Somerset did not prosper in any competitions in 1973 and we need pause only to acknowledge Cartwright's continued mastery, and contributions from Graham Burgess, beefier in his pomp, which ranged from the buccaneering to the classical. To date, if his bowling had been subtle in conception and execution his batting had flattered to deceive, for Burgess was an adherent of Platonic philosophy in that he believed every stroke should strive towards perfection. Blessed with a good eye and power to destroy, he preferred to try to bat as Barry Richards might and, lacking his concentration and, sometimes, judgement he was inclined to be enigmatic. Suddenly, in May, he was promoted to open and unleashed two superb hundreds in nine days, batting as might a prince. Frustratingly it did not last and Burgess, bucolic and popular, returned to his lower-order perch and resumed a batting career of brave moments and life as a bowler as likely to trouble the best as the worst. He was a stalwart in a side gathering strength, and a Somerset man in thought, diet and deed.

One game did stand out in 1973, if only as proof that Somerset could still pluck defeat from victory's very jaw.

Playing Leicestershire at Taunton in their first Gillette Cup game that summer, Somerset advanced cautiously – too cautiously for Close's taste – to 212, Robinson scoring 67. Smiles returned as Leicester slipped to 127/7. Chris Balderstone stood fast, having already been dropped by Jones, who also managed to kick the elusive ball into Colonel Ridley's stand. Hereabout Jim Parks complained of a sore thumb and Brian Close, informing all and sundry that he had kept in a Test match, took over, and duly caught McKenzie. Jones was recalled at 167/8 whereupon Close, finding his gloves too small, gave them to umpire Jack Crapp to hold. To Jones this was as a red rag is to a bull, and he charged in, peppering batsman and keeper with bumpers and wides. Somerset lost by 2 wickets, a devastating defeat – if one which had about it an air of Fred Karno's army.

On such days Close's leadership was too erratic for his team, including as it did such rational men as Cartwright, Parks and Taylor, not to mention a couple of blond and impressionable youngsters. And yet Close was usually forgiven, for he held no grudges and was as likeable off the field as he was forthright upon it. Nevertheless his players occasionally murmured their dissatisfaction.

Even though it was a summer of dramas as opposed to triumphs, plans were being laid to build a powerful team. On committee Len Creed had been badgering on about a young West Indian he had seen while holidaying in Antigua. He had paid his air-fare and found him matches and ground-work at Lansdown, Somerset being unable to accommodate him. Les Angell and Dickie Burrough were asked to report upon this novice and they told their committee that he 'was likely to make the grade in first-class cricket'.

In their wisdom Somerset decided to employ this Isaac Vivian Alexander Richards, this cricketer of joy, of brilliance, of laughter, this combustible mixture of pride and humility, anger and sorrow, as their overseas player in 1974. Len Creed recouped his expenses and waited to see if his hunch had been correct.

Nor was this Somerset's only bold move of that autumn. Roy Kerslake had written a report advocating that Somerset try to strengthen local club cricket, a laudable idea difficult of fulfilment, and that 2nd XI rather than Minor County cricket be played, an idea vehemently opposed by Bill Andrews, who tended to be either very right or very wrong. Finally Kerslake recommended that, besides Richards, five young cricketers be offered contracts as a first step towards creating a stronger, deeper staff and one with a Somerset flavour.

After a debate gentle by Somerset standards Botham, Slocombe, Roebuck, Marks and John Hook, an off-spinner from Weston-super-Mare who was to fall by the wayside, were signed at wages ranging from £20 to £12 a week. Besides cricket their tasks were to include helping Don Price, Buttle's deputy and successor, with his work.

Somerset approached 1974 with a lighter step than usual. They might be poor, their captain might be eccentric but he was a fighter and now he had a squad of youngsters at his command one or two of whom might make a name for themselves. As it turned out the intake of April 1974 was to include a batsman of captivating greatness, one of the most exhilarating all-rounders in cricketing history, an off-spinner of durability who was to play for England, and a batsman destined to write books and score more hundreds for Somerset than anyone save Gimblett and Richards.

31

Close endeavours

Viv Richards and Ian Botham were already chums, had been since an early under-25 game in which Botham scored runs and Richards took wickets, both having failed in their primary activity. Richards had liked Botham's reaction to his bowling failure: 'Well, Viv, you take the wickets for Somerset and I'll score the runs.' Each man trusted his instincts, was prepared to let himself go, no matter what, and both meant to enjoy their lives, and did so, when they were simple. Botham set great store by Richards's support; Viv, by temperament more suspicious, enjoyed Ian's sense of fun.

Some in Taunton wondered if Viv could succeed in county cricket, for did he not hit across the line? In fact Richards, a cracking back-foot player at first, quickly adapted to the vagaries of English pitches by reaching forward at every opportunity, thrusting his foot across and flicking nonchalantly through mid-wicket. Accordingly he managed to hold his own.

Somerset's first important fixture of 1974 was played at Swansea. Glamorgan scored 194 and Richards entered at 50/2, evenly poised. Ninety minutes later he marched off in triumph and found Close and his team lining up to applaud. Richards's 81 not out combined violence, sweetness and authority, and it gave Somerset victory with 14 overs to spare. Somerset duly reached the Benson and Hedges quarter-finals. It was time for Botham to announce himself.

Hampshire were Somerset's opponents. They arrived boasting two great opening batsmen in Greenidge and Barry Richards and the world's fastest, meanest bowler in Andy Roberts, a brooding, hostile Antiguan, a friend of Vivian Richards. It was to be an epic contest, as exciting as any at Taunton save those against Essex in 1978 and Middlesex in 1990.

First Burgess and Botham, unapologetically mixing it with the greats, took 4 early wickets, then Hampshire recovered to 182. Despite Gilliat saving Roberts for a later onslaught, Somerset batted dismally, sinking to 113/8, a débâcle grimly followed in the scoreboard where all save Botham of Somerset's new youngsters were working. Botham was still batting, joined now by Hallam Moseley, whose technique had not changed. A crowd of 6,500 was unnaturally silent, as if merely awaiting the *coup de grâce*. Not Botham, for this was to be one of his finest hours.

Moseley and Botham swung their bats irreligiously and a disbelieving crowd saw them defy Roberts. Suddenly, in the 49th over with Somerset on 152/8, Botham tried a hook and was hit on the face. Bloodied, unbowed, Botham waved help away and took a single. Next he swung Mike Taylor for 6 and promptly straight drove a thundering boundary. Soon he clouted Herman for 6 too, only for Moseley to fall to a Roberts yorker. Bob Clapp, tall, amusing, inaccurate, entered with 7 needed in 16 balls. A leg bye was run, and then Botham scampered a third run to deep-square leg, Clapp surviving with a desperate dive. With 3 needed Botham drove Herman to the cover fence and charged off, shirt spattered with blood.

Those final, heart-stopping overs had been played in an atmosphere approaching pandemonium as runs were roared and bumpers booed, Somerset had found a new hero, a man to match Woods or Alley, and a local lad to boot.

Anti-climactically Somerset were thrashed at Leicester in the semi-final, only Richards rising to the occasion. They enjoyed a run in the Gillette Cup, winning at Westcliff by 4 wickets and beating Surrey in front of a vast crowd at Taunton, with Peter Denning, ever rising in stature especially in overs cricket, striking a typically uncomplicated 112. Sadly Somerset lost a second semi-final, this time at Canterbury.

They were, perhaps, the best one-day side in the country, certainly the most exciting. On Sundays they won twelve games and lost two, reaching 52 points, a total high enough to win the league in four of its five previous seasons. Alas, they were forced to give second best to Leicester where, at a vital moment in the deciding game, Allan Jones took an age to find his way to the middle, a delaying tactic promoted, some joked, by his captain locking him in the bathroom. Close hit two hundreds on Sundays, and struck 19 sixes, a record, not bad for a man who had left Yorkshire criticizing this newfangled entertainment. Bob Clapp, between college and schoolmastering, took 34 wickets in this campaign, also a record. He bowled his overs late, probably because Close reasoned that if Clapp, a great trier, could not tell where his deliveries were going, how were the batsmen to guess?

Finishing fifth in the championship was no mean effort either, a rise of five places due largely to an increase in batting and bowling points. Close, Cartwright and Kerslake must have been happy with their new team, and excited by the potential of Richards and Botham, who roared like lions.

And yet many still opposed Close, arguing that his leadership was a handicap to a young and gifted team. Senior players contemplated a move against him, but in the end they desisted. Some found Close drove too hard and acted too rashly. Mervyn Kitchen asked to be released from his contract and, reluctantly, Somerset agreed. Allan Jones left too, apparently for good. Neither Robinson nor Clapp had flourished under his leadership, for both needed gentle encouragement and were apt to freeze upon being cursed. Cartwright worked hard to keep Close's wilder notions in check, and urged him to tighten his grip on things by moving his home to Somerset, an opinion echoed on committee. Close was being paid nearly £3,000 a year and was expected to earn it.

Financially, too, Somerset's affairs were not entirely in control. With £5,000 being spent on youngsters, expenditure had risen to £86,000 and a loss of nearly £11,000 was recorded. Inflation had not helped. Obviously this could not go on. Fortunately members, acknowledging their committee's efforts, voted overwhelmingly in favour of a rise in subscriptions from £4 to £7. Moreover 1975 was to be a year of celebration, for it was the centenary of the formation of this County Cricket Club. In 1876 it had cost £40 13s 11d to run Somerset C.C.C. In 1990 it would cost around £900,000.

A centenary appeal was launched. Inflation and rain had been formidable enemies, and Somerset's overdraft was soaring. Treasurer Hugh Rendell said, 'It has brought us to a point of crisis.'

Harold Gimblett launched his own appeal. At a dinner in Weston he attacked Somerset officials and suddenly announced he was intending to walk from John o'Groat's to Land's End to raise funds. He also asked everyone in Somerset to give 50p. A small boy in Ilminster sent his sweet money and many others did their best, one old lady barking at her son: 'To hell with my pension, send the man the money.' Delightfully impractical, born of despair and love, Gimblett's isolated campaign was doomed and he soon joined forces with orthodoxy. Somerset were helped, too, by the Somerset Wyverns, a recently formed club of exiled Somerset supporters which had already donated thousands of pounds and which was, in time, to do much good, especially for young professionals.

Unfortunately Somerset lost form in 1975, largely because injuries to Cartwright and Burgess deprived them of vital bowlers. Two catching accidents leading to shoulder injuries curtailed Cartwright's appearances, and virtually ended his career. Somerset were to urge a comeback upon him a year later, much to his horror, and Cartwright's reluctance to play led to an acrimonious departure.

Allan Jones had reappeared and took 55 wickets but relations with Close, and a crowd which loved him not, objecting with particular vigour to his lapses at long leg, did not improve and he left to play for Middlesex. Nor could Dennis Breakwell, a cheery left-arm spinner signed from Northampton with looks reminiscent of Charlie Chaplin, entirely fill the breach left by Langford and Robinson, though he batted merrily especially against spin which was to his taste and he bowled tidily if without imparting devastating turn. Moseley had endured a winter knee operation and did not play regularly.

Struggling in the field, with an attack suddenly appearing threadbare, Somerset could at least rejoice in the strides made by their youngsters, especially Botham and Slocombe.

Botham's rows with Close were legion, and involved much gesticulating and cursing on both sides. Afterwards the lion and his cub were apt to repair to the bar for a pint and a nip. Botham played every match as if it were a village game and he a blacksmith with the winning of it in his hands. As a young cricketer he had an unquenchable appetite for bowling, batting and life, and always he sought a spotlight. Bowling outswingers deceptive in their innocence, and gradually absorbing Cartwright's lessons, he was crafty and wily enough to take wickets, not least because his combative attitude led previously discreet batsmen into wild

341

shots. For the present he was a medium-pacer whose temperament rebelled against the restrictions of his craft. He wanted to take a wicket every ball, not winkle men out. Here was a cricketer who could absorb training, and yet react against it too.

Botham's batting had advanced more slowly, for here crudeness and command were enemies. As a boy, lonely and lively, he had been a swashbuckling hitter whose aggression hid a solid technique. Those who had seen him rise through Somerset's underage team hoped he would recapture this form.

Phil Slocombe was a slight, neat batsman from Weston-super-Mare. This was his first season and he scored 1,000 runs in it, using his feet to spinners and playing smooth off-drives. A worthy county career was predicted and soon Slocombe, to his delight, was being compared as a stylist with Sir Leonard Hutton. Perhaps this turned his head, led him to expect too much, for he only scored 1,000 runs once more, in 1978. To his intense frustration he could not win a place in Somerset's team as it chased glory, and in trying to adapt his game he lost confidence and skill. Weaknesses, especially against outswingers and pace, emerged and better men took his place. An outstanding fieldsman at cover, and no mean batsman, Slocombe's disappointing career ended in 1983, ironically at the very moment it might have begun to blossom as Somerset began to slip and players much less worthy than Slocombe were given a chance.

Opening regularly, Derek Taylor also scored 1,000 runs, and had Alan Knott and Bob Taylor belonged to a different era he might have won recognition, for he rarely missed a catch, though his ambit was sometimes restricted. Steady, consistent, Taylor's influence was missed when he retired at the end of the 1982 season, and egos began to run wild.

Rose was his opening partner, and he was beginning to shine. Having endured failure, Rose had tightened his defence. He did not mean to be sacked again. Denning sometimes opened with Rose on Sundays. Running hard, this pair often gave Somerset a bright start. With Richards, now a Test batsman, Botham and Close to follow, Somerset ought to have challenged for a limited-over trophy. They did not, and once again Close's leadership was subjected to scrutiny. Some officials thought his time was up, and Roy Kerslake left his post as chairman of cricket. Close's company was enjoyed, his judgement doubted.

Somerset ended with a bang and Close was appointed for 1976. Driving hard on the field, no great listener off it, his captaincy was destined to appear more impressive in retrospect than it did to contemporaries, few of whom understood what a difficult task it is to lead a county side year after year.

At least gate takings were high in 1975, for Somerset was fast restoring its reputation as an entertaining if somewhat idiosyncratic side. Alas, Jimmy James left to join Lancashire, and was replaced by Roy Stevens, a naval man whose appointment owed more to background and pension, and to a revival of Somerset's latent conservatism, than to his particular merits. His task proved beyond him, and few regretted his departure in 1979.

Losing Kerslake and James was a blow, and by September 1976 Cartwright was gone too. As Somerset cricket grew in strength so their old and vast committee stood in place ever finding fresh purpose as hope returned. Success brings with it all manner of ambitious men, and opportunists eager to assist. Having helped to raise Somerset from its lowest ebb, having ruled informally and with a personal touch, James, Cartwright, and Kerslake had lost control, their decisions being challenged by committees previously content to leave them to it.

Perhaps it was inevitable. Cricket had shaken off its cobwebs, thanks not least to limited-over cups, and had joined battle with other games as it sought headlines and cash. Players could see fortunes being made by other sportsmen and they too were impatient of cricket's stuffiness. Crowds, membership, staffs, and sponsorship were growing and so that expenditure and income had risen at a pace never previously experienced. County cricket, now, was no backwater, it was playing to a gallery. Committees no longer felt so inclined to abdicate their power.

On 2 May Cartwright, who had been his old self, collided with a fielder while running a single and, landing badly, cracked a shoulder-blade. His apparent recovery months later coincided with Somerset's surge up the Sunday League table, a surge which took them towards their first-ever trophy, and to the fulfilment of a million dreams. Cartwright was urged to play his part and refused to do so, saying he was not properly fit. He believed, too, that Somerset had promised him a permanent appointment as coach and felt let down that no such position was yet his. Tempers rose,

Cartwright was suspended and, in September, offered no further contract.

It was a dismal episode speaking of poor management on one side and a stubbornness provoked by a sense of betrayal on the other. Somerset had lost its coach, and just as his team was beginning to assert itself. Ken Palmer was offered the position but preferred to keep his white coat, whereupon Somerset turned to Peter Robinson.

In searching with ever-increasing desperation for a cup Somerset had failed to sympathize with a player who had served them so well, had failed to see a larger picture in which Cartwright might continue his work as coach. It did not help that Cartwright was a socialist – a political philosophy somewhat at odds with those commonly found upon cricket-club committees. His lack of affection for those in power may have curtailed a Test career which, some thought, had never been energetically pursued. His principles were firm and utterly misunderstood by Somerset, who could see only a man declining to play when they most urgently needed his services. And so a relationship which had done much good ended in bitterness as Cartwright moved to Glamorgan.

For Somerset 1976 was, on the field, a year of apparent disappointment which in fact, promised much. Viv Richards was away giving conclusive evidence of greatness with a string of proud, ruthless, vibrant innings against Tony Greig's England, and Somerset fielded a largely home-bred side which gave a good account of itself, especially in the championship in which five of the last eight games were won to lift them to a respectable seventh position in the championship, a rise of five places.

Denning and Rose, nip and tuck, had matured into splendid cricketers, Denning scoring his first championship hundred and continuing to bat crisply and adventurously in overs games, while Rose, having laid his foundations, restored many of his shots, and was easily Somerset's best batsman. Botham, too, had applied his mind to building an innings and his unbeaten 167, which included 6 sixes, to give Somerset an exhilarating victory at Trent Bridge, was one of the most measured innings of his career.

Other local lads played their part. Slocombe had a poor year as an opener, but Colin Dredge, all elbows and legs, appeared from Frome to clean bowl Glenn Turner with a full-toss in his

first county over while Roebuck and Marks hinted at improvement, though both were still at university and available only after
the Varsity match.

A third Oxbridge cricketer also appeared. David Gurr was tall
and possessed of a fine action which brought pace and movement.
He took 34 county wickets and soon the world appeared his to
conquer. Certainly Somerset cricketers were confident they had
found a man to spice up bowling which was a trifle genial since
Jones had left.

It was not to be. Gurr continued to bowl well as a student but
upon turning professional his nerve failed him. Within two years
he could not bring himself to bowl in public, and this insecurity
could not be removed no matter what was tried. Somerset were
patient and it was ages before they conceded defeat. Had he
been born a cricketer, as opposed to being blessed with a gift
for fast bowling, had he found within himself sufficient strength
and desire, Gurr could have become an England regular, for he
was a fine bowler. To Somerset's regret it was not for him and
he went off to sell insurance. Later he returned to give Greg
Chappell, over to play a single-wicket contest, a net. Chappell
was repeatedly beaten and asked if Gurr had been picked for the
forthcoming Ashes tour. He was, at the time, playing for a local
club 2nd XI as a batsman, and quite unable to pitch upon the cut
strip once the net was removed.

Somerset were beginning to be noticed. Taylor was picked for
MCC versus West Indies, Slocombe played for MCC against the
champions, and Botham represented England in two one-day internationals. And Brian Close, in his benefit year, was summoned
by Greig to add fight to his team as they lost to the West Indies.

Close had not played Test cricket for nine years, and for the
first time in 1976 he had omitted to enter the Test match dates in
his diary. Appetite undiminished, he scored 88 and 40 for Somerset against Clive Lloyd's men and won his recall. Close acquitted
himself manfully, scoring 2, 36 not out, 60 and 46 before being
promoted to open at Old Trafford, a move regarded by cynics
as a first step to dropping him. Close survived bombardment as
severe as any seen in cricket, took many blows on his body, scored
2 and 20 as England went one down . . . and was dropped, never
to reappear.

Rejoining Somerset's team for a Gillette Cup at Edgbaston,

Close was at once struck on his chest by Willis. For a moment his legs wobbled, for he was badly bruised, but he stood his ground and scored 69, easily Somerset's best.

Perhaps he could lead his team to a Sunday League title. He so very nearly did. Amidst mounting excitement Somerset survived a string of narrow finishes, winning successively by 2 wickets, 8 runs and 2 wickets, so that supporters drove in their thousands to Glamorgan on 5 September to see if their men could, at last, win something. They could hardly fail. Glamorgan had lost their previous six games and their spirits were low. One decent afternoon's work and Somerset would have rid themselves of their albatross.

Seven thousand people, most of them long-suffering Somerset supporters, arrived at Cardiff to watch a nervy, tense contest, a game full of mistakes and desperation. Close was particularly affected by this mood, and he charged at Glamorgan, chin forward. Alas, he dropped Allan Jones, who was to be Glamorgan's top scorer, and his fielding was marred by haste.

Glamorgan reached 191/7, and Somerset quickly lost 3 wickets in reply, including their captain's to an adventurous shot. Kitchen, back at Somerset after a year's absence, and Burgess led a staunch fight-back, proud county men in the twilight of their careers. Finally Somerset needed 3 runs off Nash's last ball. Burgess hit it hard and ran. Dredge was swift too but a vital hesitation left him inches short of completing a third, and this as gasps and shrieks and, in the end, sighs, rent the air.

Devastatingly, Somerset had let a cup slip from their grasp once again. To lose had seemed impossible yet they managed it. Close was unusually contrite, saying this game had 'been like my ruddy life, a cock-up'. For senior players it was a dreadful moment, younger men steeled themselves for a day when hope was fulfilled. And everyone else cherished Somerset still more, a county capable of winning and losing when least expected, and doing both with generosity of spirit, though the last characteristic was emphasized most by those loosely acquainted with cricket club politics.

Viv Richards had established his greatness in 1976 and returned to Somerset as a man no longer content with style, as a man in search of substance. Somerset won six championship matches in 1977 and in them Richards scored 946 runs at a rate of around 50 an hour. He scored 2,874 runs in all competitions, and hit three double-centuries. Having shed its joyous abandon, his batting was now simple and commanding, a statement of athletic greatness.

Botham was hardly less productive, taking 64 wickets and occasionally playing eye-catching innings. To widespread surprise he was picked for England's 3rd Test against Australia in Nottingham, a Test which was also Boycott's return to the fold. After a nervous start Botham erupted upon the match, taking 4 wickets in 34 balls and ending with 5/74 after 20 overs of bright swing bowling. Out of his depth at first, he was soon splashing about in the waves. He even scored a scratchy 25. A no less brilliant 4th Test followed and only an injury prevented him doing the double. England soon learned to love its recalcitrant, energetic and courageous child.

Otherwise it was a summer memorable mainly for an arrival and a retirement.

For Brian Close it was the end. Prevented by illness and injury from playing early games and unable to bowl at all, he did manage a glorious finale against Gloucestershire at Taunton, his last game. Set to chase 272, Close joined Denning with Somerset on 106/2. This pair added 144 to herald a fine victory, and to avenge defeat a season earlier when Proctor skittled Somerset after his team had followed on. Here, Denning, ever at his grittiest when chips were down, scored his second hundred of the match and Close signed off with 87.

Nor was that all. In May he led Somerset to an historic first victory over Australia in Bath, where floods had only abated days earlier. A gripping contest began with Burgess taking 5/25, swinging the ball in the valley, a spell defied only by old boy Greg Chappell (113). In reply Somerset reached 340/5, Brian Rose scoring 110 not out, adding 81 with Denning despite hints by Jeff Thomson that he meant to pin them to the sightscreens. Close did not break his duck, and took no further part in the match, having walked through a glass door at a reception. Hookes drove a hundred in 81 balls but Australia were beaten by a county for the only time that summer, Botham following his 59 and 4/98 by hitting the winning runs. It was a proud day for Somerset and Close. To beat Australia at last. Might not Harry Chidgey be smiling in his grave?

A new face appeared in this epic game. He was tall, black,

347

gentle and decidedly fast. Somerset had urgently needed a fast bowler. Littleborough of the Lancashire league had one, and would spare him for mid-week matches if they were paid £100. Joel Garner had arrived. Without him Somerset might never have won anything. With him they were to win five trophies in six years. Mind you, he was joining a side which had so nearly won so much, and a side now girding its loins once more, and with a new, young and local captain.

32

Roses all the way

Brian Rose was not a unanimous choice to succeed Brian Close as Somerset captain. Colleagues thought him too dreamy and were more inclined to support Denning's pride and grit. Derek Taylor was a candidate too, though one widely regarded as too cautious and, perhaps, too pleasantly middle-aged to assume the mantle. For his part Close advocated Mervyn Kitchen who, restored to the fold, had shown a fresh appetite for cricket and even for Ethel's notorious salads at lunchtime in the indoor school.

Rose won appointment by impressing officials with his calm yet erudite manner, and he proved to be a wise choice. At once he surprised his team with his enthusiasm, imagination and entrepreneurial skills. Though born in Kent, where his father had been stationed, he regarded himself as Somerset thew and sinew and he was determined to build up a will to win within his team so that never again would they be bridesmaids. He was fortunate, too, that his men were young, local by birth or adoption, and just as bent upon victory. Those defeats had hurt and vengeance was sought. In his early years in charge Rose seldom had any problem in motivating his side; it is the rise which is the greatest fun.

Having trained with fierce intent that spring, and having attracted all manner of new sponsorship, not least through Rose, who was apt to wonder if Somerset was quite as commercially alert as might be (not without reason, for the club had no souvenir shop and little notion of hospitality), Somerset started their championship season with a dash, beating Glamorgan by 9 wickets as Botham broke through, trouncing Gloucestershire by 10 wickets as Botham fought a diverting and eventually successful bumper war

349

with Zaheer and as Moseley took 6/35, and chasing 234 in 41 overs to beat Lancashire at Bath, a game brought to its happy conclusion by a characteristically beefy 6 from Burgess. With Botham and Moseley bowling well, and Garner able to play mid-week, Somerset had fought their way to the top of the table. Days later, Garner having skittled Sussex at Bath, they were 6 points in front.

Had Rose's men been able to concentrate their energies solely upon this championship they might have won it. But Somerset had ideas of one-day glory too. They reached the semi-final of the Benson and Hedges Cup and were drawn to meet Kent at Taunton. Surely, at last, Somerset could cast off its chains and head for Lord's. Not so. Rain spoilt the occasion and over three days of tense cricket Kent stuttered to 204, Chris Tavare scoring 56, and Somerset, batting nervously against accurate swing bowling, fell 41 runs short. Sighs could be heard from the Mendips to the Quantocks. Had anything changed? Dare not even *this* team win? One down and three to go.

Alas, Somerset could not sustain its championship charge and slipped to fifth without ever striking a bad patch. Vic Marks, now an accomplished off-spinner, returned from Oxford in July to add balance to Somerset's attack but their forces were spread too wide. As the season marched towards its climax so Somerset supporters ever more fervently began to follow their team's march towards triumph in the Gillette Cup and Sunday League.

Somerset's cup run had appeared certain to end at its first obstacle, for Warwickshire arrived at Taunton and promptly scored 292/6 in the 60 overs, a humdrum total these days yet one almost beyond conception in 1978. In reply Somerset quickly lost Rose and then began a breathtaking partnership between Denning and Richards, who survived a loud shout for caught behind off an agitated, aggressive Willis. Richards played an innings stunning in its authority and, with Denning cobbling 60 and Roebuck a swift 45, Somerset won with 17 balls to spare, and this on a windswept day and in bad light.

Glamorgan, in turn, were annihilated as Somerset reached 330/4 in 60 overs at Cardiff, Denning hitting 145 and everyone else driving merrily. For Denning these runs were sweet for his championship form was poor and had cost him his place.

A quarter-final at Canterbury, scene of so many disappointments, now faced Somerset. On a damp pitch and under misty skies Kent collapsed to 120, with Colin Dredge taking 4/23, moving the ball either way and to the unnerving length of a Frome man eager to show these toffs he could bowl. Kent depended upon Underwood, who made the ball jump disconcertingly. Botham was dropped at once off one leaping delivery, and never faced another for Roebuck and Marks took care of Underwood, defending staunchly while their partner cut loose at an easier foe. Somerset won by 5 wickets, a deceptive margin in a fraught match.

And so to Essex at Taunton for what was to be as dramatic, as hypnotic a game as any ever played even in this era of tight finishes. It was a game of valour and incident as Somerset played brilliantly and made dreadful mistakes as this game followed its frenzied course.

Gates were shut at 9.15 a.m. with thousands of chanting fans locked out. Later, at the instigation of a sympathetic official, these supporters were to be allowed in so that a county ground already packed to the halters became a seething mass of excited humanity. Nicholas Pringle, Richard Bartlett and Richard Harden, first-formers, sat in the River Stand, and elsewhere one Neil Burns had arrived to support his native Essex. All England, apparently, was watching on television as these two colourful sides battled for supremacy.

Slocombe fell for a duck and Richards appeared, a weight of history upon his shoulders. For a time he scratched around, as Lever and Turner found swing and seam. And then, quite suddenly, Richards was moving, hitting 14 boundaries and a six over cover point as he scored a sizzling 116. Roebuck hit 57, and Marks and Breakwell summoned a vibrant partnership in the closing overs to take Somerset to 287/6, a huge score in a semi-final.

All was tension. Essex set off at a gallop; Botham was inaccurate, Gooch at his best. Finally 22 were needed in 17 balls and both sides pressing hard for victory, too hard in Somerset's case. Astonishingly Derek Taylor, never a man to wear his heart on his sleeve, missed a take and four byes resulted. Next over Joel Garner, preferred to Hallam Moseley, hurled a ball towards Taylor from five yards, and only an explosion of stumps prevented overthrows. Worst of all, with 7 needed in 3 balls and Somerset spread far and wide, Dredge bowled his first no-ball of the season and it yielded a run and two overthrows. Essex needed 4 in 3 balls.

Somehow they failed, though only by a foot as Brian Rose's throw beat Lever to his crease. Amidst scenes of invading crowds and raucous cheers, blind relief in one camp, sad tears in another, Somerset reached a final. Champagne flowed freely, and players hugged each other. It was a time of hope, a team united by a pioneering spirit.

Commanding displays on Sundays took Somerset to a weekend in September in which they could win two trophies. First they had to beat Sussex at Lord's, and then, ironically, Essex at Taunton. They seemed certain to do both. They did neither.

Somerset arrived at Lord's as an exhausted and nervous team, a team drained by the Essex match, their faces white, their minds tense. At Lord's only Botham, relishing a stage, an embodiment of vitality, could free himself to give of his best. Having survived so many crises, having silenced so many doubts, Somerset's other batsmen failed badly, scoring only 207/7 in 60 overs. Sussex faltered once or twice but won easily enough in the end. Somerset supporters cheered their men and sang their songs but even their loyalty could not shorten a long journey home.

Only two counties had never won a trophy and they met a day later, Essex bent upon stopping Somerset breaking their duck. Surprisingly Somerset preferred Moseley to Garner, who had not played Sunday League cricket all summer but was now available. Moseley bowled beautifully but Rose could not stop Essex's closing surge. Chasing 190 Somerset fell 2 runs short, to their own despair and to that of a buoyant, eager crowd spilling over the boundary.

Players and supporters were devastated. A team had tried its heart out and fallen short. Viv Richards smashed his bat in the dressing-room, others were moved to tears, and few could speak. Fortunately thousands of supporters stayed to cheer and they insisted upon their players answering their calls. For hours this display of affection and intimacy continued and then the curtain fell on a wonderful and brutal season which went unrewarded.

Roy Kerslake had returned as cricket chairman now, and he worked closely with Rose, serving as a sounding-board, diplomat and negotiator, finding time, despite a busy legal practice, to serve more or less as a manager. He was, too, a bridge between committee and player, an essential link in a small club now containing famous players, powerful characters, and an uninspired committee.

For years success was to hide tensions between these two groups: conservative officialdom and modern player. Nevertheless seeds of future argument were sown in 1978. Amongst Rose's innovations was the formation of a limited company through which players traded souvenirs, yearbooks and items of clothing. Michael Taylor (no relation) arrived to promote these activities. Players felt that Somerset was commercially moribund; and with justice, for the club had been invited by Rose and Taylor to take charge of these enterprises and had been slow to react. Accordingly a company was formed out of sheer frustration. In a bigger club more imaginatively run this apparent challenge to authority could never have occurred. Bogged down by a committee structure embracing a vast general committee, all sorts of sub-committees, a management committee and several area committees of no small size, Somerset had failed to adapt to its times had been left behind by brighter cricketers. If now carts were driving horses it said much about the pace of the horse. Somerset was also slow to see that different men were playing professional cricket these days, men who fifty years earlier would have been amateurs. Marks was a farmer, Roebuck trained as a lawyer, Denning had a teaching certificate. It was no longer a matter of Them and Us. Mutual respect was essential and unfortunately there were few avenues through which it could find expression. Far too many important voices in Somerset belonged to a bygone era when committees ruled the roost and players touched the forelock.

Nor was that all. Peter McCombe, a roly-poly Scotsman of a rough if kindly type, had risen from a £4-a-day dressing-room attendant to a £65-a-week lottery manager, a task he carried out with aplomb and profit. A close friend of Richards and Kerslake and of other players, he owed his employment to their support, a situation contemplated with suspicion by a committee mystified by his friendships. Officials saw McCombe as evidence of player-power, that fate worse than death.

McCombe, wrote Dudley Doust, 'is a lovely fellow, one of life's bagmen with neither airs nor graces and, one supposes, the team's constant and subconscious reminder that they, too, are ordinary folk'. Constantly by Richards's side as companion, jester, fixer, and whipping-boy, McCombe was to be at the centre of much controversy in the years ahead, for he symbolized a divide between club and leading players. A world within a world was being created, and it was when this world went sour that the trouble started.

Such thoughts were far from the mind as Somerset players gathered for the 1979 season. Save that Garner had signed a full contract, his vacillations having ceased upon hearing that Michael Holding was interested, Somerset's squad had not changed. Had 1978 been a dress rehearsal for success or a prediction of inevitable failure?

It was to be a summer of trauma and glory.

Somerset's Benson and Hedges campaign began well with victory over Glamorgan, Gloucestershire and a Minor Counties team. Studying their table, Somerset were alarmed to discover that they must beat Worcestershire to be certain of advancing, for defeat might bring elimination on a technicality. Desperate for a trophy, Somerset cricketers were heartily fed up with technicalities, which had denied them a Sunday League title on umpteen occasions. Accordingly it was a worried, frustrated team which arrived in Worcester for the final game. Rain prevented play on the first day, allowing time for debate and further unease at the prospect of elimination, for when play did start the wicket was bound to be damp and the outfield slippery. So much was being left to chance.

Play was delayed on Thursday morning too, and despondency spread. An idea had been mooted, its origins confused by time. If Somerset lost a short game they were safe. Why not declare? Once the notion was aired it could not be returned whence it sprang. Ian Chappell would do it, opined one senior figure, and not a voice was raised in opposition. Kerslake, Rose, Denning, and Derek Taylor met and a declaration was decided upon, for no rule was being breached and, besides, the ground was deserted, though many later claimed to be present. Rose rang Donald Carr at Lord's and was told, as he understood it, that declaring was within his rights though changes to the rules must result. Carr accepted this interpretation of their conversation for a time but three days afterwards he retracted, saying he had warned Rose as to the grave consequences of such a move. Rose had no such recollection.

To concede a game was, of course, a dreadful mistake, and one which wise counsel must surely have discouraged. Rose batted first and declared after one over, giving the game away and apparently taking Somerset through the qualifying stage. At once a torrent of abuse heaped upon Somerset and upon Rose in particular. Important cricketing officials, in some cases perpetrators of far worse if more secret outrages themselves, demanded Rose be sacked and heavily fined, and Somerset be ejected from this competition for a decade.

Newspapers filled their pages with vitriol, and cricket's rulers condemned Somerset for their apparently cynical act. And yet Rose's declaration had naivety as much as cynicism at its heart. No one was interested in money, simply in winning a game, and in pursuit of this end they were blind to matters political and diplomatic. Nothing was hidden. Somerset could easily have thrown the game by batting appallingly, and bowling widely. Teams have lost such contests before. But Rose and his men had no taste for dishonesty; they could remember being denied so often previously and simply decided they had had enough of it.

For three days Rose and his team were subjected to a vicious assault, and found they must be silent. Meetings were held and Somerset duly ejected from the Benson and Hedges Cup.

Two days later Taunton was packed as Somerset prepared to play its next game. As Rose led his side on to the field 6,000 people stood and cheered, out of sympathy and solidarity as much as support. Fuelled by a belief that the establishment, its cronies and ambitious bystanders had conspired to do down rural cousins who had been too clever by half, these spectators were determined to drive their team to triumph. Rose, for his part, had learned much and he too felt spurred towards victory. Curiously this mistake borne of immature frustration allowed Somerset to cast off its inhibitions. From now on they were going to attack, as men may who believe they have nothing more to lose.

It was to be Somerset's best season. A profoundly united team could no longer tolerate defeat and fought, fearlessly this time, to win. Though finishing only eighth in the championship Somerset lost just one game and this the last match of the season at Hove when Garner, Richards and Rose were resting. Denied their Test players for a month due to World Cup commitments, and with little bowling in reserve, they could not sustain a challenge and yet managed to give a robust account of themselves, especially the batsmen amongst whom everyone shone except Slocombe, whose limitations were proving an exasperation, and Kitchen who

355

appeared past his best. Garner took 55 wickets at 13.8, and was only once to surpass this tally for Somerset. Burgess was playing only in limited-over games, for he was heavy now and the end was nigh. Popplewell had arrived from Cambridge, encouraged to join by Roebuck, and though he considered himself a moderate if cheerful all-rounder some detected substance in him. Vic Marks was playing his first full season, contributing 894 runs, taking 57 wickets and rarely being mastered in one-day cricket.

Somerset's hopes of a title rested in the Gillette Cup and Sunday League. Nor, as September approached, were these hopes forlorn. Somerset swept past Derbyshire and Kent in the Gillette Cup, Garner taking 5/11 to bowl Kent out for 60 amidst roars of delight from a partisan Taunton crowd relishing a kill. And it was a local lad, Graham Burgess, who had rescued Somerset's innings with a timely 50 not out. Thanks to Garner (4/24), Burgess (3/25) and Denning (90 not out) Somerset won their semi-final against Middlesex and reached Lord's again. This time they were fresh, for they had learned to pace themselves. Rose's team included a balance of experience, in Taylor and Burgess, a sprinkling of imported bowlers in Breakwell, Richards and Garner and gifted local lads in Rose, Denning, Roebuck, Marks, Dredge, Jennings and, of course, Botham, still a Titan. As in the 1960s and 1890s Somerset had followed its only path to success, mixing ages and origins and yet never forgetting the value of home-bred talent, for a team must be more than its constituent parts.

Good progress had been made in the Sunday League too, and a series of handsome victories, most of them batting second, lifted Somerset to second position, needing a win at Trent Bridge and Kent to lose at Canterbury on the final weekend. Despite Rose's powerful batting his strength lay in his bowling, for only once in fifteen Sunday games did a team pass 200 in their 40 overs and they, Leicestershire, ever a bogey, managed just 202. Garner's first spell was invariably mean, which helped Marks to bowl his brave spinners slow and straight, inviting risks that batsmen were loath to take as they rebuilt. Jennings, son of a carpenter from Milverton, angled his deliveries at the pads and could muster a leg cutter while Dredge, Burgess, Richards and Breakwell gave Rose a choice of bowlers. Moreover Somerset's fielding was often brilliant, with Denning, Popplewell and Richards outstanding.

Northants were Somerset's Gillette Cup opponents at Lord's.

Ten thousand fans had visited Lord's for the semi-final, astonishing their hosts, who had to open extra gates. Somerset was aflame. They had cheered their team, especially Denning, who celebrated his 90 by pouring a bottle of orangeade over himself, for reasons he could not later explain. Now these thousands returned, or as many as Lord's deigned to accommodate. They could not be disappointed on this their second pilgrimage in two years.

Somerset were different, older and wiser. To them this was no longer an ordeal. Denning nudged and scampered to 19 whereupon Viv Richards entered, and quite an entry it was. With sparkling batting he scored 117, rising to the occasion and yet never indulging his more reckless shots. It was a command performance, and it took Somerset to 269/8 in their 60 overs. Garner contributing 24 vastly entertaining runs, not least because his running was founded upon the view that a correct shot must certainly be worth at least a single.

Somerset felt confident, and their supporters cheered their appearance on the field, and sang their songs to the horror of stuffy inhabitants of this shrine. Northants lost early wickets to Garner and (vitally) Geoff Cook ran himself out at 126/2. Lamb played crisp shots, reached 78 and was then superbly stumped off Richards. Garner returned and to ecstatic yells from thousands of Somerset folk he skittled the tail, taking 6/29. Incredibly Somerset had won at last, and great were the celebrations. One hundred and four years had been a long time to wait.

And they won again on Sunday, beating Nottinghamshire by 56 runs, a notable effort considering their euphoric state. As Garner took wickets, so news filtered through of Kent's collapse, each bulletin bringing shouts from Somerset men in Trent Bridge. Soon it was confirmed. Somerset had taken not one but two trophies. Truly it was time for cider with Rosie. All Somerset joined the party, and Rose and his men paraded their cups around Taunton in a double-decker bus. Thousands cheered them on their way.

For Somerset this was a priceless opportunity. Essex had won their first trophies too. Both clubs were glamorous, colourful and increasingly rich. After decades carrying an overdraft Somerset were £100,000 in profit, and membership had risen beyond 6,000 (it was to pass 7,000 before decline began after 1981). Membership had spread into Devon and Cornwall. In 1975 there had been only six advertising boards around the ground, now there were forty.

Sponsorship had grown apace. Cricket in Somerset was on fire.

Somerset urgently needed leadership which was stable and far-sighted. They had built a team and must now build a club and a ground.

Building a ground was an easy matter, save that it cost money. In 1978 Colin Atkinson had begun a fund for a New Pavilion (for the original one still stood, having defied rain, storm and fire, and was still damp and inhospitable). Plainly Somerset needed a worthy pavilion in which sponsors, players, members and guests could feel comfortable. As Atkinson said, 'The original cost was less than a quarter of a million and ended up more than £400,000. We've been paying off the bank at a rate of £50,000.'

By 1990 Somerset's interest repayments had reached £35,000 a year, but they had a new pavilion and they could be proud of it. Moreover Mrs Webb and her son Harry arrived to take care of the catering and bar, and Somerset swiftly rose from worst to best in the significant areas. In time this splendid pair handed on to Janet Mill and Frank Betts, who also worked long hours and to a standard high in quality and profit, earning Somerset tens of thousands of pounds a year.

At Rose's insistence a communal bath was included in the home dressing-room at an extra cost of £10,000 and at Eric Hill's insistence the pavilion attic was not used for the Press, who remained in their ramshackle cupboard close to the line of play.

Building a ground was one thing, a club quite another. Colin Atkinson had been ferociously attacked by members for his appeasement of Lord's over the Worcestershire declaration. Many called for his head, for Somerset supporters hold Lord's in little affection and are suspicious of officials whose ambitions lie in that direction. Kerslake publicly defended Atkinson for his role. Rose had clearly been in the wrong.

And then, in this glorious hour, Kerslake himself resigned as club chairman. Exasperation was apt to overtake him when he could not get his way. Rather than fight it out he was inclined to withdraw, for confrontation was not to his taste. He wanted to build a family atmosphere and had found his committee obstructive. Bent upon holding his team together, Kerslake defended his men and supported their demands even in the face of concerted attacks from unwieldy committees. He was, himself, no cunning

358

manipulator of meetings, and no compromiser either. He wanted it done his way or he would have no part of it.

For its part Somerset officials felt that Kerslake allowed his emotions to cloud his judgement, especially so far as Viv Richards was concerned. They saw McCombe and Mike Taylor finding roles, heard tales of outlandish social conduct and wondered where it all might lead. Kerslake asked for support and did not receive it as enthusiastically as he felt entitled to expect. He had given of his time and energy and wondered if it was worth it. Too many battles had to be fought even to hold such ground as had been won.

So it was to be hereafter. After a fearful rumpus, with members packing meetings in open rebellion, Kerslake was persuaded to resume his responsibilities as chairman of cricket though he refused to stand as club chairman. But the rifts never healed. Faults lay on both sides. Somerset's committees were ridiculously large, far too numerous, and full of men with little experience in business or cricket and a philosophy of life entirely at odds with professional realities. As a club Somerset was incapable of reforming itself – could see no need to do so for membership was booming and their team winning. These committees were convinced of their own merit and rejected all notions of a small, single, elected committee of seven people empowered to run things, arguing that Somerset was a members' club in which everyone was entitled to a say. Kerslake wanted to be a Murray-Anderdon and was refused.

Kerslake was himself flawed. After all, he had survived just one year as captain before being eaten up by a rougher element. A man of integrity and loyalty, he lacked those powers of persuasion which might have converted sceptics to his cause and he could with justice be accused of blindness to the faults of those he admired. In trying to promote his vision he failed to see signs of decay, and accordingly did not correct them. In short he had many of those qualities which signify greatness, but had a number of weaknesses too. Enlightened in his attitudes rather than wise in his judgements, Kerslake was to feel let down by a club he had never carried with him, a club in which enlightenment had only a minority voice, and by players whom he was apt to indulge. Once he had lost his club he continued working with his players until his way forward was blocked. He was not a man who could communicate his convictions; rather he was silent and reserved, and to remove obstacles proved beyond his power. If ultimately he failed because he could not win support, he did, at least, help to bring success to Somerset. Garner apart, this team was scarcely his creation, and being so ambitious perhaps it could scarcely fail. Yet Kerslake allowed passion and enthusiasm to find their expression and, with Rose, he protected players from distractions and made certain that there was no slip betwixt cup and lip.

Roy Stevens left as secretary in 1979 and was replaced by David Seward, a local schoolmaster who was to find himself caught between committee and players, an uneasy situation even for a man of calibre. He felt his committee had not given him a sufficiently free hand.

Richards and Garner were away in 1980, touring England with the West Indies, and in their place Somerset signed Hugh Gore, a left-arm seamer from Antigua who arrived overweight and was soon injured, and Sunil Gavaskar, India's greatest batsman.

Gavaskar was to illuminate Somerset cricket by playing several innings of immense brilliance. Few will forget his hundred against Sylvester Clarke at his most horrid at The Oval, his scintillating partnership with Rose at Canterbury or an astonishing 123 against a powerful Middlesex attack in a Benson and Hedges game at Taunton. Nor will his partner forget a flick off his pads which ended on a tent roof in Bath (we were playing at the Recreation (not County) Ground – he was not *that* good!).

Oddly, though, Gavaskar had a moderate season, undone by damp pitches and threatening clouds. He was not a man for a treadmill, rather a cricketer of inspiration whose peaks were awesome in their majesty. A mild, amusing man, he did not care to reveal his more quixotic and rugged characteristics at Somerset and was fondly regarded by colleagues, who managed to brush him with Somerset humour, tolerance and patience.

Burgess had retired, his work done, ending a career combining honest talent and exasperation (he was apt to sit on a chair while slaughtering team mates at table tennis during pre-season training) which weakened Somerset bowling – already without Garner and Botham, who had succeeded Brearley as captain of England. Brian Rose, batting with the freedom of a golfer on a tee who can see no traps ahead, was picked for England and Vic Marks was called up for limited-over internationals and, unsurprisingly, Somerset had a modest season in knock-out cricket. Incredibly and significantly they managed to finish equal fourth in the championship and second in the Sunday League.

To end so respectably placed in the championship was a splendid effort, and one to be repeated in 1984. Somerset had lots of excellent cricketers, besides its famous men.

Having won only once before 25 July, Brian Rose leading a charge to beat Worcestershire by 8 wickets, scoring 150 not out, Somerset promptly won successive games, thanks largely to their bowlers. Moseley and Dredge skittled Kent at Taunton while Jeremy Lloyds, a stylish left-hander from Blundells who could also turn his off-breaks, took 11/95 to beat Worcestershire at Clarence Park. In a wet summer these three victories were enough to lift Somerset to fourth place, far, far behind Middlesex and Surrey. Botham took only 18 championship wickets, and Breakwell (13) and Jennings (13) were ineffective too. Botham did, though, offer one devastating innings, his 228 against Gloucestershire brightening a gloomy May.

Even without Garner, Somerset's bowling was never collared on Sundays. Dredge (3/8 in 8 overs against Surrey), Marks, and Moseley being helped by Popplewell, a cheerful and adaptable cricketer who also constructed combative innings in various forms of cricket.

All told it was a year of surprise, a year cherished by many, not least Brian Rose who enjoyed batting with Gavaskar and leading a team suffering no resentment. Sadly it ended on a sour note. Gavaskar had been forced to return early to Bombay to pick an Indian touring team. Fulfilling his obligations, he flew back to Somerset to play in the final game against Warwickshire. Rose wanted him to play but Botham, acting as captain for Rose who was injured, and Richards, whose tour commitments had ended, objected and Kerslake bowed to them. Disgracefully Gore was preferred to Gavaskar, whose season ended in humiliation. And Somerset lost by 10 wickets. It boded ill for the future, and spoilt happy memories of Popplewell's brave 79 not out against Glamorgan a week earlier and his brilliant unbeaten partnership of 179 with Breakwell helping to bring victory over Kent in July.

For English cricket 1981 was the year a phoenix rose from the Ashes. It was Botham's year, as England's swashbuckling hero fought back from misfortune. Botham's batting and bowling inspired a country, and all summer people stood in their dozens outside television shops to catch the latest episode. And yet in June Botham had lost the England captaincy and returned to Taunton forlorn and forsaken. What effect such a swing of fortune had upon this powerful, calculating, earthy man from Yeovil cannot be said. Certainly he was never so at ease with his world again, for he had been let down, he believed, by those without affection for him, and he felt terribly alone. Now he emerged as a people's champion, a brave, buccaneering cricketer imitated by every child in every backstreet game. It was, he had always felt, his destiny and from time to time he was to try to recapture his place in a nation's heart – mistakenly perhaps for 1981 had been a joyous accident, as events swept him along.

For Somerset 1981 was hardly less dramatic a year and with a stronger will they might have won their first championship. As ever Joel Garner was the key to their hopes and for once, Garner was fit for nearly every game. He took 88 wickets and was seldom less than devastating as Somerset won ten of their twenty-two games, enough usually for a championship pennant but not this time as Nottinghamshire and Sussex won eleven each.

Had Garner played in every match he would certainly have taken 100 wickets and probably a championship medal too. As it was he missed two critical games, against Sussex at Taunton, which Somerset lost by 6 wickets on a green pitch, and against Northampton at Clarence Park, where Somerset were beaten by 2 wickets on a dodgy wicket. Dredge, Botham, Moseley and Marks bowled manfully in these contests but could not do quite enough.

It was Joel's year. Surging in head down, he gathered himself at delivery in a whirl of elongated arms and legs, leant back and hurled his missiles at batsmen often intimidated by his presence. Neither Garner nor any of his illustrious colleagues was ever paid a vast sum for playing for Somerset, though Garner had private arrangements of his own, unlike Richards. They liked playing for Somerset, in those years, and did not allow money to deflect them. Suspicion and mistrust, fostered by a breakdown in the club and by gossip spread by ill-chosen friends had not yet displaced the former club characteristics of goodwill and enjoyment.

If Joel was on song so were Somerset. If he was running in upright, resembling a man running in water, they usually won. He took 10/116 to beat Lancashire, who had once rejected him, 6/29 he bowled out Nottingham, 7/41 against Leicester, where Viv Richards scored 196 in another win, 7/25 to rout Hampshire, 7 cheap wickets in the Kent match and 4/25 against Warwickshire.

It was a *tour de force*. Garner was never to take 50 wickets in a season for Somerset again.

Rose had a quiet year, undone by harsh experiences with England in the Caribbean. A fellow of domestic inclinations, like so many other Somerset men, he did not always appear comfortable in a larger, more hostile world. Otherwise the batsmen scored well, and in Jeremy Lloyds and Nigel Popplewell Somerset had two capable cricketers in reserve. For once Somerset had a squad of fifteen players good enough to play county cricket. Truly times had changed.

Besides their championship challenge, which did not really begin until August when Somerset won seven out of nine games, losing narrowly to Northampton, and had Essex following-on (a series of results seldom equalled in their history), Rose's men also finished second in the Sunday League, a matter of celebration for umpteen years and lamentation now.

Highlights of the season included Jeremy Lloyds' maiden hundred against Holding on a Manchester pitch not entirely above suspicion, whereupon Garner and Botham bowled Somerset to victory by delivering 34.2 consecutive overs; Richards's memorable encounter with Jeff Thomson at Lord's, all cut and thrust; a match-saving last-wicket partnership between Brian Rose and Peter Roebuck at Bath, during which this pair of temporary crocks, fearing a cock-up, sent off their runners; and Somerset's first win at Sheffield since 1902, Richards scoring 153 and Colin Dredge snaring 6/43.

To top off another vibrant season, a season in which a promising side reached its fullest maturity, Somerset won the Benson and Hedges Cup for the first time. Until Lord's everyone played their part superbly. At Lord's Garner (5/14) and Richards (132 not out) imposed themselves in a manner which brooked no argument. Garner proved himself to be the greatest one-day bowler, with Vintcent van der Bijl his only rival, while once

Clarke's onslaught had been resisted Richards was master of all he surveyed. Somerset supporters went home relishing a crushing victory – and this at headquarters. They went rejoicing in a team, and a club, which had risen to dominate county cricket, and had done so in style. And the dialect poets had found fresh voice:

Zummerzet '81

Our cap'n's the best, so it's hardly surprisin'
That Brian Rose 'as kept on risin'.
If the world is just it should soon happen
The our Rose'll climb to be England's cap'n.

One day Ian Botham, our national hero,
Will score 300, an' take ten for zero.
Renowned from the Kop to the Caribbean,
The Big Guy's truly Hercul-Ian.

To see the great Viv the whole world's eager.
He's from a Zummerzet village – Antigua.
When he's in, a feast o' battin's sure.
When he's out, no dressin'-room window's secure.

Big Bird's as long as a giant banana,
But plenty o' wickets he'll always garner.
He bowls the ball from such a height,
You crick your neck just watchin' the flight.

Derek's many Taylor-made catches
Help us to win a lot of matches.
His age is a subject we just won't mention
(But he'll soon be stumpin' off for his pension.)

Roebuck is eddicated – he bats an' he writes.
He could have an England cap in his sights,
But he stands so funny – in a kind of arc,
A bit like a human question mark.

Hallam's been over here for so long,
He could play for England, but his accent's wrong.
When he decides to give up pitchin',
There's a job waitin' for him – in Big Bird's kitchen.

364

Dredge's arm's a sky-scraper, a bit like Garner's,
And when wickets fall 'Herbie' Goes Bananas.
Dasher's still dashin' away. Ain' 'e fit!
Well he's got to be – it's for his own benefit.

An England prospect from Oxford's Parks,
Vic in most matches makes his marks.
For 'insured' success, Lloyds is essential,
But don't bank on him if he's in the Prudential.

We're making plans for Nigel to tell
The pop world how to popple well.
But Keith's got to go 'cos there's no rhymes for Jennings.
His name is as difficult as Denning's.

An' the lack o'rhymes is bad for Slocombe.
He comes from Weston. Shoulda come from Crowcombe.
But Dennis gives us a rhyme to make well:
Because his left-arm spinners break-well.

For Russom and Olive, Ollis and Gard,
Spiller, Davis, Felton, Palmer it's hard
To find a place. Their time's not yet,
But for golden futures some-r-set.

This poem now I'd like to end
By thankin' everybody's friend:
Roy bears his burdens with a grin –
'Cos all his burdens are borne by Lynne.
To both, our thanks for all their bounty,
Which helps make ours a champion county.

(David Henry Wilson)

Inevitably it was not as simple as it appeared. Dennis Breakwell
was released in September, and was appointed to coach in schools
and junior cricket on a self-supporting basis. He is still carrying out
this task cheerfully. McCombe had raised £25,000 in his lottery in
1980 and though profits fell to £17,000 in 1981 it was surprising to
find him under pressure. For ever and a day schemes have been
afoot at Somerset to squeeze more money from supporters and
businesses. By and large these ideas have been too ambitious,
for they have failed to take into account Somerset's quiet, modest

ways. So many whiz-kids have arrived with bright notions which, sadly, have floundered on the rocks of rural life. Somerset has too small an industrial base and money market to warrant easy promotion. Essex's rise was due, in part, to the spread of the new money-men of free-market enterprise into such accessible towns as Chelmsford and Colchester. Somerset could boast only a fading landed gentry and an ailing farming community. Essex rose, in part, on the back of the Futures market; Somerset declined with old money and private-school cricket. Membership had fallen to 5,400 largely because subscriptions had increased. Somerset's new pavilion was open now, and Colin Atkinson's fund to pay for it had reached £105,000. Soon profits from catering and bar sales, hitherto negligible, helped to reduce the deficit. And plans were made to build executive boxes atop the indoor school, lay artificial pitches, and improve behaviour and dress amongst players. Nigel Popplewell was to be provided with a new sweater, as according to one committee man 'his present one looks untidy on the field'. Popplewell was uncertain if cricket was a serious enough profession, for he was from a legal family and his misgivings were expressed by the scruffiness of his attire.

Two faithful servants had left by autumn 1981. Tom Tout had worked as scorer and fiery administrator practically since the dawn of time and now he retired from a club he served for love rather than money, as so many other men and women have done. Don Price, groundsman since Buttle's departure, was forced to give up work because his hips had failed him. He was given a framed picture and a cheque for £1,407. Gordon Prosser was appointed in his place at a wage of £6,500. It was the first time an outsider had served as head groundsman since the club was founded and only upon the arrival of Phil Frost, trained by Price, was the unbroken line repaired.

Sadly in other areas, and most particularly in appointing captains and secretaries, Somerset has been extraordinarily reluctant to promote insiders. And yet it is as plain as day that our best captains, administrators and groundstaff have all been Somerset men; for this is a county which runs on passion and resents opportunism.

Somerset was at its peak. Rose's team – in so far as it was still his team – was feared and to play at Taunton was to enter a fervent arena with partisan crowds and a charged atmosphere spoilt only by a loutish element interested largely in lager and Botham. Travelling towards triumph had been hugely enjoyable; arrival had not been so bad; now people were wondering if staying might not bring with it some pain. Ever more within the club battle lines were being drawn. No shot would be fired until victories were fewer and further between and some had not yet chosen upon which side to fight. Rose was beginning to lose command of his team, and Kerslake of his club. If struggle were not inevitable in April 1982 it certainly was by September. Senior management and leading cricketers followed different stars, adhered to hostile philosophies, liked different people. So long as Kerslake was in position these factions could be kept apart. Once he withdrew it was over.

To finish sixth in the championship in 1982 was a respectable effort, and to win eight Sunday games after losing the first three was a worthy fight-back. Moreover Somerset could still boast a large portion of home-bred players, for Jeremy Lloyds, blond and imitative in his insecurity, emerged as a regular county cricketer, forming an opening partnership with Peter Roebuck which allowed Rose and Denning to retreat to quieter pastures in their twilight years. To add to his 965 championship runs Lloyds took 43 wickets and caught 28 catches, most of them at slip. Plainly he was maturing into an important player. So much depends upon personality. Lloyds had disciplined his previous errant talents. Nigel Popplewell, too, had used his brains and his fearlessness to tighten his game so that success could be expected rather than merely yearned for.

Of the locals, Mark Davis arrived, a left-arm seamer with a temperament too affable and a physique too comfortable long to survive the rigours of pace bowling in county cricket. Richard Ollis, Neil Russom and Gary Palmer, Ken's son and just sixteen years old, also appeared as men likely one day to carry the torch of Somerset cricket, a task which was to prove beyond them. Nearly every youngster introduced in the 1970s succeeded. Nearly every player introduced in the early 1980s failed. In part, no doubt, this was due to a want of talent, in part it is evidence of a more fundamental decline.

These failures could not yet be forecasted and optimism was still all around. And why not? On 24 July 1982 Somerset returned to Lord's once more and were once more victorious. Kent had been

367

beaten by 3 wickets in the quarter-final and Sussex swept aside with terrible authority at Taunton a fortnight later. So impressive were Somerset hereabouts that teams seemed to crumble before their eyes. So it was at Lord's, Nottingham appearing white of face and fretful of manner as they collapsed to 130 all out, a total Somerset collected with contemptuous ease. Garner again was at his glorious best as he took 3/13, and Marks gave crafty support (2/24) as did every bowler in a quintet which, thankfully, now could include Hallam Moseley who was at last deemed to be an English cricketer. Roebuck and Richards, who was not called up to hit a fourth cup final hundred, took their team to victory.

To Somerset these occasions were now enjoyable days in the metropolis, to their opponents they were ordeals at which must be faced a relaxed, confident team boasting a scything fast bowler and a devastating batsman, both eager to display their pre-eminence.

To the naked eye Somerset had everything, an exciting, gifted and committed team, enthusiastic support, a new pavilion and trophies in the cabinet. Yet within two and a half seasons they were bottom of the championship and broken. It was as if a tree growing into glorious maturity had suddenly been stricken by an apparently incurable disease. This Benson and Hedges Cup was the last of those days of wine and roses: for a time, hereafter, enough games were won to disguise deterioration but ever more it was obvious that a spirit had been lost as Somerset fragmented.

33

Sweet and sour

Following their Benson and Hedges victory Somerset went to Bournemouth for a county match. For reasons incomprehensible to his colleagues Viv Richards did not play in this game, though he did appear at the ground. Garner was outstanding, taking 11/80 on a dubious pitch; but Somerset, set to score just 83 in their 2nd innings, slumped to ignominious defeat by 10 runs.

Richards's withdrawal, so untypical in a cricketer hitherto extraordinarily conscientious, did not cause Somerset's defeat nor did it provoke irresistible decline. Rather it was symptomatic; all was not well, partly in Richards' life and certainly in his county club. Both were suffering from hubris.

A cancer of unease and lack of confidence had begun insidiously to spread through Somerset's cricketing body. Apart from a suspicion, keenly felt by some colleagues, that Rose was being given undue credit, this cancer had at its origins the world within a world built during the heady rise. Into this world had come Mike Taylor, now in charge of the club shop and assorted commercial activities, Peter McCombe, who had been removed from his post as lottery manager and put into a never-never land of busy inactivity, and of course Kerslake himself, still selflessly giving of his time.

Within months all were to depart their posts, and none of them as a result of an overnight campaign. Disputes arose about the performance of contracts and liabilities that had been incurred by the club. Taylor was made redundant in 1983. At first he had worked for the players' company and upon this being merged with the club he was employed by Somerset, who found him too garrulous and too close to the players, a mortal sin in their eyes, for sides had to be taken. They did not consult their marketing committee, including as it did Rose and Popplewell, before removing Taylor, who sued for wrongful dismissal and lost, victim of his own loquaciousness.

McCombe, too, had been under pressure for years, his position constantly protected by Kerslake and Richards. By now he was called players liaison officer and paid £81 a week, after tax. Moves were made to sack McCombe in 1982 and an unholy row broke out. Three committee men offered to pay his wages themselves. Arguments rumbled on for twelve months, and in September 1983 the committee, representing 6,618 members, unanimously agreed that Somerset could not afford to employ him any longer.

Money, of course, was not the issue. Rather a committee was determined to re-establish its power. Besides snapping at the heels of McCombe and Taylor they were also reluctant to employ Dennis Waight, who had arrived as trainer and physio in 1981, and refused to pay his air-fare. Kerslake stepped into the breach.

Somerset's old guard had little idea of running a modern sporting club, especially one containing such powerful egos and such outstanding talents, and they carried on as if it were 1957 not 1982. They saw the players' company, the omnipresent and down-to-earth McCombe, and Waight as evidence of players reaching beyond what was appropriate, and they blamed Kerslake. For his part Kerslake did not grasp that to grant every wish was to invite a debilitating decadence. Somerset had achieved greatness and did not know what to do with it. Racked by internal divisions, they had lurched diametrically from one extreme to the other, straying too far from principle. Accordingly when decline began there was too little in place to resist it. Within a year players hitherto prepared and proud to play for modest wages were rejecting their lives at Somerset.

Too easily Somerset said no, too easily its cricket chairman said yes. Kerslake had helped to build a strong team but he had not carried his club with him, and those close to him could feel his frustrations, which added to their insecurity.

If ever a chance existed of Somerset and Kerslake living in harmony – or if not in harmony, for with such vast committees this is too much to ask, at least in mutual toleration – it ended when David Seward resigned as secretary in June 1982. What followed is open to various interpretations and remains critical.

Bill Alley exacts vengeance for his failure to play Test cricket for Australia by clean bowling Bob Simpson, Australia's captain, in 1964

Lord's 1967. Roy Palmer is almost run out by Alan Knott, Kent's wicket-keeper, in the thrilling Gillette Cup final which Somerset narrowly lost. Even 'Kipper' Cowdrey is excited

At last, Somerset's first major trophy: Brian Rose holds aloft the
Gillette Cup in 1979

Viv Richards,
in relaxed and
violent mood

Ian Botham,
undoubtedly one of
Somerset's greatest
players

Big Bird Garner
swoops to deliver
another
thunderbolt.
Without him,
Somerset's trophy
cupboard might
still be bare

Brian Rose succeeded Brian Close as captain in 1978 and proved to be an inspired choice

Nigel Popplewell, the all-rounder, who was unsure whether cricket was a serious enough profession and eventually retired to become a lawyer

Chris Tavare batting. Take that!

Peter Roebuck's off drive

Vic Marks whose bowling
skills won Somerset many
matches over the years,
here seen batting in 1986

Steve Waugh, the
Australian batsman who
joined Somerset in 1987

Two of Somerset's
successful overseas
players: Martin Crowe
(left), the impassioned
New Zealander and Jimmy
Cook (right) the steadfast
South African

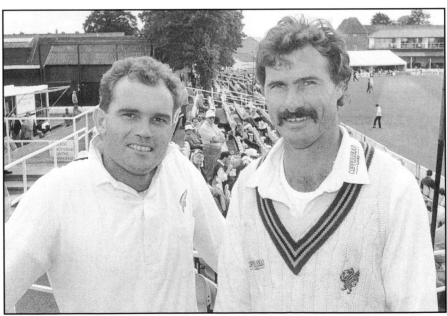

Kerslake was expected to abandon his lucrative legal career in favour of the secretaryship, a job he might combine with that of team manager. To do so meant serving notice to his law firm by 30 June. But Somerset did not accept Seward's resignation until 1 July and accordingly Kerslake felt unable to apply. Somerset officials say they were astonished when Kerslake arrived for the interviews and promptly sat on their side of the table; for his part Kerslake suspected a plot to obstruct his appointment, a plot constructed by the very forces of conservatism he had been resisting for years.

Disgusted, Kerslake did not apply for re-election to the committee in 1983 and he never returned. Richards and his other friends were no less infuriated by this débâcle and one, Peter White, a local garage-owner and committee man, angrily condemned Somerset at a meeting.

What was the truth? Beyond argument senior officials did not want Kerslake to be secretary, or at any rate did not want to be steamrollered into appointing him, for he was already powerful and they were not confident of his judgement in pursuance of power, believing he might turn a blind eye to activities offensive to them. But they could not, in truth, block Kerslake. Had he fought he could not have been stopped. As it was, he was unprepared for further conflict, especially on his own behalf and withdrew. Somerset had made a martyr of its most important influence, at least in the eyes of players close to him. Somerset now had three factions: committee, Kerslake and his supporters (not that he sought any), and a wedge of players wary of both.

If nothing else, this episode proved that communications had broken down irrevocably. An innocence had been lost.

Rather than Kerslake Somerset chose Tony Brown as its new secretary. To some this appeared a provocative appointment, for Brown was a Gloucestershire man, and a supposed hard-liner who had fiercely condemned Rose's 1979 declaration. Moreover relations with Somerset players had taken several curious turns during his playing career, and cricketers have long memories. It was as if a gauntlet had been thrown down. Nor was Brown, a fine cricketer, enough of a diplomat to soften these objections. And he was being paid £15,000 a year, more than Richards or Garner. Somerset had not meant to be provocative, and saw Brown as a cricketer who might be able to converse with players currently hostile to their committee. In this supposition they were mistaken.

No one present at Taunton on 14 September 1982 could doubt the depths to which Somerset had already plummeted. After leading Lancashire by 142 runs, Richards and Botham to the fore, Somerset took the field on the final day with Lancashire 56 runs behind and 4 wickets down. Rather than finish things off, Botham, acting captain, allowed his best bowler to take the field in gym shoes. Lancashire scrambled to a lead of 133 against a team hardly bothering to disguise its lack of interest and Somerset were skittled out for 119 by David Lloyd. It was a profoundly cynical performance and no one said anything.

This was Derek Taylor's farewell match. After a long and worthy career he had decided to emigrate to Australia where he had found work as an insurance salesman, a task to which he brought his customary earnestness. His loss was a blow, for he was Rose's closest ally, and a bulwark against brewing storms. Trevor Gard, as much a craftsman as Taylor and a proud Somerset man too, could take the catches but he could hardly be expected to bring stability.

Without Taylor and Kerslake by his side Brian Rose was nearly naked as he began his final season as captain in 1983. Having lost the England captaincy Ian Botham was keen to take charge at Somerset, as was evident enough as the season gathered pace. He had, in fact, expected Rose to resign at the end of 1982 and was nonplussed when he showed no inclination so to do.

Hallam Moseley did not play a game in 1983, wear and tear ruining his lithe body, Joel Garner played only fitfully (taking 35 wickets) and since Botham was often at Test matches and Rose absent through injury it was a bedraggled Somerset team which took to the field under a variety of captains that summer. Rose and Botham, his vice-captain, had spells in charge and when both were away Richards took over. During the World Cup, Somerset battled on with only Roebuck and Denning left of the senior players.

Roebuck's leadership of a young team surprised officials and colleagues, for it forced him out of his shell and revealed unsuspected pride and determination. Accordingly towards the end of the Bath Festival he was asked, unofficially, if he would consider taking charge of the team until September. Somewhat surprised, Roebuck replied that Somerset had a vice-captain in Botham and that if they did not care for him they should sack him. He would not do their job for them.

Roebuck believed those officials had realized that Botham was bound to be made captain in 1984, realized what a potentially unwise move this would be and yet were not resolute enough to avoid it. Botham had many outstanding characteristics but insiders knew well enough that to invite him to lead the club might well prove to be irresponsible.

Somerset sank to tenth position in 1983, and could win only three games, at Lord's under Botham, against Glamorgan under Roebuck and at Leicester, where Richards hit 216, Botham 152 and where an embattled Rose played his last county match as Somerset's captain, a fortuitous injury preventing further play and rendering irrelevant attempts hereabouts to depose him.

Into this atmosphere strode Julian Wyatt, son of a Somerset farmer, and Stephen Booth, a left-arm spinner from Yorkshire. Booth was a bright, engaging character with a Yorkshireman's love of cricket and life, and with proper care he might have answered Somerset's prayers, for in years ahead such spinners were to prove elusive. Wyatt had a simple technique, an eye for the ball, and talent enough provided he could change his game once county bowlers detected its flaws. Alas, he was to be unlucky, a career frustrated by untimely injury, want of opportunity and slowness in absorbing lessons. In better times, and when staffs were smaller, he might have made it. He tried hard for several years, found moments of glory and days of disappointment, and in his departure Somerset lost a cricketer of passion.

As ever this season had its moments, even in championship matches. At Bath Nigel Popplewell launched so violent an assault upon Gloucestershire's bowlers that he reached his 100 in 41 minutes, and was only denied the Lawrence Trophy by O'Shaughnessy who was fed his century in 35 minutes of insulting cricket. Popplewell was capped for his efforts, recognition for his willed transformation from colt to thoroughbred. In September Nigel Felton, recently signed, hit 173 not out against Kent, a club which had rejected him. Quick on his feet, living on his wits, he appeared certain to mature into a productive left-hander, a useful asset for Denning was near the end.

In limited-overs cricket Somerset remained supreme, being denied a second Sunday League title only because Yorkshire won more away games, and beating Kent to win the NatWest Trophy, a game to which a deposed Kerslake was smuggled by the players, and at which he was presented with a new suit, two courses staunchly advocated by his wife.

Richards, Denning, Roebuck and Botham batted in their various and mostly energetic styles to score most of the runs on Sundays while Marks, Dredge, Garner and Richards were especially economical bowlers. Somerset's pattern of play embraced an early strike by Garner, batsmen pinned down by Marks and a gradual strangulation thereafter by an experienced, persistent and professional attack.

No less was evident in the NatWest Trophy as Somerset, led by Botham, held Lancashire to 163/6, bowled out Sussex for 65, Gard taking 5 catches, and arrived at Lord's for a semi-final at Lord's as hot favourites.

For Botham the stakes were high. To be certain of appointment as Somerset captain he must take his team to a final. Middlesex scored 222/9 and Botham took guard with Somerset having crept to 43/4. Soon they had slipped further to 52/5 with Popplewell in and only Marks to follow. Botham now played what was, in all probability, his greatest innings, for he had not been relieved of pressure as in 1981, rather he was carrying a heavy burden. Middlesex bowled superbly, fielded adroitly and yet still they could not stop him. Quite simply Botham imposed his will upon the game, constructing an innings massive in its certainty. For three long hours he resisted Middlesex, never taking a risk, collecting runs with shots of force and control. At tea he sat quietly in his corner, contemplating work to be done. No one studying him that day could have failed to grasp his extraordinary powers, for here was a man so often happy to rejoice in vulgarity silently picking his way forwards. Failure never appeared possible and yet to play one ball badly was to lose.

Popplewell and Marks, doughty cricketers both, gave game support and by the time Emburey was called upon to deliver the final over scores were level. Thrusting a pad out, poking with sudden nervousness, Botham somehow survived the ordeal of blocking out, for Somerset had lost fewer wickets. He charged from the field as a bull might who is suddenly released after years of captivity. He had done it, Somerset were going to Lord's. And he was going to be captain. He had a bulldozer for a will.

374

And so for the fifth time in six seasons Somerset appeared in a cup final. This time Kent offered valiant opposition and lost by only 24 runs in a game reduced to 50 overs. Somerset played competently rather than brilliantly, for it was a muggy, moody day upon which it was hard for either side to relax. Still a cup-winner's medal was not something about which to be blasé. In seven years since Somerset has not returned to Lord's. Moreover one man played his part magnificently that day. Trevor Gard had been waiting patiently in the wings since his début in 1976, never once considering playing for another county, for he set no great store by foreigners, which included anyone born outside Somerset. Now, on his first big occasion, he stumped Aslett and Chris Cowdrey, removing bails and dancing a jig, for they were vital wickets and difficult chances. By taking them Gard left his mark upon Somerset cricket. In all he gave fifteen years of unassuming service to Somerset cricket, and though he ended where he began, in the 2nd XI, he did not complain, preferring to carry on with his duties, pausing only to observe that 'with so many chiefs about we need a few Indians', whereupon he would repair to his shooting or his ferreting, at heart a countryman.

Despite enduring if doomed resistance, Botham was appointed captain for the 1984 season. His first task was to select an overseas cricketer to replace Richards and Garner, who had tour commitments. His choice fell upon Martin Crowe, an impassioned, committed cricketer of a maturity far beyond his twenty-one years. Once again Somerset had gambled upon a relatively obscure cricketer and once again their judgement was to be triumphantly vindicated. Batting along clean, precise, classical lines and with courage and fast footwork Crowe survived a poor start (he had been unnerved by Dredge's famous nip-backer in spring practice) to score 1,870 runs and to hit six hundreds, many of them exhilarating.

Besides these runs Crowe also took 44 wickets with his mixture of inswing and leg-cut and generally infused a previously downcast bunch of youngsters with enthusiasm. Where Richards was instinctive Crowe was analytical, where Richards was tired he was fresh. Of course to compare the bubbly Crowe of 1984, with worlds still to conquer, with mighty Vivian Richards, now beyond his pomp as a county cricketer, was unfair. Yet, inevitably, this was the comparison made by those new to the club, be

375

they players or officials. Moreover Crowe knew nothing of recent battles and was not bogged down by suspicion, disappointment or jealousy. Accordingly he brought to Somerset cricket a vitality, even an innocence, characteristics long since in decline. Crowe had a messianic streak, an urge to uplift those around him, and in Somerset's floundering young players he found a group plainly in need of such work.

With Crowe in such form and with Roebuck enjoying his best season, scoring 1,702 runs, moving fearlessly towards success rather than merely away from failure (a change brought about by a flourishing writing career) and narrowly missing Test selection, Somerset were seldom short of runs. Alas, Peter Denning who had endured a cartilage operation in the winter, could play only five games and he announced his retirement in September, ending a career which had seen Somerset rise from the very depths to unimagined heights. He had played his part, especially in overs cricket, in which he had collected seven man-of-the-match awards and 4,565 Sunday runs, a record. A man entirely without pretension, he could be stubborn to the point of cussedness, and had adopted for himself a role which captured his contempt of smooth words and smooth people rather than his warmth and generosity, which softer traits he was reluctant to reveal in a world he considered harsh and corrupt. Despite his growling manner, people liked playing with him, not least because he was unselfish. More than most he was everything he could have been as a batsman, never straying far from what he knew. His character is best caught by his reaction to dismissal, a circumstance which finds few men at their best. Whatever had unfolded Denning simply unbuckled his pads and lit a small cigar. To enquiries about a leg-before decision he would mutter, 'Must have been out.' So far as tactics went he would limit his opinions to: 'We've got to fight.'

Into Denning's breach stepped Nigel Popplewell, batting at first wicket down and showing unsuspected tenacity. To his own surprise he scored 1,116 runs, in a style entirely different from his student days, when to make hay while the sun shone seemed the wisest course. Vic Marks was in superb form too, scoring 1,000 runs for the first time, and playing with dazzling if rustic brilliance throughout August. Marks rarely felt obliged to leave a ball alone and he seldom hit a delivery in a direction easy of prediction, save to those long of his acquaintance, and accordingly when in form he collected runs at a rapid if unobtrusive pace. He also bowled 808 overs and took 86 wickets at an average under 26, and to top it off he captained the side with diplomacy and no little success, during Botham's absences.

To score runs was expected in 1984, to take wickets less so, and yet Somerset bowled well, thanks largely to Marks, Crowe, Dredge, Booth, and Mark Davis, who took 66 wickets (at 23/77), most of them in his first spell, which was usually hostile. Fit after being chased around the Quantocks by a mother determined to get him fit, Davis bounced in off a short run and darted his deliveries across batsmen, generating pace, bounce and movement even on docile pitches. Had his later spells been as dangerous he might have played for England; as it was he was mentioned at meetings. Of those 66 wickets, 53 were caught, many of them in the slips; for the time being his angle surprised batsmen. To sustain his threat he would need to introduce an inswinger, for a bowler must constantly find new deliveries to unsettle batsmen. This proved beyond Davis, who faltered hereafter.

Lacking Garner and with Hallam Moseley having refused to sign a contract conditional upon him being fit in April, Somerset could not challenge in one-day cricket, though they reached two quarter-finals and might with any luck have beaten Kent in one. Nevertheless Somerset had much in which to rejoice, not least Wyatt's brave 45 and 69 against the West Indies, a match-winning third-wicket partnership of 319 between Roebuck and Crowe against Leicestershire, and a profit of £73,000 to boot, and this without quite as many financial statements as had been released amidst a confusion of forgotten bills a year earlier. And membership had held firm, more or less, falling from 6,098 to 5,923.

Crowe's *tour de force* was his astonishing double of 70 not out and 190 against Leicestershire. His 70 embraced an angry riposte to Andy Roberts, who had been bowling bumpers to Somerset tailenders. Afterwards Crowe was furious that he had sacrificed mastery over himself and in the second innings, entering as Somerset tottered at 3/2, chasing 341 on a pitch presumed dodgy, he constructed an innings extraordinary in its command, memorable in its driving straight of mid-on. Somerset won by 6 wickets and Crowe's was one of the greatest innings played in the county colours. Perhaps he needed a certain anger to unleash the full fury of his will.

377

And yet, bit by bit, good men were being lost, so that Somerset moved ever more unsteadily towards its future. Denning and Moseley had retired, and Phil Slocombe too, a departure born of a frustration which had also had its effect upon technique and temperament. Had Slocombe arrived rather than left in 1983 the distinguished career he had felt to be his might have been granted. Sadly Peter McCombe was gone too, victim of a heart attack provoked by a way of life which never allowed tomorrow to dictate to today.

These losses could not be avoided. Of more significance was the departure of Jeremy Lloyds to Gloucestershire, for no Somerset man had left for another club since Roy Virgin in 1972. Lloyds had batted capably yet had drifted down the order, as Wyatt, Felton, Popplewell, and Ollis, a Keynsham lad, were given opportunities. Lloyds suspected, rightly, that Botham and cohorts admired neither his cricket nor a personality in which insecurity found expression in affectation. He brought to Gloucestershire his speculative and sharply turning off-breaks, and a batting talent which was at its most productive on the counter-attack. Lloyds was wise to leave for plainly he was being judged more by the supposed nature of his character than his cricket. Not that either, properly seen, was remotely objectionable. But Lloyds did not simply move away. He appeared at a committee meeting and told Somerset's management that their cricket team was poorly led and that cynicism and glorification of the individual was certain to spread unless tackled at once. Somerset cannot have been surprised by this message; but nothing was done.

For Botham the winter of 1985 was to be a watershed. By now his dreams had moved from heroism to fantasy. Pursued by scandals, never running fast enough, or along a straight enough path, to outstrip them, he decided to spend a few months at home, playing soccer for Scunthorpe. He wanted some peace and quiet. On the other hand he also wanted to be a celebrity, to hear again those unrestrained cheers of 1981. By now he had surrounded himself with flatterers, followers and bohemians, none of whom appeared able to restrain him or to make him laugh at himself in the old way. Having sampled glory, he now had an appetite for power in the execution of which he was handicapped by an inability, noble of birth, to see any fault in those he cherished.

378

Two events spoilt Botham's winter. First he was convicted of possessing 1.9 grammes of cannabis and fined £100 by Scunthorpe magistrates. Secondly he appointed Tim Hudson as his manager. A mixture of hippy, entrepreneur and opportunist, Hudson told Botham he could conquer Hollywood. He said he was a flamboyant character in a staid world, and should be making millions. Botham lapped it up, and took to wearing splendidly striped blazers and straw hats and began, to widespread surprise, to appear blond and bedraggled. Harmless stuff, in its way, and cheerful too provided it was merely a bit of fun. But Botham's ego had been engaged and he did not realize that he was straying too far from his talents, from his cricket, and that it was all sound and fury. Hudson did not mislead Botham, rather he was Ian's alter ego, a 1985 projection of that reckless, overpowering child who had dared to hook Andy Roberts in 1974, a child who had resented being mistaken for a ruffian by adults in collars and ties, a child who had been seeking the companionship of chums and the admiration of a boggled public ever since.

Botham was driving a car with no brakes. Hearing of his drugs conviction Somerset considered sacking him and decided not to by a vote of 12/2. Botham had issued a statement saying he was 'totally opposed to the use of drugs by any sportsman'.

Excited by Hudson's ideas, and goaded by his conviction, Botham started 1985, his last year as captain, in supreme form. By May's end he had scored 473 runs off the 345 deliveries bowled to him in first-class cricket. At the crease he was a storm, a violent, rolling thunder which charged the atmosphere at its every appearance. These runs were scored not with the flashy hits of a Jessop but with the authority of a Hammond. His assault upon Marshall one damp morning in Taunton remains etched in the memory of those who saw it. All told he scored 1,280 runs for Somerset in 1985, at an average of 91.43.

Viv Richards was on song too, hitting 1,836 runs at an average of 76.5. And yet Somerset finished bottom and in total disarray. In March supporters were hoping for a championship, by May, and notwithstanding enjoyment derived from individual brilliance, most were disgusted. A closer study of the figures revealed that Botham and Garner took 44 county wickets between them. Stephen Booth paid a heavy price for being overbowled, rapidly losing confidence. Everyone could see that Somerset's captain had lost interest in county cricket save as a vehicle for his genius.

Nor did it help that Viv Richards and Joel Garner lingered in the Caribbean that spring, leaving Somerset to open its various campaigns without them. Seeing Marshall and Greenidge already in full swing, Somerset supporters felt let down. Somerset lacked morale, leadership, and purpose. Some blamed their committee for this breakdown, others argued that star players were failing to set an example. Umpires and opposing teams scoffed, paying only lip service to Somerset's supposed stature. To many this fall was shocking in both its speed and its depth. Unsurprisingly membership dropped by 400, though a handsome profit of £51,610 was recorded, reducing Somerset's repayments for its New Pavilion.

Botham and Richards were not the only players to shine in 1985. Vic Marks took 8/17 against Lancashire at Bath, bowling his off-spinners with guile and phlegm on a Recreation Ground pitch which Buse and Langford might have appreciated. And Nigel Popplewell, promoted to open, proved himself to be a superb player, tight in defence, especially on the back foot, and selective in attack. His 172 on a testing Southend pitch was as close to a masterpiece as can be constructed by those denied greatness.

But, like Lloyds a year earlier, Popplewell had seen enough. He could follow other careers, had no need to tolerate this insulting way of playing county cricket. Accordingly in mid-season he decided to retire and to become a lawyer. And like Lloyds too, he did not go quietly but wrote a forthright letter to the committee.

Somerset's cricket team had lost lots of good men, and had failed to replace them satisfactorily. Just as Richards, Botham and Garner felt less inclined to lift their team so it depended ever more upon them. Inevitably this led to tensions, especially with those who had not experienced these cricketers in their pomp. Somerset had failed either to sign or to produce good cricketers. None of any significance had been signed in the early 1980s because Roy Kerslake believed he could find local youngsters to follow Rose, Denning, Botham, Marks and Roebuck. Now it was because Botham did not want outsiders to invade his patch and could not persuade his friends to enter it. Bedevilled by rumours and headlines, Somerset was not an attractive proposition for honest and ambitious cricketers.

Nor were players being produced. Popplewell had been lucky to arrive while all was well, besides which he was bright. Those appearing later entered a club in trouble and failed to advance.

Botham resigned as captain days before he was due to be sacked. He had not believed anyone dare dismiss him not least because, of his rivals, Marks was supposed to be too soft and Roebuck too eccentric. Upon resigning he contacted Richards to say they would be leaving at the end of 1986. Roebuck was chosen to replace him, chosen in the belief that he alone was strong enough to repair the damage. Upon hearing of Botham's message and thoroughly alarmed, Roebuck wrote to Richards expressing his hope that they could work together, as they had done in the old days. Without interference it might have been possible. Alas, forces on both sides were at work to guarantee it was not.

Having lost the captaincy, Botham joined the dispossessed. For a time he contemplated moving his tent elsewhere, but Somerset was his home and he decided to sign a contract for one year. It had been a heavy defeat, one which stung.

Another row broke out in the winter of 1985. Fire officials had found the Old Pavilion to be unsafe. Rather than spend £60,000 on rebuilding it Somerset's committee decided, by 11 votes to 8, to demolish it and build afresh at a cost of £123,500. At once a fierce debate began as opponents, led by Peter White, forced a new meeting to be called and saved their beloved pavilion by 18 votes to 8. It had been an acrimonious debate, at the end of which a white elephant was saved. A proper building could have been erected, with 300 seats and excellent facilities. Sentiment decreed that this chance was missed. Lovely as the Old Pavilion is, history insists that its survival was as serious a mistake as the preservation of a sprawling and over-populated committee system.

Fortunately it was not all tears. Isaac Vivian Alexander Richards did, on Saturday, 1 June, play as magnificent an innings as can ever have been played at Taunton. Taking guard at 11.44 a.m. Richards proceeded to score 322 runs in 294 minutes, unleashing shots devastating in their power, unerring in their judgement and conclusive in their statement of greatness. Only in their dreams can most men contemplate let alone execute such a knock. A map of his shots bears reproducing:

I.V.A. RICHARDS – 1 June 1985
v. Warwickshire at Taunton
322 runs

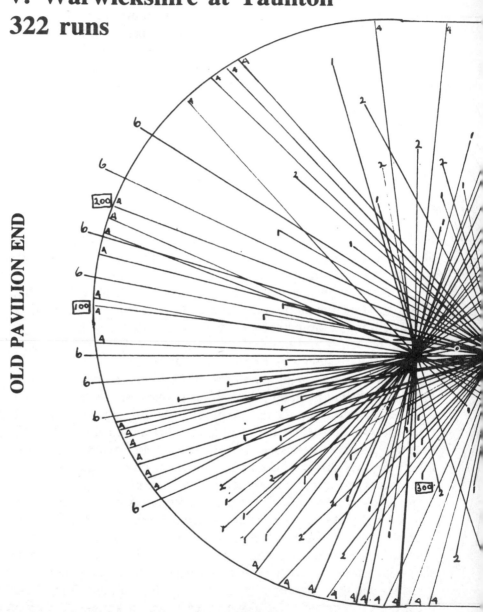

OLD PAVILION END

Recorded by Simon Richards and Simon White

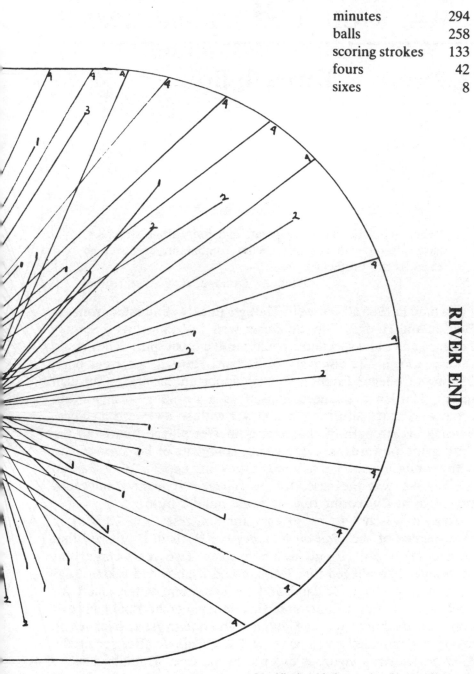

minutes	294
balls	258
scoring strokes	133
fours	42
sixes	8

RIVER END

Verified and drawn by David Oldham

34

Through fire

'When the differences are great, and the parties strangers, men quarrel with courtesy. What combatants are ever so eager as two brothers?'

Anthony Trollope, *Barchester Towers*

For a time in 1986 all was well. Though quickly eliminated from the Benson and Hedges Cup, Somerset won 4 of their first 5 Sunday League games and spectators could sense a fresh spirit. They could rejoice, too, in the discovery of Richard Harden, a former pupil of King's College, Taunton. Seizing opportunities arising through injury, Harden announced himself as a resolute batsman with a range of shots surprising in a player with so awkward a stance. Sensing his strength of character Somerset played him from the third game onwards in every game, confident of his survival. So many youngsters are not as good as they first appear. With Harden the reverse was the case, for he rejected style and embraced pragmatism. By scoring runs he could build a future.

Alas, it was not to be so easy for Somerset. On 18 May in the columns of the *Mail on Sunday*, Ian Botham confirmed that he had 'taken pot', if only as a youngster. Two years earlier this newspaper had alleged that Botham and friends had taken drugs on a tour of New Zealand and he had immediately sued for libel. Anticipating a court case this newspaper had built up evidence on Botham's life and found it to contain parts over which decorum demanded a veil be drawn. Accordingly after seeing the *Mail on Sunday*'s vigorous defence of the case, Botham decided that discretion was the better part of valour. For him it was another defeat.

Once more Somerset was distracted by scandal. Nor was that all. Other newspapers were threatening to print further and grimmer allegations, and desisted from doing so only because saturation point had been reached on Botham stories. Lord's summoned Botham for a disciplinary hearing and suspended him for two months, punishment for his acknowledged offence.

Botham was outraged, and threatened to emigrate to Australia where he imagined, erroneously as it emerged, a more democratic mood awaited him. It was not in Ian's nature to distinguish between liberalism and licence, and therein lay his problem. Upon hearing that he might be asked to play a 2nd XI game before returning to Somerset's colours he said he would leave Somerset if any such request was made, that Richards and Garner would go with him and that these players had no confidence in Tony Brown. He added that Garner's benefit was being undermined by club social functions. He was an angry man in open rebellion.

In time tempers cooled, and Botham returned home to rest. TCCB solicitors and Somerset officials investigated a variety of matters and concluded no further charges could be made. Somerset was asked to pay £9,000 towards the TCCB's legal costs and declined to oblige on the grounds that nearly all these supposed events had occurred when he was representing England.

Distracted by these affairs spirits slowly declined in Somerset's cricket team. Gloucestershire and Kent had been handsomely beaten by mid June but Somerset could win only one more county match, Roebuck scoring 147 not out and Marks an unbeaten 71 as their team reached Worcestershire's target of 340 in 77 overs at Clarence Park in August. Again it was a season with moments, Botham hitting 175 not out in a trice one Sunday in Wellingborough, Richard Bartlett, from Taunton School, scoring 117 not out on his first class début at Oxford, Rose returning to form after two quiet seasons, and Marks and Harden adding 187 to rescue Somerset from 108/4 against Sussex. All of these were local men. But too many overs were being bowled by too many moderate bowlers, so that Somerset could not hope to win with any regularity. And, in truth, the team had lost its will to win years before.

Things fell apart within the team. Men screamed their anger and frustration in the dressing-room and sometimes in the oppos-

385

ing dressing-room too; men picked and chose their games, trying hard when it suited and otherwise returning to their own world, for no one was around, friend or foe, to lift sights from immediate enmities to distant horizons. Nor would such inspiration have been easy, for the divisions were great, especially between playing staff and administration. Men felt they were due much and owed little. For far too long heads had been buried in the sand, as if the nastiness would all go away, as if it were some minor fault rather than a terrible divide. Roebuck in particular was angry for he felt let down by those he had hoped to help, by those to whose support he had felt entitled. Failure was not a problem, for Somerset's cricket history was a history of failure. But a lack of commitment was intolerable. He did not mean to spend the next few years of his life playing for a team or club entirely without worth. Popplewell and Lloyds had been lost. Somerset's cricket team had become a patch and woe betide those who would invade it.

Much of this was hidden from outsiders, hidden within a dressing-room, which leaked only to umpires and opponents, who could scarcely miss the arguments. Somerset was a hotch-potch of men from the same generation, men used to success and now, experiencing failure, of inadequate cricketers mostly signed when hubris began around 1982, and of bewildered, intimidated youngsters who enjoyed the sense of private danger in the air and yet could find no advance in their careers. Ever more Richards and Botham were living in a world apart, and scarcely hiding their contempt for officials, and some colleagues.

In Botham's case the reasons for his conduct were apparent, for he was seemingly being led a merry dance by his own fantasies. Moreover those newspapers which had previously defied him now rejected him; feeling spurned and weary, Botham was in a sour mood. A fellow can be in one place for too long, find himself suddenly amongst people who do not so readily share the huge, glorious joke. Richards was a more complicated case, for here was a man who had been, and could be again, an inspiration and a joy. And yet now to be near him was to be near a volcano, and those who had not risen with him were dismayed.

Upon reflection it is plain that two things were gnawing away at Richards's temper. First he was unused to playing in a poor team, unused to finding himself surrounded by such mediocrity. Somerset had failed to rebuild at the top, a charge for which Kerslake and Botham were especially answerable. Richards could not respect many of his colleagues and in many cases his judgement proved correct, for most fell by the wayside. He was a victim of years of inertia. Secondly he had around him men whispering dark words about Somerset's intentions, outcasts, most of them, and with axes to grind. Richards lost all faith in Somerset, suspected plots to remove him. And yet no such notions existed, until the end of July anyhow. Richards was dragged down by these rumours, and they became a self-fulfilling prophecy. No one, at the time, understood his worries for they were never expressed. To a depressing degree Richards was undone by those who were, and who remain, his friends, and by a want of wisdom and communication within a club many of whose servants were manifestly out of their depth. Those battles had left scars everywhere.

Had Somerset's new captain been a man of diplomacy and patience it is possible that this gradual disintegration might have been endured. As it was, Roebuck found himself caught between warring factions for neither of which he much cared. At first he believed he could persuade his senior cricketers to his side with remembrances of things past and portrayals of things future. Having restored morale he might hope to use his influence to bring about a change in management attitudes, specifically by the creation of a small duly elected and alert committee. To his disappointment he found these tasks beyond him. Three captains had tried and failed in four seasons. Perhaps the divisions were too deeply entrenched. Maybe Somerset needed to start afresh. Membership was tumbling. It was a view widely held.

A showdown was inevitable. And then, quite suddenly, Somerset were presented with a dilemma. Towards the end of July Essex asked for permission to approach Martin Crowe, who had played a few 2nd XI games for Somerset in 1985. Crowe wanted to play county cricket in 1987 and was unwilling to wait for his opportunity until 1988, when the West Indies would be on tour in England. Essex were seeking a new overseas batsman because Allan Border had decided not to fulfil the second year of his contract. Border's decision set in motion a scarcely contemplated series of events. Had he stayed a second season Somerset would have carried on as before, reluctantly, unhappily, hardly knowing where lay a solution to its difficulties.

At once an impromptu meeting was called. Was Somerset prepared to release Crowe? To refuse implied that Richards and Garner might not be retained for 1987. Immediately it was apparent that a majority at this *ad hoc* meeting of management and cricket committee personnel were heartily fed up with the status quo, a sentiment with which Roebuck, speaking last here and at every subsequent gathering, now concurred.

Somerset had hoped that Crowe might return with Richards and Garner in 1987 in preparation for their absences in 1988. Plainly this was not feasible, for it had all gone far beyond compromise. Brian Langford, cricket chairman, was in difficulty for he had told Richards that he would be offered a contract for 1987, a statement made in an effort to silence Richards's doubts, during a conversation of which Roebuck knew nothing. Langford was compromised by his efforts at appeasement.

Michael Hill, club chairman since 1983, was the leading advocate of change. A successful farmer with a bumbling manner, almost the last of the landowners who used to be so influential, he was easily underestimated but his convictions were sincere, firmly held and keenly pursued. No doubt the revelations about Botham's private life, and the failure of Viv Richards to take a random drugs test in Bristol that July, had hardened his opinions. They certainly brought a sombre tone to the meeting. After Lloyds and Popplewell had left, and after all those battles, morale seemed to have been restored – as in Prague in spring before the tanks rolled in.

From this meeting onwards it was plain that Somerset was intent upon crying enough. Their duty, they decided, lay with the present and the future, not the past, no matter how glorious. Rebels, hereafter, were to talk at length about those largely happy years of breakthrough from 1974 to 1981, as if they were a golden era capable of revival; in talking of the past little reference was ever made to 1985 and 1986, to a slide comprehensible to few save those within.

At a series of later official meetings, Somerset confirmed its decision to release Richards and Garner, and to sign Crowe. To reach a final decision took a month of painful and secret debate, during which period, of course, committee men led a strange and false life, avoiding public consultation for it would certainly bring a storm of trouble and leave them with too little time for contemplation, or a change of heart. Once opinions were made public they were entrenched. And once they were public a ferocious outcry must begin.

Accordingly for a month Somerset officials debated in private and were silent elsewhere. Astonishingly – for Taunton is a place where gossip spreads like a new strain of 'flu – no word of this matter crept out and when at last, towards the end of August, the decision was confirmed and announced it seemed brutal in its suddenness and its want of consideration. Concentrating upon the merit of their judgement, Somerset did nothing to present its case well, did nothing to assuage the hurt certain to arise in the hearts of Garner and Richards. Roebuck did, once, visit Richards's home to see if he felt tired of county cricket but his reception was hostile. He had also consulted many people whose opinions he valued, and found most of equivocal opinion, which did not prevent several pronouncing themselves rebels later. Many ran from opinion, some positioned themselves for every eventuality, offending no one and taking advantage of whatever outcome ensued. People found out about themselves and their erstwhile friends. It was an extraordinary time.

Somerset conveyed its decision in a manner which appeared cavalier, hardly realizing that two such distinguished servants could not be summoned one Saturday morning and told that their services were no longer required, for this had not seemed to be the issue. No insult had been intended.

Richards and Garner were outraged by their rejection, Garner less so perhaps for he had already intimated that hereafter he only wanted to play one-day cricket, besides which he was no blind supporter of his Test captain. Beyond argument they ought to have been consulted and every avenue explored. Unfortunately there was no one to bang heads together to see if anything could be resolved, no channels for discussion. Only the wildest of optimists could have hoped for a resolution, despite which it ought to have been tried. Fearing an ignominious end to this season, Somerset delayed their decision as long as they could, and paid the price of seeming not to care.

Somerset's decision was by no means unanimous. Colin Atkinson, whose role as president it was to offer thoughtful advice, to steer Somerset away from its more reckless notions, a role

389

he played with consummate skill, joined Brian Langford on the benches of equivocation. Both were to fight for their club, in their various ways, when battle commenced. Three members of the management and cricket committee voted against it.

An announcement was made on 23 August and at once a campaign started, a campaign which was to be as violent as any cricket club has ever known, a campaign which included death threats to Roebuck and Crowe (and possibly others), included the arrival in Taunton of reporters seeking stories, investigating the private lives of the main parties in the affair, one which included all manner of vicious allegations, spread with particular energy by ill-informed rebels. Seven men resigned when the general committee met to confirm Somerset's decision, a septet which included Peter White and David Challacombe, the club doctor. These men rallied to a banner demanding justice for the fallen heroes, a banner also carried by Roy Kerslake, Peter Denning and many who had enjoyed the drama and charisma of Somerset cricket from 1978 to 1982.

Others, and especially members, spoke out for the club, were thankful that this time, in contrast to 1953, something had been done. Catching a general feeling, one wrote: 'Full marks for the decision, no marks for the means.' Doubts felt by these supporters were quelled once insults began to be hurled, for this nastiness was itself evidence of a club in abject disarray. It seemed as if a patch had been invaded.

Upon hearing of Somerset's decision Ian Botham joined forces with the rebels, denouncing Somerset and vowing to leave if their decision stood. Many wished he had shown such passion in the previous seasons. Botham's threat was ineffective for his recent performances were more savoured by occasional spectators than club members, those who would be called upon to choose sides.

Officials hoped Botham might stay, no matter what. Isolated he might concentrate his energies upon cricket. Of course Botham grasped this quickly, realized that his closest friend Trevor Gard could no longer be certain of selection (for a rival had been approached) and concluded that he must move elsewhere if he lost, for above all he sought companionship. Botham lashed out because he was fighting for his survival as a man. In defeat he duly left though with a regret he could not allow himself to admit. Many wondered if he would find it as easy elsewhere, be it in Worcester or Brisbane, for Somerset was used to Botham and his ways, and wanted only to re-engage that formidable pride.

Signatures were gathered in a petition calling for a special meeting at which a no-confidence vote on the committee could be taken and efforts made to reinstate Joel and Viv. Arrangements were made for a debate and a vote in November at the Bath and West Showground in Shepton Mallet.

In the meantime Somerset was divided into factions *for* and *against*. A large majority of players, opponents, umpires, reporters and members accepted the club's judgement for there were stables to be cleaned. But plainly Somerset could be accused of disloyalty, and it was around this accusation and an apparent litany of broken promises, that Kerslake and Bridget Langdon, a supporter from Yeovil constantly swinging between temper and tears, yet genuine in her emotions, built their case. They said Richards and Garner had been let down, not least by Roebuck. It was an opinion, some thought, which might just as well have been turned upon its head.

For two months a propaganda war was fought on television networks, radio and newspapers were filled with facts, half-truths and downright lies. Being organized and motivated the rebel campaign set off with a bang, shaking a committee unprepared for such mounted hostility and unwilling to swap insults. Soon Somerset organized its reply, capable officials taking charge of their effort. Roebuck had intended to fly to Australia in October but felt obliged to defend himself once Botham had launched his assaults, which were of devastating brutality. A rebellion needed a target, and this one chose Roebuck, whom Botham called a Judas.

This is not the place to recall every twist in argument during those two months. At times the central points were lost as accusations were flung far and wide. Somerset had finished seventeenth in 1985 and sixteenth in 1986. Membership was dwindling, young players were failing and new ones could not be signed. Evidently the chemistry was wrong and a majority decided it was time for change. It was as simple and as startling as that.

To concentrate unduly upon the misdeeds of a Yeovil all-rounder clearly affected by the extremity of his sudden rises and falls, of a great West Indian batsman who had previously bubbled with joy and was now torn between love and hatred, and a mild, calculating, ageing, fast bowler with no relish for county

391

cricket is to cast unfair shadows for they had made a magnificent contribution. Everyone needed a change.

Colin Atkinson took the chair in Shepton Mallet. For Somerset important speeches were made by Michael Hill, still astonishingly underestimated, Brian Langford, Philip Squire, appointed club's doctor in 1986 to which position he had brought fresh judgement, and Nigel Popplewell, who broke his silence with a short, telling speech explaining his reasons for retiring and his dismay at the lack of commitment shown by those who had been released. His speech was loudly applauded for, though it did not sway many votes, it gave authority to a case hitherto unsatisfactorily put. It was also a courageous speech and one which was to affect Popplewell in years ahead, for he had not anticipated the backlash, having not sampled the depth of passion involved. Practically alone of those who gave voice to their thoughts on Somerset's behalf, Popplewell had nothing whatsoever to gain.

David Challacombe condemned Roebuck as divisive, and others chastised Tony Brown as incompetent. Peter Denning argued that Somerset needed a fast bowler not a batsman, and said Garner should have been kept. Here he struck a chord. Throughout the meetings and debates no effort had been made to separate Richards and Garner. And yet, beyond Somerset, they were not close friends and Garner was often critical of Richards in his writings. In truth Garner had scarcely been mentioned in the debate at all, his chief fault being a fondness for his armchair at home. Indubitably these cases should have been separated, lest both be tarred with one brush. Many reluctant to defend Richards were keen to protect Garner, whose image was far less tarnished. This was curious, for Richards had given much more of himself to his cricket club.

Strong arguments could, too, be made for signing a fast bowler, if not for retaining Garner, who was certainly near the end. Somerset had traditionally preferred batsmen because they could play a large part in one-day competitions, of which there were three. Roebuck had concluded that Somerset needed four new bowlers, not one, and believed a batsman could help to prop up his side while these men were found. Eventually he made the jump from releasing Richards and Garner to signing Crowe.

After a dramatic, strangely warm meeting and a debate of depressingly poor standard, two votes were taken, a no-confidence motion being defeated by 1,828 votes to 798 and a call for the committee to resign being beaten by 1,863 to 743 – convincing margins. Afterwards Roebuck called for a radical restructuring of Somerset's outdated committee system and for fresher, more intimate relations off the field; to fail to improve management was to betray members and supporters.

35

Having a go

Brian Rose had been appointed as a cricket manager, in all save name, during those fraught months towards the end of 1986 and with Roebuck he set about raising a cricket team. Apart from Richards and Garner who had been released, and Botham who left in protest, four other young cricketers had departed, including Stephen Booth and Murray Turner, a local pace bowler. Crowe, plainly, would strengthen the batting while Nigel Felton and Jon Hardy, an elegant, affable left-hander signed from Hampshire, who was at his best against fast bowlers and upon hard pitches, had for some time been demanding a fair chance and could be expected to flourish. But Vic Marks apart, Somerset's bowling was in a sorry state, especially as Colin Dredge had injured a shoulder during the winter and might not bowl a ball in 1987.

Botham's move to Worcestershire left a hole and obviously men were needed to occupy positions 7 to 11. By autumn plans were already afoot to sign Neil Burns, a bright, earnest wicket-keeper and batsman from Essex whose ambitions had hitherto been thwarted at his home county, and Graham Rose, a powerful lad from Tottenham who had been thought a paper tiger at knowing Middlesex. They were cricketers hand picked from strong clubs which were not eager to lose them. Burns was signed to replace Trevor Gard, whose concentration had wavered during Botham's period as captain, and whose limitations as a batsman were a handicap in a team denuded of Lloyds, Popplewell and Botham. Gard continued to keep wicket for the 2nd XI, recapturing his lost form at times and he led them capably, instilling high professional standards until his retirement in 1990.

Working throughout the winter Brian Rose found two bowlers, Neil Mallender of Northants and Adrian Jones of Sussex. Empowered to act quickly and independently by a cricket committee suddenly impatient of delay, Rose flew to New Zealand to settle with Mallender, a skilful, honest and accurate pace bowler who had been frustrated by docile pitches and a want of purpose at Northampton. Jones was a different case entirely. Already twenty-six, Mallender's age, he had accomplished little and carried a reputation for being moody and prone to injury. To sign him was a gamble, for it was against medical and cricketing advice and failure would certainly bring retribution from those recently dispossessed.

Somerset started their 1987 season depending heavily upon these new men, upon Crowe, Felton and Hardy, and of course upon Marks's durability. Crowe and Roebuck, in particular, were under a pressure experienced by few county cricketers, for bitter enemies were waiting upon their fall and friends could offer only encouragement. Membership and sponsorship had increased, contrary to predictions of bankruptcy made by rebel scaremongers, so they did at least realize that support outweighed hostility.

Fortunately Somerset started at a gallop, winning their first three Benson and Hedges games to reach the quarter-finals. Moreover Rose announced himself with a thundering 95 on his county début against Lancashire and Burns hit a scintillating 52 too. In years ahead both men tried to consolidate their batting talent, as Popplewell had done, so that they were less often frustrated by want of technique. In Burns's case it was a matter of working hard at his defence for to his dedication and thoughtfulness was added an impulsive streak which needed to be harnessed. Rose simply needed to feel secure enough to release his aggression, which he did in 1990, and in no uncertain terms, hitting as powerfully as ever did Wellard or Botham.

Crowe, Roebuck and Marks were prominent, and Somerset rose to eleventh in the championship, a finish widely considered satisfactory after their years of disgrace. Had Roebuck not broken a finger and missed eight matches a higher finish might have been achieved. He missed the Benson and Hedges quarter-final against Northants at Taunton too, and Somerset lost in a low-scoring game by 29 runs. Highlights of the year included Crowe's astonishing 155 not out in a Benson and Hedges qualifying game in Southampton, where he added 269 for the third wicket with Roebuck, a record partnership in limited-over cricket. Also, fighting hard, Somerset rose to fourth place in the Sunday League, for their bowling was rarely collared.

For many it was enough. Somerset had a personable, determined, if slightly colourless team which had, at least, repaired the club's reputation by batting to the last man in every match. But Roebuck, intolerant of opposition and impatient with mediocrity, was not satisfied, for while Somerset had lost only three county matches they had won only two and, under pressure, they had leant too heavily upon the elder statesmen. In particular Somerset had lost to Buckinghamshire in the NatWest Trophy, and failed to chase Northamptonshire's modest target in their Benson and Hedges quarter-final. Certainly his team, capably led by Marks in his absence, had fought back courageously but still they had shown, in parts, a weakness of temperament. Players who had complained most bitterly about Richards had performed no better in his absence.

Believing Somerset must continue to move forwards in search of excellence Roebuck began the 1988 season determined to prevent a consolidation around the humdrum, an attitude which risked further battles. Power to him was simply a means of doing something worthwhile, not an end in itself, a thing to be risked not protected. He did not want to preside over an ordinary team, one forever promising jam tomorrow, or over a club ruled by outdated committees the banishment of which had been promised during the 1986 turbulence.

Somerset began 1988 in poor form, especially Roebuck and Crowe, both suffering a reaction from their intense efforts a season earlier. Crowe was soon complaining of a back injury and a stress fracture was diagnosed. Later it emerged that salmonella poisoning was at the heart of his trouble, weakening him to injury and stress. After playing five county games, two of which he won with clinically constructed hundreds, innings born of a fierce, sometimes black will, Crowe was obliged to return to New Zealand for a period of rest and recuperation. Batting was never an easy matter for him, for he was an analytical man who could play to his best only after summoning a depth of commitment, mental and physical. Being capable of such commitment he was inclined to dismiss those around him whose approach was more

396

carefree, believing their sacrifices were too small, for which their team suffered. As an acknowledged Test batsman of high calibre Crowe was not as easy a companion as in 1984, and some felt him too ruthless. Roebuck thought him much improved, a demanding adult where once had been a callow youth.

Into Crowe's shoes stepped Stephen Waugh, a fighting young cricketer from Sydney who could hit a ball hard all around the wicket in a style which eschewed glamour, relying instead upon power generated by wrist, judgement won by a sharp eye and a tough streak which emerged whenever there was a match to be won. Waugh had played a few breathtaking innings for Somerset in 1987, taking hundreds off Courtney Walsh in Bristol and Sylvester Clarke at The Oval, rescuing his team on both occasions, cutting loose as stubborn tail-enders offered support. Now he recaptured this dazzling form, scoring 1,314 runs in fifteen matches, regularly giving Somerset a chance of victory.

Thanks to Crowe and Waugh, and to capable bowling by Mallender, Rose, Marks and Jones, who again hardly missed a game, Somerset won five matches in 1988, only one less than in the previous three seasons combined. By August they were fourth in the table, a marvellous effort for their bowling resources were stretched by injuries, this despite the appearance of youngsters such as Daren Foster, a slight lad from Haringey College blessed with a whippy action and suffering from an insufficient respect for accuracy, and two Somerset born and bred bowlers in Matthew Cleal, an outswinger raised in Yeovil, and Harvey Trump, an off-spinner whose father had captained Devon for years.

To observers it seemed as if Somerset were pressing ahead, challenging themselves to force victory or defeat, sifting good players from modest ones, promoting promising youngsters perhaps too quickly but promoting them anyhow so that at Bath their average age was twenty-three, and six locals were playing. But Roebuck had been pressing on too urgently and had neglected to carry elements in team and club with him.

Suddenly, in August, battle resumed. Roebuck was furious that no effort had been made to reduce Somerset's committee from forty-one to single figures, and that democracy, represented by postal ballots, was in decline. He believed Essex and Lancashire were models of properly run clubs and had hoped Somerset might be humble enough, and wise enough, to copy them. Some improvements were made, more power being given to the chief executive so that decisions could be made speedily if necessary, but so far as committees went things were getting worse, with intelligent, experienced men leaving out of frustration.

Roebuck believed the lessons of 1983–6 had not been absorbed, argued that the difficulties which had bedevilled Somerset cricket for decades, hidden at times by diplomatic individuals such as Kerslake and Jimmy James, had not been resolved. In July Tony Brown decided to accept an appointment at Lord's. Somerset's new chairman, John Gardner, announced that no current employee would be considered for this position. Possibly it was meant as a gentle way of telling Brian Rose he would not be given the job. It emerged as an insult to everyone at Somerset, for no one associated with the club could even apply. Believing this to be an outrageous state of affairs Roebuck complained bitterly and was reprimanded by his employers for this indiscretion.

Things were moving towards a denouement. Exasperated, Rose resigned from his cricketing and commercial responsibilities to begin working in industry. Perhaps he could be forgetful, and certainly his paperwork caused alarm in some quarters, yet his passion for Somerset cricket had never flagged and many considered he deserved at least to be considered as a candidate for the position of chief executive. Perhaps, like Kerslake and others, he was condemned because he was close to the players.

By now Roebuck was in high dudgeon. To cap it off, a letter was sent to every player, young and old, from a member of his cricket committee, saying that reports of discontentment in the camp had been heard, thus offering an ear to those feeling unhappy. Somerset's move away from mediocrity threatened one or two careers and those involved manipulated friends of immature judgement. Teenagers had been sent an official letter openly critical of Roebuck, who rightly felt humiliated. And so he resigned as captain. Evidently he had taken the club as far as he could, away from its divided, defeated state of 1985, hopefully towards a happier future in which young players had a chance to succeed. He had failed to carry his club with him and thought it time for Vic Marks to take the strain. It was a time for diplomacy. Roebuck's departure sent such a strong signal to the club that Vic Marks could depend upon firm support, especially once Gardner resigned as chairman during the winter.

Few cricketers can have given Somerset better service than

398

Victor Marks, and none can have won more games. He had played six Tests and it might have been more, for he was too easily mistaken for a rustic. Competitive, born with native cunning and a flair he would not analyse lest it be lost, Marks had taken guard in his last three Test innings with England tottering and each time he scored 50. Throughout his career scarcely a game went by without him coming up with something.

For years he had been freely tipped as a potential captain of Somerset. But Marks was not a fellow for clubs, had no taste for intrigue and was accordingly not seriously considered either in 1983 or in 1985. Humility and a hint of indolence prevented any fight for power, scepticism stopped him tilting at windmills and conservatism inherited from his farming family discouraged radical thought. He loathed disharmony and was best suited to lead in times of peace. Had he been appointed in 1982 much trouble might have been avoided but this idea was never mooted for there were too many strong characters eager for power. Now it was probably too late for Marks's generation had left and his own energy was draining away.

Nevertheless during his period in office he brought to Somerset three notable characters and played his part in choosing a new chief executive in Peter Anderson, an energetic and garrulous character who had played for Devon and investigated corruption in Hong Kong, qualifications evidently deemed to be ideal. Marks brought to Somerset his old university chum Chris Tavare, whose wife was a Somerset girl, and a new overseas player in James Cook, a hitherto obscure South African. In choosing both men he took into account their mild and steadfast temperaments, and their brilliance as cricketers.

Besides these players, Marks also persuaded Somerset to appoint Jack Birkenshaw as manager, filling a gap left by Brian Rose's departure. To Birkenshaw, a Test cricketer, Test umpire and acknowledged coach, was given the task of lifting Somerset cricket to the highest ranks.

In many respects 1989 was an enjoyable season, though it was not spectacularly successful. Jimmy Cook introduced himself as a batsman of the highest pedigree, sitting on his back foot, scarcely moving foot or bat, ever vigilant, putting the ball to the fence as if he were removing the top from an egg. Tall, moustachioed and polite he was an Edwardian figure, one who could be imagined arriving in a charabanc. To sign a thirty-six-year-old South African batsman who had never played Test cricket was an audacious move and one which was vindicated as, without ever setting the pulse racing, and hardly ever making a mistake, Cook scored 2,241 first-class runs and played a stream of masterly limited-over innings, if never quite on the big occasions when, perhaps, he tried too hard.

Freed from internecine warfare at Kent, Chris Tavare was hardly less of an inspiration, and if his championship form was patchy he played three one-day innings as fine as any produced in Somerset colours. On his début he struck 120 not out in 34 overs of a Sunday game, and in two vital cup games, both against Essex, he contributed vibrant hundreds, combining astonishing power with cool calculation. Set a target, Tavare was at his best.

Lacking penetration, and with Marks himself overbowled and out of sorts, Somerset slipped to fourteenth in the championship in 1989 winning four games but taking few bowling points. Mallender and Rose were injured too often, while Adrian Jones, fast and furious in spells, suffered from lapses of concentration. At his fittest and sharpest Jones was impressive: at his worst he was wayward and expensive. Nevertheless he was once more fit for every game, a tribute to his durability.

After two years of painful reconstruction, Richard Harden returned to first-team cricket as a tighter, harder player, reminding everyone that it is not how much talent a man has but what he does with it. A loss of confidence in August cost him his 1,000 runs but he had learnt to play off the back foot and to wait for the ball and was here to stay. He was, in fact, the first born and bred cricketer to establish himself in Somerset's team since the vintage crop of the 1970s.

Lots of youngsters were tried including Nick Pringle, Richard Bartlett, Harvey Trump, Matthew Cleal and Jon Atkinson, son of Colin, and while all showed promise none proved mature enough to demand a regular place. Julian Wyatt, alas, suffered a poor summer and to the disappointment of supporters of his simple style, passion for Somerset cricket and polite manner, he was not retained. He had played several stirring innings and his fielding had been outstanding.

By and large it was the experienced players who served Somerset best, especially on big occasions. Having won all their qualifying games, Somerset were drawn to meet the Combined Universities at Taunton in a quarter-final of the Benson and Hedges Cup. Somerset reached 252/5, Roebuck scoring 102. So brilliant was the students' reply that they needed 30 runs in 6 overs with 7 wickets left. Hereabouts Marks introduced Roebuck to bowl what might be described as fastish off-breaks, a mode of delivery which captain and bowler had discovered at some careless moment a month or so earlier. Suddenly their opponents panicked, Hussain slashing at Jones, who had summoned an aggressive spell upon his return, and everyone else caught midway between swiping and pinching singles.

Incredibly, and to the delight of a large crowd basking in warm sunshine, Somerset won, Roebuck taking 2/19 in his 4 overs and Jones being just as tight. It was not the only time in 1989 that Somerset's new captain and new bowler managed to extract victory from defeat's very jaw.

And so to a semi-final. Despite accurate bowling from Marks and Roebuck, Essex scored 293/5 in their 55 overs and few in a packed Rack Field gave Somerset a chance. Cook and Roebuck started well once more but it was after tea, with 200 needed in 30 overs, that the fireworks began. In 99 balls and against overwhelming odds, Chris Tavare struck a hundred dazzling in its stroke-play if, sadly, doomed in its effect. Despite all manner of heroics, especially from Jones, a swashbuckling tail-ender whose spirit usually exceeded his concentration, Tavare could not quite take Somerset home, and by 4 runs they failed to reach Lord's for the first time since 1983. These games were vastly enjoyed by enthusiastic crowds relaxing in a calmer county ground.

Tavare played an innings hardly less rousing against Essex in the NatWest Trophy, adding 195 with Roebuck to give Somerset a famous victory. Alas it was to no avail for a batting collapse in the second round, in which Tavare again stood like a beacon surveying a stormy sea as he scored 79 not out, denied Somerset advancement.

All told it was a season of rich days and captivating last hours, a season in which Somerset's batting was usually solid and sometimes inspired, and their bowling honest if rather predictable. Somerset could field no left-arm bowler, fast or slow, and while Jones and Mallender were capable of early wickets they were seldom given enough support. Not for the first time Somerset needed a strike bowler and a left-arm spinner, for which sacred creatures they duly scoured this earth.

In August Vic Marks announced his retirement from county cricket. Aged thirty-four, he had played 275 county games for Somerset, scored 9,742 runs and taken 738 wickets in 8,811 overs. Besides he had played in 249 one-day games, scoring 3,616 runs and taking 225 wickets at a respectable average and – more importantly – with remarkable economy for so tantalizing a bowler. He had done his bit and when a letter arrived from the *Observer* offering a position as its cricket correspondent, an offer which could not wait a year, he decided to hang up his helmet. For Somerset of course the loss was considerable for he was two cricketers in one. Colin Atkinson, Somerset's president, struck the right note at the presentation by saying that Vic would be missed more as a man than as a cricketer. Everyone understood no slight was intended upon his play. His players struck the right note too. They gave Marks a rocking chair.

Possibly he had inherited the captaincy too late to bring to it these resources of drive and combativeness which had carried him through an outstanding career. Nevertheless he had led with humour and his season had included moments of glory amongst its frustration. And, thankfully, he was retiring gracefully, without recrimination or resentment, while people were asking 'Why?' rather than 'Why not?'

Chris Tavare was duly appointed captain for 1990 and with Jackie Birkenshaw and Peter Robinson, still coaching day and night come hail or shine in the old indoor school upon which executive boxes had been built years earlier, he set about strengthening Somerset's staff and bringing to it a greater professionalism. By now Felton and Foster had left and Colin Dredge, plagued by injury, had returned to his family in Frome shortly to begin working as an engineer. So far youngsters such as Bartlett, Pringle, Atkinson, Cleal and Trump had not broken through and these new leaders were not inclined to wait upon the hope of their doing so.

Throughout its history Somerset has needed to import bowlers and now they signed two Dutchmen, Roland LeFebvre (twenty-seven) an engaging, whippy medium-pacer who could also bat, and was a trained physiotherapist and an accomplished pianist and Adrian Van Troost, a skyscraper of seventeen years not yet out of school. Both immediately showed intelligence, humour and talent which boded well for their futures. LeFebvre played regularly in 1990 and if his wicket tally and batting averages did not please him he was nevertheless asked to bowl many telling overs in tight finishes and was at his best when the chips were down, both of which were significant for the future.

Ian Swallow arrived from Yorkshire to replace Marks and proved to be an honest, bright cricketer who could bowl accurately if without undue penetration. Andrew Hayhurst (twenty-seven), appeared from Lancashire as a ready-made cricketer who could take wickets with his strong outswingers and, more importantly, was a solid enough batsman to score runs at first wicket down, for years a voodoo position. Fighting with the tenacity of a man who had been waiting years for just such a chance, driving and cutting hard through the covers, Hayhurst enjoyed a productive first season, especially in championship cricket. Sharper running between the wicket and a wider range of shots to leg might bring even greater rewards, especially in overs matches.

Thankfully local men did well too, Harden scoring heavily, confirming his standing as a respected county batsman, one decidedly difficult to remove, while Pringle and Bartlett dominated 2nd XI cricket, taking their team to a limited-over final, and were denied games on a bigger stage only by the excellent form of those in possession. Ian Fletcher, Harvey Trump and Jeremy Hallett, all Millfield schoolboys, announced themselves too, while Gareth Townsend and Mark Lathwell, from Devon, made appearances speaking of promise. Andrew Caddick, a tall New Zealander determined to qualify by residence for English county cricket, promised much on a solitary appearance against Sri Lanka. He could be a regular in 1992. Ken MacLeay, a wily and capable cricketer with West Australia, found he could play for a county and he too was signed as Somerset spread its net wide, rather in the manner of John Daniell.

These men will join a side solid in batting, for Cook, Tavare, Hayhurst, Harden, Burns, and Rose all partook of the run-orgy of the dismal 1990 season, batting with disciplined habit. But Somerset's bowling wanted variety and thrust. Hopefully Hallett and Trump will be Somerset's first home-grown bowlers of substance since Dredge and Marks. As Caddick, MacLeay and others arrived so news broke of Jack Birkenshaw's decision to take a job nearer to his home in Leicester, leaving behind a club tumbling towards financial difficulty as inexperienced officials risked a surge in spending. Birkenshaw could be congratulated for his enterprise in finding good bowlers in improbable places.

Those who arrive join a club blessed with proud, patient, and passionate supporters. Of all the county cricket clubs this is the one most beloved, for it has charm, intimacy, and a doomed warmth captured by the old battle-cry, 'Have a go at 'un!'

Even since the great days of 1890 Somerset cricket has been full of character, and characters, men such as Tyler, Nichols, Woods, Lyon, Andrews, Hazell, Stephenson, Rumsey, and Denning, men whose every move speaks volumes. Hitters abound too, in Wellard, Earle, Hill, Fowler, Tremlett, and Botham. Memories of old favourites such as Robson, Alley, and Burgess linger too. Everywhere in this county so insultingly abbreviated by legislation nearly twenty years ago people clutch pints of scrumpy and recall heroes, failures, and valiant victories; for every Somerset man, stationed near or far, seems to follow his team. Only anonymity or half-heartedness brings rebuke. Cricket matters here as it does in Leeds, though fortunately expectations are lower.

And yet it is a desperately flawed, exasperating club too, one which has never known how to rule itself, one which accordingly stumbles along, occasionally making decisions audacious in their brilliance and otherwise searching for that elusive combination, wisdom and harmony. From 1981 onwards it has been a club blighted by committees too vast to be sage. Throughout its history Somerset has been enthusiastically supported by men and women of intelligence and judgement; seldom have such followers found their way on to Somerset's governing body, though good intentions abound.

Nevertheless this is on the whole a happy club, if one in which hard times are never far away. This is a county in which cricket is well played at schools and badly played at clubs, and a county suspicious of snobbery and pretension. Somerset cricket has an atmosphere of its own, one in which hope is eternal, one which defies every sling and every arrow, even those fired by supposed friends.

Our tale is at an end. What has been missed? Of the 500 or so men who have played first-class cricket for Somerset around 190 attended public schools, including seventeen Etonians. Few, very few, emerged from clubs. Somerset CCC was committed to amateurism, both by instinct and by economic strength. Luckily local schools, private and state, foster cricket, and especially Millfield under Meyer and Atkinson, and Taunton School, and they have produced lots of hopeful cricketers in the past ten years.

Some men have been neglected. Cricketers such as M. R. H. M. Herbert (Eton), Thomas Coleridge Spring (Blundells) and Douglas Smith have hardly been mentioned, yet between them they made sixty somewhat undistinguished county appearances. And my old friend John Luff is not here. Luff is a Pickwickian, an advocate of the Loch Ness Monster, an important local businessman, councillor, politician, and a man who has served on Somerset committees for years, a staunch supporter of the Weston Festival. Always he has spoken seriously when it mattered and hilariously when it did not, rather in the manner of Sir Spencer Ponsonby-Fane, whose great-grandson still eagerly follows Somerset's fortunes, as do the relations of the various Greswells, Whites and Spurways who adorned the scene in years gone by.

Hard times may lie ahead, for this club of 115 summers has not yet caught up with its age. Somerset depends upon a stream of imported talent, a supply of locals of genuine promise, wise stewardship, a few pounds in the bank and strong leadership, a combination found during three or four celebrated periods. When such times will return cannot be foreseen, for too much depends in this club upon chance. Until Somerset arranges its affairs properly a challenge cannot be sustained, and even if matters are duly organized it will not be easy, for cricket in Somerset remains a game loved rather than mastered. Nor has character been lost. Included in the current arrangements, rather a hotchpotch, is a captain who like Archdale Wickham is interested mostly in butterflies, a coach who likes Pavarotti, several fast bowlers scarcely less keen on beer than Andrews and Wellard, an aged dressing-room attendant who had, he insists, a trial with Somerset in 1935 and a Dutchman who can play Mozart piano concertos. And Somerset still wins hearts. Men such as John Cleese, Leslie Crowther, Jeffrey Archer, Dennis Silk (lately Warden of Radley College), Lord Rippon, John Biffen, and Tom King die a thousand deaths during a Somerset semi-final. Decidedly it will last another 115 years and decidedly they will be diverting. Whether or not they will contain a first championship cannot safely be said. If they do many will die with a smile upon their face and fellows like Murray-Anderdon, Robson, Daniell, Tremlett and Woods will have a spring in their step as they wander through their heavenly repose.

Appendix

Records
and
Statistics

The following records refer to first-class matches for Somerset and are correct to the end of the 1990 season.

Officials

President/Chairman (Joint Title Till 1953)

1891–1915	Hon Sir Spencer Ponsonby-Fane, Bt
1916–22	H. E. Murray-Anderdon
1923	A. E. Newton
1924	The Marquis of Bath KG
1925	Lt-Col Sir Dennis F. Boles, Bt
1926	Col H. M. Ridley
1927	Rev Preb A. P. Wickham
1928	Col H. M. Ridley
1929	L. C. H. Palairet
1930	V. T. Hill
1931–32	Major A G Barrett
1933	Lt-Col W. O. Gibbs
1934–35	Lt-Col Sir Dennis F. Boles Bt
1936	The Duke of Somerset
1937–46	R. C. N. Palairet
1947–49	J Daniell
1950–53	Major G E Longrigg

President

1954–60	The Bishop of Bath and Wells
1961	J. C. White
1962–65	W. T. Greswell
1966–67	Lord Hylton
1968–71	E. F. Longrigg
1971–76	R. V. Showering
1976–	C. R. M. Atkinson

Secretary

1891–94	T. Spencer and H. E. Murray-Anderdon (Joint)
1895–1907	H. E. Murray-Anderdon and S. M. J. Woods (Joint)
1908–10	H. E. Murray-Anderdon
1911–12	G. Fowler
1913–19	R. Brooks-King
1920–22	S. M. J. Woods
1923–31	A. F. Davey
1932–36	J. Daniell
1937–49	Brig E. H. Lancaster
1950	N. J. C. Daniell
1950–55	Air Vice-Marshal M. L. Taylor
1955–69	R. Robinson
1970–75	A. K. James
1975–79	R. G. Stevens
1979–82	D. G. Seward
1982–88	A. S. Brown
1988 -	P. W. Anderson

Chairman

1954–59	A. H. Southwood
1960–69	E. F. Longrigg
1969–71	Lt-Col G. C. G. Grey
1972–73	C. R. M. Atkinson
1974–76	H. W. Hoskins
1977–78	L. G. Creed
1979	R. C. Kerslake
1979–82	J. M. Jeffrey
1983–87	M. F. Hill
1988	J. Gardner
1988–	R. Parsons

Captain

1882–84	S. C. Newton
1885	E. Sainsbury
1886–90	*not applicable*
1891–93	H. T. Hewett
1894–1906	S. M. J. Woods

1907	L. C. H. Palairet	1955	G. G. Tordoff
1908–12	J. Daniell	1956–59	M. F. Tremlett
1913–14	E. S. M. Poyntz	1960–64	H. W. Stephenson
[. . .]		1964	W. E. Alley (Acting
1919–26	J. Daniell		Capt)
1927–31	J. C. White	1965–67	C. R. M. Atkinson
1932–37	R. A. Ingle	1968	R. C. Kerslake
1938–46	E. F. Longrigg	1969–71	B. A. Langford
1947	R. J. O. Meyer	1972–77	D. B. Close
1948	N. S. Mitchell-Innes	1978–83	B. C. Rose
	G. E. S. Woodhouse	1984–85	I. T. Botham
	J W Seamer	1986–88	P. M. Roebuck
1949	G. E. S. Woodhouse	1988–89	V. J. Marks
1950–52	S. S. Rogers	1990–	C. J. Tavare
1953–54	B. G. Brocklehurst		

Competitions Record

Year	County Championship Position	Year	County Championship Position	Year	County Championship Position	Gillette/ NatWest Trophy Stage Reached	J Player/ Refuge League Position	Benson & Hedges Cup Stage Reached
1891	5=	1926	14	1963	3	1st Round		
1892	3	1927	14	1964	8	Qtr-Final		
1893	8	1928	14	1965	7	Qtr-Final		
1894	6	1929	15	1966	3	Semi-Final		
1895	8=	1930	13=	1967	8	Final		
1896	11	1931	13	1968	12	2nd Round		
1897	11	1932	7	1969	17	1st Round	16	
1898	13=	1933	11	1970	13	Semi-Final	15	
1899	13=	1934	15	1971	7	1st Round	5	
1900	11	1935	14	1972	11	2nd Round	7=	Eliminated In Group
1901	12=	1936	7	1973	10	2nd Round	11	Eliminated In Group
1902	7	1937	13	1974	5	Semi-Final	2	Semi-Final
1903	10	1938	7	1975	12	2nd Round	14	Qtr-Final
1904	12	1939	14	1976	7	2nd Round	2=	Eliminated In Group
1905	15	1946	4	1977	4	Semi-Final	9=	Eliminated In Group
1906	11=	1947	11=	1978	5	Final	2	Semi-Final
1907	14	1948	12	1979	8	Winners	1	Eliminated In Group
1908	16	1949	9	1980	5	1st Round	2	Eliminated In Group
1909	11	1950	7=	1981	3	1st Round	2	Winners
1910	16	1951	14	1982	6	Qtr-Final	9	Winners
1911	16	1952	17	1983	10	Winners	2	Eliminated In Group
1912	14	1953	17	1984	7	Qtr-Final	13	Qtr-Final
1913	16	1954	17	1985	17	Qtr-Final	10=	Eliminated In Group
1914	15	1955	17	1986	16	2nd Round	6	Eliminated In Group
[. . .]		1956	15	1987	11	1st Round	4	Qtr-Final
1919	5=	1957	8	1988	11	2nd Round	12	Eliminated In Group
1920	10	1958	3	1989	14	2nd Round	10	Semi-Final
1921	10	1959	12	1990	15	2nd Round	8=	Semi-Final
1922	10	1960	14					
1923	9	1961	10					
1924	8	1962	6					
1925	15							

Somerset Playing Record

	Years	P	W	D	L	Td	Abd
Derbyshire	1912/90	104	29	31	44	-	2
Essex	1895/1990	119	26	44	48	1	1
Glamorgan	1921/90	131	30	64	37	-	1
Gloucestershire	1882/1990	184	51	65	68	-	1
Hampshire	1882/1990	174	47	65	62	-	1
Kent	1884/1990	144	33	36	75	-	-
Lancashire	1882/1990	126	20	36	70	-	2
Leicestershire	1920/90	78	28	31	19	-	-
Middlesex	1891/1990	140	22	40	78	-	-
Northamptonshire	1912/90	100	23	46	31	-	1
Nottinghamshire	1892/1990	96	23	47	26	-	-
Surrey	1883/1990	145	25	46	74	-	1
Sussex	1892/1990	155	38	53	63	1	1
Warwickshire	1905/90	105	27	48	30	-	-
Worcestershire	1901/90	152	51	52	48	1	1
Yorkshire	1891/1990	136	12	45	79	-	-
Oxford University	1892/1990	30	8	11	11	-	1
Cambridge University	1892/1985	26	10	9	7	-	-
Australia	1882/1989	26	1	11	14	-	-
South Africa	1901/60	11	1	1	9	-	-
India	1911/86	10	2	6	2	-	-
West Indies	1923/88	13	1	5	7	-	-
New Zealand	1927/90	10	0	6	4	-	-
Pakistan	1954/82	5	1	3	1	-	-
MCC	1882/91	4	1	2	1	-	-
Philadelphians	1897/1903	2	1	1	-	-	-
Pakistan Eaglets	1963	1	0	1	0	-	-
Combined Services	1959	1	1	0	0	-	-
Totals		2228	512	805	908	3	13

P	W	L	Td	No Dec.	No Play	P	W	L	Abd	P	W	L
21	12	9	-	-	1	2	2	-	-	4	2	2
19	9	10	-	-	3	5	1	4	-	3	2	1
22	14	6	1	1	-	12	9	3	-	2	1	1
21	14	7	-	-	1	10	5	5	-	-	-	-
19	10	9	-	-	3	12	5	7	1	2	-	2
21	9	12	-	-	1	7	5	2	-	6	3	3
21	8	11	-	2	1	2	-	2	-	7	3	4
20	5	13	-	2	2	3	-	3	-	4	2	2
22	12	8	-	2	-	6	2	4	-	3	2	1
20	10	8	-	2	2	1	-	1	-	5	3	2
21	14	6	-	1	1	2	2	-	-	3	3	-
20	14	5	-	1	2	3	1	2	-	2	2	-
22	11	10	1	-	-	6	4	2	-	5	3	2
22	16	6	-	-	-	1	-	1	-	5	2	3
20	6	12	-	2	2	3	1	2	-	2	-	2
21	12	8	-	1	1	2	2	-	-	3	2	1
332	176	140	2	14	20					-	-	-

Minor Counties						8	8	-	1	-	-	-
Combined Universities						6	6	-	-	-	-	-
						91	53	38	2	-	-	-

	P	W	L
Bedfordshire	1	1	-
Berkshire	2	2	-
Buckinghamshire	2	1	1
Devon	1	1	-
Dorset	1	1	-
Durham	1	1	-
Hertfordshire	1	1	-
Northumberland	1	1	-
Shropshire	1	1	-
	67	40	27

Principal Records

Highest Innings Totals:

675-9 Dec.v Hampshire (Bath) 1924
630 v Yorkshire (Leeds) 1901
592 v Yorkshire (Taunton) 1892
584-8 v Sussex (Eastbourne) 1948
566-5 Dec.(In 100 overs) v Warwickshire (Taunton) 1985
561 v Lancashire (Bath) 1901
560-8 Dec.v Sussex (Taunton) 1901

Lowest Innings Totals:

25 v Gloucestershire (Bristol) 1947
29 & 51 v Lancashire (Manchester) 1882
31 v Gloucestershire (Bristol) 1931
31 v Lancashire (Manchester) 1894
33 v Lancashire (Liverpool) 1908
35 v Yorkshire (Bath) 1898
35 v Derbyshire (Derby) 1935

Highest & Lowest Totals For & Against Counties & Tourists

VERSUS	FOR SOMERSET HIGHEST	LOWEST	AGAINST SOMERSET HIGHEST	LOWEST	BEST BATTING FOR SOMERSET	BEST BOWLING FOR SOMERSET
Derbyshire	508	35	495-7 Dec	37	219 M.D.Lyon	8-30 A. Young
Essex	488	48	692	69	174* J. Daniell	8-67 B. A. Langford
Glamorgan	535-2 Dec	40	574-7 Dec	52	313* S.J. Cook	9-51 J. C. White
Gloucestershire	534-6 Dec	25	550-5 Dec	22	241* I.V.A. Richards	9-46 J.C. White
Hampshire	675-9 Dec	37	672-7 Dec	44	292 L.C.H. Palairet	9-62 W. T. Greswell
Kent	503	50	601-8 Dec	55	222* P.B. Wight	8-23 B.A. Langford
Lancashire	561	29	801	48	202* R.J.O. Meyer	9-26 B.A. Langford

Team						
Leicestershire	528	61	490	41	216 I.V.A.Richards	7-41 J. Garner
Middlesex	523-9	35	596	52	231 H. Gimblett	9-38 R.C. Robertson-Glasgow
Northamptonshire	501-5 Dec	55	506	95	205 B.C. Rose	8-41 B.A. Langford
Nottinghamshire	459-4 Dec	62	585-5 Dec	62	221* P.M. Roebuck	9-33 E.J. Tyler
Surrey	507-6 Dec	36	811	35	204 I.V.A. Richards	10-49 E.J. Tyler
Sussex	584-8 Dec	54	559	47	310 H. Gimblett	9-51 A.A. Jones
Warwickshire	566-5 Dec	50	494-5 Dec	44	322 I.V.A. Richards	9-58 J.C. White
Worcestershire	628-7 Dec	56	590	42	257* L.C. Braund	10-76 J.C. White
Yorkshire	630	35	549-9 Dec	73	217* I.V.A. Richards	9-41 L.C. Braund
Australia	376	59	609-4 Dec	85	136 M.D. Lyon	8-35 E. Robson
India	506-6 Dec	128	432-9 Dec	64	141* M.M. Walford	6-52 A.W. Wellard
New Zealand	349-5 Dec	67	544-9 Dec	128	156 C.J. Tavare	8-28 J.C. White
Pakistan	502-6 Dec	215	456-6 Dec	99	189 M.J. Kitchen	6-38 B.A. Langford
South Africa	440-9 Dec	68	438	96	107* S.S. Rogers	6-61 J. Bridges
West Indies	345	112	482-6 Dec	78	88 D.B. Close	6-40 W.H.R. Andrews

Record Wicket Partnerships

1st Wicket: **346** - H.T. Hewett (201) + L.C.H. Palairet (146) v Yorkshire (Taunton) 1892
273* - N.A. Felton (156*) + P. M. Roebuck (102*) v
Hampshire (Taunton) 1986
258 - A.E. Lewis (120) + L.C.H. Palairet (194) v Sussex
(Taunton) 1901
255 - B.C. Rose (133) + P.A. Slocombe (103*) v Gloucestershire (Taunton) 1979

2nd Wicket: **290** - J.C.W. MacBryan (132) + M.D. Lyon (219) v
Derbyshire (Buxton) 1924
262 - R.T. Virgin (162) + M.J. Kitchen (189) v Pakistan
(Taunton) 1967
258 - P.M. Roebuck (201*) + A.N. Hayhurst (119) v
Worcestershire (Worcester) 1990
251 - J.C.W. MacBryan (148) + A. Young (125*) v
Glamorgan (Taunton) 1923

3rd Wicket: **319** - P.M. Roebuck (128) + M.D. Crowe (190) v Leicestershire (Taunton) 1984
300 - G. Atkinson (190) + P.B. Wight (155*) v Glamorgan
(Bath) 1960
297 - P.B. Wight (125) + W.E. Alley (183*) v Surrey
(Taunton) 1961
285* - S.J. Cook (313*) + C.J. Tavare (120*) v Glamorgan
(Cardiff) 1990

4th Wicket: **310** - P.W. Denning (98) + I.T. Botham (228) v Gloucestershire (Taunton) 1980
256 - C.J. Tavare (156) + R.J. Harden (104) v New
Zealand (Taunton) 1990
251 - I.V.A. Richards (204) + P.M. Roebuck (112) v
Surrey (Weston-Super-Mare) 1977
229* - S.J. Cook (147*) + R.J. Harden (101*) v Essex
(Chelmsford) 1989

5th Wicket: **235** - J.C. White (113) + C.C.C. Case (122) v Gloucestershire (Taunton) 1927
227 - I.V.A. Richards (217*) + D.B. Close (91) v Yorkshire (Harrogate) 1975
222 - P.A. Slocombe (78) + B.C. Rose (173*) v Gloucestershire (Bristol) 1982
221 - D.B. Close (138*) + P.A. Slocombe (102) v Gloucestershire (Bristol) 1975

6th Wicket: **265** - W.E. Alley (156) + K.E. Palmer (125*) v Northants (Northampton) 1961
213 - N.D. Burns (166) + G.D. Rose (85) v Gloucestershire (Taunton) 1990
201* - R.J. Harden (102*) + V.J. Marks (89*) v Kent (Bath) 1989
196 - M.F. Tremlett (100) + P.B. Wight (162) v Middlesex (Bath) 1959

7th Wicket: **240** - S.M.J. Woods (144) + V.T. Hill (116) v Kent (Taunton) 1898
189 - J.C. White (142) + R.A. Ingle (101) v Hampshire (Southampton) 1935
182 - S.S. Rogers (101) + H.W. Stephenson (82) v Northants (Frome) 1950
177 - I.T. Botham (134) + J.C.M. Atkinson (79) v Northants (W-S-M) 1985

8th Wicket: **172** - I.V.A. Richards (216) + I T Botham (152) v Leicestershire (Leicester) 1983
163 - M.D. Crowe (113) + J.W. Lloyds (73*) v Lancashire (Bath) 1984
153* - I.V.A. Richards (181*) + C.H. Dredge (34*) v Pakistan (Taunton) 1982

9th Wicket: **183** - C.J. Tavare (219) + N.A. Mallender (87*) v Sussex (Hove) 1990
183 - C.H. Greetham (141) + H.W. Stephenson (80) v Leicestershire (W-S-M) 1963
179* - N.F.M. Popplewell (135*) + D. Breakwell (73*) v Kent (Taunton) 1980

10th Wicket: **143** - J. Bridges (99*) + H. Gibbs (41) v Essex (W-S-M) 1919
139 - P.R. Johnson (117*) + R.C. Robertson-Glasgow (49) v Surrey (Oval) 1926

First Class Career Figures (Somerset Only)

QUAL: BATSMEN – 5,000 RUNS; BOWLERS: 250 WKTS; W/KEEPERS – 200 DISMISSALS

Player	Career	M	Runs	H.S.	Batting Avge	100s	Season 1,000s	Bowling Runs	Wkts	Avge	B.B.	5 wkts	Season 100 w	Ct/St
W.E. Alley	1957-68	350	16644	221*	30.48	24	10	16264	738	22.04	8-65	30	1	267
W.H.R. Andrews	1930-47	224	4833	80	15.60	2	2	17541	750	23.39	8-12	40	4	91
G. Atkinson	1954-66	271	14468	190	32.08	21	8	236	4	59.00	4-63			159
K.D. Biddulph	1955-61	91	468	41	6.78			7457	270	27.62	6-30	10		10
I.T. Botham	1974-86	172	8686	228	36.04	16	2	12970	489	26.52	7-61	22		133
L.C. Braund	1899-1920	281	12209	257*	25.38	13	2	19135	684	27.98	9-41	44	1	360
D. Breakwell	1973-83	165	3777	100*	21.22	1		9337	281	33.23	6-38	6		59
J. Bridges	1911-29	214	2414	99*	10.10			17528	684	25.63	7-41	48		126
G.I. Burgess	1966-79	252	7129	129	18.91	2		13543	474	28.57	7-43	18		120
N.D. Burns	1987-90	92	3148	166	29.98	3		8	0					189/15
H.D. Burrough	1927-47	161	5316	135	20.92	4		14	0					83
H.F.T. Buse	1929-53	304	10623	132	22.69	7	1	18908	657	28.77	8-41	20		151
T.W. Cartwright	1970-76	101	2422	127	18.92	1		7698	408	18.87	8-94	29	1	62
C.C.C. Case	1925-35	255	8515	155	22.17	9	3	128	0					46
G. Clayton	1965-67	89	1741	106	14.75	1								209/33
D.B. Close	1971-77	142	7567	153	39.41	13	5	2586	74	34.95	5-70	1		140
B. Cranfield	1897-1908	125	1250	42	10.33			13858	563	24.61	8-39	43	2	60
J. Daniell	1898-1927	287	9826	174*	21.79	8		158	6	26.33	1-4			215
P.W. Denning	1969-84	269	11559	184	28.68	8		96	1	96.00	1-4			132
C.H. Dredge	1976-88	194	2182	56*	13.98			13338	443	30.10	6-37	12		84
T. Gard	1976-89	112	1389	51*	13.75			8	0					178/39
J. Garner	1977-86	94	1170	90	18.00			6121	338	18.10	8-31	22		47
H. Gimblett	1935-54	329	21142	310	36.96	49	12	2054	41	50.10	4-10			234
C.H.M. Greetham	1957-66	205	6723	151*	21.97	5	2	5529	195	28.35	7-56	5		95
W.T. Greswell	1908-30	115	2416	100	15.49	1		9787	453	21.60	9-62	31	1	90
H.L. Hazell	1929-52	350	2280	43	8.17			22941	957	23.97	8-27	57	2	248
W.C. Hedley	1892-1904	84	2395	102	18.14	2		5276	254	20.77	8-18	14		55
G. Hunt	1921-31	233	4954	101	15.43	1		12686	386	32.87	7-61	11		198

Player	Career	M	Runs	HS	Avge	100	Runs	Wkts	Avge	BB	5wi	10wm	Ct/St
R.A. Ingle	1923-39	309	9483	119*	19.1	10	26						124
P.R. Johnson	1901-27	229	10201	164	25.83	17	212	3	70.67	1-18			142
A.A. Jones	1970-75	118	442	27	6.05		8456	291	29.06	9-51	13		32
M.J. Kitchen	1960-79	352	15213	189	26.41	17	109	2	54.50	1-4			156
B.A. Langford	1953-74	504	7513	68*	13.58		34599	1390	24.89	9-26	85	5	224
J. Lawrence	1946-55	281	9094	122	20.39	3	19683	791	24.88	8-41	37	2	258
F.S. Lee	1929-47	328	15252	162	27.99	23	749	23	32.57	5-53	1		156/12
J.W. Lee	1925-36	241	7852	193*	21.11	6	14627	493	29.67	7-45	19		122
A.E. Lewis	1899-1914	208	7633	201*	21.32	9	11893	513	23.18	8-103	39		106
B. Lobb	1955-69	115	624	42	5.20		8729	369	23.66	7-43	15	1	24
J.G. Lomax	1954-62	211	7516	104*	20.76	2	8231	235	35.03	6-75	3		310
E.F. Longrigg	1925-47	219	8329	205	24.57	10	93						121
W.T. Luckes	1924-49	365	5708	121*	16.22	1	565	8	70.63	3-43			586/243
M.D. Lyon	1920-38	123	6231	219	31.00	12	61						108/31
J.C.W. MacBryan	1911-31	156	8371	164	31.00	16							100
C.L. McCool	1956-60	138	7913	169	33.82	12	6144	219	28.05	8-74	10		137/1
J.W. McMahon	1954-57	115	645	24	6.14		9115	349	26.12	8-46	20	1	52
V.J. Marks	1975-89	275	9742	134	30.53	4	24271	738	32.88	8-17	37	5	114
H.R. Moseley	1971-82	205	1502	67	12.41		13184	547	24.10	6-34	16		76
A.E. Newton	1891-1914	197	3069	77	12.08		4						297/119
G.B. Nichols	1891-99	134	2793	74*	13.69		6867	291	23.60	6-75	7		62
L.C.H. Palairet	1891-1909	222	13851	292	35.79	27	3374	87	38.78	4-32			209
K.E. Palmer	1955-69	302	7567	125*	20.73	2	17665	837	21.11	9-57	44	4	154
I.V.A. Richards	1974-86	191	14698	322	49.82	47	4239	96	44.15	4-36			164
P.J. Robinson	1965-77	180	4887	140	21.53	3	7969	291	27.38	7-10	10		168
E. Robson	1895-1923	424	12439	163*	17.67	5	29846	1122	26.60	8-35	56		258
P.M. Roebuck	1974-90	289	15379	221*	38.73	30	2127	36	59.08	2-22			142
B.C. Rose	1969-87	251	12342	205	39.26	23	289	8	36.12	3-9			113
F.E. Rumsey	1963-68	153	766	45	7.66		10829	520	19.79	8-26	28		78
H.W. Stephenson	1948-64	429	12473	147*	20.02	7	135						695/311
D.J.S. Taylor	1970-82	280	6800	179	22.52	4	12						578/74
M.F. Tremlett	1947-60	353	15195	185	25.93	15	9468	326	29.04	8-31	11		239
E.J. Tyler	1891-1907	177	2875	66	11.59		19285	865	22.29	10-49	74		114
R.T. Virgin	1957-72	321	15458	179*	28.52	22	321	4	80.25	1-6			300
A.W. Wellard	1927-50	393	11432	112	19.34	2	36898	1517	24.32	8-52	104	8	342
J.C. White	1909-37	410	11375	192	18.77	6	39606	2167	18.02	10-76	185	14	391
P.B. Wight	1953-65	321	16965	222*	32.75	27	2061	62	33.24	6-29	1		197
S.M.J. Woods	1891-1910	299	12637	215	25.07	18	13408	556	24.12	8-51	36		203
A. Young	1911-33	310	13081	198	25.40	11	9928	388	25.59	8-30	9		218

Most Appearances for County

504	B.A. Langford	1953-74	309	R.A. Ingle	1923-39
427	H.W.Stephenson	1948-64	304	H.F.T. Buse	1929-53
424	E. Robson	1895-1923	302	K.E. Palmer	1955-69
410	J.C. White	1909-37	299	S.M.J. Woods	1891-1910
393	A.W. Wellard	1927-50	289	P.M. Roebuck	1974-90
365	W.T. Luckes	1924-49	287	J. Daniell	1898-1927
353	M.F. Tremlett	1947-60	281	L.C. Braund	1899-1920
352	M.J. Kitchen	1960-79		J. Lawrence	1946-55
350	H.L. Hazell	1929-52	280	D.J.S. Taylor	1970-82
350	W.E. Alley	1957-68	275	V.J. Marks	1975-89
329	H. Gimblett	1935-54	271	G. Atkinson	1954-66
328	F.S. Lee	1929-47	269	P.W. Denning	1969-84
321	P.B. Wight	1953-65	255	C.C.C. Case	1925-35
321	R.T. Virgin	1957-72	252	G.I. Burgess	1966-79
310	A. Young	1911-33	251	B.C. Rose	1969-87

Batting Records

Highest Individual Innings (Somerset)

322 I.V.A. Richards v Warwickshire (Taunton) 1985
313* S.J. Cook v Glamorgan (Cardiff) 1990
310 H. Gimblett v Sussex (Eastbourne) 1948
292 L.C.H. Palairet v Hampshire (Southampton) 1896
264 M.M. Walford v Hampshire (Weston-super-Mare) 1947
257 L.C. Braund v Worcestershire (Worcester) 1913

Most First Class Centuries (Somerset)

49	H. Gimblett	24	W.E. Alley
43	I.V.A. Richards	23	F.S. Lee
30	P.M. Roebuck	22	R.T. Virgin
27	L.C.H. Palairet	21	G. Atkinson
	P.B. Wight		B.C. Rose

1,000 Runs for Somerset – Most Seasons

12	H. Gimblett	9	M.F. Tremlett
10	P.B. Wight		R.T. Virgin
	W.E. Alley		P.M. Roebuck
	I.V.A. Richards	8	F.S. Lee
			G. Atkinson

2,000 Runs (First Class) for Somerset

PLAYER	YEAR	MATCHES	INNS	N.O.	RUNS	AVERAGE
S.J. Cook	1990	24	41	7	2608	76.70
I.V.A. Richards	1977	20	35	2	2161	65.48
S.J. Cook	1989	23	41	4	2241	60.56
W.E. Alley	1961	32	58	11	2761	58.74
R.T. Virgin	1970	24	47	0	2223	47.29
F.S. Lee	1938	28	51	6	2019	44.86
P.B. Wight	1962	30	55	9	2030	44.13
H. Gimblett	1949	28	50	3	2063	43.89
P.B. Wight	1960	34	61	5	2316	41.35
H. Gimblett	1952	29	55	1	2134	39.51
G. Atkinson	1961	29	53	1	2005	38.56
M.F. Tremlett	1951	30	55	0	2071	37.65
G. Atkinson	1962	32	61	5	2035	36.33

Oldest Player to Score 2,000 Runs in Season
W. E. Alley (42 yrs) 1961

Youngest Player to Score 2,000 Runs in Season
G. Atkinson (23 yrs) 1961

Most Centuries in Season
10 - W.E. Alley (1961); 9 - I.V.A. Richards (1985), S.J. Cook (1990);
  8 - S.J. Cook (1989); 7- F.S. Lee (1938); H. Gimblett (1946);
  R.T. Virgin (1970); I.V.A. Richards (1977 & 1981); P.M. Roebuck
  (1984)

Fastest 100s
41 Minutes - N.F.M. Popplewell (143) v Gloucestershire (Bath) 1983
49 Minutes - I.T. Botham (138*) v Warwickshire (Edgbaston) 1985

Fastest 200s
135 Minutes - S.M.J. Woods (215) v Sussex (Hove) 1895
165 Minutes - I.T. Botham (228) v Gloucestershire (Taunton) 1980

Fastest 300
276 Minutes - I.V.A. Richards (322) v Warwickshire (Taunton) 1985

Oldest to Score Century
Ernest Robson (51 yrs) 111 Runs In 1921

Youngest to Score Century
A.T.M. Jones (18 yrs 104 days) 106 v Leicestershire (Leicester) 1938

Youngest to Score Century on Début
R.J. Bartlett (19 yrs 194 days) 117 v Oxford Univ (The Parks) 1986

Century in Each Innings
1908 – P.R. Johnson 164 & 131 v Middlesex (Taunton)
1925 – J. Daniell 174* (carried bat) & 108 v Essex (Taunton)
1928 – R.A. Ingle 117 & 100* v Middlesex (Taunton)
1938 – F.S. Lee 109* (carried bat) & 107 v Worcestershire (Worcester)
1949 – H. Gimblett 115 & 127* v Hampshire (Taunton)
1952 – H. Gimblett 146 & 116 v Derbyshire (Taunton)
1961 – W.E. Alley 183* & 134* v Surrey (Taunton)
1965 – R.T. Virgin 124 & 125* v Warwickshire (Edgbaston)
1977 – P.W. Denning 122 & 107 v Gloucestershire (Taunton)
1980 – B.C. Rose 124 & 150* v Worcestershire (Worcester)
1982 – J.W. Lloyds 132* & 102* v Northants (Northampton)
1989 – S.J. Cook 120* (carried bat) & 131* (carried bat) v Nottinghamshire (Trent Bridge)

Most Sixes in an Innings
12 – I.T. Botham v Warwickshire (Edgbaston) 1985

Most Sixes off Consecutive Balls
5 – A.W. Wellard off T.R. Armstrong v Derbyshire (Wells) 1936 (30
   Runs off over)
5 – A.W. Wellard off F.E. Woolley v Kent (Wells) 1938 (31 Runs off
   over)

Players Achieving the 'Double' in Somerset Matches
2 – J.C. White (1929) – 1,064 Runs 150 Wkts (1930) – 1,008 Runs 115
Wkts
2 – A W Wellard (1933) – 1,055 Runs 104 Wkts (1935) – 1,232 Runs 105
Wkts
2 – W H R Andrews (1937) – 1,063 Runs 137 Wkts (1938) 1,001 Runs 124
Wkts
1 – K E Palmer (1961) 1,036 Runs 114 Wkts
1 – W E Alley (1962) 1,915 Runs 112 Wkts

Oldest Player to Achieve Double
W.E. Alley (43 yrs) as above

Youngest Player to Achieve Double

K.E. Palmer (24 yrs) as above

100 Wickets or More – Most Seasons

14 – J.C. White
8 – A.W. Wellard
4 – W.H.R. Andrews
    B. A. Langford
3 – K.E. Palmer

2 – B. Cranfield
    H.L. Hazell
    J. Lawrence
    F.E. Rumsey

Most Wickets in a Season

169 – A.W. Wellard (1938) avge 19.24
150 – J.C. White (1929) avge 15.17
147 – J.C. White (1922) avge 15.07
147 – J.C. White (1923) avge 15.32
144 – J.C. White (1924) avge 15.12
143 – A.W. Wellard (1936) avge 18.22
140 – A.W. Wellard (1937) avge 23.71
139 – J.C. White (1921) avge 16.10
137 – W.H.R. Andrews (1937) avge 19.72

Oldest Player to Take 100 wickets in a Season

A.W. Wellard (44 yrs) 119 wkts in 1946

Youngest Player to Take 100 wickets in a Season

B.A. Langford (22 yrs) 1958; W.T. Greswell (22 yrs) in 1912

Ten Wickets in an Innings

E.J. Tyler 34.3 – 15-49-10 v Surrey (Taunton) 1895
J.C. White 42.2 – 11-76-10 v Worcestershire (Worcester) 1921

Sixteen Wickets in a Match

J.C. White 16-83 (8-36, 8-47) v Worcestershire (Bath) 1919

Most Maiden Overs in Succession

H.L. Hazell 17 (105 Balls) v Gloucestershire (Taunton) 1949

Dismissals in Career by a W/Keeper

1007 (698 ct 309 st) H.W. Stephenson 1948-64
 827 (586   241) W.T. Luckes 1924-49
 661 (587   74) D.J.S. Taylor 1970-82

415 (297 118) A.E. Newton 1891-1914
242 (209 33) G. Clayton 1965-68
217 (178 39) T. Gard 1976-89
204 (189   15) N.D. Burns 1987-90

Dismissals in a Season by a W/Keeper

86 (50 ct 36 st) H.W. Stephenson 1954
85 (71 14) G. Clayton 1965
84 (74 10) G. Clayton 1966
83 (38 45) H.W. Stephenson 1949
79 (74   5) H.W. Stephenson 1963

Most Dismissals in an Innings by a W/Keeper

6 H.W. Stephenson v Glamorgan (Bath) 1962. G Clayton v Worcestershire (Kidderminster) 1965. D.J.S. Taylor v Hants (Bath) 1982 and v
Sussex (Taunton) 1981

Most Dismissals in a Match by a W/Keeper

9 A.E. Newton v Middlesex (Lords) 1901
  H.W. Stephenson v Yorkshire (Taunton) 1963

Most Catches in a Career-Fielder

381	J.C. White 1909-37	267	W.E. Alley 1957-68
355	L.C. Braund 1899-1920	259	J. Lawrence 1946-55
344	A.W. Wellard1927-50	253	E. Robson 1895-1923
308	R.T. Virgin 1957-72		

Most Catches in a Season-Fielder

41	R.T. Virgin 1966	36	J. Lawrence 1951
38	P.J. Robinson1967	35	R.T. Virgin 1964
37	L.C. Braund 1906	34	J. Lawrence 1947
37	J. Lawrence 1949		

Most Catches in an Innings

5 - L.C. Braund v Worcestershire (Taunton) 1909. G. Hunt v Hants
(W-s-M) 1928. P.J. Robinson v Lancashire (W-s-M) 1968

Most Catches in a Match

7 - C.J. Tavare v Sussex (Taunton) 1989

Limited Overs – Principal Records

John Player/Refuge Assurance League

Highest Innings Totals

For: 360-3 v Glamorgan (Neath) 1990 (LR)
Against: 288-5 by Hampshire (W-S-M) 1975

Lowest Innings Totals

For: 58 (18.2 overs) v Essex (Chelmsford) 1977
Against: 72 (19 overs) by Nottinghamshire (Bath) 1982

Highest Aggregate of Runs

541 – Somerset 271 v 3 v Warwickshire 270-5 (W-S-M) 1990

Largest Victory

By 220 runs v Glamorgan (Neath) 1990 (LR)

Most Runs in Career

I.V.A. Richards 4745 (1974-86); P.W. Denning 4565 (1969-84);
P.M. Roebuck 4039 (1975-90)

Most Runs in Season

S.J. Cook 902 avge – 64.42 (LR) (1990);
I.V.A. Richards 578 avge – 52.55 (1975)

Highest Individual Innings

175* I.T. Botham v Northants (Wellingborough) 1986
148 G.D. Rose v Glamorgan (Neath) 1990

Most Sixes in Career

I.V.A. Richards 146; I.T. Botham 123

Most Sixes in Season

I.V.A. Richards 26 (LR) I.T. Botham 23

Most Sixes in Match

I.T. Botham 13 (LR) v Northants (Wellingborough) 1986

Most Appearances

P.W. Denning 191 (1969-84); D.J.S. Taylor 183 (1970-82)

Highest Partnerships

223 (3rd wkt) S.J. Cook (136*) and G.D. Rose (148) v Glamorgan (Neath) 1990 (LR)

179 (5th wkt) I.V.A. Richards (93) and I.T. Botham (106) v Hampshire (Taunton) 1981

176 (1st wkt) S.J. Cook (114) and P.M. Roebuck (63) v Glamorgan (Taunton) 1989

Most Wickets in Career

H.R. Moseley 222 (1971-82); G.I. Burgess 172 (1969-80)

Most Wickets in Season

R.J. Clapp 34 (1974) (LR with C E B Rice)

Most Economical Bowling

B.A. Langford 8-8-0-0 v Essex (Yeovil) 1969 (LR)

Hat Tricks

R. Palmer v Gloucestershire (Bristol) 1970; I.V.A. Richards v Essex (Chelmsford) 1982

Most Catches in Career – Fielder

P.W. Denning 68 (1969-84); I.V.A. Richards 62 (1974-86)

Most Catches in Season – Fielder

I.V.A. Richards 11 (1978)

Most Catches in Match – Fielder

P.J. Robinson 4 v Worcestershire (Worcester)

Most Dismissals in Career – W/Keeper

D.J.S. Taylor 177 (1970-82); N.D. Burns 71 (1987-90)

Most Dismissals in Season – W/Keeper

D.J.S. Taylor 24 (1981); N.D. Burns 23 (1989)

Most Dismissals in Match – W/Keeper

D.J.S. Taylor 4 v Lancs, Essex (1972) & Notts (1978)
N.D. Burns 4 v Derbyshire (1987) & Northants (1990)

Benson & Hedges Cup

Highest Innings Total
For: 321-5 v Sussex (Hove) 1990
Agst: 303-7 by Derbyshire (Taunton) 1990

Lowest Innings Total
For: 98 (39.3 overs) v Middlesex (Lords) 1982
Agst: 68 (32 overs) by Combined Universities (Taunton) 1978

Highest Aggregate of Runs
613 Somerset 310-3 v Derbyshire 303-7 (Taunton) 1990 (CR)

Most Runs in Season
C.J. Tavare 346 (1989) S.J. Cook 329 (1990)

Highest Individual Innings
177 S.J. Cook v Sussex (Hove) 1990; 155* M.D. Crowe v Hants
(Southampton) 1987

Best Partnerships
269* (3rd wkt) P.M. Roebuck (110*) & M.D. Crowe (155*) v Hants
(Southampton) 1987 (CR)
241 (1st wkt) B.C. Rose (137*) & S.M. Gavaskar (90) v Kent (Canterbury) 1980 (CR)

Most Wickets in Season
A.N. Jones 17 (1989); J. Garner 16 (1981); I.T. Botham 15 (1981)

Best Bowling Performance
J. Garner 11-5-14-5 v Surrey (Lords) 1981 Final

Hat Trick
N.A. Mallender v Combined Universities (Taunton) 1987

Most Catches in Season – Fielder
T.W. Cartwright 6 (1975); I.T. Botham 6 (1984)

Most Catches in Match – Fielder
T.W. Cartwright 4 v Glamorgan (Taunton) 1975

Most Dismissals in Season – W/Keeper
D.J.S. Taylor 15 (1982)

Most Dismissals in Match – W/Keeper
D.J.S. Taylor 8 v Combined Universities (Taunton) 1982 World Record Limited Over

Gillette/Nat West Trophy

Highest/Innings Total
For: 413-4 v Devon (Torquay) 1990 (Trophy Record)
Agst: 299-5 by Hampshire (Taunton) 1985

Highest Aggregate
590-14 wkts v Glamorgan (Cardiff) 1978

Biggest Victory
By 346 runs v Devon (Torquay) 1990 (Trophy Record)

Most Runs in Season
I V A Richards 361 (1978) 266 (1979) C J Tavare 261 (1990)

Highest Individual Innings
162* C J Tavare v Devon (Torquay) 1990

Fastest Century
G.D. Rose 42 mins (36 balls) v Devon (Torquay) 1990 (Trophy Record)

Most Wickets in Season
17 J. Garner (1979)

Best Bowling Performance
R.P. Lefebvre 9.3-6-15.7 v Devon (Torquay) 1990

Most Catches in Season – Fielder
4 – R.T. Virgin (1966) C.R.M. Atkinson (1967) K.E. Palmer (1967) I.V.A. Richards I.T. Botham

Most Dismissals in Season – W/Keeper
10 G. Clayton (1967)

Most Dismissals in Match – W/Keeper

5 T. Gard 5 v Sussex (Hove) 1983

Best Partnerships

195 (3rd wkt) P.M. Roebuck (102) + C.J. Tavare (101) v Essex (Taunton) 1989

189 (4th wkt) C.J. Tavare (162*) + G.D. Rose (110) v Devon (Torquay) 1990

188 (2nd wkt) P.M. Roebuck (98) + M.D. Crowe (114) v Sussex (Hove) 1984

SOMERSET 100 APPEAL
ROLL OF HONOUR

1880	Mr G.J. Laird-Portch	1931	Mr K.W.H. Clothier
1912	Mr J.D. Huxtable		Mr T.A. Waller
1915	Mr D.A. Coombs		Eva Edwards
1921	Mr E.H. Bremridge		Mr P. Tyley
	Mr F.J. Farmer		Mr J.B. Hauser
	Mr S.F. Palmer		Mr P.A.C. Cattell
	Mr L.G. Creed	1932	Lord Rippon
	Mrs A.J. Lewis		Mr F. Criddle
1922	Mr R.J. Trott		Mr C. Wildblood
1923	Lt.Col. E.E. Jones		Mr L.J.C. Cavill
	Mr C.B. Lace		Mr G.A. Scammell
1924	Mr R.N. Tovey		Mr G.T.R. Thomas
	Mr J.H. Crossman		Mr J. Harriman
1925	Mr L. St.Vincent Powell	1933	Mr L.C. Evans
	Mr P.H. Daly	1934	Mr A.W.H. Cross
	Mr R.V. Criddle		Mr J.G. Luckes
	Mr D.A. Hawkins	1935	Mr D.J.E. Inchbald
1926	Mr T.R.I. Morrish		Mr R.F. Ash
	Mr J.E. Martin		Mr N. Dunford
1927	Mr W.J.F. Arnold		Mr J.A. Cheston
	Mr M.S. Blundell		Clar Robbins
	Rev. H.J. Thomas		Mr R.T. Patten
	Mr H.W.H.F. Taylor		Mr C.J.P. Barnwell
	Mr R. Gill		Mr F.R. Barter
1928	C.H.F. Blake	1936	Mr L.J. Harris
	R.S. Skinner		Mr R.N. Barnes
1929	Mr R. Harris		Elsie M. Willett
	Mr C.J. White		Mr K.C. Dunthorn
1930	Mr A.S. Underdown		Mr. T.A. Broad
	Mr R.R. Curry		Mr. R.J. Ewens
	Mr J. Young		Mr M.W. Earle
	Mr F.J. Endacott		Mr P.J.L. Lee
	Mr L.J. Wright		Mr R.J. Fussell
	Mr W.R. Lee		Mr B.E.W. Whitehead
	Mr B.F.W. Ashman	1937	Mr S. West

Mr K.J. Butler
Mr G.W.J. Moore
Mr P.T.H. Young
Mr T.B. Harding
1938 Rev. Canon A.E.H. Rutter
Mr G.H. Tolson
Mr A.C. Hopkins
Mr H.D.J. Manley
Mr G. Holcombe
Mr D. Tuffin
Mr A.C. Emery
1941 Mr R.A.F. Ings
1942 Mr A.J. Burton
1945 Mr R. Steeds
Mr J.H.F. Mackie
Mr W.B. Lawley
Dr R.G.H. Bunce
Mr S.P. Bennett
1946 Mr A. Gould
Mr G.G. Gatehouse
Mr R.J. Mason
Mr A.J. Bowden
R.A.A. 'Bob' Moore
Mr D.G. Short
Mr G. Turner
Mr R.B. Cheetham
Mr C. Usher
Dr J.A. Lane
Mr A.J. White
Mr D. Gabbitass
Mr. J. Cartwright
Mr K.W. Duckett
Mr R.D. Russell
Mr R.D. Appleyard
Mrs R.H. Thomas
K.K. Board
Mr C.J. Clothier
Mr J. Cartwright
Mr D. Giles
Mr B.R. Pepperall
Mr N.G. Pepperall
Mr A.J. Gardner
Mr M.F. Hill
Mr C. Lambourne
Mr D.G. Burchell
Mr W.R. Gatehouse
Mr P.E. Heywood-Bawden
Mr A. Irish
Mr J. Stanley
Mr S.F. Chilcott
Mr A. Restorick
Mr J.R. Weaver

Mr D. Kitson
Mr K.B. Miles
Mr D. Smith
Mr H.W.M. Brewer
Mr A.H.G. Clark
1947 Mr A.V.R. Hillier
Mr T. Wanless
Mr M.S. Beacham
Mr A. Beaven
Mr E.J. Pullen
Mr J. Hobbs
Mr & Mrs A.J. Toley
Mr A.A. Chapman
Mr G. Sanders
Mr R.D. Bigwood
Mrs E.M.B. Clark
Patricia M. Bayley
Mr I.E. Hardwidge
Mr E.C. Bryant
Mr E.C. Palmer
Jill Symonds
Mr K.A.W. Wills
Mr H.J. Weber
Mr D.A. Potts
Ann S.H. Grieve
Mr M.A. Gilson
Mr N.B. Johnson
1948 Mr P.J.C. Warren
Mr H. Pinn
Mr R.G. Banwell
Mr J. Pike
Mr G.M. McLennan
Mr J.T. Robson
Mr J.Marshall
Mr J.W. Hart
Mr D.G.A. Russell
Mr H.L. Compton
Mr B. Andrews
Mr S. Ashman
Mr M.J. Gumm
Mr A.S. Hollis
Vivian Horn
Mr B. Harrington
P. Rich
Mr R.L. Roe
1949 Mr D.J. Horn
Mr W. Tregoning
Mr J.C. Stoyle
Dr M.W. Kennedy
Mr G. Mannell
Miss M.A. Hamilton
1950 Mr W.E. Venn

Mr E.E. Moorman
Mr C. Chambers
Mr A.W. Cornell
Mr B.J. Howell
C.D. & Mrs B.M. Vian
Mr H.J. Lansdowne
Mr B.L. Butcher
Barbara von Tyszka
Mr S.J. Tucker
Mr G.E. Parfitt
Mr J. Brunt
Mr B.Downton
Mr E.J. Luce
Mr N.D.H.Q. Coombes
Olive W. Owens
O.B.N. Paine

1951 Mr P.J. Lane
Mr P.R. Lockett
Mr E. Isbell
Mr M.J.W. Richards
Mr T.R. Boobyer

1952 Mr C. Jiggens
M.H.T. Gairdner
Mr R.D. Vaughan
Mr D.W. Brown
Mr C. Bull
Mr C. Little
Mr P.J. Oram
Mr M.A. Small
Mr D. Robertson
Mr F. Dibble

1953 Mr A.H. Strong
Mr R. Stallard
Mr R.F. Sims
Mr J.W. Churchill
Mr W.J. Burt

1954 Mr I.W. Martin
Mr R.H. Yeoman
Mr T. Ackroyd
Mr G. Brock
G.W. & Mrs J.M. Vian
B.A. Duke
Mr L.C. Till
Mr F. Sheppard
Mr P.D. Richardson
Mr E.C. Chapman
Mr T.R. Houghton
Mr A.J. Martin

1955 Mr H. Clowes
Mr I. Jenkins
Mr R.J. Pratten
Mr G.W. Dance

Mr R.C.F. Squibbs
Mr H.C.W. Warren
Mr S.F. Reeves
Mr T. Mills

1956 Rt Hon. Sir Edward Du Cann
Mr C. Twort
Mr J.C. Grundy

1957 Mr R.H. Beattie
Mr P.J.L. Hazel
Mr A.J. Beard
Mr T. Churchill
Mr A.K. Miles

1958 Mr J. Sharp
Mrs C. Walker
Mr D.H. Till
Mr D. Hall
Mr D.K. Stocker
Mr P. Spellissy
Mr G.A. Ellis
Mr J.H. Lee

1959 Mr G. Latham
Mr R.K. Hockey
Mr K. Salway
Mr M.F. Powell
Mr E.J. Howe
Mr M.J. Padfield

1960 Mr R.I. Griffiths
Mr S.G. Porter
Mr F.R. Darby
E.W. Dauncey
Mr A. Steeds
Mr S.G. Thorne
Mr G. Read
Mr N. Abbott
Miss A.U. Chapman
Mr H.R. Baker
Mr E.J. Thomas
Mr J.C. Blanshard
Mr A. Starr

1961 Mr A.M. Warner
Mr W.B. James
John & Barbara Hamlin

1962 Mr J.H.F. Williams
Mr N.S. Lyddon
Mr P.R. Steer
Mr M. Peart
Mr S. Vaitilingam
Mr J.D. Wilcock
Mr K. Chafey

1963 Deborah J. Amos
Mr G.S. Strongitharm
Mr A.G. Burt

Mr K.R. Scott
Mr C.B. Wadsworth
Mr G.S. Daw
Mr & Mrs W.J. Hobbs
Mr B.G. Staples
1964 Bgdr R.H. Bright, CBE
Mr P. Such
Mr R.M. Ash
Mr B. Lumley
Mr D. Hucker
Mr D. Trist
Mr T. Rendle
1965 Mr P.E. Taylor
Mr N.J. Cross
Mr D. Lang
Mr D. Wood
Mr D. Male
Mr D.P. Watts
Mr B.J. Bown
1966 Mr M. Usher
Eileen Taylor
Mr R.E. Snelling
Mr N.J. Cooper
Mr A.G. Aplin
Mr A.J. Russe
Mr G.J. Merson
1967 R.L. & S.J. Cummings
Mr K.N. Lee
Mr K. Russell
Mr C.R.M. Atkinson
Mr S. Carrow
Mr & Mrs R.S.S. Lodge
Mr D.J. Holmes
Mr A.H.O. Codling
1968 Mr T.J. Bell
Mr M. Purnell
Mr M.J. Pavey
Mr E. Beilby
Mr D.J. Sperring
Mr D.M. Doig
Mr B.A. Ridge
1969 Mr N. House
Mr P. Maksimczyk
1970 Mr C. Shaddock
Mr G. Wheeler
Mr R.W.H.T. Cross
Mr M. Talbot
Mr D. Godfrey
Mr E.A. Boffey
Mrs F.S. Kilkenny
Cmdr N.R.H. Rodney RN
Mr C. Rodney

Mrs S.P. Maunder
Mr M. Ridewood
Mr M.A.T. Puddy
Mr S.J. Howard
Mr D.J. Cockram
Mr C.L. Banks
Mr C. Tate
Mr M.D.R. Buck
1971 Mr & Mrs J. Playll
Mrs P. Broach
Mr D.A. Thorogood
1972 Mr R. Parsons
Mr R. Brumby
Mr C. Ford
Mr F.J. Bourne
Dr P. January
Mr R.W. Tucker
1973 Mr S.A. Wood
Mr K.R.G. Hopkins
1974 Mr P.B. Rand
Mr P. Gael-Rew
Mr & Mrs C.P. Chidgey
Mr A.L. Hargreaves
Mr A. Rodber
1975 Mr W.R. Hawkins
Mr M.J. Hughes
Mr M. Leat
Mr M.F.A. Ward
Mr D.M. Singleton
Mr J.R. Pike
Mr J.P. Belcher
Mr T. Jay
Mr D.J. Pearce
Mr J.R. Leahy
Mr P.K. Jones
Sally Grieve
Mr A.H. Stringer
Mr S.K. McIntyre
Miss A. Ridge
1976 Mr K.E. & A. Tyrrell
Mr A.B. Horlock
Mr R.J. Brocklebank
Mr A. Whiteway
Mr C.J. Campbell
Mr P.J. Burton
Mr C.J. Chrisp
Margaret Bennett
Rosemary J. Blanshard
1977 Mr D. Lush
Mr C.J. Webber
Mr P.E. Price
Mr J.S. Beeston

Mr M. Brush
Mrs S. Smith
1978 Bgdr E.D. Smith
Mr N. Hobbs
Mr M. Jackman
Mr J.R. Thompson
Mr R. Davey
Mr G.A. Padfield
Mr R.N.W. Farquhar
Mr R.W. Gooden
Mr A.E. Ranger
Mr R. Minson
Mr M. Williams
Mr D.P. Ashman
Mr G.E. Brownsey
Mr S.G. Trees MVO OBE
1979 Mr D. Wall
Mr G.C. Sharp
Mr D.W. York
Mr B. Hutchinson
Mr R. Parsons
Dr J.V. Beaverstock
Lord Courtenay
Mr D. Golding
Mr B. Green
1980 Mr A. Hole
Mr & Mrs Symes
Mr E. Dymond
Mr M.B. Russell
Mr D.S. Rowe
Miss N.J. Crossman
Mr J.P. Dyke
Margaret & David Alston
Mr D. Goddard
1981 Mrs J.V.V. Day
Mr B.J. Whitlock
Mr J. Braid
Mr D.J. White
1982 Mr P. Brackner
Gianna Caiger
Mr M.P. Harris
Mr S. Grenfell
1983 Mr T.C. Taylor
Mr T. Anderson
Mr & Mrs Naftel
Mr K. Cock
Pamela M. Thorne
Mr F.C. Thomas
Mr W.F. Cole MBE
Mr P.O. Goldsworthy
1984 Mr W.J. Smith
Mr W.B. Greenhill

Mr H.A. Puttick
Mr D.R. McArthur
Mr N.R. Laverick
Mr H.S. Norbury
Mr J.N. Morse
Mrs B.M. Ryley
Mr D. Fasey
Mr J. Fasey
Mr B.E. Williams
Mr B.R. Veale
1985 Mr R.G. Brett
Mr V. Ashley
Mr G.L. Holt
Mr R.J. Pincham
Mr P.J. Butterworth
Mr S.J. Balcombe
Mr M. Mattiuzzo
Mr J.K. Hopping
Mr D.J. Carter
Mr G. Turner
Mr D.S. Phipps
Mr M. Williams
1986 Mr E.J. Diment
Mr A.M. Mitchem
Mr A.G.T. McCulloch
Mr P.J.H.C. Sheppard
Mr L. Halsey-Barrett
Mr M.E.C. Maggs
Mr. M.A. Hearn
The Rev. D.C. Flatt
1987 N.N.S. Mackay FRCS
Mr E. Booth
Mr F.E. Dethridge
Mr. A.S. Trayford
Mr F. Stevens
Mr M.C. Graves
Mr G. Wolstenholme
Mr B. Skittrall
Deborah B. Tarrant
1988 Mr & Mrs P.W. Anderson
Mr G.H. Burdge
Mr J.M. Ellison
Mr J. Fulwell
Mr N. Brooking
Mr M.W. Stanley
Mr S.W.H. Boobyer
Mr A.R. Evanson
Mr M.D. Wallace
Mr J.V. Gore
Mr R.J.G. Mackey
Mrs P.J. Jackson
Mr A. Jackson

Mr R.J.B. Hughes
Mr J.L. Gill
Mr T.L. Whitmarsh
1989 Mr A.M. Barrett
Mr C.J. Bisby
Mr D. Towells
Mr G.E. Wilson
Mr C.J. Edwards
Mr M.R.T. Salter
1990 Mr L.A. Teear
Mr B.G. Skinner
Mr A.E.P. Wood
Mr T. McCormack
Mr C.H. Williams
Mr R.A. Pinches
Mr E.R. Crowe
Mr D.C. Higginson
Mr B. English
The Levan Family
Mr C.A. MacLucas
Mr P.J. Talbot
Mr J.C. Luker
Mr N. Southwood
Mr A. Payne
Mr S.F. Hannan
Jeanne Titcombe
Mr E.J. Cullingford
Mr I.K. Warren
Mr E. Halden

Mrs B. Cullingford
Andre Jozwiak
1991 Mrs J.M.F. Walmesley
Mr K.R. Watkin
Mr J. Scott
Mr W.P. Kelly
Mr S.J. Kingshott
Mr D.F. Robinson
Mr G.J. Dicker
Mr G. Dicker
Mr W.G. Galton
Mr A.J. Bradbury FCIB
Mr R.J.B. Champion
Mr M.J. Ryan
Mr G.V. Summers
Mr B. King
Mr C.H. Tink
Mr S.M. Maidment
Mr N.P. House
Mr D. Cole
Mr D.R. Catchpole
Mr N.G. Reading
Mr S. Lovegrove
Mr D.J. Perkins
Mr J. Westcott
Mr H. Counsell
Mr W.G. Newton
Mr P.S. Blacker

Index

Ainslie, Rev C., 12
Alley, W.E., 275–7, 287, 290–1, 292, 301, 302, 322
amateurism v professionalism, *see* professionalism v amateurism
Amor, S., 137
Anderson, P., 399
Andrews, W.H.R. ('Bill'), 187, 190, 211, 221, 228, 236, 237–8, 244, 299, 325
Angell, L., 251
arranged declaration, *see* Barnwell, J.
Atkinson, C., 293–4, 302–3, 320, 325, 389–90
Atkinson, G., 266, 283, 288, 290, 310–11
Atkinson, J., 400

Baig, A.A., 288
Bailey, A., 91
Bailey, C.A.H., 87
Baldock, W., 171, 221
Bajana, M., 108
Banes-Walker, C., 114
Banks, P. d'A., 114
Barlow, C., 155
Barnwell, J., 197–8, 229
Barnwell, L., 322
Barrett, Major A. G., 178
Bartlett, R., 385
Barwell, T., 284, 322
Bastard, E., 29, 30
'Beaune, Admiral', *see* Martyn, H.
Bennett, G., 162
Benson and Hedges Cup:
  v Combined Universities, 400–1; declaration controversy, 354–5; v Essex, 401; v Glamorgan, 338, 354; v Gloucestershire, 354; v Hampshire, 338–9; v Kent, 350, 367–8; v Leicestershire, 339; v Minor Counties,

354; v Northamptonshire, 395; v Nottinghamshire, 368; semi-final, 339, 350, 368, 401; suspension from, 355; v Sussex, 368; quarter-final, 338–9, 367–8, 377, 395, 400–1; winners, 363–4, 367–8; v Worcestershire, 354
Bernard, C., 74
bicycle racing, 25–6
Biddulph, K.D., 268–9
Birkenshaw, J., 399, 403–4
Bisgood, Bert, 97, 113
'Bishop', the, *see* Wickham, A.
Bligh, A., 137
Boles, Sir Dennis, 153
Booth, S., 379–80, 394
Botham, I.T.:
  acting captain, 372, 374; Ashes success, 362; attacks Roebuck, 391; captains England, 360; captains Somerset, 375; character, 378; drugs, 379, 384; friendship with Richards, 338; joins rebellion, 390; leaves Somerset, 394; loses England captaincy, 362; one-day internationals, 345; relationship with Close, 341; resigns Somerset captaincy, 381; six-hitting record, 195; soccer career, 378; suspended by Lord's, 385; Test debut, 347; *see also* Hudson, T.; rebellion
Boundy, G.O., 247
Bowerman, A., 77
Braund, L.C., 75, 86–7, 110, 128
Breakwell, D., 341, 365
Bridges, J., 107, 110–11
Brocklehurst, B., 255–6, 266–7
Brooks, A.J., 23
Brooks, Dickie, 322
Brooks-King, R., 107
Brown, Tony, 371, 398

Bryant, E., 280, 288
Buck, Bill, 324
Burgess, A.W., 137
Burgess, G.I., 307, 335, 360
Burns, N.D., 394
Burrington, G., 81
Burrough, H.D. ('Dickie'), 171–2
Buse, H.F.T. ('Bertie'), 171, 214, 239–40,
    256–7
Buttle, C., 139–40, 170, 209, 230–2, 239,
    257, 270, 289, 305–6, 333

Caddick, A., 403
Caesar, Bill, 228
Caesar, J., 11
Cameron, J.H. ('Snowball'), 213
Carter, C., 324
Cartwright, T.W., 327, 343–4
Case, C.C.C., 156, 172–4
Cassan, E.J.P., 8, 15
Castle, F., 227
Challen, J.B., 18, 49
Chappell, G.S., 321–2, 325
Chidgey, H., 106, 107
Clapp, Bob, 340
Clarence Park, Weston-super-Mare, 206
Clark, S., 176–7
Clarkson, Tony, 326, 332
Clayton, G., 303
Cleal, M., 397
Close, D.B., 330, 332, 334, 345, 347
club cricket, 4, 5
Coke, F.S., 26
Collings, E., 155
Conibere, J., 250
Considine, S., 129
Cook, S.J., 399–400
Coope, M., 235
Cooper, R., 334
county cricket, decline of, 307–8
County Ground, 103–4, 155, 221
Cranfield, B., 72, 78–9
Creed, L., 336
Cricketers Association, 314–15
Critchley-Salmonson, H.R.S., 107, 108
Crowe, M., 375–6, 377, 387, 388, 390,
    396–7
'Crusoe', see Robertson-Glasgow, R.C.

Daniell, J.:
    born, 100; captains Somerset, 97, 119,
    126–8; character, 100–2, 126–8;
    dies, 297; England selector, 100, 133;
    Homburg hat, fielding in, 127; joins
    Somerset, 75; motivation of bowlers,
    127; plays rugby for England, 100;
    Secretary, 179; resigns as Secretary,
    208, 250; war service, 101

Daniell, N., 247–8
Daubney, Rev. E.T., 8
Davey, A.F., 141, 178
Davies, Tony, 250
Davis, M., 367, 377
Dean, J., 7
Dean, W., 252
Deane, C.G., 114
death threats, 390
Denning, P.W., 326, 335, 376
Deshon, Captain, 257
Devon Wanderers, 77
Doddington, H.P., 12–13, 15
Doughty, D., 298
Dredge, C.H., 344, 402
'Drink up thy Zider', 317
Dunlop, C., 64

early history:
    in England, 2, 10, 13; in Somerset,
    1–14
Earle, G.F., 145–6, 180
East Somersetshire, 34
Ebdon, P., 68
Eele, P., 296, 304
Elers, C.G., 8
Evans, A., 19
Ewens, P., 140, 155

Felton, N., 373, 394
Fernie, H., 139–40, 209, 230
Fletcher, G., 221
Fletcher, I., 403
Flowers, 77
football pool, 255
Forman, H., 106
Foster, D., 397
Fothergill, A., 23–4, 26
Fowler, Bill, 19, 28
Fowler, Gerald, 28, 107
Fox, H.F., 29
Foy, P., 107
Francis, T.E.S., 138
Frederick, Prince of Wales, 2–4
Frost, R., 251, 255, 261, 299
Fussell, P., 266

Gamlin, H., 68, 71
Gard, T., 372, 374
Gardner, J., 398
Garner, J., 348, 354, 362–3, 380, 388–92
Garnett, T.R., 218
Garrett, H., 110, 114
Gavaskar, S., 360, 361
Gay, L., 89
Gentlemen v Players, 142, 290
Gerrard, R., 198, 221

Gill, G., 72, 73–4
Gillette Cup:
  v Derbyshire, 356; v Essex, 351–2; final
    318–19, 352, 356–7; v Glamorgan,
    298, 350; v Kent, 318–19, 339, 350–1,
    356; v Lancashire, 309–10, 317–18; v
    Leicestershire, 316, 321, 335–6, 339; v
    Middlesex, 356; v Northamptonshire,
    316, 328, 356–7; v Nottinghamshire,
    300–1, 328; semi-final, 310, 317–18,
    339, 351–2, 356; v Surrey, 339; v
    Sussex, 301, 309, 352; quarter-final,
    305, 350–1; v Warwickshire, 310, 316,
    345–6, 350; winners, 356–7; v
    Yorkshire, 305, 309; see also Nat West
    Trophy
Gimblett, H.:
  2000 runs in season, 248; 310 v Sussex,
    243; benefit, 253; character, 203; fails
    trial for Somerset, 199; debut,
    199–202; fire service, 139, 204;
    Lawrence Trophy (fastest 100), 202;
    mental breakdown, 204, 263–4;
    picked for England, 245; plays for
    England, 203, 217; plays for Somerset
    Stragglers, 198; tours India, 248
Gore, H., 360
Grace, W.G., 26
Grand Hotel, Swansea, scandal at, 278–9
Graves, P., 57–8
Greetham, C.H.M., 267, 276, 278, 310
Greswell, W.T. ('Bill'):
  born, 104; debut, 97, 104; inswinger,
    104; last appearances, 175; President,
    105, 299; sent to Ceylon, 105; war
    service, 105
Greswell, W.H.P., 15
greyhound racing, 289
groundsmen:
  Frost, P., 366; Godsmark, 54; Hortop,
    33; Mettam, 54, 91; Morley, 25, 27;
    Price, D., 337, 366; Prosser, G., 366;
    Underwood, 27; see also Buttle, C.;
    Fernie, H.; Robson, E.
Gundry, J.P., 12
Gurr, D., 345

Hall, G., 293
Hall, H., 29
Hall, T., 258–9
Hallett, J., 403
Hambling, M., 137
Hancock, R.E., 114
Harden, R., 384, 400
Hardy, J., 394
Hardy, P., 94, 115
Harris, J., 253
Harvey, K.G., 242

Hawkins, L., 162
Hayhurst, A., 403
Haywood, E., 155
Hazell, H.L., 171, 205, 221, 240–1, 244,
  254, 263
Hedley, Captain W.C., 60, 72
Hen Coop, 103, 142
Henley, E.F., 12
Herbert, M.R.H.M., 155–6
Herting, F., 288
Hewett, H.T., 43, 48–9, 66–67
Heygate, H., 119–20
Heyward, T., 11
Hill, Eric, 222, 245–6, 260–1
Hill, Evelyn, 157
Hill, Maurice, 332
Hill, Mervyn, 157, 158
Hill, Michael, 388, 392
Hill, V.T., 63–4, 171
Hilton, J., 265
Hippisley, H.E., 106, 114
Hobbs, J., 157–8
Holmes, T., 324
Hook, J., 337
Hope, P., 155–6
housing, players', 255, 279
Hudson, T., 379
Hunt, B., 181
Hunt, G., 175, 181, 187
Hylton-Stuart, B. de la C., 108
Hyman, Bill, 110, 113

Ingle, R.A.:
  average, 183; born, 182; captains
    Somerset, 183, 196; character, 183;
    debut, 140; loses captaincy, 210, 213
Irish, F., 249–50

Jackson, J.A.S., 129
James, J., 329, 343
John Player League, see Sunday League
Johnson, K.H.R., 242
Johnson, P.R., 98–9, 159
Johnson Park, Yeovil, 274
Jones, Adrian, 395
Jones, Allan A., 327, 340, 341
Jones, J., 137
Jones, T., 216–17

Keith, G., 284
Kenley, A.A., 12
Kerslake, R.C., 302, 320, 322, 342, 352,
  358–60, 371
Key, L.H., 125, 137
Khan Mohammad, 252
Kinnersly, K., 185
Kirwan, Rev. J.H., 7
Kitchen, M.J., 293, 313, 334, 340

439

Kitson, D., 252

Lambert, G., 281
Lancaster, Brigadier E.H., 208–9, 247
Lang, H., 12
Langdale, G., 226–7
Langdon, B., 391
Langford, B.A., 257, 277, 280, 302, 323, 328, 332, 388
Lansdown CC, 5, 6, 10–11
Latham, M., 290
Lathwell, M., 403
Lawrence, J.M., 225–6, 229
Leat, E.J., 114
Lee, Frank, 171, 186–7, 192–3, 214, 236
Lee, Fred, 94, 160
Lee, J.W., 160, 192–4, 221
Leeston-Smith, F.A., 34
LeFebvre, R., 402–3
Lewis, A.E., 79, 90–1
Lindo, C.V., 299
Linney, K., 185
Lloyd, M., 19
Lloyds, J., 361, 367, 378
Lobb, B., 269, 275
Lomax, J.G., 265
Lomax, I., 291
Longrigg, E.F. ('Bunty'), 156, 174, 209–10, 215, 221, 224, 230, 325
Longrigg, Major G.E., 250
Lowry, T., 138, 146–7
Luckes, W.T., 156, 194, 226, 241
Luff, J., 405
Lyon, B., 149
Lyon, M.D. ('Dar'):
    career in Africa, 150; character, 150; joins Somerset, 149; return to England, 151, 198; resigns from MCC, 150; stands for parliament, 150; supports eight ball over, 214; war service, 221

MacBryan, J.C.W., 109, 140, 151, 152
McCombe, P., 353, 354, 369–70, 378
McCool, C.L., 272–4, 286
MacLeay, K., 403
McLennan, I.A.C., 242
McMahon, J.W., 265–6, 279
McRae, F.M. ('Peter'), 206–8, 221
Madden-Gaskell, J., 162
Mallender, N., 395
Marcon, Rev. W., 7
Marks, V.J., 350, 360–1, 376, 398–9, 402
Marriott-Doddington, H.P., see Doddington, H.P.
Marshall, J.A.B., 8
Marshall, A., 138
Martin, J., 306

Martyn, H., 88–9
Massey, W.M., 19
Mayo, C., 162, 221
Mermagen, P., 178
Mettam, see groundsmen
Meyer, R.J.O.:
    Cambridge blue, 232; captains Somerset, 212–13, 232–3; career in India, 232–3; character, 233; founds Millfield School, 233; joins Somerset, 205; return to England, 233; unusual stratagems, 234–5; wartime fixtures, 222
Minor Counties Championship, 307
Mitchell, C., 254
Mitchell-Innes, N.S. ('Mandy'), 163, 185, 196–7, 242–3
Molyneux, P.S.M., 212
Monk, H., 12
Montgomery, Bill, 91
Moore, Bob, 260–1
Moorlands, Glastonbury, 275
Morgan, Bert, 107
Moseley, H.R., 329–30, 378
Murdoch, Major E.H., 30
Murray-Anderdon, H.E., 32–3, 107

Narayan, Prince, 106
NatWest Trophy:
    v Buckinghamshire, 396; v Essex, 401; v Kent, 374–5; v Lancashire, 374; v Middlesex, 374; quarter-final, 377; semi-final, 374; v Sussex, 374; winners, 374–5; see also Gillette Cup
Newman, C., 12
Newton, A.E., 61–2
Newton, S.C., 20
Nichols, G.B., 36–7
North, 88
Northway, E., 176
Northway, R., 175–6

O'Keeffe, K., 330, 333–4
Old Pavilion, see Somerset CCC
Ollis, R., 367

Palairet, L.C.H.:
    archer, 48; captains Somerset, 48, 95; plays for England, 48
Palairet, R., 64, 209
Palmer, G., 367
Palmer, K.E., 267, 270, 290, 299, 324
Palmer, R., 306, 329
Palmer, W.W., 15
Parks, H., 250
Paull, R., 307
Peake, Rev. E., 15
Pearson, A., 291

440

Pencarves, C., 12
Penny, W.G., 141
Phillips, F., 74
Pickles, L., 270
Pilch, F., 8
pitches, ill-prepared, 231, 239, 256–7, 305–6, 314
'player-power', 353
poems (*see also* 'Drink up thy Zider'):
    'Alphabet on the Somerset XI, 1892', 65; 'Eight matches played and eight matches won', 51; 'Harold Gimblett's Hundred', 200–2; 'How come is that this agricultural youth', 203; 'How Robson Made the Winning Stroke', 131–2; 'In a zecond-class carriage a cricketer zat', 88; 'Summerzet 'gin Yarkzheer', 84–5; '...Then Zammy rushes down the pitch...', 57–8; 'VOWER VOR ZEBEM', 168–9; 'Zummerzet '81', 364–5
Ponsonby-Fane, Sir Spencer, 32, 54
Pontifex, A., 19
Poole, S., 15
Poore, Major, 75
Popham, Rev. E., 68
Popplewell, N., 356, 366, 373, 376, 380, 392
Porch, R.B., 71
Portman, Lord, 139
Potbury, F.J., 29
Powell, L. St V., 217
Poyntz, E.S.M., 95, 109, 112
Price, Bill, 81
Priddy, J., 162
Pringle, N., 400
professionalism v amateurism, 2, 9, 92–3, 101–2, 117–19, 132–3, 138–9, 156, 163, 186–7, 193–4, 228–9, 246–7, 271
professionals, 1, 2, 6, 10, 11, 164, 246, 312
'Prophet', the, *see* Daniell, J.
Pullen, W.W.F., 26
Pulman, Rev. W.W., 15

Rack Field, Taunton:
    bought by Taunton Athletic Society, 25; freehold bought by Somerset CCC, 72; grandstand built, 27; improved, 44; lease bought by Somerset CCC, 33; *see also* County Ground
Radcliffe, O.G., 34–5
Raikes, T.C., 149
rebellion, 390–3
Recreation Ground, Bath, 77
Redgate, S., 7
Redman, J., 245
Reed, Rev. F., 15, 19

Refuge Assurance League, *see* Sunday League
Richards, I.V.A., 336, 338, 369, 380, 381–3, 386–92
Richardson, T., 94
Ricketts, A.J., 82
Rippon, D., 112, 122–4, 297
Rippon, S., 112, 123–5, 162, 212
River Stand, 270
Roberts, J., 324, 332
Roberts, R., 260–1
Robertson-Glasgow, R.C., 129, 147–9, 159
Robinson, C.J., 51
Robinson, E., 248
Robinson, P.J., 304
Robinson, R., 274
Robson, E.:
    character, 129; dies, 132; joins Somerset, 72; joins umpires list, 132; groundsman, 130; plays soccer for Derby County, 130; singer, 130; testimonial, 132; winning hit v Middlesex, 130
Roe, B., 292, 310
Roe, W., 19, 20–2
Roebuck, P.M., 372–3, 376, 381, 387–93, 396, 397–8
Rogers, S.S., 247, 255
Rose, B.C., 326, 329, 335, 342, 349, 354, 360, 362, 394, 398
Rose, G., 394
Rowdon, G., 206
Rumsey, F.E., 295–6, 314–15, 322
Russom, N., 367

Saeed, Y., 270
Sainsbury, C., 7
Sainsbury, E., 19, 20, 34
Samson, O., 94, 114
Sanders, A.T., 82, 133
Seamer, J., 185, 242–3
Sedgebeer, C., 222–3
Seward, D., 360, 370
Shirreff, A., Squadron Leader, 279, 281
Showering, R., 332
Shrewsbury, A., 164
Silk, D.R.W., 272, 279
Slocombe, P., 342, 345, 378
Smith, D., 73
Smith, F.A., *see* Leeston-Smith, F.A.
Smith, R., 249
Somerset:
    early club matches, 11; first game in, 3; first club formed in, 5
'Somerset':
    v Devon, 8–9, 15; v Dorset, 7; v Wiltshire, 6; first game as county club,

12; *see also* Yeovil and County CC

Somerset CCC:

2nd XI combined with Gloucestershire, 323; appeal for funds, 340–1; averages, 136–7, 177; bureaucracy, 286; buys Rack Field lease, 33; buys Rack Field freehold, 72; captaincy, rotating, 242; competitions won, 307, 356–7, 363–4, 367–8, 374–5; elected to County Championship, 50, 54; formed, 16–17; finances, 18, 20, 44–5, 58, 64, 72, 80, 89, 94, 106, 109, 111, 112, 116, 134, 141, 158, 161, 171, 178, 195, 206, 221, 244, 274, 285, 299, 304–5, 307, 308, 314, 323, 325, 326, 330, 334, 340, 357, 366, 377; first-class debut, 28; first game, 18; first professionals, 23; first trophy, 357; First World War, 114–16; internal dissent, 111, 277, 325, 359, 367, 370–1, 386–93; investigated by MCC, 121; lottery, 323, 329, 365; New Pavilion, 358, 366, 380; Old Pavilion, 142, 170, 305, 381; playing record: 1899–1922, 144; 1919–39, 219–20; 1946–55, 225; plays at other grounds, 186; Ridley Stand, 142; Second World War, 221–3; supporters' rebellion, 260–3; vote of confidence, 263; vote of no confidence, 325, 393; youngest player, 26; *see also* Benson and Hedges Cup; groundsmen; Minor Counties Championship; NatWest Trophy; 'player-power'; rebellion; Sunday League

Somerset v Australia, 27, 66, 72–3, 75, 94, 105, 159–60, 175, 188, 244, 274, 290–1, 347; v Civil Service, 18; v Derbyshire, 113, 157, 175, 205, 275, 328; v Devon, 18, 24, 52–3; v Dorset, 19; v Essex, 133–4, 156–7, 184, 199–202, 267; v Glamorgan, 142, 229, 245, 288, 292, 300, 333, 349, 373; v Gloucestershire, 26, 29, 32, 56, 66, 68, 69–70, 103, 140, 143, 174, 184, 188–9, 216, 235, 294, 300, 330, 349–50, 385; v Hampshire, 19, 23, 30–1, 32, 35, 43, 50, 77, 97–8, 164, 184, 244, 289, 302, 306, 328; v Incogniti, 18; v India, 204, 226, 283; v Kent, 55–6, 69, 73, 97, 216, 257, 274, 361, 385; v Lancashire, 28, 29, 43, 55, 62, 68, 70–1, 95, 97, 184, 257, 280–1, 288, 372; v Leicestershire, 174, 216, 258, 309, 373; v MCC, 24, 56; v Middlesex, 43, 50, 51–2, 55, 62, 69, 75–7, 87, 91, 95, 130, 135–6, 164, 226, 234, 248, 267, 275, 297, 373; v Northamptonshire, 205, 211, 218, 291, 309, 362; v Nottinghamshire, 62, 66, 274, 280, 292, 297, 300, 306, 309, 334; v Pakistan, 292, 314; v South Africa, 68, 79, 142; v Staffordshire, 45, 50; v Surrey, 32, 55, 56–7, 62, 66, 73, 91, 149, 157–8, 159, 211–12, 300, 302; v Sussex, 23, 68, 69, 79–80, 119–22, 140, 243, 292, 330, 333, 350, 362, 369; v Warwickshire, 43, 45, 50, 291, 307; v West Indies, 142, 162, 218, 298, 377; v Worcestershire, 180, 217–18, 245, 306, 328–9, 330, 361, 385; v Yorkshire, 56, 62, 65, 79, 81–6, 87, 95, 113, 140, 175–6, 180, 226, 244, 283, 292

Somerset Stragglers CC, 92, 106, 141

Somerset Stragglers Pavilion, 92

Somerset Wyverns, 341

Sparks, J., 6

Spencer, T., 50–1

Spring, T.C., 405

Spurway, F.E., 137

Spurway, R.P., 68

Stanley, 77

Stephenson, H.W., 249, 286–7, 301–2

Stevens, R., 343, 360

Sully, H., 284

Sunday League, 325, 326, 328, 331–2, 339–40, 346, 352, 356, 357, 373–4

Supporters Club, 230, 255–6, 270, 279, 326

Sutton, L.C., 114

Swallow, I., 403

Tankerville-Chamberlayne, 34

Tate, H., 29

Taunton Athletic Society: formed, 19; grandstand built, 25; sells Rack Field lease, 33

Taunton CC: buys Rack Field, 25; founded, 5

Tavare, C., 399, 400, 402

Taylor, D.J.S., 327, 342, 345, 372

Taylor, M., 369–70

Taylor, Air Vice-Marshall M.L., 248, 250, 274

Terry, F., 30

Thomson, J., 347, 363

Toller, M., 77

Tordoff, G., 253, 267–8, 271

Tout, T., 366

Townsend, G., 403

Trask, J., 29

Trask, W., 29

Tremlett, M.F., 233–4, 249, 252, 258, 271–2, 278–9, 280, 282, 284–5

Trestrail, Major, 94

'Trimnell, S.', 125; *see* Rippon, S.

Tripp, G., 269–70, 284

Troost, A. Van, 402

Trott, A., 95–6

Trump, H., 397

Tudway, H., 114
Turner, M., 394
Tyler, E.J.:
  average, 46; benefit, 75; business
    ventures, 47; joins Somerset, 46; plays
    for England, 46; 'throwing', 46, 77–8

Virgin, D., 250
Virgin, R.T., 278, 312–13, 327–8
Voules, G.B., 12
Voules, S.C., 8, 10, 12–13

Walford, M.M., 227–8
Walker, M., 252
Watts, H., 218, 221
Waugh, S., 397
Wellard, A.W., 160, 170, 176, 185, 190–2,
  195, 214, 221, 246
Welman, F., 29
Welman, T., 15–16
Westcott, 68
Western, E., 15, 16
West of England v MCC, 7
Weston-super-Mare, 111, 113
Wharton, L.E., 137
White, J.C.:
  Australian tour, 154, 166–8; average,
    154; captians England, 154, 170;
    captains Somerset, 161; character,
    152; debut, 97; dies, 297; 'double',
    185; dropped by England, 170;
    England selector, 154; farm, 153; last
    season, 212; plays for England, 154;
    presentation following tour of
    Australia, 170; resigns from Somerset
    captaincy, 182
Whitehead, A., 277–8
'White Mouse', the, see Robinson, C.J.
wicket-keeping gloves, 62

Wickham, A., 60–1
Wight, P.B., 256, 282–3, 306–7
Willetts, T., 307
Wilson, C.J., 24
Windsor, R., 324
Winter, C., 30
Winter, C.A., 138
Winter, J., 19, 24, 72
Wisden, 63, 74, 75, 78, 93, 106, 108, 109,
  121, 135, 140, 167, 251, 280, 297
Wisden, J., 10–11
Wood, G.R., 63
Woodcock, Rev. P., 15
Woodhouse, G.E.S., 163, 243
Woods, S.M.J.:
  Assistant Secretary, 74; averages, 41;
    born, 39; at Cambridge University,
    39–40; captains Somerset, 40, 67–8;
    debut, 36; dies, 95; plays for
    Australia, 40; plays for England, 40;
    plays rugby for England, 40; Poynton
    on, 38; resigns as Secretary, 141;
    Secretary, 128; sent to England, 39;
    stops playing, 42; war service, 41
Wright, E.F., 15
Wright, O., 87
Wyatt, J., 400
Wynyard, Captain, 75

Yeovil and County CC:
  formed, 11; v Devon, 12; see also
    Somerset CCC
Young, A., 160
Young, T.:
  average, 174; benefit, 175; character,
    174; dies, 175, 208; ill-health, 175; war
    service, 175
Young, W.A.R., 45

443